# Lloyds Bank

# Tax Guide 1997-98

## SARA WILLIAMS AND JOHN WILLMAN

PROFILE BOOKS

Published by Profile Books Limited
Registered Office:
62 Queen Anne Street, London W1M 9LA


This edition published 1997

Consultants: Brian Clutterbuck, Jonquil Lowe and Jane Vass
Desk-top publishing and design: Paul Taylor
Editorial team: Penny Williams, Ashley Hickie and Nicky White
Index: Moira Greenhalgh


Printed in Great Britain by The Bath Press


A CIP catalogue record for this book is available
from the British Library


ISBN 1 86197 034 X

Profile Books

# Lloyds Bank Tax Guide 1997-98

Sara Williams is the editor-in-chief of *The AIM Guide* and former editor of *Small Company Investor*. For a number of years she wrote for *Which?*, including the *Which? Tax Saving Guide* and the *Which? Book of Tax*. She has also contributed many articles on personal finance and tax to newspapers and magazines. She is the author of the *Lloyds Bank Small Business Guide*. Sara Williams is a former investment analyst and lecturer in finance. She has been a public interest member for LAUTRO (Life Assurance and Unit Trust Regulatory Organisation), a council member of the Consumers' Association, and she is on the authorisation committee of the Institute of Actuaries.

John Willman is the features editor of the *Financial Times*. He has written extensively on personal finance and tax for *Which?*, including the *Which? Tax Saving Guide* and the *Which? Book of Tax*. Formerly publications editor at Peat Marwick McLintock (a firm of accountants), he was the editor of *Assessment and Taxes*, published by the Inland Revenue Staff Federation. He is the author of *Make Your Will, How to Sort Out Someone's Will* and the *Which? Guide to Planning and Conservation*.

# CONTENTS

AN OUTLINE OF INCOME TAX
1    How income tax works                                      1
2    Income, reliefs and allowances                            5
3    Your tax inspector                                        11
4    Tax changes for the year starting 6 April 1997            25

SAVING TAX
5    Seventy-five ways to save tax                             28
6    Marriage and divorce                                      37
7    Home and tax                                              50
8    Saving and investing                                      62

THE BASIC TAX RETURN
9    How to fill in your tax return                            75
10   Income                                                    80
11   Reliefs                                                  106
12   Allowances                                               128
13   Other information                                        137

SUPPLEMENTARY PAGES
14   Employment                                               140
15   Share schemes                                            174
16   Self-employment                                          184
17   Partnership                                              214
18   Land and property                                        218
19   Foreign                                                  231
20   Trusts etc                                               239
21   Capital gains                                            245
22   Non-residence etc                                        270

HOW TO CALCULATE YOUR TAX

23    Keeping an eye on your tax affairs              280
24    Filling in the tax calculator                  295
25    Case studies in filling in the tax calculator  327


APPENDICES

A     Tax-free income                                339
B     Grossing-up tables                             342
C     Inheritance tax                                345
D     Useful leaflets                                356


INDEX                                                360

# A MESSAGE FROM SIR BRIAN PITMAN LLOYDS TSB GROUP CHAIRMAN

The start of the 1997/98 financial year has seen a revolution in personal taxation with the introduction of self assessment. The changes introduced mean that millions of taxpayers will now calculate for themselves how much tax they owe or are owed and be responsible for all the associated work. There are also important changes regarding the retention of records of income and expenditure.

Everyone who completes a tax return is affected by these changes and so now it is more important than ever that individuals understand taxation and their own personal position.

The Lloyds Bank Tax Guide, now appearing in its 12th year, has achieved a reputation as a ready means of understanding the world of personal taxation. It provides clear, simple and accurate information and this year has been completely rewritten to aid in the understanding and completion of the new self assessment forms.

With our Tax Guide, our Personal Tax Management Service and the comprehensive range of financial services that we offer, our aim is to provide solutions to meet our customers' needs in an ever changing financial world.

This guide will help readers both to work out correctly the tax which they should be paying and to plan their financial affairs in a tax efficient manner.

I hope that you will find the Lloyds Bank Tax Guide useful.

*Brian Pitman*

© Lloyds Bank Plc 1997

# ACKNOWLEDGEMENTS

A tax guide of this type can not appear without the help and hard work of a multitude of people. In particular, we would like to mention the support and enthusiasm of Sue Crawley at Lloyd Bank, along with Tony Gibbons. Both Sue and Tony have helped us navigate a number of pitfalls. Alone we would not have succeeded.

In addition, Stephen Brough and Andrew Franklin at Profile Books and Stephen Page and his team at Fourth Estate have shown determination and commitment to bring the guide to as wide an audience possible.

Thank you.

*Sara Williams and John Willman*

NOTE
Both of us – along with everyone at Lloyds Bank and Profile Books Ltd have made strenuous efforts to check the accuracy of the information. If by chance a mistake or omission has occurred, we are sorry that neither we, Lloyds Bank or the Publisher can take responsibility if you suffer any loss or problem as a result of it. But please write to us c/o Profile Books Ltd if you have any suggestions about how we can improve the content of the guide.

Dear Reader

A lot of uncertainty surrounds the year ahead:

- Will there be a change of government? And will these mean tax changes before 1997?
- Will new self-assessment forms be published or the existing ones revised? And how will you deal with them?

You can get free help to overcome these problems. Please tick the box below if you would like (one box only please):

☐ a guide to filling in your capital gains tax calculator

☐ an early autumn update (available only if a new government introduces a mini budget)

☐ a guide to checking your Revenue Calculation Slip (sent to you if you ask the Inland Revenue to work out your tax bill)

☐ a guide to checking your Correction Notice (sent to you if you work out your own tax bill and your tax inspector spots an error)

Photocopy this page and send it to Ashley Hickie, Lloyds Bank Tax Guide, 62 Queen Anne Street, London W1M 9LA along with an A4-sized self-addressed envelope with a 38p stamp stuck on.

---

Like a post-budget update? Available in December. Tick this box below:

☐ Please send me a post-budget update in December

Photocopy this page and send it back to Ashley Hickie, Lloyds Bank Tax Guide, 62 Queen Anne Street, London W1M 9LA along with an A4-sized self-addressed envelope with a 26p stamp stuck on.

# HOW INCOME TAX WORKS

## CHAPTER 1

Last year your tax inspector worked out what you owed in income tax on the basis of information you and possibly others supplied – through your tax return and various other forms.

This year you can work out your own tax bill if you wish. It is known as self-assessment. You fill in your tax return, and you can also complete a tax calculator and work out the amount of tax you should pay. Or you can work it out yourself without using the tax calculator. Working out your own tax bill could have advantages. But at the outset, you might find it a daunting prospect. This guide, which is completely independent and written with you in mind, should help.

Self-assessment is the biggest upheaval in the tax system for years. A fundamental shift of responsibility has occurred away from the Inland Revenue to you the taxpayer. You now operate the tax collection system for yourself – you provide the records, fill in the form, work out your tax bill (although you can ask your tax inspector to do it for you), and you must make sure your payment is made on time.

There are a myriad of changes, especially for those of you who fill in a tax return (some 9.5 million people, including the self-employed, higher rate tax-payers, pensioners and anyone who gets untaxed income or large amounts of investment income).

There are new:
- tax returns (pp. 13, 75)
- dates by which you have to fill in your tax return (p. 14)
- penalties you have to pay if you don't stick to all the rules (p. 19)
- rules about records which you must now keep (p. 12)
- dates to pay your tax bill (p. 15)
- rules about which income you will pay tax on (p. 80)
- rules for partners (p. 214)
- dates for reporting income (p. 12)

- obligations which taxpayers must stick to (p. 12).

In summary, the whole tax procedure has been tightened up with penalties and responsibilities for the taxpayer made clearer.

The self-assessment regime began on 6 April 1996. From that day, you have been required by law to keep the records you need to back up what you put in your tax return. Failing to do so might mean a penalty of up to £3,000.

The new-style tax returns should land on your doorstep during April 1997. These will cover your income and gains in the tax year ending on 5 April 1997. However, many aspects of the tax regime have not been changed by the introduction of self-assessment; for example, what is income (see p. 5) and how income tax, capital gains tax (see p. 245) and inheritance tax (see p. 345) are worked out. The range of taxes you might pay has not altered, and the way in which the tax rules are changed is just the same.

## The taxes you might pay

There are a number of different ways in which the government raises money from taxpayers. Some of the taxes are as follows:

- income tax – some of your income is taxed at varying rates
- capital gains tax – some of the gains you make on investments or possessions may be taxed at varying rates
- inheritance tax – when you die, some of the money you leave to others could be taxed
- National Insurance – this is paid only by people who are earning, employees, employers, the self-employed or partners.

This guide explains how and in what way these taxes are raised. But there are other taxes which the guide does not explain. These include council tax, corporation tax, value added tax, stamp duty and excise duties.

## How tax rules are changed

Parliament is responsible for changing the tax rules. The government of the day, advised by the Inland Revenue, produces a Budget, currently held towards the end of November. Changes will apply from the start of the next tax year, which runs from 6 April to the following 5 April.

The Finance Bill with the changes suggested in the Budget will be published in January, debated in Parliament and the Finance Act passed before 5 May.

## A simple guide to income tax

There are many complexities and exceptions in the way that income is taxed.

What follows is a broad brush approach to how income is taxed and give some important relationships:

Taxable income = (Income − Reliefs − Allowances)
Total income = (Income − Reliefs)
Income tax = Taxable income x the rate(s) of tax

**Income** is made up of what you earn from your job or self-employment and what you receive as income from other sources, such as investments. But not all the money you receive is income (see p. 5) and some income you receive is tax-free (see p. 339). Some income you receive has had tax deducted (called *net* − see pp. 6 and 63) and some income is paid without tax deducted (called *gross* − see pp. 6 and 342). Savings income (see p. 62) is a special case: much of it is paid with lower-rate tax deducted and no further tax to pay unless you are a higher-rate taxpayer.

**Reliefs** are amounts which you pay out and on which you get tax relief. They reduce your income before your tax bill is worked out. With some reliefs you get tax relief at your highest rate of tax, for example, pensions contributions. With other reliefs, the amount of tax relief is restricted to a certain figure, regardless of the rate of tax you pay; for example, mortgage interest to buy your home.

**Allowances** are amounts to which you are entitled because of your personal circumstances. They reduce your income before your tax bill is worked out. But some allowances, for example married couple's allowance, get a reduced rate of tax relief.

---

## Example

Jessica Jones has income from self-employment of £10,000. She pays £1,000 into a personal pension scheme and she can claim a personal allowance for the tax year ending 5 April 1998 of £4,045, Her taxable income is:

|  | £ |
|---|---|
| Income | 10,000.00 |
| Less Reliefs: pension contributions | 1,000.00 |
|  | 9,000.00 |
| Less personal allowance | 4,045.00 |
| Taxable income | 4,955.00 |
| Less:  tax at 20 per cent on first £4,100 | 820.00 |
|          tax at 23 per cent on next £855 | 196.65 |
| Total tax bill | 1,016.65 |

**Taxable income** is the figure on which you work out your tax bill. The amount of your income tax depends on how much taxable income you have and what rate of tax is paid on it (see below).

**Total income** is a figure that is not important for most taxpayers, but it is for the elderly (those in receipt of age-related allowances). The amount of total income determines whether you can receive these allowances in full or in a reduced amount (see p. 38). Total income can also affect some taxpayers paying life insurance premiums (see p. 67).

Total income is the amount you have after you have deducted some reliefs from income, but before deducting allowances. The reliefs you deduct to arrive at total income include pensions contributions, the gross amount of charitable covenants and charitable donations under Gift Aid and the pay-roll giving scheme, the gross amount of maintenance payments and some loan interest (but not on a mortgage to buy your home). Premiums for private medical insurance are not deducted.

## The rates of tax

There are three different rates of tax:

- lower rate tax (20 per cent for tax years ending on 5 April 1997 and 1998)
- basic rate tax (23 per cent for tax year ending on 5 April 1998 and 24 per cent for tax year ending on 5 April 1997)
- higher rate tax (40 per cent for tax years ending 5 April 1997 and 1998)

The levels at which these rates apply can vary from year to year. Here are the levels of income for each of these rates for the tax years ending 5 April 1997 and 5 April 1998:

### Tax year ending 5 April 1997

| Income band £ | Size of band £ | Tax rate % | Tax on band £ |
|---|---|---|---|
| 0 – 3,900 | 3,900 | 20 | 780 |
| 3,901 – 25,500 | 21,600 | 24 | 5,184 |
| Over 25,500 | | 40 | |

### Tax year ending 5 April 1998

| Income band £ | Size of band £ | Tax rate % | Tax on band £ |
|---|---|---|---|
| 0 – 4,100 | 4,100 | 20 | 820 |
| 4,101 – 26,100 | 22,000 | 23 | 5,060 |
| Over 26,100 | | 40 | |

# INCOME, RELIEFS AND ALLOWANCES

## CHAPTER 2

Income, reliefs and allowances are the three elements in determining your income tax bill – and the three ways in which you can minimise the size of it. Look for opportunities to arrange your income to be tax-free (see p. 339 for a comprehensive list). In the case of a married couple, seek to distribute the income between the two of you to the greatest advantage. And don't forget to claim all your reliefs and allowances, including those from the past that you might have forgotten. You will find tax-saving tips throughout the guide; many of them are gathered together on pp. 28 to 36.

## INCOME

Your income will be made of money or goods you receive or anything you get in return for a service – but not all money you receive counts as income (see below). The following will all normally be considered as income:

- what you earn from your work, including a job (see p. 140), a partnership (see p. 214) or self-employment (see p. 184). This includes salary, fringe benefits and business profits
- rent from letting out property (see p. 218)
- income from investments, such as interest, dividends and distributions (see pp. 62 and 80)
- pensions (from the state, your previous employer or your own plan)
- social security payments, such as jobseeker's allowance
- maintenance income, if the arrangement was made before 15 March 1988
- casual, occasional or miscellaneous income, such as freelance earnings, income received after you close a business, income from guaranteeing loans, dealing in futures, income from underwriting, certain capital payments from selling UK patent rights, accrued income including from gilt strips (see p. 87)
- income from a trust.

### Payments that are not income
Some payments you receive are not income. For example:

- presents and gifts
- loans
- lottery prizes
- gambling winnings (unless it is your way of making a living)
- what you make from selling an asset (unless this is how you make a living)
- what you receive under a maintenance agreement made on or after 15 March 1988
- money you inherit.

Although these payments are not income, there may be other tax to pay on them – for example, capital gains tax or inheritance tax.

### Tax-free income
There are many examples of income that is tax-free, including premium bond prizes or interest on National Savings Certificates. A comprehensive list is given on p. 339.

### How is income paid to you
Income can be paid to you without any tax deducted *(gross)* or with tax deducted *(net)*. The tax can be deducted at the lower rate, the basic rate, the higher rate, or all three rates. The table on the right lists types of income, whether or not they are paid with tax deducted and if any further tax will be due. There are more details of income in Chapter 10.

If you need to give a figure for gross income when you have received net income, there are ready reckoners which help you to gross it up in Appendix B on p. 342.

## RELIEFS

You make certain choices in your life. You might choose to buy a home using a mortgage. Or you might save now to give yourself a pension (over and above the state pension) when you retire. The government decides that it wants to encourage certain of your actions – for example, buying your own home, saving for a pension. So it allows you to deduct some or all of what you pay for these from your income before working out your income tax bill. These items are known as reliefs, outgoings or deductions.

A further advantage of reliefs is that they may lower the rate at which you pay tax. For example, if you pay pension contributions it might mean you pay tax at the basic rate of 23 per cent rather than the higher rate of 40 per cent. When this happens it means that the cost to you of some of these pay-

# Types of income

| Type of income | Tax deducted? | At what rate? | More tax to pay? [1] |
|---|---|---|---|
| Earnings from a job | yes | LR, BR, HR | no |
| Taxable fringe benefits | yes, from earnings | LR, BR, HR | no |
| Pension from your former employer | yes | LR, BR, HR | no |
| Bank, building society interest | yes | LR [2] | yes – HR |
| British Government stocks [3] | yes | BR | yes – HR |
| Income from annuity | yes [4] | BR | yes – HR |
| Dividends from shares | yes | LR | yes – HR |
| Distributions from unit trusts | yes | LR | yes – HR |
| Income from an executor before a will is sorted out | yes | BR | yes – HR |
| Income from a trust | yes | BR | yes – HR |
| Income from self-employment | no | | yes |
| Income from a partnership | no | | yes |
| Social security benefits | no [5] | | yes |
| Maintenance payments | no | | sometimes |
| Rent from property | no | | yes [6] |

Key: LR = lower rate; BR = basic rate; HR = higher rate

(1) There could, of course, be more tax to pay if insufficient has been collected.

(2) Non-taxpayers can have interest paid without tax deducted – see p. 64.

(3) Tax is not deducted on stocks bought through the National Savings Stock Register (ask at the Post Office) or on War Loan (however it was purchased).

(4) Tax is deducted from the part of the annuity which counts as income, not the part which counts as a return of the capital.

(5) But if you return to work, tax if due will be deducted from your earnings.

(6) But rent in the Rent a Room scheme is tax-free up to a limit. (For more details see p. 218.)

ments after tax can be low.

### How you get tax relief

There are three ways in which you can get tax relief:

- you can make a lower payment by deducting the amount of the tax relief from the payment and keeping it yourself – for example, for your mortgage to buy your own home you pay interest on up to £30,000 of a loan in MIRAS after deducting tax relief of 15 per cent
- you can get your tax relief through the PAYE system. It will be included in your Notice of Coding and thus you will pay less tax on your salary each month
- you can get your tax relief by claiming it in your tax return. If you are going to work out your own tax bill you would deduct the amount in your calculation and pay less tax. Or your tax inspector will work out the bill allowing for the deduction.

The table on the right lists types of reliefs and how you get them. There are more details about reliefs in Chapter 11.

## ALLOWANCES

Everyone is entitled to an allowance to deduct from their income to ensure that some income is tax-free. This is called the personal allowance. But the amount of the allowance varies with age. There are other allowances that you may be able to claim – but these depend on your personal circumstances. There are details of allowances in the tables on p. 10 and in Chapter 12.

# Types of relief

| Type of relief | Amount of relief | How do you get tax relief? |
| --- | --- | --- |
| Charity: covenant | LR, BR or HR | LR, BR: make lower payments<br>HR: either PAYE code or tax bill |
| Charity: single payments (Gift Aid) | LR, BR or HR | LR, BR: make lower payments<br>HR: either PAYE code or tax bill |
| Enterprise Investment scheme (up to £100,000) | 20% | through your PAYE code or tax bill |
| Home income scheme | BR | make lower payments or through your PAYE code or tax bill |
| Interest on a loan to pay inheritance tax | LR, BR or HR | through your PAYE code or tax bill |
| Interest on business loans | LR, BR or HR | through your PAYE code or tax bill |
| Job expenses | LR, BR or HR | through your PAYE code or tax bill |
| Maintenance payments[1] | LR, BR or HR | through your PAYE code or tax bill |
| Mortgage interest to buy your home | 15% | make lower payments if the loan is in MIRAS |
| Mortgage interest on a home you let | LR, BR or HR | a lower tax bill on rental income |
| Pension contributions | LR, BR or HR | through PAYE system |
| Personal pension payments | Employees<br>BR or HR<br><br>Self-employed<br>LR, BR or HR | Employees<br>BR: make lower payments<br>HR: through PAYE code or tax bill<br>Self-employed<br>a lower tax bill |
| Private medical insurance for people aged 60 or over | BR | make lower payments |
| Training for NVQ and SVQ – level 5 | BR or HR | BR: make lower payments<br>HR: through PAYE code or tax bill |

Key: LR = lower rate; BR = basic rate; HR = higher rate

(1) Under old rules, see p. 44

# Details of allowances

| Allowance | Age | Tax year ending 5 April | Amount |
| --- | --- | --- | --- |
| Personal | up to 65 | 1997 | £3,765 |
| | | 1998 | £4,045 |
| | 65-74 | 1997 | £4,910[1] |
| | | 1998 | £5,220[1] |
| | 75 plus | 1997 | £5,090[1] |
| | | 1998 | £5,400[1] |
| Married couple's | up to 65 | 1997 | 15% of £1,790 |
| | | 1998 | 15% of £1,830 |
| | 65-74 | 1997 | 15% of £3,115[1] |
| | | 1998 | 15% of £3,185[1] |
| | 75 plus | 1997 | 15% of £3,155[1] |
| | | 1998 | 15% of £3,225[1] |
| Blind person's | any | 1997 | £1,250 |
| | | 1998 | £1,280 |
| Additional personal | any | 1997 | 15% of £1,790 |
| | | 1998 | 15% of £1,830 |
| Widow's bereavement | any | 1997 | 15% of £1,790 |
| | | 1998 | 15% of £1,830 |

(1) The amount of these allowances is reduced if total income is above a certain amount. In the tax year ending 5 April 1997 the allowances were reduced if total income was £15,200 and over and in the tax year ending 5 April 1998 the income limit is £15,600. For more details see p. 30.

# YOU AND YOUR TAX INSPECTOR

## CHAPTER 3

The popular image of the tax inspector is probably close to that of Hector, the character the Inland Revenue has used over the last year to publicise the change to self-assessment. In reality, your tax inspector is nothing like the pin-striped, bowler-hatted Hector. On the contrary, the whole of the Inland Revenue has been reshaped and updated over the last few years – a process which still continues and isn't due to be completed until 2002.

The Inland Revenue is in the middle of a fundamental change in organisation, helped along and precipitated by technological improvements and the switch to self-assessment. The process includes making the Revenue's working practices less cumbersome, reorganising the tax office structure and improving the service to customers. A major programme to rewrite tax laws without using jargon is also being implemented.

Under the old system, you might have needed to correspond with several different offices if you had different sources of income. And yet another office dealt with the collection of tax. Self-assessment has streamlined all this. You should have just one tax district, one tax reference and one calculation of income tax due.

For most taxpayers, the plan is that your Taxpayer Service Office will send out your tax return, process it when you send it back and issue your PAYE code. In most cases, it will be the only tax office you need to deal with. Specialist Taxpayer District Offices will check that employers operate the PAYE system properly and chase up non-payers and tax evaders. A network of high-street Taxpayer Enquiry Centres will provide a face-to-face service, where

> ## TAX-SAVING IDEA
> Make sure you keep all your records, including the originals of certificates and your working papers. If you don't, you may end up paying more tax than you should because you can't provide the evidence to back up your tax return. And don't forget you can be fined for not keeping your records.

taxpayers can talk to tax staff who will be able to call up their records on computer screens and deal with queries.

## YOUR OBLIGATIONS

### New source of income or capital

Under self-assessment, if you don't receive a tax return, you must notify your tax inspector of any income or capital gains, which have not been previously declared, within six months of the end of the tax year in which you make the income or gain. This is a more stringent requirement than the old system which allowed you 12 months.

There are certain circumstances in which you don't have to notify your tax office. This applies, for example, if all the income comes under the PAYE system or if the income is dividends from shares which is paid with tax deducted at 20 per cent and you pay tax at no more than the basic rate.

You should also note that even if you do not know the amount of your new source of income or capital gain by the deadline by which you must tell your tax office you should not delay. You must tell your tax office of a new source as soon as you know of it.

### Records

A new requirement is to keep records, for example, original copies of dividend vouchers, bank statements, certificates of interest received and any certificates showing foreign tax deductions, which you need to complete your tax return. This requirement started from 6 April 1996, so you should have been keeping your records already. If you don't have the original certificates,

> ## EXAMPLE
> Roger Rose is an employee paying tax under the PAYE system. He buys some shares in a UK company in October 1996 and receives a dividend of £84 some two months later. He also decides to do some freelance consulting on the side, as well as his job. He doesn't know how much income that will bring in, since part of his payment will be in the form of commission. He begins his business on 1 September 1996.
>
> Although he knows exactly how much income he will receive on his shares in the tax year ending 5 April 1997, he doesn't need to declare this income to the tax office until he fills in his tax return. This is because dividend income is paid with basic rate tax deducted. However, although he doesn't yet know what he will earn from his freelance business, he must tell his tax office by 6 October 1997 (that is, six months from the end of the tax year in which the income is earned).

you can complete your tax return using information that can be verified by an external source. But to get a tax refund you must have the originals. You also need to keep a copy of the working papers that you used to work out your calculations.

If you don't run your own business or have letting income, the period to keep records is one year from the date by which you must send back the tax return (31 January). However, this period is extended if there should be an enquiry into your affairs. Records must be kept until the enquiry is complete.

The period to keep records is also extended if you send in your return late or need to correct it after you have sent it in. The documents need to be kept until one year after the end of the quarter in which you amended the return or sent it in late. Quarters end on 31 January, 30 April, 31 July and 31 October.

> ## Example
>
> Ashley Hickie is a self-employed journalist. He also has some savings, such as unit trusts and a building society account. He completes his tax return for the year ended 5 April 1997, including carrying out the calculation of his own tax bill and returns it by 15 January 1998. Ashley must keep the dividend vouchers and certificate of interest, plus the working papers on this, until 31 January 1999. The records of his business and the working papers relating to it need to be kept much longer. He has to preserve them until 31 January 2003.

If you run your own business or receive any income from letting, you need to keep records for five years from the date by which you should send in your tax return (31 January). The records should include what you receive and spend in your business, for example, sales and purchase invoices.

The failure to keep records can result in a swingeing penalty (see p. 19).

## THE NEW TAX RETURN

Tax returns have been completely revised to cope with self-assessment. A fundamental change is that the information you will be asked to give in your 1997 tax return will be about just one tax year – the year ending on 5 April 1997. You need to give details about your income, deductions and allowances for that tax year. Before self-assessment, your tax return covered two years – it looked back at the tax year just ended for income, deductions and capital gains and forwards to the tax year just beginning for allowances.

Another change is that while there used to be at least three types of tax return available (called Form 11P, Form 11 and Form P1), from 6 April 1997, there is now one basic tax return of eight pages. The new form is sent to everyone who should receive a tax return. But there are also a lot of supplementary pages for particular types of income – self-employment, trusts, employment, share schemes, partnerships, land and property, foreign, capital gains and non-residence. You may not receive any of these or, in an extreme case, you might receive nine different supplements to the basic return. For more details about these supplements, (see p. 76).

In the past, it was acceptable to use such phrases as 'as returned' or 'as agreed' for income or the value of benefits. But the new return requires that you fill in the correct figure – otherwise you will not be able to work out how much income tax or capital gains tax you owe. This means you must get hold of the documents you need, including Forms P60 (your income from your job and the tax you have paid on it), P45 part 1A (your income and tax to date when you leave your job), P11D or P9D (your fringe benefits and expenses for the year), P2 (your notice of coding). Your employer has the responsibility to supply you with these forms (but not P2) by certain dates (see p. 22).

### Deadlines for your tax return

There are two important dates to bear in mind. If you want to ask the Inland Revenue to work out your tax bill on your behalf, as your agent, rather than yourself or a tax adviser, your tax return must be sent in by 30 September. This is the date by which you must also submit your return even if you do your own tax calculation if you want any previous underpayment (£1,000 or less) to be deducted through the PAYE system, rather than you paying it with the rest of your tax bill.

There is a different date set for returning your tax return if you or your tax adviser choose to calculate what you owe in income tax. This is 31 January.

If you have missed the 30 September deadline and decide that after all you want the Revenue to calculate the

---

**TAX-SAVING IDEA**

If you are an employee paying tax under the PAYE system and you have some other income, for example from investments, on which you will need to pay tax, you should send in your tax return with your tax calculation by 30 September. If you do this, and the amount of tax due is £1,000 or less, you will not have to pay tax on this extra income by 31 January. Instead, it will be included into your PAYE code for the following tax year and you will pay tax on it with your monthly salary, thus spreading out and delaying the payment of your tax bill.

tax due, you can still ask for this to happen. But your tax inspector won't guarantee to do this by the 31 January slot, so you may end up paying a penalty for late tax payment.

Where a tax return has been issued after 31 October, you are given three months to complete it and send it back to your tax office. But if the return is issued after 31 July and you want your tax inspector to calculate the tax due, it must be returned within two months.

**TAX-SAVING IDEA**
If you are sent a tax return, try to work out your own tax bill under self-assessment. Try not to leave it to your tax office. You must not calculate the bill incorrectly or hide any income, but you will be able to present the figures in your own way.

### If you don't send in your tax return
Failing to send back your completed tax return means you can be charged a penalty (see p. 19) and allows the Inland Revenue to issue what's called a determination. Your tax inspector produces an estimate, to the best of his or her belief and using the best information available, of how much tax you should pay. The tax shown on this determination is payable; you cannot appeal against it or postpone it.

The only way you can overturn this estimate is to complete your tax return and self-assessment. You must do this within five years of the date by which you should have sent it in, or, if it is later, within a year of the determination by your tax inspector.

Your tax inspector cannot make a determination if five years have passed since the date by which you should have sent in your tax return. There will also be penalties and interest to pay (see p. 19).

## TAX PAYMENTS
Under the old system, different tax bills on different types of income were paid at different times. Under self-assessment, after completing your tax return, either you or your adviser or your tax office work out the amount of tax due on all types of income and capital gains. When you return your tax return, at least by the following 31 January, you send in the amount of tax that you have calculated as being due. This is the final bill for income tax for the year.

### Interim payments
Self-assessment of income tax requires interim payments on account. These

will be based on what you paid in income tax the previous year. The estimate will be what was due in the previous year, less amounts deducted at source, what is deducted through the PAYE system, tax credits and so on. There is no adjustment for changing levels of income, tax rates or allowances, but you can ask for it to be adjusted.

For any one tax year, apart from those paying through the PAYE system, the income tax due will be paid in three instalments. The first interim payment on account normally half the amount of tax you paid in the previous year less any capital gains tax and tax deducted at source will be on 31 January during the tax year. The second interim payment on account (one-half of business profits) will be on 31 July following the end of the tax year. The final balancing income tax payment or repayment will be made after completion of the tax return on 31 January following the end of the tax year. Any capital gains tax due will also be paid with this third instalment.

However, there are rules which mean that these interim payments will not be required if they are small. Working on the basis of the tax due for the previous tax year, if the total tax payable, net of tax deducted at source (including PAYE), is less than £500 or if tax deducted at source (including PAYE) is more than 80 per cent of the total income tax plus Class 4 National Insurance due, then interim payments won't be required.

> **TAX-SAVING IDEA**
> Always check your Statement of Account to see if you can claim a reduction in interim payments. Don't pay more tax than you can show is likely to be due.

The effect of this new system will be that income tax will be paid either monthly through the PAYE system or half-yearly on 31 January and 31 July. Under the old system, tax due on some income was only paid on the one day; for example, higher rate tax on 1 December following the tax year and tax due on property and untaxed investment income on 1 January. All this income is now added together and tax is paid at the same time.

Employees can put off paying a final tax bill of £1,000 or less by asking for it to be included in next year's PAYE code. To achieve this, you have to send in your tax return, along with your tax calculation, by 30 September.

## Statement of Account
During autumn 1996, you may have received a Statement of Account giving an estimate of what you should pay on 31 January 1997 and the same figure will be due on 31 July 1997. This estimate is based on the tax you paid

for the tax year ending 5 April 1996. For how to check this statement (see p. 291). And for how to appeal against it if you think that you won't be paying as much tax in the current tax year as is given in the Statement of Account (see p. 291). You will need to use form SA303 to claim to reduce your payments on account.

### Interest and surcharges on unpaid tax
Interest is payable on tax which is paid late or unpaid. It will be automatically charged on tax not paid by 31 January, or the date by which it should be paid if a tax return has been issued late. If the tax is still not paid after 28 days, there is a surcharge of five per cent of the unpaid tax. A further five per cent surcharge of the amount of tax still unpaid after six months is imposed. Interest will be added to any unpaid surcharge, starting 30 days after the notice of the surcharge. The rate of interest will be based on the average rate of borrowing.

## CHANGES TO YOUR TAX RETURN

### Mistakes and corrections
Sometimes you may not know a figure with 100 per cent accuracy by the time it comes to fill in your tax return. What you have to do is to put in your best estimate and work out the tax due on that. When you can supply the final figure, you should do so. If there is more tax to pay, you will have to pay interest (or it could be a repayment interest if a refund is due) but no surcharges or penalties.

It's also possible that you might make a mistake when you complete the return. You can correct an error at any time within 12 months after the date the return should be sent back – 31 January.

If you don't spot a mistake but the Inland Revenue picks up an obvious error, such as an arithmetical mistake or a misunderstanding of principle, your tax office will correct the return within nine months of the date the return was sent in.

Either you or your tax office can correct mistakes. Any tax due as a result of the revised self-assessment should be paid either by the normal payment date or 30 days after the making of the self-assessment.

### Enquiries
The new self-assessment system gives your tax inspector the right to enquire into your tax return without giving any reason. A tax enquiry can be made into the return of an individual, a trustee, a partnership or a company. An

enquiry can be made only once into the same tax return.

An enquiry is quite different from your right as a taxpayer or your tax inspector's right to correct or amend your tax return (see previous page).

Your tax inspector must give you written notice of an enquiry. If you sent in your tax return on time, the notice must be made by 31 January the following year. If you sent in your return late, the notice of an enquiry can be issued up to a year after the end of the quarter in which you sent in your return (quarter ends are 31 January, 30 April, 31 July and 31 October). With an amended tax return, the notice can be issued up to a year after the end of the quarter in which you amended it.

Once the Inland Revenue has said it is going to enquire into your tax return, you are not able to amend it until after the enquiry is complete.

Your tax inspector has the right to demand that you produce certain documents. When you receive a notice of an enquiry, you may also receive a notice to produce these within 30 days. You can produce copies, but your tax inspector may insist on seeing the originals. You can appeal within 30 days against this notice to produce documents.

You can also appeal to the general commissioners (see p. 21) if you consider that an enquiry should not have been undertaken or is being continued unnecessarily. The general commisioners can issue a notice to the Inland Revenue requiring it to close the enquiry.

If your tax return or its amendment is the subject of an enquiry your tax inspector will issue you with a formal notice telling you it is completed, how much tax you are considered to owe (if any) and requiring you to amend your self-assessment. You may also be required to amend your self-assessment before the completion of an enquiry if your tax inspector decides that it is too low. You will be given 30 days to amend your self-assessment in line with your tax inspector's conclusions. In certain conditions, you can also use this 30-day period to amend your self-assessment yourself with any changes which you had notified to your tax inspector. If you don't amend your self-assessment, your tax inspector has 30 days in which to do it for you. You can appeal against this Revenue amendment.

### What your tax inspector can do if an enquiry has been completed
While a second enquiry cannot take place, the law allows a discovery assessment if you have been acting fraudulently or negligently. A discovery assessment cannot be made if it is a mistake of arithmetic or principle on your part.

Nor can it be made if the correct information was available to the Inland Revenue and it should have been possible to work out the correct tax.

A discovery means that your tax inspector has discovered that some income or gain on which you should have paid tax has not been included in your self-assessment, or the assessment is too low, or the amount of relief given is too much. A discovery assessment would be to collect the tax due. You can appeal against a discovery assessment (see next page).

If tax is overpaid, there will be a compensating repayment of interest. The interest repayable will be based on average investment returns available at that time less tax that would be paid.

## PENALTIES, APPEALS AND COMPLAINTS

### Penalties
A whole raft of penalties has been introduced to ensure the self-assessment system runs smoothly and taxpayers carry out their obligations:

- if you don't tell your tax office about a new source of income or capital gain within the required time limit, the maximum penalty imposed can be the amount of tax which would be assessed for that tax year. Interest can be charged on this penalty
- if you don't keep the records required under the self-assessment system, a penalty of up to £3,000 could be imposed. But there are certain exceptions to this, for example, if the documents which you have not kept are dividend vouchers or interest certificates – because there are other ways in which this income can be verified. Interest can be charged on this penalty
- failing to make the annual returns required from employers under the PAYE system and construction industry scheme by 19 May following the year of assessment would bring penalties of £100 for each month (or part of a month) by which they are overdue
- you are allowed to claim that you should not make interim payments of your tax bill (see p. 293), either because you will have no tax bill or because it will be covered by payments deducted at source (for example, earnings under the PAYE system or savings income paid with tax deducted). If you make an incorrect statement fraudulently or negligently, the maximum penalty is the amount or additional amount you would have paid on account if you had made a correct statement. Interest can be charged on this penalty
- if you fail to deliver your tax return, you can be fined £100 and a further penalty of up to £60 a day may be set by the commissioners for each day it is late starting from the day you are notified by the commissioners –

but this is only likely to happen if your tax office believes you may owe a substantial amount of tax. If your tax return is still not delivered six months after it was due you can be fined a further £100, and a delay of a year would mean that you could be charged a penalty of the amount of tax that would have been due. You can appeal against these penalties to the commissioners

- if you are in a partnership and you fail to deliver your partnership return, you can be charged the same penalties as above, but not the tax-geared penalty. There is no provision for reducing the £100 penalty
- if you fraudulently or negligently deliver an incorrect return, you can be charged a penalty equal to the amount of tax that would have been due
- if you don't produce the documents your tax inspector asks for during an enquiry, you can be charged a penalty of £50. If you still don't come up with the documents, a daily penalty can be imposed. The amount will be £30, but it could rise to £150 if your tax inspector chooses to take it to the commissioners.

Penalties which are based upon an amount of tax that is due can be limited by certain factors which your tax inspector could take into account. These include disclosure, cooperation and gravity.

A claim for tax relief, allowance or tax repayment must be made in a tax return, unless it couldn't be included at that time or within the arrangements for correcting a return. If you make a claim independent of a return, you will need documentary proof and you must keep all the records relating to the claim. If you do not keep your records, you may be fined a penalty of up to £3,000 for each and every claim.

## Appeals and complaints
You have the right to appeal against:

- an assessment which is not a self-assessment
- an amendment to your self-assessment by the Inland Revenue after an enquiry into your tax return
- an amendment of a partnership statement where a loss of tax is discovered
- a disallowance, in whole or in part, of a claim or election included in a tax return.

You have to give written notice of appeal within 30 days after the issue of the notice of assessment, amendment or disallowance. But if you want to appeal against an amendment by the Revenue as a result of an enquiry, you cannot appeal until you have received notice that the enquiry is complete.

Even though you are appealing against the tax, it is due unless you also apply to postpone payment of the tax.

If you disagree about the amount of the tax bill, you should first of all exhaust the avenues within the Inland Revenue to try and reach an agreement. It is always worth appealing to your tax inspector – he or she may not have made the original decision. However, if it becomes clear that the two of you are not going to agree, there remains the options of appealing to the commissioners – and if that doesn't work you could appeal to the High Court, then to the Appeal Court and ultimately to the House of Lords.

There are two types of commissioners. The general commissioners are not tax experts, but often local people acting in the same way as magistrates. There will be a clerk with expert knowledge on hand to advise them. The second group are known as special commisioners. These are part of the Civil Service and tax experts in their own right.

If you are dissatisfied with the way the Inland Revenue handles your tax affairs, you should first complain to your tax inspector. If you get no satisfaction, you should direct your complaints to the regional controller responsible for your tax office (ask the tax office for the name and address). If this doesn't work, you should channel your next communication to the independent Revenue Adjudicator. The Adjudicator's remit covers matters such as excessive delay, errors, discourtesy or the way your tax inspector has exercised his or her discretion. Complaints about your tax bill must be dealt with through the normal appeals procedure.

## THE PAYE SYSTEM

The government has used companies to collect tax from their employees for many a year. Your employer is an unpaid tax collector for the Inland Revenue using the PAYE system – Pay As You Earn. Every time employees are paid an amount of money, tax is deducted from the earnings and sent in a batch to the collector of taxes.

Your employer needs various bits of information to operate this system. The aim is that at the end of the tax year, each employee will have had the correct amount of tax deducted, although this does not always happen. Underpayments of tax might be collected in the following year through the PAYE system or in a tax bill at the end of the year.

Under the self-assessment system, an underpayment of tax which is calculated in a tax return, as long as it is £1,000 or less, and as long as you have returned your tax return by 30 September, along with your calculation of the tax you owe, can be included in your PAYE code for the next tax year. This means that you will not have to pay the lump sum direct to the Inland Revenue, but it will be deducted in monthly instalments from your salary.

The Inland Revenue will tell your employer what your PAYE code is and will also supply tax tables so that your employer can deduct the right amount of tax. If the number in your code is 405 for example, you will be entitled to £4,059 free of tax for the tax year. If you are paid monthly, you will receive one-twelfth of £4,059 (that is £338) each month. If you are paid weekly, you will receive £4,059 divided by 52 each week free of tax. This would be £78.

The PAYE system is flexible and can be adjusted during the tax year. If you are entitled to more allowances, for example, because you got married, you should tell your tax inspector who should issue a new PAYE code. Your monthly after-tax earnings should rise once the new code has been received by your employer

For how to check a Notice of Coding, see Chapter 23.

Your employer must give you certain forms by required dates so that you can use them to fill in your tax return. You should receive your P60 for the tax year ending 5 April 1997 by 31 May 1997. Form P9D or Form P11D should be received by 6 July 1997. Chase your employer if you don't receive them. You don't want to send in your tax return late because your employer is inefficient.

## DEADLINES

### From 6 April 1996

- Employees keep copies of all Notices of Coding (Form P2)
- Employees keep Form P45 part 1A on any change of employment
- Employees keep Form P160 on retirement
- Employees keep records of business miles and any other expenses that are tax deductible
- Keep dividend counterfoils, certificates of interest from banks, building societies and so on

### Within 60 days

- Tell your tax office you disagree with the statement of taxable social security benefits you receive from the benefit office

*On or before 31 January 1997*

- Make first interim payment on account of tax due for tax year ending 5 April 1997 according to the Statement of Account sent out in the last few weeks of 1996

*On or before 5 April 1997*

- Claim for allowances and deductions for tax year ending 5 April 1991
- Apply to allocate the married couple's allowance to the wife or to split equally between the two of you for the tax year ending on 5 April 1998

*April 1997*

- Self-assessment tax returns sent to taxpayers

*On or before 31 May 1997*

- Form P60 should have been given to all employees by employer

*On or before 4 June 1997*

- Choose to pay tax in instalments on exercise of option in the tax year ending 5 April 1997 to acquire shares through an approved scheme

*On or before 6 July 1997*

- Form P9D (or Form P11D) should have been given to employees receiving fringe benefits by employer, plus details of other benefits provided by someone else

*31 July 1997*

- Second interim payment of tax due for tax year ending 5 April 1997

*On or before 30 September 1997*

- Send in tax return if you want Inland Revenue to work out tax due
- Employees who have underpaid tax by £1,000 or less should send in their tax return, along with tax calculation, so that tax will be collected through the PAYE system

*On or before 5 October 1997*

- Tell your tax inspector about any new source of income or capital gain for year ending 5 April 1997

*On or before 30 January 1998*

- Claim to reduce payments on account for the tax year ending 5 April 1997 (see p. 293)
- Tell your tax inspector if you have reduced your payments on account by too little

- Send in your tax return, along with calculation of any income and capital gains tax due, plus payment for any unpaid tax for the year ending 5 April 1997
- Make first interim payment on account of tax due for tax year ending 5 April 1998 (statement received from Inland Revenue based on previous year's tax bill or your own self-assessment calculation)
- Choose to carry back personal pension payment made in the tax year ending on 5 April 1997 to the tax year ending on 5 April 1996

*On or before 5 April 1998*

- Claim for allowances and deductions for tax year ending 5 April 1992

*On or before 31 January 2000*

- Setting losses made in a new business for the tax year ending 5 April 1997 against other income
- Setting business losses made in the tax year ending 5 April 1997 against other income

*On or before 31 January 2003*

- Claim for allowances and deductions left out of tax return by mistake for the tax year ending 5 April 1997
- Claiming unused relief for retirement annuities and personal pension schemes for tax year ending 5 April 1997
- Setting business losses against future profits of the same business.

# TAX CHANGES FOR THE TAX YEAR STARTING 6 APRIL 1997

## CHAPTER 4

In his November 1996 budget, the Chancellor resisted any temptation to make big cuts in taxes ahead of the general election. While there was a further cut in the basic rate of income tax and some other reductions, there was also some tightening up, particularly in tax loopholes.

This guide has gone to press before the general election was held. The changes described here do not include any new elements introduced by a new government. We are proposing to send out a free update in the autumn – if you would like to receive a copy of this, see p. ix on what to do.

## Income tax rates
The basic rate of income tax was cut from 24 per cent to 23 per cent, the lower rate stayed at 20 per cent and the higher rate at 40 per cent. The income band for the lower rate of tax was widened by £200 to £4,100 (more than would be required under indexation to keep pace with inflation). This change means a quarter of taxpayers are already paying tax at no more than 20 per cent, which is the government's widely publicised objective for the basic rate. The income band for the basic rate was also increased by £600 in line with inflation.

The rate of tax which applies to income from discretionary trusts remains at 34 per cent.

## Allowances for income tax
Allowances were once again raised, some in line with the indexation rules, some by a larger amount. Personal allowances for those aged under 65 were increased by £280 from £3,765 to £4,045 (up 7.4 per cent) and age-related personal allowances for those aged 65 and over by £310 (up 6 per cent). These personal allowances were increased by £200 more than required by indexation.

Other allowances were increased by the amount required to keep them in line with inflation over the last year. They include married couple's, widow's bereavement, additional personal and blind person's – see p. 10. The tax relief on maintenance payments is linked to the married couple's allowance and will be £1,830 for the tax year ending 5 April 1998. Apart from the blind person's allowance where the relief is variable depending on your rate of tax, the rate of tax relief remains at 15 per cent.

The income limit for the age-related allowances was increased from £15,200 to £15,600, corresponding with the rise in prices.

## Capital gains tax and inheritance tax
The tax-free slice for capital gains was increased in line with the indexation rules from £6,300 to £6,500 (and for most trusts from £3,150 to £3,250).

The rate for inheritance tax was unchanged at 40 per cent. Inheritance tax will not become payable from 6 April 1997 until the value of taxable gifts is £215,000 or more (the previous threshold was £200,000).

## Employees
Employees who work away from their normal place of work will be able to claim travelling and subsistence expenses from 6 April 1998. So if you travel from home to a site, for example, this would apply to you. And if you have to work away from the workplace on a temporary basis, you will be able to claim as an expense the amount additional to what you spend on travel between home and the normal workplace.

The profit-related pay scheme is to be phased out. Over the next three years, the amount of pay which can be free of tax will be reduced, until on or after 1 January 2000, there will be no tax relief. The full details are in Chapter 14.

If you pay for your own vocational training, but were unable to claim tax relief because you have been getting public financial assistance, for example, a career development loan, the budget introduced measures to change this – see p. 117.

The Chancellor bumped up the tax on the private use of free fuel provided by employers for company cars. From 6 April 1997, the scale charges were increased by 13 per cent for petrol cars and 15 per cent for diesel cars. For the full details see Chapter 14.

## Savings and property
The Rent a Room scheme was freshened up by the budget. From 6 April 1997, the amount of rent from letting furnished accommodation in your main or only home which is tax-free is raised from £3,250 a year to £4,250.

After a flurry of changes in the last few years, there was little change for savings. The rate of tax on savings income remains at 20 per cent (with an extra 20 per cent to pay for higher rate taxpayers).

The cap on earnings for pension schemes (see p. 109) was increased from £82,200 to £84,000 in line with indexation. This applies to people who contribute to a personal pension scheme, joined an occupation pension scheme set up since 14 March 1989 or joined any occupation scheme from 1 June 1989.

## Businesses

The Chancellor broadened the rules for the Enterprise Investment Scheme and venture capital trusts (VCTs). From 26 November 1996, it was no longer necessary for the activities of each individual company in a group to qualify for the relief, simply the group as a whole. It was also made easier for managers of a venture capital trust to raise more money through an existing trust, rather than having to go to the expense of setting up a new one. This was achieved by giving the trust a further period of three years to invest the second amount of capital raised. These changes were designed to stimulate further investment in unquoted companies.

Another measure to improve investment in unquoted companies introduced a clearance scheme to allow companies to approach the Inland Revenue for a ruling on whether investment in their shares will qualify for capital gains tax reinvestment relief. This will help investors in companies traded on the Alternative Investment Market (which count as unquoted) as well as investors in companies that has shares which are not traded at all.

If your business spends more than £100,000 a year on long-life plant and machinery, the amount of your capital allowances is cut from 25 per cent a year to six per cent. Long life means an expected working life when new of 25 years.

## The tax crackdown

The Chancellor announced an initiative to bring in more tax by reducing tax avoidance and evasion. He proposed that £800 million would be spent over the next three years to bring in an estimated extra £2 billion a year.

# SEVENTY-FIVE WAYS TO SAVE TAX

**CHAPTER 5**

Here are 75 tips to cut your tax bill. None of them requires you to turn your life upside down in search of tax savings.

## All taxpayers

- Make sure you keep all your records, including the originals of certificates and your working papers. You can be fined for not keeping your records (p. 12).

- Keep careful records – apart from the legal requirement, it could help you pay less tax. Note down all the expenses you could claim: if you are an employee (see p. 169); if you are self-employed (see p. 197); if you let out property (see p. 221).

- Don't be late sending in your tax return. The 1997 tax return must be sent back by 31 January 1998 if you want to avoid an automatic £100 penalty (see p. 19).

- Always check your tax forms. As soon as you receive a Coding Notice or a Statement of Account, make sure your tax inspector has got the sums right. If you get a statement of taxable benefits, you must appeal against it within 60 days (see p. 96).

- If you are asked to make payments on account, check that you're not paying more than you need to. The figures will be based on last year's tax bill. If you expect your income to be lower this year or your allowances and reliefs to be higher, you can make reduced payments (see p. 293).

- Investigate the past. It may not be too late to claim an allowance or deduction you have forgotten about. Some of the more important deadlines for claims are given on p. 22.

- If you want to give money to charity, think about covenants, payroll-giving schemes and Gift Aid – you'll get tax relief on the gifts. There are more details in Chapter 11 (p. 106).

- Look closely at any gifts you make to charity by covenant or through Gift Aid. If you are a non-taxpayer or pay tax at the lower rate, you will not be able to keep all the tax relief you deduct at the basic rate from the gifts (p. 124). If your husband or wife pays tax, it may be better if he or she makes the gifts.

## Married

- If you are married, consider reorganising your investments so your investment income is paid to the partner who pays least tax on it.

- Married couples where one partner has a low income and can't use up all their allowances can transfer the married couple's allowance and blind person's allowance to their partner (see p. 40).

- If you are single and there is a child under 18 living with you at the start of the tax year, you may be able to claim the additional personal allowance, the same amount as the married couple's allowance (£1,790 for the tax year ending 5 April 1997, £1,830 for the tax year beginning 6 April 1997). You may also be entitled to claim this allowance if you are married but separated, or a married man whose wife is totally unable to look after herself (see p. 133).

- If you are separated or divorced and paying maintenance under arrangements made before March 1988, it could pay you to change the way you get tax relief on the payments (see p. 146).

- If you separate from your husband or wife, don't agree to make their mortgage payments as part of any maintenance arrangements – you won't get tax relief on mortgage interest. Give the money to your ex-spouse and he or she can claim the tax relief (see p. 48).

## Employees

- If you pay tax under the PAYE system and have some other income, for example from investments, on which you will need to pay tax, make sure you send your tax return back by 30 September – even if you are working out your own tax bill. If the amount of tax due is £1,000 or less, the tax on this extra income will be deducted from your earnings under PAYE in the tax year which begins on 6 April 1998 – not as a lump sum by 31 January.

- If you are an employee, see if you can negotiate the introduction of share option schemes (p. 174). These can be free of income tax.

- There is a long list of fringe benefits which are tax-free whatever your level of earnings – try to take advantage of them in your negotiations with your boss. These perks are still free of tax: entertainment by your suppliers or customers at cultural or sporting events (within certain rules); air miles (which enable you to make cheap flights); and non-cash gifts costing up to £100 from a third party, (see p. 147).

- Fringe benefits which are not tax-free can still be a tax-efficient way of being paid. The taxable value put on them may be much lower than the value to you. There is a rundown of how they are taxed in Chapter 14 (p. 146).

- If you have a company car, keep an eye on your business mileage as the end of the tax year approaches or if you are about to change your car. If your business mileage is approaching a rate of 2,500 or 18,000 miles a year, try to use the car for work enough to qualify for the reduction in the tax bill if you travel more than either of these amounts on business (see p. 156). Keep good records of your business mileage so you can substantiate your claims.

- If you plan to keep a company car for some years, you will pay less tax if it is registered just before the end of the tax year (April 5). The taxable value of a car which is more than four years old at the end of the tax year is reduced by one-third (see p. 156). If you buy a car just after the start of a tax year, it will be almost five years old before you get the reduction.

- Be aware that if you want a large, luxurious company car, you will be taxed fairly heavily for the privilege (see p. 156). Do your sums carefully before accepting a company car if you are just below the limit for paying higher rate tax (£26,100 in the tax year beginning 6 April 1997). If you have the option, consider taking a cheap, lightly taxed company car and taking the rest of the car allowance in cash which you can invest in a tax-free investment, such as additional contributions to your pension plan.

- Working parents should try to persuade their employers to provide child-care facilities, as this fringe benefit is tax-free. Your private childcare arrangements are not eligible for tax relief (see p. 148).

- If you often work away from home and think you may be affected by changes in what expenses you can claim (see p. 170), start keeping a note now of your costs of normal commuting. It may help you to establish what costs of travel you can claim.

- If you can arrange your work so you count as self-employed rather than an employee, you will be able to claim a wider range of expenses, (see p. 197). But remember there may be disadvantages in not having the protection of employment law. For more about the distinction between employees and the self-employed, see pp. 140 and 184.

- If you borrow to buy shares in a company where you work, you may be able to get tax relief on the loan (see p. 119). The company must be largely owned by its employees or you must have a large stake in it.

- If you are unemployed and not claiming social security benefits, ask your tax inspector for a rebate of tax paid when you were working.

- If you are working abroad, you can get tax relief on all your earnings there if you observe a few simple rules about the length of time you spend in the UK (see p. 166).

## Self-employed

- If you leave a job to become self-employed, ask your tax inspector for a rebate. It will help your finances, although not cut your actual tax bill.

- If you are self-employed or in partnership and your turnover is less than £15,000 a year, take advantage of the ability to send in three-line accounts (see p. 195). This won't save you any tax, but it may cut your book-keeping and accountancy fees.

- The introduction of self assessment means that earnings from self-employment are now taxed on a current-year basis. There are opportunities to save tax in the transition from a preceding year basis, (see p. 186).

- You can still claim as an expense for your business something you use partly for business and partly in your private life, for example, using your home for work, sharing the car (p. 198).

- When you first start your business, claim capital allowances on any equipment you already own but take into the business, for example, a car, desk and so on (see p. 207).

- You do not have to claim all the capital allowances you are entitled to. It may save you more tax to claim less and carry forward a higher value to the next year when your profits may be higher or your personal allowances lower (p. 206).

- If you are married and run your own business, consider employing your spouse if he or she does not work. It could save money if you pay your spouse just under the lower earnings limit for National Insurance contributions (p. 211).

- If you are in business and buying assets, see if they can be treated as short-life assets. The cost can be reclaimed over five years, whereas the writing-down allowances available on other sorts of assets mean the cost is reclaimed much more slowly (see p. 206).

- If you make a tax loss in your business, there are several ways this can be used to reduce tax on other income. Choose the one that will save you the most tax (see p. 209).

## Investments
- The government offers lots of tax incentives to persuade you to save for a pension. Take advantage of them. Chapter 8 (p. 62) and Chapter 11 (p. 106) tell you how to take them up.

- If you're approaching retirement, consider making extra contributions towards a pension. If you work for an employer, you can get tax relief on additional voluntary contributions (AVCs) to your employer's scheme (p. 69). With contributions to a personal pension scheme, you can get tax relief on a higher proportion of your earnings as you get older (p. 109).

- Take advantage of the rules that allow you to backdate contributions to personal pensions (see p. 111). You may be able to get a higher rate of tax relief – for example, if you paid tax at the higher rate in a previous tax year. If you haven't made the maximum contributions allowed in previous tax years, you can claim the unused relief up to six years later to make a bigger contribution (see p. 112).

- If you pay tax at the top rate of 40 per cent, tax-free investments can be attractive. Even if you could get a higher rate of return on a taxable investment, the after-tax return could be considerably lower.

- Non-taxpayers investing in banks, building societies and other investments where tax is deducted from the income should claim it back from the Inland Revenue. With interest from banks and building societies, you can arrange for it to be paid without deduction of tax if you are a non-taxpayer (see p. 64).

- If you want to give some capital to your children, any income it produces over £100 a year will be counted as yours. Choose investments that produce a tax-free income or gain (see pp. 83 and 246).

- If you are elderly, watch out for the income trap – the level of income where the extra allowances paid to people aged 65 or over are withdrawn. The withdrawal is phased, but it means you are effectively taxed at a higher-than-normal rate on each extra £1 of income (see p. 39). Consider tax-free investments if this is the case.

- If you invest in shares, investment trusts or unit trusts, make sure you invest the maximum through personal equity plans (PEPs) – there's no tax to pay on the income or gains. You can invest up to £9,000 a year in PEPs – and a couple can invest double that amount. If you buy shares in a privatisation issue, transfer these into your PEP (see p. 71).

- Investing in a tax exempt special savings account (TESSA) means tax-free interest on up to £9,000 of savings – as long as you can leave the money for the full five years (p. 72).

- If you receive shares through an employee profit-sharing scheme or a savings-related share option scheme, transfer the £3,000 maximum for a tax year into a single-company PEP (see p. 71). This will mean no income tax on the dividends and no capital gains tax when you eventually sell the shares.

- Investors should consider having some investments which give a capital gain rather than income. There is a tax-free allowance of net capital gains (£6,500 in the tax year beginning 6 April 1997) which you can make each tax year (see p. 262).

- If you took out a life insurance policy before midnight on 13 March 1984, the chances are that you get tax relief on the premiums (currently at 12.5 per cent). However, altering the policy (for example, increasing the benefits unless this is done automatically under the policy) could mean losing the tax relief (see p. 67). Consider carefully before altering – perhaps you can achieve your objective in another way.

- If you get income from trusts, it comes with a tax credit – you can reclaim some or all of this if it is more than you should have paid (see p. 240).

Unless you pay tax at the higher rates, you are almost certainly entitled to a tax rebate on income from discretionary trusts.

- People investing in a new business can claim tax relief on up to £100,000 in a tax year through the Enterprise Investment Scheme. There is also generous tax relief for investing in venture capital trusts (see p. 72).

- If you get income from investments abroad on which you have paid foreign tax, tax credit relief can reduce the amount of UK tax you pay (see p. 236).

## Homeowners

- The cost of borrowing money to buy a home can be reduced by the tax relief on mortgage interest paid on up to £30,000 of loans. You can get the tax relief on a range of loans – it doesn't have to be a mortgage. You can use the loan to buy a home anywhere in the UK or Ireland – even if it is a caravan or houseboat. Chapter 24 (p. 50) tells you the rules so you get the maximum relief.

- A married couple can choose to share the tax relief on mortgage interest however they like. If some split other than an equal one would save you tax, make an allocation of interest election (see p. 53 for when it would pay to do this).

- If you have a home improvement loan taken out before 6 April 1988, consider carefully before you replace it with another loan with a lower rate of interest. You would not be able to claim tax relief on the interest paid on the replacement loan (see p. 55).

- You can be away from your home for quite long periods and still get mortgage interest tax relief (the various concessions you can claim are on p. 55). You'll also need to keep an eye on the capital gains tax position – don't lose private residence relief which means you pay no capital gains tax on your only or main home (see p. 59).

- Do you have more than one home? You may have to pay capital gains tax when you sell your second home (p. 58). But you can choose which of your homes counts as your main one, make sure you nominate the home that is likely to incur the biggest capital gains tax bill.

- Do you want an income of over £80 a week tax-free? If you let out a room in your home under the rent a room scheme, you can take £4,250 of gross rent a year tax-free. This relief can reduce your tax bill even if the income is higher (see p. 218).

- If you let out your home, you might do better to switch from mortgage interest tax relief to claiming the interest as an expense against letting income. You get the tax relief at your highest rate of tax and there's no £30,000 limit on the loan (see p. 56).

- If you let out your second home, try to make sure you meet the conditions for the rent to be taxed as income from furnished holiday lettings (p. 220). You can claim a wider variety of deductions against tax, and you may be able to avoid capital gains tax when you sell the home.

- You can claim a tax allowance for the wear and tear incurred in letting out furnished property (see p. 228).

- If you have made a loss letting out property, you may be able to use this to reduce other parts of your tax bill (see p. 230).

- If you've let out part or all of your home, lettings relief could mean no capital gains tax to pay when you dispose of it (see p. 60).

## Capital gains tax

- Try to use the tax-free allowance for capital gains tax every year – you can't carry over unused allowances to other years. You can always sell some shares showing a profit and buy them back a little later to make a gain that uses up the allowance. This is known as bed and breakfasting (see p. 263).

- Husband and wife are each entitled to the tax-free allowance of net capital gains (see p. 263). Consider reorganising your possessions so each of you can use up the limit before either starts paying capital gains tax.

- If you are going to dispose of assets, split the disposals over several years. You can then claim the tax-free allowance for capital gains to reduce the bill each year.

- If you are facing a capital gains tax bill on the disposal of one large asset, you could sell assets that are showing losses to set against the gain. If you don't really want to get rid of these other assets, you can buy them back some time later (see p. 264).

- If you own valuables such as antiques, a second home or collectables, keep careful records of what they cost you to buy and maintain. You could face a capital gains tax bill when you dispose of them – allowable expenses can reduce the tax bill (p. 257).

- If you are thinking of making a gift to charity of an asset which is showing a loss, think again. It would be better to sell the asset and give the money to the charity (see p. 246).

- Do not forget to claim losses if you dispose of something like shares or valuables at a loss. Losses can be set off against taxable gains, and carried over to later years. But you must claim them within time limits (see p. 264). Keep careful records so you don't forget them later!

- If you have a big capital gains tax bill, think about investing the gain in growing companies. Reinvestment relief can defer the bill (see p. 267).

## Inheritance tax

- Draw up a will. There are simple steps you can take to minimise the tax payable on your estate when you die and to reduce the complications for those you leave behind (see p. 345). Making a will helps you to start thinking about inheritance tax.

- Make as full use as possible of the gifts you can make which do not fall into the inheritance tax net. Gifts on marriage and those made out of normal income are tax-free (p. 347).

- Share your wealth with your husband or wife so you can each make tax-free gifts. There is no capital gains tax to pay on gifts between a married couple (p. 263).

- Use life insurance to blunt the impact of inheritance tax. Policies written in trust go straight to the beneficiary and don't form part of your estate (see p. 350). If you pay the premiums out of your normal spending, they are tax-free gifts (see p. 347).

- If you own a small business or farm, take professional tax advice. There are extensive tax reliefs which can mean you pay little or no capital gains tax (p. 274) or inheritance tax (p. 351), but they are complicated and need careful planning.

- There are steps you can take to reduce an inheritance tax bill after a death (see p. 353). In particular, you can rearrange inheritances in ways that reduce the amount of tax.

# MARRIAGE AND DIVORCE

## CHAPTER 6

Married couples are treated as two independent taxpayers by the Inland Revenue. They are taxed on their own income and gains and have their own allowances. Each is responsible for filling in their own tax return and paying their own tax bills.

However, there are some aspects of the tax system which recognise that husband and wife are more than just two individuals living together. One is that the Chancellor still blesses marriage with the wedding gift of an extra income tax allowance – the married couple's. Another is they can transfer some allowances between them in certain circumstances. Gifts between husband and wife don't normally fall into the net for capital gains tax or inheritance tax. And by sharing their wealth, a couple can each use their tax-free allowances to reduce the amounts paid in tax.

This chapter explains the opportunities to save tax in marriage. It sets out the rules for what happens when marriages come to an end, and the taxation of maintenance payments. And it gives some brief guidance on what happens if you are widowed. For how marriage affects mortgage interest tax relief, see p. 53, and information about capital gains tax is on p. 263, and on inheritance tax on p. 347.

## MARRIAGE

### Married couple's allowance
A husband and wife are each entitled to a personal tax allowance in the same way as single people. And if they are 65 or over during the tax

> ## TAX-SAVING IDEA
> If one of you pays tax at a higher rate than the other, you should consider giving investments which produce a taxable income to the partner who would pay least tax on the income.
>
> Gifts between married couples must be genuine – you can't hand them over with strings attached. If you are reluctant to give away the investments completely, consider putting them into joint names with your spouse so the income is shared equally (see p. 41).

year, they can claim the higher amounts of personal allowance for older people (see below). This personal allowance is deducted from total income (see right) in arriving at the taxable income on which the individual's tax bill is calculated

But they can also claim married couple's allowance which can be allocated to either the husband or the wife, or split equally between them. Unlike the personal allowance, the married couple's allowance reduces their tax bill by a fixed amount – it is not used to reduce their income for tax purposes. For the tax year beginning 6 April 1997, for example, the allowance is £1,830 for people under the age of 65. Tax relief is given at 15 per cent against this amount – giving a maximum tax-saving of £274.50 for the tax year.

## EXAMPLE

Janet Lardon is a high flier on a salary of £60,000 a year and income from shares and savings accounts of £5,000 a year before tax. She pays tax at the higher rate of 40 per cent on her earnings – and that will be the rate for any additional income from investments.

She decides to share the investments with her husband Ted, who pays tax at the basic rate only. She puts them in their joint names, so £2,500 of the investment income is taxed as his. He has to pay tax on dividends and interest only at the lower rate of 20 per cent (see pp63,64), so they save higher rate tax of 20 per cent of £2,500, that is £500 a year.

The married couple's allowance goes automatically to the husband. However, the husband and wife can ask their tax inspectors to set it against the wife's income – they should both sign Inland Revenue Form 18 before the start of the tax year it is to apply to. The same procedure would be required if they subsequently wanted the allowance switched back to the husband.

## TAX-SAVING IDEA

If one of you does not pay tax, allocate the married couple's allowance to the partner who does. If this means changing the current allocation, do it before 6 April 1998 if you want it to come into force for the tax year which begins on that date.

Either partner can ask for half the allowance to be allocated to their income – again this must be done before the start of the tax year.

### For those aged 65 or over

As with the personal allowance, there are higher rates of married couple's allowance for people who are 65 or over at any time during the tax year. The figures for this tax year and the last tax year – and the maximum tax-savings – are given in the table below.

| Age of older partner during tax year | Tax year ending 5 April 1997 | | Tax year ending 5 April 1998 | |
|---|---|---|---|---|
| | maximum allowance £ | maximum tax-saving £ | maximum allowance £ | maximum tax-saving £ |
| Under 65 | 1,790 | 269 | 1,830 | 275 |
| 65-74 | 3,115 | 467 | 3,185 | 478 |
| 75 and over | 3,155 | 473 | 3,225 | 484 |

As with the married couple's allowance for under-65s, it will normally be given to the husband. It can be switched to the wife or split equally between the pair – but only the amount under-65s get can be allocated in this way. The extra allowance for those aged 65 and over always goes to the husband.

This additional amount is gradually reduced if the husband's 'total income' is above a certain level – even if the couple are getting the allowance because of the wife's age. Total income is broadly all your income less deductions such as pension contributions (see p. 4).

If the husband's total income in the tax year ending 5 April 1998 is £15,600 or more, his personal allowance is first reduced by £1 for each extra £2 over the limit until he is getting the same allowance as the under-65s. This would be when his 'total income' had reached £17,950 (£18,310 if 75 or over). Then the married couple's allowance is similarly reduced until it is the same as for the under-65s. This would be when his total income reached £20,660 (£21,100 if he is 75 or over, or £20,740 if he isn't but his wife is.).

If the husband is under 65, he won't get the higher personal allowance, so if his total income is over £15,600 it will immediately start to reduce the married couple's allowance. He will end up with the same allowance as under-65s if total income is £18,310 (£18,390 if his wife is 75 or over).

---

## TAX-SAVING IDEA

If one of you is 65 or over and the husband's 'total income' is £15,600 or more in the tax year which began on 6 April 1997, see if you would save tax by giving investments that produce a taxable income to the wife. Even if the husband is under 65, his total income could be reducing the amount of married couple's allowance you get.

The total income limit for the tax year ending on 5 April 1997 was £15,200.

## Transfer of allowances because of low income

If either husband or wife has a tax bill which is too low to use up all their married couple's allowance, they can ask to have the unused part deducted from the tax bill of their spouse. You can do this after the end of the tax year in which you got the allowance – and it can cover the extra allowance paid to a husband where one of you is 65 or over. (See p. 130 for how to claim this.) The same is true if you get blind person's allowance and can't fully use it because your income is too low. It can be transferred to your partner even if not blind.

You have up to five years and ten months after the end of the tax year to transfer the unused allowances. So for the tax year ending 5 April 1997, you can make a claim any time up to 31 January 2003. But if you know in advance that your income will not be big enough to benefit from these allowances, you can ask your tax inspector to transfer the part you estimate will be unused to your spouse's PAYE code.

## Allowances in the year of marriage

In the tax year of your marriage, you get a proportion of the married couple's allowance. The proportion depends on the date of the wedding (see table on the right).

If a man has a child living with him when he marries, he can carry on claiming the full additional personal allowance for single parents (which is the same as the married couple's allowance) instead of a fraction of the married couple's allowance. He can't claim additional personal allowance after the

> ## Example
>
> Jasper Duffy, 68, has a total income of £19,750 – of which £9,300 a year is from savings and investments. Because his total income is over the £15,600 limit, it reduces the amount of personal allowance he gets to the amount for under-65s. But it is also high enough to reduce the married couple's allowance the Duffys get by £1 for each £2 over £17,950.
>
> He decides to share his savings and investments equally with his wife Ellen, whose total income is well below the £15,600 limit. He puts them all into their joint names, which means only half the income they produce is his. This reduces his total income by half of £9,300 = £4,650 to £15,100.
>
> The Duffys will thus get the full amount of married couple's allowance for people aged 65 and over. And Jasper will get the full higher personal allowance for those aged 65 and over.

tax year he marries unless his wife is totally unable to look after herself throughout the tax year (see p. 133).

If a woman has been claiming additional personal allowance, she can claim it for the year she marries, but not after.

| Date of marriage before | Tax year ending 5 April 1997 | | Tax year ending 5 April 1998 | |
| --- | --- | --- | --- | --- |
| | maximum allowance £ | maximum tax-saving £ | maximum allowance £ | maximum tax-saving £ |
| 6 May | 1,790 | 268.50 | 1,830 | 274.50 |
| 6 June | 1,641 | 246.15 | 1,678 | 251.70 |
| 6 July | 1,492 | 223.80 | 1,525 | 228.75 |
| 6 August | 1,343 | 201.45 | 1,373 | 205.95 |
| 6 September | 1,194 | 179.10 | 1,220 | 183.00 |
| 6 October | 1,045 | 156.75 | 1,068 | 160.20 |
| 6 November | 895 | 134.25 | 915 | 137.25 |
| 6 December | 746 | 111.90 | 763 | 114.45 |
| 6 January | 597 | 89.55 | 610 | 91.50 |
| 6 February | 448 | 67.20 | 458 | 68.70 |
| 6 March | 299 | 44.85 | 305 | 45.75 |
| 6 April | 150 | 22.50 | 153 | 22.95 |

## Jointly owned assets

If you have investments which are jointly owned, your tax inspector will assume the income from them is split equally between you. If the investments are not owned in equal proportions, you can have the income divided between you to reflect your actual shares of it. You do this by both signing a declaration of beneficial interests on Form 17 (available from tax offices) and sending it to your tax inspector.

The new split of joint income applies from when the declaration is signed – it can't be backdated. If you acquire new assets on which the 50:50 split is not to apply, you must make a further declaration. Note the split for income will also be used to allocate any gain on selling an asset between you when you dispose of it (see p. 263).

## SEPARATION AND DIVORCE

You should tell your tax inspector when you separate – even if you have yet to make a deed of separation or seek a court order. The Inland Revenue will treat you as no longer living with your husband or wife if you have parted in circumstances that make it look as if the separation is permanent.

You should tell the Inland Revenue even if you weren't paying tax before – contact your local tax office (under Inland Revenue in the telephone book). You will be asked to fill in a form about the separation and provide documentation about it. You must also tell your tax inspector if you get back together again or remarry.

## Tax allowances

Each of you retains your personal allowances. And each of you will also retain any married couple's allowance you were getting before the separation – but only for the rest of the tax year.

If either of you has a child under 18 living with you at the start of the tax year, you can claim additional personal allowance – worth the same as married couple's (see p. 133).

---

## EXAMPLE

Joe and Jenny Barrett separate on 15 April 1997. They have three children under 18, one of whom is to live with Joe while the other two will live with Jenny. Before separation they split the £1,830 married couple's allowance between them.

For the tax year beginning 6 April 1997, each will get the personal allowance of £4,045, an additional personal allowance for having a child living with them of £1,830 and half the married couple's allowance – £915. That makes total allowances of £6,790. Of this total, tax relief is at 15 per cent only on the £2,745 of additional personal and married couple's allowances.

In the tax year which begins on 6 April 1998, each will get the personal allowance and additional personal allowance. Neither will then be entitled to married couple's allowance.

---

Where a couple separated on or before 5 April 1990, the husband could go on getting married couple's allowance as long as he wholly maintained his wife by making voluntary payments. This can continue until the couple divorce.

## Maintenance payments

Maintenance can take several forms, including direct payments of cash or the provision of support such as a home. Where this is provided voluntarily – that is, payment cannot be enforced – the person paying it gets no tax relief and the person getting it does not have to pay tax on what they receive.

But most maintenance payments are made under enforceable agreements, such as a deed of separation, court order or assessment by the Child Support Agency. There is some tax relief for most enforceable maintenance payments, provided they are enforceable in the UK or another country in the European

Economic Area (the EU plus Iceland, Liechtenstein and Norway).

But the amount of tax relief the giver gets on maintenance payments – and how the recipient is taxed on them – depends on when the arrangements were made. What follows below is an explanation of the rules that have applied to new arrangements made in the last nine years or so.

The old rules (pre-1988 or so) are set out on p. 44 – and apply to the following:

- court orders made on or before 30 June 1988, provided they had been applied for on or before 15 March 1988
- maintenance agreements made on or before 14 March 1988 – if you wrote to your tax inspector on or before 30 June 1988
- any agreement made on or after 15 March 1988 which replaces such court orders or agreements – provided the person who receives the payments is unchanged.

### Rules for new maintenance arrangements

Under the new rules for arrangements since 1988, any maintenance payments you receive are tax-free. This applies even if you remarry and payments continue for a child, for example.

Thus the person receiving the maintenance can have other income up to the amount of the personal allowance (£4,045 for the tax year beginning 6 April 1997) before paying income tax.

If you make enforceable maintenance payments to an ex-husband or ex-wife, you can get tax relief equivalent to the married couple's allowance – that is get tax relief of 15 per cent of the payments you make up to the level of the married couple's allowance (£1,830 in the tax year beginning 6 April 1997). If you are already getting tax relief under the old rules below, it is deducted from the amount you can get under the new rules.

You don't get any tax relief on payments made direct to a child, or to someone you weren't married to. Lump sum payments are excluded – as are any payments which already qualify for tax relief (such as mortgage interest payments). The tax relief ends if the ex-spouse remarries.

The maximum you can get under the new rules is the same however many former spouses you are making maintenance payments to. But it is in addition to any other tax allowances, such as part or all of the married couple's allowance you are allowed to keep during the year of separation.

You get the tax relief on these maintenance payments through your PAYE code (see p. 280) or through an adjustment to your tax bill. You do not deduct any tax from the maintenance payments you make.

## Rules for old maintenance payments

If the maintenance arrangements were made before the 1988 deadlines listed above, the old rules for the taxation of enforceable maintenance payments apply. They also cover any agreements made since those deadlines which replace, vary or add to such arrangements.

## Taxation of payments received

Under the old rules, payments received by an ex-wife or ex-husband are tax-free only within limits. The limit is the married couple's allowance, which is £1,830 for the tax year beginning 6 April 1997, plus any increase in maintenance payments made since the tax year ending 5 April 1989. If you get more than this, the excess is added to your taxable income and you pay tax on it at your top rate. If you remarry and continue receiving the maintenance, you no longer get the £1,830 tax-free.

Anything paid direct to a child under a court order is fully taxable – though again, not any increase on the court order paid since the tax year ending 5 April 1989. The child will be entitled to a personal allowance to set against the income. Once the child is 21, the payments become tax-free.

Payments to a child under a legally binding agreement are tax-free. If these are paid after deduction of basic rate tax, the child may be able to claim a refund if it is more than he or she should have paid.

## Tax relief on payments made

Under the old rules, you can get tax relief on maintenance you pay to an ex-wife or ex-husband, and on some payments to your children. You cannot get tax relief on payments to an unmarried partner.

The maximum amount you get tax relief on is the amount you got tax relief on in the tax year ending 5 April 1989. You get tax relief at 15 per cent on what you pay, up to the amount of the married couple's allowance – £1,830 in the tax year beginning 6 April 1997. If the amount qualifying for tax relief is more than the married couple's allowance, you get tax relief on the excess at your top rate of tax.

If you pay more maintenance now than in the tax year ending 5 April 1989, you won't get any tax relief on the increase. So if you got tax relief on payments of £3,000 in the tax year ending 5 April 1989, that is the maximum

# Example

Lewis and Monica Lomax separated on 6 October 1992. Their three children live with Monica, and Lewis makes enforceable maintenance payments of £90 a week (£4,680 a year) from his salary of £25,000 a year. Monica has a job which pays £12,500 a year.

Monica will pay no income tax on the maintenance payments. In the tax year beginning 6 April 1997, Monica's tax bill will be calculated as follows:

| | | |
|---|---|---|
| Earnings | | £12,500.00 |
| Less personal allowance | | £4,045.00 |
| Taxable income | | £8,455.00 |
| | | |
| Tax due: | 20 per cent of £4,100 | £820.00 |
| | 23 per cent of £4,355 | £1,001.65 |
| | | £1,821.65 |
| Less additional personal allowance: 15 per cent of £1,830 | | £274.50 |
| Total tax | | £1,547.15 |

So Monica's after-tax income is £12,500 less £1,547 tax plus maintenance of £4,680 – a total of £15,633 for the tax year beginning 6 April 1997.

Lewis's tax bill for the same tax year is calculated as follows:

| | | |
|---|---|---|
| Earnings | | £25,000.00 |
| Less personal allowance | | £4,045.00 |
| Taxable income | | £20,955.00 |
| | | |
| Tax due: | 20 per cent of £4,100 | £820.00 |
| | 23 per cent of £16,855 | £3,876.65 |
| | | £4,696.65 |
| Less tax relief on maintenance payments: maximum is 15 per cent of the £1,830 married couple's allowance | | £274.50 |
| Total tax | | £4,422.15 |

Thus Lewis has an after-tax income of £25,000 less £4,422 tax, less maintenance payments of £4,680 – a total of £15,898 for the tax year beginning 6 April 1997.

on which you will get tax relief in the tax years ending 5 April 1997 and 1998. With payments to a child, you get tax relief only if they are paid under a court order to a child under the age of 21.

## Example

Conrad Murdoch pays £3,000 a year maintenance to his former wife Theresa and £2,000 direct to each of his two children under a court order which falls under the old rules. In the tax year ending 5 April 1989, he paid £2,500 to Theresa and £1,250 to each of the two children – a total of £5,000. He earns £40,000 a year, while Theresa earns £9,500.

In calculating her tax bill for the tax year beginning 6 April 1997, Theresa first calculates how much of her £3,000 maintenance payment is taxable. She can deduct two sums from it:

- the £1,830 married couple's allowance for the tax year
- the £500 increase she received over what she was given in the tax year which ended on 5 April 1989.

Thus she can deduct £1,830 + £500 = £2,330 from the £3,000 of maintenance she received – leaving just £670 which is taxable. Theresa's tax bill is calculated as follows:

| | | | |
|---|---|---|---|
| Earnings | | £9,500.00 | |
| Taxable maintenance payments | | £670.00 | |
| Total income | | | £10,170.00 |
| Less personal allowance | | | £4,045.00 |
| Taxable income | | | £6,125.00 |
| Tax due: | 20 per cent of £4,100 | £820.00 | |
| | 23 per cent of £2,025 | £465.75 | |
| | | | £1,285.75 |
| Less additional personal allowance: 15 per cent of £1,830 | | | £274.50 |
| Total tax | | | £1,011.25 |

So Theresa's after-tax income is her £9,500 earnings, plus £3,000 maintenance payments, less £1,011 tax – £11,489 for the tax year which began on 6 April 1997.

## Switching from the old rules to the new

It could pay you to switch to the new rules if you would get more tax relief on the maintenance payments you make.

This could happen if you made maintenance payments of less than £1,830 in the tax year ending 5 April 1989 and you are now paying more than this. Under the old rules, you are restricted to tax relief on what you paid then; under the new rules, you would get tax relief on the equivalent of the married couple's allowance – £1,830 for the tax year beginning 6 April 1997.

But if you switch to the new rules, you would lose any tax relief on payments

The two children can each deduct the personal allowance of £4,045 from the maintenance they receive in the tax year beginning 6 April 1997. As this is more than the £2,000 they each get, they pay no tax on their maintenance payments. Each of them could have another £4,045 – £2,000 = £2,045 of income before paying tax.

In calculating his tax bill for the tax year ending 5 April 1997, Conrad first calculates how much of his maintenance payments qualify for tax relief. He can get tax relief on no more than he paid in the tax year ending 5 April 1989 – £5,000. He will get tax relief at 15 per cent on the first £1,830 of this, and at his top rate of tax on the remaining £5,000 – £1,830 = £3,170. His tax bill will be as follows:

| | | | |
|---|---|---|---|
| Earnings | | | £40,000.00 |
| less allowances: | | | |
| maintenance allowable at top rate | | £3,170.00 | |
| personal allowance | | £4,045.00 | |
| Total allowances | | | £7,215.00 |
| Taxable income | | | £32,785.00 |
| Tax due: | 20 per cent of £4,100 | £820.00 | |
| | 23 per cent of £22,000 | £5,060.00 | |
| | 40 per cent of £6,685 | £2,674.00 | |
| | | | £8,554.00 |
| Less tax relief on first £1,830 of | | | |
| maintenance payments at 15 per cent | | | £274.50 |
| Total tax | | | £8,279.50 |

Thus Conrad has an after-tax income of £40,000, less £8,280 tax, less maintenance payments of £7,000 – a total of £24,720 for the tax year which began on 6 April 1997.

you make to your children under a court order.

You can switch from the old rules for taxing maintenance payments to the new rules, simply by filling in Inland Revenue Form 142. To have the payments taxed under the new rules, you must tell your tax inspector within a year of the end of the tax year in which you made the pay-

# EXAMPLE

Conrad and Theresa Murdoch look at whether it would pay them to switch to the new rules. They quickly see they are better off sticking to the old rules where Conrad gets tax relief on £5,000 of payments; under the new rules, his tax relief would be limited to £1,830 of payments in the tax year which began on 6 April 1997.

ments. So for payments you make in the tax year beginning 6 April 1997, you must make the change on or before 5 April 1999. Once you have made the change to the new rules, you cannot go back to the old ones.

## What happens to your home?

Once you are separated, you are likely to need two homes. You can each get tax relief on interest you pay on loans to buy your only or main home (see p. 50).

However, if you pay the interest direct to the lender on behalf of your ex-spouse, you won't get tax relief (unless you bought the home for the ex-spouse on or before 5 April 1988 – see p. 55). The best financial arrangement is for you each to pay the mortgage for the home you live in.

## Capital gains tax and inheritance tax on separation

You can carry on making gifts to your ex-husband or ex-wife in the year of separation without falling

> ## EXAMPLE
> Damian Boland makes enforceable maintenance payments of £1,900 a year to his ex-wife Debbie under an agreement originally drawn up in 1986 to support her and their child. But he has been steadily raising the amount over the years – he paid £1,300 in the tax year ending 5 April 1989. So the amount he gets tax relief on under the old rules is pegged at £1,300. He gets tax relief of 15 per cent of £1,300 – £195 a year.
>
> Under the new rules, Damian would get tax relief on maintenance payments up to the level of the married couple's allowance – £1,830 for the tax year ending 5 April 1997. He would be better off switching, when he would get tax relief of 15 per cent on £1,830 = £274.50. And since the married couple's allowance has risen each year in line with other tax allowances, the value of the tax relief should rise.

into the net for capital gains tax. After this, gifts may lead to a capital gains tax bill in the same way as for any other gifts (see p. 266).

However, if one of you moves out of the family home and gives or sells it to the other within three years of the separation, there will be no capital gains tax to pay. Even after that, there may be no capital gains tax if your ex-spouse is still living there and you have not claimed any other property as your only or main home.

If you bought a home for your ex-spouse on or before 5 April 1988, there will be no capital gains tax to pay when you dispose of it, as long as the ex-spouse has lived in it rent-free ever since.

Gifts between a separated husband and wife are free of inheritance tax (see

p. 347). Once you are divorced, gifts may fall into the inheritance tax net unless they are for the maintenance of the ex-spouse or any children.

## WIDOWED

When your husband or wife dies, you keep the married couple's allowance for the rest of the tax year in which the death happens. And if you have living with you a child or children under 18 at the start of the tax year, you can get additional personal allowance.

Widows can also get widow's bereavement allowance – £1,830 for the tax year beginning 6 April 1997. The amount of tax relief is restricted to 15 per cent in the same way as for married couple's allowance. This allowance can also be claimed in the tax year after the one in which you are widowed.

You can go on getting additional personal allowance for as long as a child who is under 18 at the start of the tax year is living with you.

# HOME AND TAX

**CHAPTER 7**

Buying a home is probably the biggest purchase you will make. Your mortgage payments are almost certainly the largest outgoing in your household budget. And your home is also likely to be your most valuable asset.

This chapter tells you how to keep the cost of the mortgage as low as possible by claiming all the tax relief you are entitled to on the interest. It also explains how to make sure you don't pay a hefty capital gains tax bill if you sell your home for a lot more than you paid for it.

## MORTGAGE INTEREST TAX RELIEF

You can get tax relief on interest you pay on loans of £30,000 or less to buy your only or main home. Your only or main home is normally the one you live in for most of the time, although you may be able to get tax relief on loans for homes you are not currently living in (see p. 55).

The rate of tax relief is 15 per cent. So every £1 of interest you pay within the £30,000 limit will be reduced by 15p tax relief to 85p. A gross interest rate of 8 per cent will then be 6.8 per cent after the tax relief.

### How you get the tax relief
In most cases, you get the tax relief in the form of lower monthly payments to the lender. For example, if £100 interest is due on your mortgage, you pay £100 minus tax relief of 15 per cent: £100 – £15 = £85. You get the tax relief even if you don't pay tax, or you pay less than the tax relief you get.

This system is known as mortgage interest relief at source (MIRAS) and the scheme is operated by most lenders such as building societies, banks and insurance companies. They reclaim the tax relief direct from the Inland Revenue.

MIRAS does not include loans which are only partly for buying a home. If this applies to your loan – or your lender is not in MIRAS – you will have to claim the tax relief direct from the Inland Revenue (see p. 118). In this case, you will get tax relief only if you have enough income to pay tax.

## Which loans qualify for relief?

The relief is available on loans to buy a house or flat, leasehold or freehold, in the UK or the Republic of Ireland. You can also claim it for a houseboat designed to be used as a home. And loans for a caravan (or mobile home) used as your only or main home are also eligible.

You can get tax relief on the interest paid on most sorts of loans used to buy your only or main home, including personal loans from banks and other lenders. The loan doesn't have to be a mortgage secured on your home to qualify. But you won't get tax relief on interest paid on a bank overdraft or credit card debts – even if these are incurred on your home. And there's no tax relief on interest for loans which have to be repaid within a year of being taken out, unless the lender is a bank, stockbroker or discount house.

You can still get the tax relief if part of the loan is used to pay the costs of buying the home such as stamp duty, valuers' fees, legal bills and insurance premiums (for example, for a mortgage indemnity policy). And if the loan is increased because you fall behind on the payments or to cover insurance premiums, the amount of loan on which you can get mortgage interest tax relief can be increased by up to £1,000 (or 12 months' payments arrears, if greater).

If you remortgage your home to change lenders or borrow more, you will get mortgage interest tax relief on the new loan provided you got it on the old loan it replaces.

## Bigger mortgages

If your loan to buy your only or main home is more than £30,000, you get the tax relief on only a proportion of the interest. For example, if your loan is £40,000, the proportion of interest on which you get tax relief is:

$$\frac{£30,000}{£40,000} = \frac{3}{4}$$

If your loan is in MIRAS, it will automatically give you the right amount of tax relief.

If you are buying your home with two or more loans which add up to over £30,000, you get the tax relief on the earliest loans first, up to the £30,000 limit. For example, if you had a loan of £25,000 topped up with another £10,000 loan, you would get tax relief on all the interest on the first loan.

That would leave unused mortgage interest tax relief of £30,000 – £25,000 = £5,000. So you would get tax relief on the following share of the interest on the second loan:

$$\frac{£5,000}{£10,000} = \frac{1}{2}$$

Your loan could creep up above £30,000 if you miss some interest payments (or don't increase your payments when the mortgage rate goes up). You can get tax relief on all the interest you pay as long as no more than £1,000 of interest is added to the loan.

## Bridging loans

If you take out a bridging loan to buy a new home before you have sold your old one, you can get tax relief on the interest for up to £30,000 of the bridging loan, as well as on £30,000 of loans on your old home. This second lot of tax relief is available for up to 12 months (longer if you can persuade your tax inspector that there is good reason for the delay in selling your old home).

It doesn't matter which of the homes you live in during the transitional period. But you will have to pay back the second lot of relief if you do not move into the new home at the end of the bridging period.

## Home income schemes

People aged 65 or over can get tax relief on a mortgage loan taken out as part of a home income scheme. Under such a scheme, an insurance company lends up to £30,000 against the security of the home. The loan is used to buy an annuity which pays a regular income that leaves the home-owner with money to spend after making the mortgage payments.

Provided 90 per cent or more of the loan is used to buy the annuity, tax relief is given on the interest payments at the basic rate of tax. This means the rate of tax relief was 24 per cent in the tax year ending 5 April 1997, and 23 per cent for the tax year beginning 6 April 1997.

In practice, these schemes make financial sense only for people in their seventies, when the rate of income paid by the insurance company in return for the lump sum is high enough to more than cover the mortgage costs. Some types of home income schemes have led to losses for investors in recent years. Avoid schemes where the income can vary up or down, or where interest on the mortgage can be added to the loan.

## Rolling the mortgage over to a new home

Normally, when buying a new home you pay off the old loan and take out a new one. However, if you carry a loan over from one home to another, you can go on getting tax relief on the loan.

This concession was introduced in 1993 to help people who wanted to move but could not repay their mortgages because their homes were worth less than the loan outstanding (this is known as negative equity). Provided the lender agreed, they could sell the home and carry the loan over to the new one.

This provision can also be useful if you have taken out a fixed-rate mortgage for a set term and want to move before the end of the term. Repaying such a loan early usually involves paying several months' interest as a penalty, so you can instead roll the loan over to your new home.

## Married couples

A married couple get tax relief on interest they pay for loans of £30,000 or less in total. If the loan is in one of their names only, that person gets all the tax relief. With a mortgage in their joint names, the mortgage interest tax relief will be divided 50:50 between them. But you can allocate the tax relief between husband and wife in any way you choose, simply by signing a form.

For loans covered by MIRAS it makes no practical difference how the relief is allocated. However, if the loan is outside MIRAS and one partner pays little or no tax, the couple should allocate all the interest to the other partner to get the tax relief in full.

To change the way relief is allocated, both husband and wife must sign Form 15. You have up to a year after the end of the tax year to make the choice. So for the tax year ending 5 April 1997, you have until 5 April 1998 to send in Form 15.

The allocation can be varied from year to year, simply by filling in a new Form 15. To revert to a 50:50 split, you should withdraw the allocation on Form 15-1.

## Newlyweds

If a newly married couple each owned homes before marriage and move into one of them after the wedding, they can go on getting tax relief on the interest on the other for up to a year. Alternatively, they may decide to buy a new matrimonial home. In this case, they can go on getting tax relief on the mortgage interest for the two other homes for up to a year after the wedding –

effectively getting three lots of tax relief.

## Sharers

If two or more single people buy a home together, or a married couple buy with another couple or single person, the tax relief is restricted to interest on £30,000 of loans per home – irrespective of the number of people sharing it.

For example, two single people would share between them the tax relief on the interest paid for £30,000 or less of loans (that is on £15,000 of loans each). Where a married couple shares with a single person, the couple would get tax relief on interest they pay on two-thirds of the £30,000 limit (£20,000) with one-third (£10,000) for the single person.

If a sharer has a loan smaller than his or her entitlement, the unused part can be transferred to the other sharers – the example shows how this works.

Sharers who took out loans before 1 August 1988 to buy a home in which they still live are each entitled to tax relief on £30,000 of mortgage interest. So two single people who have shared a home since before that date can get tax relief on the interest paid on up to £60,000 of such loans. These rules continue to apply until the loans are paid off, replaced with a new loan or switched to a new home. If two such sharers marry, the maximum

# EXAMPLE

Len Mallory, Norma Openshaw and Peter Quince decide to buy a house, with a one-third share each. Each of them has some savings, so they end up with different loans: Len of £12,000, Norma of £7,000 and Peter of £14,000.

The three are jointly entitled to tax relief on interest of up to £30,000 of loans. This is divided equally between them, so each is entitled to tax relief on interest on up to £10,000 of loans.

Norma's £7,000 loan is less than her £10,000 entitlement – so she gets tax relief on all the interest she pays. That leaves £10,000 – £7,000 = £3,000 of her entitlement unused. This can be divided between Len and Peter so they can get tax relief on more than £10,000 of loans.

Norma's unused £3,000 entitlement is divided between Len and Peter in proportion to the amount by which their mortgages exceed £10,000:

Len's mortgage is £2,000 over the £10,000 limit; Peter's excess is £4,000.

The total of their excesses is £2,000 + £4,000 = £6,000. So Len will get £2,000 ÷ £6,000 = $1/3$ of Norma's unused £3,000 allowance, that is £1,000. Peter gets £4,000 ÷ £6,000 = $2/3$, that is £2,000.

This means Len will get tax relief on £11,000 ÷ £12,000 = $11/12$ of the interest he pays. Peter will get tax relief on £12,000 ÷ £14,000 = $6/7$ of his mortgage interest.

amount of loans on which they can get tax relief immediately falls from £60,000 to £30,000.

## Home-improvement loans
If you took out a loan before 6 April 1988 to improve your only or main home, the interest paid on it could be added to the interest paid on loans to buy it when calculating your mortgage interest tax relief. You can go on getting the tax relief for such home improvement loans for as long as they last. But if you pay off the loan and replace it with a new one – at a lower rate of interest, say – you won't get tax relief on the interest on the new loan.

## A home for an ex-spouse or dependent relative
You could get tax relief on a loan taken out on or before 5 April 1988 to buy or improve a home for a separated or former spouse or dependent relative. You can go on getting the tax relief on such loans as long as the ex-spouse or dependent relative continues to live in the home as their only or main residence. If you pay off such a loan and replace it with a new loan – at a lower rate of interest, say – you won't get tax relief on the interest on the new loan.

Dependent relatives are:
• your mother or mother-in-law if widowed, separated or divorced
• any relative of yours or your spouse who is unable to look after themselves because of permanent illness, disablement or old age (over 64 at the start of the tax year).

The tax relief is given only if the dependent relative lives in the home rent-free.

## Absence from home
Mortgage interest tax relief is meant for your only or main home. But you can be away from the home for up to a year without losing tax relief on the mortgage interest payments. And if you have moved out but not yet sold the home, you can go on getting the tax relief for up to a year (longer if you can persuade your tax inspector that selling the home is proving difficult).

You may also be able to go on getting tax relief if work takes you away from home. If you work for an employer who requires you to live away from home, you can go on getting mortgage interest tax relief for up to four years provided you're expected to return within that period. If you're still away after four years, the tax relief ends. But if you move back in for at least three months, further such absence of up to four years is allowed.

Servants of the Crown who move abroad because of their jobs can be away indefinitely without losing the tax relief. So can those who have to live in job-related accommodation, provided they intend to live in it eventually. Job-related accommodation is living accommodation provided for one of the following reasons:

- it is necessary to live in it to do the job properly – for example, a residential housekeeper
- it is customary to live in it for that sort of work and living there helps do the job better – a hotel manager
- it is essential for security reasons.

There is a similar exemption for the self-employed who have to live in work-related accommodation (for example, over the shop or at the club). They can go on getting mortgage interest tax relief on their own homes provided they intend to live in them eventually.

## Working from home

If you use part of your home for business, you may still be able to go on getting mortgage interest tax relief through MIRAS – provided the business use is incidental. For example, if you occasionally work from home or use part of it on occasions as an office or place to store work tools.

If you start to use your home for more substantial work or business purposes, tell the lender. The loan may have to leave MIRAS, although you should still be able to get mortgage interest tax relief on it (and perhaps also set off some of the interest against business income – see p. 198).

## If you let your home

If you let out no more than one-third of your home, you can go on getting mortgage interest tax relief through MIRAS. But if you let out more than one-third, you should tell the lender and your tax inspector. You will no longer get mortgage interest tax relief through MIRAS – although you can claim it directly from the Inland Revenue if you are still entitled to it.

Whether or not you are in MIRAS, you may be better off not claiming mortgage interest tax relief but deducting the interest from rental income when working out the profit or loss of your letting business (see p. 222). There are several possible advantages:

- all the interest qualifies for tax relief – mortgage interest tax relief covers interest on £30,000 of loans only
- the tax relief is at your highest rate of tax – not just the 15 per cent given for mortgage interest tax relief
- if the interest is more than your property income in one tax year, you can carry forward the loss to set against property income in the future.

If your loan is not in MIRAS, you can choose each year whether to claim mortgage interest tax relief or set the interest against letting income (see p. 222).

If your loan is in MIRAS, you have to opt out of it if you want the interest to be set against letting income. Write and tell your tax inspector within 22 months of the end of the tax year in which you first want this to happen. So if you want the interest paid in the tax year ending 5 April 1997 to be set against letting income for that year, tell the tax inspector by 5 February 1999. Once you have opted out of MIRAS, you will not be able to return to it unless the letting business ends.

## CAPITAL GAINS TAX ON HOMES

If you sell most types of investments (including property) for more than you paid for them, there may be capital gains tax to pay (see Chapter 21 p. 245). But if you sell your only or main home, there is normally no capital gains tax to pay unless the garden is excessively large (see below) or you are making a business out of buying and selling homes. This exemption from capital gains tax is known as private residence relief.

However, if you own more than one home, only one of them qualifies for private residence relief. And you might lose the relief if you use the home for business, leave it for prolonged periods or let it out. If you do have to pay capital gains tax on selling a home, it can mean a hefty tax bill – the gain, adjusted for inflation, is taxed at your top rate of income tax.

### Which homes?

Private residence relief is given for your only or main home, whether it is a house or flat, freehold or leasehold, and wherever in the world it is situated.

You must occupy the home exclusively as your residence if it is to be free of capital gains tax. If part of the home is used for work or business, you may have to pay tax on part of the gain (see p. 59). And letting out some or all of your home can also mean a capital gains tax bill (see p. 60).

If you live in a caravan or houseboat, there's normally no capital gains tax to pay on it, even if it is not your only or main home. Caravans and boats count as wasting assets with a useful life of 50 years or less – and are thus outside the net for capital gains tax (see p. 247). But if you own the land on which a caravan stands, you might have to pay capital gains tax if you sell it, unless the caravan was your only or main home.

A home which an ex-spouse or dependent relative lives in rent-free is also free of capital gains tax provided it fell into this category on or before 5 April 1988 (see p. 43 for who qualifies). This exemption lasts only as long as the ex-spouse or dependent relative continues to live in the home.

## Gardens

Private residence relief applies to both your home and garden. But there are rules to stop people taking advantage of it to avoid capital gains tax on dealing in land.

If the area of your home and garden exceeds half a hectare, there may be tax to pay on the gain you make on the excess. The gain on any excess will be free of tax only if you can convince your tax inspector that a garden of that size is appropriate for the home (for example, it is a Capability Brown garden designed for the house).

If the area of the home and garden is less than half a hectare, you can sell part of the garden without having to pay capital gains tax. But if you divide the garden to build a second home which you sell off, there could be tax to pay on the gain. And if you sell the home and keep some of the land, there may be capital gains tax to pay when you eventually sell the land.

## If you own more than one home

If you own more than one home, you can choose which of your homes is your main one and thus free of capital gains tax. It doesn't have to be the one you live in most of the time, or the one on which you get mortgage interest tax relief.

So you should think about which home is likely to make the largest gain and nominate it for private residence relief. You must make your choice and tell your tax inspector in writing within two years of buying the second home. Newlyweds who have kept the two homes they owned while single should tell their tax inspector which is to get private residence relief within two years of the marriage.

You can alter your choice at any time, but you cannot backdate the change by more than two years. Again, write and tell your tax inspector that you wish to change your choice and when you want the change to run from.

If you don't nominate one of your homes for private residence relief, your tax inspector will decide – probably on the basis of which home you spend the most time at. You can appeal against this decision in the normal way (see p. 20), but you will have to produce proof that the other home really is your main one.

## Working from home

If any part of your home is used exclusively for work, there may be a capital gains tax bill when you sell the home. This applies to work for your own business (if you are self-employed) and work for an employer.

So if you use one or more rooms entirely for work (as an office or workshop, for example), there will be tax to pay on a proportion of the gain when you come to sell the home. You will have to agree the proportion with the tax inspector, who may calculate it by reference to the number of rooms you use or their floor area. If you claim a proportion of the rent and council tax as business expenses (see p. 197) or as expenses of employment (see p. 169), the same proportion of the gain is likely to be taxable. But in modest cases you may be able to persuade your tax inspector to allow you the expenses without out a capital gains tax bill.

For details of how the taxable gain will be worked out, see Chapter 21 p. 245. If there is a tax bill, it can be deferred if you buy another home used partly for business (see roll-over relief, p. 275). You may also be able to claim retirement relief if you are aged 50 or over or suffer ill-health (see p. 274).

## Away from home

If you don't live in your home for all the time you own it, you might lose some of the private residence relief – even though it is the only home you own or you have nominated it as your main home. Normally you will have to pay capital gains tax on the following proportion of the taxable gain:

$$\frac{\text{Number of complete months of absence}}{\text{Number of complete months of ownership}}$$

Only months of ownership or absence since 31 March 1982 count in working out the proportion – gains before that date are outside the scope of the tax (see p. 260).

In practice, you can be away from the home for considerable spells of absence without losing any private residence relief. You can retain it during absence for the following periods:

- the first year of ownership while you are building, rebuilding or modernising the home, or because you can't sell your old home. This can be extended for another year if you can convince the tax inspector it is necessary. To retain the exemption, you must move in within the one-year (or two-year) period
- the last three years of ownership – even if you have already moved out

- any other absences totalling up to three years, provided you live in the home both before the first absence and after the last.

You may also be able to retain private residence relief if work takes you or your spouse away from home. If you work for an employer who requires you to live away from home in the UK, you can go on getting private residence relief for up to four years of absence, provided you return to the home afterwards (unless you are prevented by the job). If your employer requires you to work abroad, you can get private residence relief on your home indefinitely.

Provided you intend to live in your home in the future, private residence relief continues if you or your spouse are required to live in job-related accommodation (see p. 55). Self-employed people who have to live in work-related accommodation (for example, over the shop or at the club) can go on getting private residence relief on their own homes as long as they intend to live in them eventually.

You can add together some or all of these reasons to continue getting private residence relief for longer periods of absence – as the example shows.

## Capital gains tax on lettings
There is no capital gains tax to pay if you take in a lodger who is treated as a member of the family – sharing your living rooms and eating with you. But in other circumstances, there may be capital gains tax to pay

## Example
Linda March bought a house on 24 June 1986. On 6 July 1989 her employer sent her on an overseas posting lasting until 10 November 1991. On Linda's return to the UK, her employer sent her to work away from home until 15 August 1995. She lived in the home until 22 October 1995, when she bought a new home, eventually selling her old home on 27 February 1997.

During the ten years and nine months Linda owned the home, she was absent for three periods totalling seven years and three months. But she will get private residence relief for the entire time she owned the house:

- the two years and four months from July 1989 to November 1991 count for private residence relief because they are a period of employment spent entirely abroad
- the three years and nine months from November 1991 to August 1995 are less than the four years of employment elsewhere in the UK possible without losing private residence relief
- the year and four months from October 1995 to February 1997 are part of the last three years of ownership.

when you sell a home that has been let out wholly or in part.

If you let out the whole house for a period, the gain attributable to that period is taxable.

If you let part of your home, you may have to pay capital gains tax on the part that is not occupied by you. If you let two of your six rooms, for example, a third of the gain on selling the home is taxable (less if you haven't let the two rooms for all the time that you've owned the home).

However, there may still be no capital gains tax to pay if you can claim lettings relief, for homes which have been wholly or partly eligible for private residence relief. Lettings relief reduces the taxable gain by £40,000, or the amount of private residence relief if this is lower – the example shows how it works.

### Property dealings

If you regularly buy and sell houses for profit, there might be a capital gains tax bill when you sell one – even if you have been living in it as your only or main home. This is meant to catch people who are making a business out of doing up unmodernised homes for sale.

> # EXAMPLE
>
> Jane Mortimer lived in a home for four years and then let it out for six. She sold it making a gain (after allowing for inflation – see p. 259) of £50,000.
>
> Jane qualifies for private residence relief for the four years she lived in it, plus the following three years – seven years in all. The gain attributable to the remaining three years is $^3/_{10}$ of the £50,000. This £15,000 is taxable.
>
> Jane next works out how much lettings relief she is entitled to. The amount is the lower of £40,000 or the value of private residence relief on the house, which is £50,000 – £15,000 = £35,000. She can reduce the gain by £35,000; that means no taxable gain on the letting.

If your property dealings are on a substantial scale, you could find yourself classified as a dealer in land. You would then have to pay income tax on the profits like any other self-employed person (see p. 184).

# SAVING AND INVESTING

## CHAPTER 8

The ordinary saver faces a wider choice of investments than ever before. Banks, building societies and National Savings are vying to look after your spare cash. Many more people have become shareholders through employee share-ownership schemes and by buying shares in privatised industries. And millions of people are saving for their retirement through personal pensions.

To encourage savings, the government has introduced a series of tax incentives for investors. These include a reduced rate of income tax for interest and dividends – 20 per cent for basic rate taxpayers, rather than the 23 per cent on other sorts of income for the tax year beginning 6 April 1997. There is an impressive array of tax concessions to make saving through pension schemes – employers' or personal – rewarding. Investing in long-term life insurance policies can produce a tax-free return. There are special tax rules to tempt savers into personal equity plans (PEPS), tax exempt special savings accounts (TESSAs), the Enterprise Investment Scheme (EIS) and Venture Capital Trusts (VCTs).

This chapter guides you through the various types of investments and how they are taxed. And it also tells you the rules to follow if you want to cash in on the tax breaks offered by the government.

## INCOME TAX ON INVESTMENTS

Income from some investments is tax-free (that is, there is no income tax to pay). For a list of these, see p. 83.

All other investment income is taxable. With more and more investments, tax is deducted from the income before it is paid to you. There is no further tax to pay on such income unless you pay tax at the higher rate. If you should have paid less tax than was deducted, you will normally be able to get a refund.

## Interest paid after deduction of tax

Interest on most kinds of savings is now normally paid after tax has been deducted from it. This applies to building society accounts, bank accounts, government stock (gilts), local authority loans and bonds and National Savings First Option Bonds.

On these types of interest, tax is deducted at 20 per cent from the gross income before it is handed over to you. There is no further tax bill if you pay tax at the lower or basic rate only on your income – which is the case for the vast majority of taxpayers. If you pay tax at the higher rate, there will be extra tax to pay on this income (see p. 65). If your income is too low to pay tax, you should be able to reclaim some or all of the tax which has been deducted (see overleaf).

The savings income is treated as the top slice of your income. This means it does not reduce the amount of earnings or other income that can be taxed at the lower rate of 20 per cent – £4,100 for the tax year beginning 6 April 1997.

---

### GROSSING-UP

If you receive investment income after some tax has been deducted from it, what you receive is known as the net income. But you may need to work out how much the income was before tax was deducted from it (the gross income).

You can find the gross income by grossing-up the net income (that is the income after deduction of tax) using the ready reckoners in Appendix B, (p. 342), or by using the following formula:

$$\text{Amount paid to you} \times \left( \frac{100}{100 - \text{rate of tax}} \right)$$

For example, if you receive £50 of income after tax has been deducted at 20 per cent, the grossed-up amount of the income is:

$$£50 \times \left( \frac{100}{100 - 20} \right)$$

$$= £50 \times \frac{100}{80}$$

$$= £62.50$$

---

## Shares and unit trusts

Dividends from UK companies and distributions from authorised unit trusts are paid with a tax credit – the amount is given on the tax voucher which comes with the dividend or distribution. If you pay tax at the lower or basic rate only on your income, you will pay no extra tax.

The tax credit is 20 per cent of the gross dividend or distribution. So if you receive a dividend of £80, the grossed-up amount of this dividend is £100 (see previous page for how to gross up). The tax credit will be £100 – £80 = £20.

## Too much tax deducted?

If too much tax has been deducted from savings income (or the tax credit with shares and unit trusts is more than you should pay), the excess can be claimed back. This would happen if the rest of your income is below the level at which you pay tax – as the next example shows.

### EXAMPLE

Sonny Dasgupta pays tax at 40 per cent on his income. National Savings certificates offer him an average return of 5.35 per cent a year tax-free over five years. He could get 7.5 per cent a year over the same period in a bank high interest account.

Sonny invests in the National Savings certificates, since that will give him 5.35 per cent a year whatever his tax rate. The interest rate he would get on the bank account after paying tax at 40 per cent would be 60 per cent of 7.5 per cent that is 4.5 per cent a year.

To claim back the tax, ask your tax inspector for Tax Claim Form R40. Fill this in and send it back with the certificates showing the amount of tax deducted (the bank or building society can supply these) or the tax credit vouchers that come with share dividends and unit trust distributions. You can send in the completed form before the end of the tax year to get the repayment as soon as possible, provided you've had all the income for the tax year paid to you after tax has been deducted and the amount of tax involved is more than £50.

If your income is too low to pay tax at all, you can arrange with the bank or building society to have interest paid without deduction of tax. Fill in Form R85 which is available from banks, building societies and post offices, as well as from tax offices. A copy is in Inland Revenue leaflet IR110 *A guide for people with savings*, which also contains useful hints on checking

# Example

Niall O'Halloran is 12 years old and has no income apart from the interest he gets on £3,000 given to him by his grandparents. During the tax year beginning 6 April 1997, he gets interest of £150 which is paid after deduction of tax at 20 per cent.

Like all taxpayers, he is entitled to a personal allowance of £4,045 for the year. Since his taxable income is much less than the personal allowance, he can claim back the tax deducted from it.

To work out the size of his rebate, Niall grosses up the net amount of interest he received:

$$£150 \times \left( \frac{100}{100-20} \right)$$

$$= £150 \times \frac{100}{80}$$

$$= £187.50$$

So the gross amount of interest Niall received was £187.50. Since he can claim back all the tax deducted, he will get a rebate of £187.50 – £150 = £37.50.

whether you will pay tax or not.

Arranging for interest to be paid without deduction of tax not only saves you the trouble of claiming back the tax that has been deducted, it also means you get the money much earlier. However, interest on joint accounts can be paid without deduction of tax to just one of the two account-holders only if the bank or building society can arrange it. There are hefty penalties for making a false declaration.

## Higher rate tax on income paid after deduction of tax

If you get savings income after tax has been deducted or credited and pay tax at the higher rate of 40 per cent, there will be a further tax bill to pay – as the next example shows.

The higher rate tax will be collected by the Inland Revenue either through the payments you have to make under the new self-assessment system (see p. 15) or from your earnings through PAYE (see p. 21).

## Example

Niamh Fagan gets £640 interest on her building society account in the tax year beginning 6 April 1997. Tax has already been deducted from the interest at 20 per cent before it is credited to her account, so this £640 is the net (that is, after deduction of tax) amount.

To work out the gross (before deduction of tax) amount of interest, Niamh must add the tax back to the net amount. The grossed-up amount of interest is:

$$£640 \times \left( \frac{100}{100 - 20} \right)$$
$$= £640 \times \frac{100}{80}$$
$$= £800$$

In other words, Niamh has paid £800 − £640 = £160 in tax and this covers her basic-rate tax on the interest.

If Niamh should pay tax at 40 per cent on this interest, her overall tax liability is 40 per cent of £800 = £320. Since she has already paid £160 in tax, she has to pay only £320 − £160 = £160 in higher rate tax. This leaves her with £640 − £160 = £480 of interest after higher rate tax has been paid.

## INVESTING FOR CAPITAL GAINS

One way of reducing your income tax bill is to invest for capital gains rather than income. Capital gains tax is paid on increases in the value of investments – for example, if the value of shares or property rises. But there's no tax to pay if your total net capital gains in the tax year beginning 6 April 1997 are below £6,500. A husband and wife can each make total net capital gains of this amount before paying capital gains tax.

If capital gains tax is due, the taxable gain is added to your income and taxed at the same rate as interest or dividends. But you can make paper gains of more than the £6,500 limit, because of the deductions you can make in calculating your total net capital gains. These include expenses incurred in acquiring, owning or disposing of the investment, an allowance for increases due to inflation and losses made on other investments. For more about capital gains tax, see chapter 21, p. 245.

# LIFE INSURANCE POLICIES

Life insurance can be used as a form of investment, since some types pay out a tax-free lump sum when the policy matures. There are various conditions to be met if the proceeds of a life insurance policy which pays out in your lifetime are to be tax-free – in particular, that the policy involves paying regular premiums for at least ten years. With most endowment, unit-linked and whole life policies, these conditions are normally met so you don't have to pay tax on the proceeds. There may be some tax to pay if you cash in a savings-type life insurance policy after less than ten years or three-quarters of the term, if this is shorter (see p. 100).

Some insurance companies make a deduction from the proceeds of unit-linked policies to cover their capital gains tax. This deduction is your share of the company's tax bill, not a tax charge on you personally – so you can't claimit back if you don't pay capital gains tax.

## Tax relief on life insurance premiums

With certain types of life insurance policies taken out before 14 March 1984, you were able to get tax relief on the premiums (within limits). Provided you haven't substantially changed the policy, you can go on getting the tax relief which is now $12^1/_2$ per cent of the premiums. In most cases you get it by paying reduced premiums to the insurance company – you pay $87^1/_2$ per cent of the gross premium and the insurance company reclaims the $12^1/_2$ per cent tax relief from the Inland Revenue.

You can get tax relief on no more than £1,500 of gross premiums (£1,312.50 of net premiums) in any tax year – or one-sixth of your total income if this is greater. If you pay more than the limit, the Inland Revenue will reclaim the excess tax relief you have been given by paying reduced premiums.

If you change the policy, you may lose the tax relief. For example, you will lose the tax relief if you extend the term of the policy, increase the cover or convert it to a different type of policy. But you won't lose the tax relief if the value of the policy increases automatically as part of the policy (for example, if it increases by 5 per cent every year). Check with the insurance company.

# PENSIONS

The government offers handsome tax incentives to encourage you to provide for your retirement by saving with an employer's pension scheme or through your own personal pension. These mean that saving for the future through a pension often provides a better return than any other type of investment:

- there is tax relief on your contributions to the scheme (within limits)
- any employer's contributions made for you are not taxable as your income or as a fringe benefit
- the fund the money goes into pays no income tax or capital gains tax
- you can trade in some pension to get a tax-free lump sum when you retire.

## Employers' pension schemes

The tax incentives for saving through an employer's pension scheme are available only if it is approved by the Inland Revenue. Approved schemes must offer benefits within set limits:

- the maximum pension is two-thirds of your final salary
- the maximum tax-free lump sum is $1^1/_2$ times your final salary
- the maximum lump sum payment which can be made on death in service (that is life insurance cover) is four times your final salary.

There are also limits on the benefits that can be paid out to widows and widowers. For example, the maximum widow's or widower's pension is two-thirds the pension the deceased would have got.

There is a further restriction on the pension benefits from an approved scheme set up on or after 14 March 1989, or if you joined an older scheme on or after 1 June 1989. The amount of final salary which can be taken into account is limited by a pension scheme earnings cap of £84,000 for the tax year beginning 6 April 1997 (£82,200 for the tax year ending 5 April 1997). If the cap applies to you, the maximum amounts you can begin to draw in the tax year which began on 6 April 1997 are:

- a pension of £56,000 (two-thirds of £84,000)
- a lump sum of £126,000 ($1^1/_2$ times £84,000)
- a payment for death in service of £336,000 (four times £84,000).

Other benefits such as widow's and widower's pensions are also subject to the pension scheme earnings cap.

### Contributions to an employer's scheme

The amount you are required to contribute to an employer's pension scheme is decided by your employer, but cannot exceed 15 per cent of your earnings (this can include the value of fringe benefits). Provided the pension scheme is approved by the Inland Revenue, you get tax relief at your highest rate of tax on these contributions. Your contributions will be deducted from your income before working out how much tax has to be paid under PAYE (although your National Insurance contributions are worked out on your full pay, that is, before deduction of pension contributions).

However, if the scheme was set up on or after 14 March 1989, or you joined it on or after 1 June 1989, contributions are restricted to 15 per cent of earnings up to the pension scheme earnings cap mentioned above. For the tax year beginning 6 April 1997, that means you can get tax relief on maximum contributions of 15 per cent of £84,000, that is £12,600.

If you leave an approved pension scheme within two years of joining, your pension contributions can be repaid only after tax has been deducted at a flat rate of 20 per cent, to recover the tax relief you have had.

### Additional voluntary contributions

Very few people qualify for the maximum permitted amount of an employer's pension – if only because job changes usually mean losing some pension entitlement. If you are in this position and want to save for your retirement, you should consider additional voluntary contributions (AVCs). These enjoy the same tax benefits as an approved pension scheme, so should grow faster than if you invested the money yourself.

You can choose between two different ways of investing your AVCs:

• through your employer's pension scheme (in-scheme AVCs)
• by making your own arrangements with an insurance company, bank, building society or unit trust manager (free-standing AVCs).

You get full tax relief on AVCs, provided the total amount you contribute in pension contributions does not exceed the 15 per cent limit. So if your employer's pension schemes contributions are 6 per cent, you can pay up to 15 – 6 = 9 per cent in AVCs.

AVCs can be used to increase the pension you will get, the widow's or widower's pension and your life cover. But you can increase the tax-free lump sum you will get only if the AVCs began on or before 7 April 1987. You cannot use AVCs to buy pension benefits greater than the maximum limits set by the Inland Revenue for approved schemes. If you inadvertently contribute so much that the benefits would exceed the limits, some of the AVCs will be paid back when you retire, with a deduction to cover the tax relief you have had on the contributions.

## Personal pensions

If you save through a personal pension scheme, you can build up a fund with an insurance company, bank, building society or other pension provider that provides you with an income for retirement. Your employer can also contribute to your personal pension, as will the government if you contract out of the state earnings-related pension scheme (SERPS) into an appropriate personal pension scheme.

The amount of pension you draw depends on the size of the fund – which in turn depends on the amount contributed and the investment performance of the fund. However, there are limits on the size of the tax-free lump sum you can take. The maximum is quarter of the fund accumulated from yours and your employers' contributions, with a cash limit of £150,000 if you took out the personal pension on or before 26 July 1989.

There are also limits on the amount you can contribute. The maximum is a percentage of your net relevant earnings (see p. 108). The percentage depends on your age at the beginning of the tax year – the maximum contributions are on p. 109. You can claim extra tax relief by backdating contributions to a previous tax year or claiming unused tax relief for up to six previous tax years (see p. 111). If your employer makes a contribution towards your personal pension, the maximum you are entitled to contribute is reduced by the amount your employer contributes. But contributions by the government towards an appropriate personal pension do not count towards the limit.

If you die before drawing the pension, you will normally get back the premiums you've paid, usually with interest. But many personal pension providers also offer some sort of optional life insurance cover, and you can get tax relief on the premiums for this up to a maximum of 5 per cent of your net relevant earnings. Whatever is spent on this life insurance cover is deducted from the maximum amount you can contribute to your personal pension.

Note that personal pensions taken out before 1 July 1988 are known as retirement annuities, with somewhat different rules (see p. 113).

# PERSONAL EQUITY PLANS

If you are 18 or over, you can invest in various stockmarket investments without paying income tax or capital gains tax if you do it through a personal equity plan (PEP). You can invest up to £6,000 in a PEP in any tax year, by single lump sum, regular monthly instalments, or several payments.

Your money is invested in shares, unit trusts, investment trusts or certain types of corporate bonds, convertible shares and preference shares. The shares must be listed on the Stock Exchange or quoted on broadly equivalent exchanges in another EU countries. Unit trusts and investment trusts must invest at least 50 per cent of their funds in such shares or bonds. Where less than 50 per cent is invested thus, the maximum you can invest in such unit and investment trusts is £1,500.

You can also invest £3,000 in any tax year in a single-company PEP which holds shares in only one company (they are sometimes known as corporate PEPs). These are normally set up by the company that issued the shares, often for employees in share-ownership schemes – such as savings-related share option schemes (see p. 177) and employee profit-sharing schemes (see p. 175). Such employees can transfer their shares into a single-company PEP up to the £3,000 limit. There will be no capital gains tax to pay on the transfer, no income tax on the dividends and no capital gains tax on the profits on selling the shares – provided the transfer takes place within six weeks of the shares being issued.

A husband and wife can each invest up to £6,000 in general PEPs and £3,000 in single-company PEPs – up to £18,000 together in any tax year. The only time you would pay tax on PEP proceeds would be if some of your money were held as cash on deposit and earned interest which was paid out to you. If more than £180 of interest was paid out to you in a year, the plan manager would have to deduct tax at 20 per cent and hand this over to the Inland Revenue. The net interest is treated in the same way as any other interest you receive after deduction of tax. Higher rate taxpayers would face an additional tax bill (see p. 65).

If you buy newly issued shares (in a privatisation, say), you can put them into your PEP, as long as your total investment in the PEP remains within the limit for the tax year. You wouldn't then have to pay income tax on the dividends and capital gains tax when you sell them. You must do this within six weeks of the share allocation being announced.

## TAX EXEMPT SPECIAL SAVINGS ACCOUNTS (TESSAS)

If you are 18 or over, you can save up to £9,000 over five years without paying income tax on the interest if you do it through a tax exempt special savings account (TESSA) with a bank or building society.

You can build up the £9,000 by regular savings (up to £150 a month), by lump sum deposits or a combination of both. But no more than £3,000 can be invested in the first year (unless it is the capital from a previous TESSA that completed its five years within the last six months). The maximum in each of the remaining years is £1,800. A husband and wife can each invest up to £9,000 in a TESSA, a total of £18,000.

If you need income from your TESSA, you can draw out up to 80 per cent of the interest. But you must leave at least 20 per cent – the equivalent of the tax which would have been deducted from the interest with a normal savings account. If you draw out more than this – or withdraw any of the capital – the TESSA comes to an end and tax will be deducted from all the interest added to your TESSA at the 20 per cent rate for savings income. If you are a higher rate taxpayer, there could be extra tax to pay (see p. 65). If your income for the tax year is too low to pay tax, you might be able to claim back some or all of the tax deducted (see p. 64).

## INVESTING IN GROWING BUSINESSES

### Enterprise Investment Scheme

If you invest £500 or more in the shares of certain unquoted trading companies issued on or after 1 January 1994, you can get tax relief on the investment – provided you hold the shares for five years or more. Investments in Enterprise Investment Scheme approved investment funds which invest in such companies also qualify – even if the investment is less than £500. If you dispose of the investments after the five years is up, there will be no capital gains tax to pay when you sell.

You get income tax relief on up to £100,000 of such investments in any tax year at 20 per cent. But if you make the investment on or after 6 April 1997 and on or before 5 October 1997, half the investment up to a maximum of £15,000 can be set off against your income for the tax year ending 5 April 1997. With a married couple, both husband and wife can each invest up to these limits.

In addition, if you are investing the proceeds from selling some other asset, you can put off paying tax on any capital gains on those proceeds (see

p. 267). This reinvestment relief is available for gains you make on or after 29 November 1994 – provided you reinvest them within a period starting one year before and ending three years after making them. For more about reinvestment relief.

The companies you can invest in must be unquoted; this includes those with shares traded on the Alternative Investment Market. They must also be trading companies, which excludes those engaged in banking, insurance, share-dealing, dealing in land or property, leasing and legal or accountancy services. The company must be trading in the UK, but it does not have to be registered or resident in the UK. You can't claim the tax relief until the company has carried out its qualifying trade for at least four months, and you lose it if it ceases to do so within three years.

You won't get tax relief on investments if you are connected with the companies – broadly this means being an employee or director or owning over 30 per cent of the shares. In deciding how much of a company you own, you must include the holdings of connected persons – your spouse and you and your spouse's children, parents and grandparents (but not brothers or sisters) – and associates such as business partners. Once you have made your Enterprise Investment Scheme investment, however, you can take part in the active management of the company as a paid director (or business angel) provided you had not been connected with the company before you made the Enterprise Investment Scheme investment.

If you sell the shares within five years, you lose relief on the amount you sell them for (that is, if you sell them for more than they cost you, you have to pay back all the relief). If you sell the shares after five years and the company still qualifies under the scheme there will be no capital gains tax to pay on any gain you make. If you make a loss, this can be set off against other income or capital gains – reducing your overall tax bill for the year.

*Business expansion scheme*
The Business Expansion Scheme, which used to offer tax relief on a wider range of investments than the Enterprise Investment Scheme, came to an end on 31 December 1993. But although no new investments have been possible under the Business Expansion Scheme since, there is still no capital gains tax to pay when you sell these investments made after 18 March 1986.

## Venture capital trusts
If you buy new ordinary shares in a venture capital trust (VCT) which invests in or lends money to certain unquoted trading companies, you can get tax relief on an investment of up to £100,000 in any tax year. A venture capital

trust is similar to an investment trust and must be quoted on the Stock Exchange. Unquoted trading companies are defined in broadly the same way as for the Enterprise Investment Scheme.

You get income tax relief at 20 per cent on your investment, provided you hold the shares for five years or more. Any dividends paid out by the Venture capital trust and gains you make when you sell your Venture capital trust shares are tax-free. In addition, you can claim reinvestment relief (see previous page).

# HOW TO FILL IN YOUR TAX RETURN

## CHAPTER 9

When you receive your tax return for the tax year ending 5 April 1997, this is what you should have:

- an eight-page booklet entitled Tax Return. We show you how to complete these pages in chapters 10 to 13. The booklet is white and blue
- a green Tax Calculation Guide. There are three versions of the tax calculation guide. We show you how to complete this tax calculator in Chapter 24 and give you some examples in Chapter 25
- supplementary pages for the tax return to cater for your individual circumstances – there are nine sets of supplementary pages (see below). We explain how to complete these pages in Chapters 14 to 22
- a Tax Return Guide. This consists of 30 pages which explain how to complete the eight pages of the tax return (see above) plus how to fill in the Employment supplementary pages. The cover of this tax return guide is blue and white.

## What you should do next
### Step 1
Make sure you have the correct supplementary pages.

### Step 2
If you are missing one or more of the supplementary pages, contact the Inland Revenue. From the beginning of April the Orderline is open every day from 8 am to 10 pm, except on Christmas Day. The phone number is 0645 000 404.

### Step 3
Gather together all your records and supporting documentation which you should have been keeping since 6 April 1996.

### Step 4
Fill in your supplementary pages FIRST, using the advice in chapters 14 to 22 of this Guide.

## Step 5
After filling in the supplementary pages, complete the tax return.

## Step 6
If you are not going to work out your tax bill yourself, send in your tax return and supplementary pages by 30 September 1997.

## Step 7
If you want to calculate your own tax, use Chapter 24 and the tax calculation working sheet in your Tax Calculation Guide.

## Step 8
If you are an employee and the tax you owe is £1,000 or less, choose to send in your tax return, supplementary pages and tax calculation by 30 September. Then you can ask to pay your tax bill through the PAYE system on a monthly basis starting in April 1998.

## Step 9
Otherwise send in your tax return, supplementary pages and tax calculation guide by 31 January and send your final tax payment for the tax year ending 5 April 1997 at the same time.

## THE SUPPLEMENTARY PAGES

On page 2 of the basic tax return you are asked nine questions. You have to answer yes or no to each of these questions. If you answer YES to a question you will need to fill in the corresponding supplementary page. If you have not been sent that page or pages automatically you will need to ask for it from the Orderline (see p. 75).

### Employment

You are required to fill in the pink Employment supplementary page if you come into any of the above categories. The Inland Revenue will regard you as an employee even if you work on a part-time or casual basis. There are more guidelines on who counts as an employee in Chapter 14 (p. 140).

### Share schemes
If you receive your shares or options under one of the special approved schemes which is tax-free and you kept to the rules of scheme, you aren't

required to complete this purple supplementary page. You will have to fill it in if in the tax year ending 5 April 1997 you have received shares or options in any other way or you have broken the rules of an approved scheme. Chapter 15 on p. 174 gives a lot of background information on share schemes and guides you through the completion of this supplementary page.

## Self-employment

If you carried on a trade, profession or vocation as a self-employed person during the tax year ending on 5 April 1997 you need to complete this orange supplementary section. Chapter 16 on p. 184 has guidelines on who counts as self-employed.

If you are in partnership you need to complete a different set of supplementary pages (see below).

## Partnership

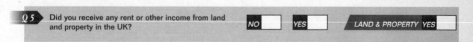

If you are in business with one or more partners, you should answer YES to this question and complete a set of turquoise supplementary pages. There is a short version and a long version. You will find guidance on which version you should complete in Chapter 17 (p. 214).

## Land and Property

Did you receive any rent or other income from land and property in the UK? NO YES  LAND & PROPERTY YES

You need to complete the red supplementary page if you receive income from land and property, furnished holiday accommodation, or providing furnished accommodation in your home during the tax year ending 5 April 1997. However, if you provide additional services, such as meals, you will need to complete the Self-employment supplementary pages, as you are considered to be carrying on a trade. You can get more guidance by turning to Chapter 18 (p. 218).

## Foreign

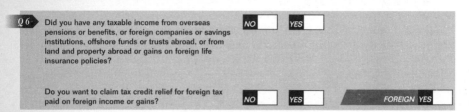

There are four olive supplementary pages which have space to give details about your foreign savings, pensions and benefits, property income and other investment income from abroad. Ask for it if you received any such income in the tax year ending 5 April 1997. You will need to fill it in even if you got no income, but you first got income from this source before 6 April 1994. If you turn to Chapter 19 (p. 231) you will find more information on what is foreign income and how it is taxed.

## Trusts etc

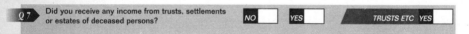

You need to complete the brown supplementary page if you were a beneficiary, a settlor or had income from the estates of someone who had died. You can find more information and guidance on filling in the supplementary page in Chapter 20 (p. 239).

## Capital gains

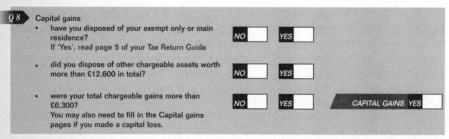

You must complete this blue supplementary page if you have made a capital gain (with some exceptions – see below) or you wish to claim an allowable capital loss for the tax year ending 5 April 1997.

You won't need to return the supplementary page if your gains were less than £6,300 (which is the tax-free slice for the year) and if the gain was from selling your home and it is free of tax and the other assets which you disposed of (leaving out assets which on which gains are tax-free) were less than £12,600 altogether for the year. For more information on which gains are tax-free and guidance on whether the gain on selling your home will be taxable or not, see Chapter 21 (p. 245).

## Non-residence etc

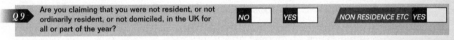

Q9  Are you claiming that you were not resident, or not ordinarily resident, or not domiciled, in the UK for all or part of the year?  NO  YES  NON RESIDENCE ETC YES

For the tax year ending 5 April 1997, if you consider yourself to be not resident in the UK, or not ordinarily resident (or not for part of the year), or not domiciled or resident but resident in a country with which the UK has a double taxation agreement, then you will need to complete this green supplementary page. Chapter 22 (p. 276) will give you guidance.

# INCOME

## CHAPTER 10

The first stage in working out your income tax bill for the tax year ending 5 April 1997 is to find your taxable income. The basic tax return on pages 3 and 4 sets out various different types of income, such as income from savings and investments, pensions and benefits, maintenance income received and other bits and pieces. You should complete this section to tell your tax inspector what types of income and how much of each type you received. You may find it helpful to read Chapter 8.

This is not the only way in which your tax inspector will find out about your income. It is your obligation to notify any new source of income within six months of the end of the tax year in which you first get it. There are also supplementary pages, including Employment, Self-employment and Land and property, where you must give details of other sorts of income.

You don't need to enter in the tax return any income which is tax-free. A comprehensive list is given in Appendix A (see p. 339).

## INCOME *for the year ended 5 April 1997*

The new system of self-assessment has brought changes in the year in which income is taxed. For the year ending 5 April 1997 income is taxed on a current year basis, so your income tax bill for this year is based on the income you received before 6 April 1997. Under the previous system, some income was taxed on a preceding year basis, including income from self-employment, and income from some investments such as some interest from National Savings and British Government stocks. If you made these investments before 6 April 1994, for the tax year ending 5 April 1997 there are transitional rules which apply to make the switch from the preceding year to the current year basis (see p. 83).

# SAVINGS AND INVESTMENT INCOME

**Q 10** ▶ Did you receive any income from UK savings and investments? | NO | YES | If yes, complete boxes 10.1 to 10.32 as appropriate. Include only your share from any joint savings and investments

You can get an income from your investments or savings in the form of interest or dividends; for example, interest on a building society account or dividends from shares. While the income from both these sources can be paid out to you, this is not always the case. For example, interest can be added to your account rather than paid out, and with distributions from unit trusts (a form of dividends) it can be reinvested if you choose. It counts as income whether it is paid out to you or not. If you have any investment income (unless it is tax-free, see p. 83), you should tick the YES box at Q10 and fill in boxes 10.1 to 10.32.

Only enter details of investments you own. If you own an investment jointly, you need to enter only the amount in the tax return which is your share. If you are married, the income from a jointly-owned investment will be split equally. But if you own an investment in a different proportion, the income can be split to reflect ownership (see p. 41).

There are many opportunities for tax saving and tax planning with investments. Turn to Chapter 5 and Chapter 8 which should help you maximise your tax-efficient investing.

If you are the beneficiary of a bare trust, that is one in which you have an immediate absolute title to (a share of) the capital and income, you should enter the amount of your share of the income on page 3. Your trustee will be able to give you the details of your share.

Your income from investments includes income from investments which you have given to your children (aged 17 or less on 6 April 1996). You need to enter details if the amount of the income is £100 or more before tax in a tax year.

> ## TAX-SAVING IDEA
> Take advantage of the many ways you can save which are free of tax: pensions, TESSAs, PEPs, many National Savings products. These are especially helpful if you are a higher rate taxpayer. If you pay tax at the basic rate, you need to look more carefully. For example, the expenses on a PEP may be more than the tax you save.

**Which investment income should not be included on page 3 of your tax return?**

You shouldn't include in your tax return any investment income which is tax-free (see box). If all your investment income is tax-free, tick the NO box at Q10.

These other types of income may be taxable but should go elsewhere in the tax return. They include:

- income from an annuity under a personal pension plan or retirement annuity contract or trust scheme. These should be included on page 4 under Q11
- gains on UK life insurance policies or life annuities or capital redemption policies. These should be included on page 4 under Q12
- a share of any partnership investment income should be entered in the Partnership pages
- accrued income charges on British Government stocks should be included on page 4 of the tax return under Q13
- annual payments from UK unauthorised unit trusts should go on page 4 under Q13.

**The documents you need**

Get together all your dividends vouchers, interest statements or tax deduction certificates and trust vouchers.

---

**EXAMPLE**

Sidney Barrow has the following investments and accounts: National Savings Certificates, a personal equity plan, a TESSA account and a bank current account which pays interest on credit balances. If he didn't have the bank current account he could tick the NO box. But the interest payable on his bank current account means that he has to tick the YES box.

**TAX-SAVING IDEA**

Married couples who have different tax rates should adjust their investments between the two of them so the investments are in the name of the person paying the lower rate of tax.

# TAX-FREE INVESTMENT INCOME

Some investment income is free of income tax. This income does not have to be entered in the tax return at all. Income from the following investments is tax-free:

- premium bonds
- a TESSA account (tax exempt special savings account), but not if you closed your account before the five years was up
- a PEP (personal equity plan), but not if you withdraw more than £180 in interest
- SAYE schemes
- National Savings Ordinary account (but only up to the first £70 of interest)
- National Savings Certificates, including the index-linked ones
- National Savings Children's Bonus Bonds
- Ulster Savings Certificates, if you normally live in Northern Ireland and you bought the certificates or they were repaid while you were living there
- shares in venture capital trusts

There are other less obvious forms of investment income which are also tax-free and don't need to be entered in the tax return:

- interest awarded by a UK court as part of a claim for damages for personal injury or death. There is an extra-statutory concession which means that this can also apply to awards from a foreign court
- if you are a trustee, before-tax interest which is paid out direct to beneficiaries from the payer, but through your authority.

# INTEREST

■ *Interest*

You should enter in the appropriate boxes the actual amount of interest you received in the tax year ending 5 April 1997. If you received income from more than two investments of the same type, you simply add the two figures together and put them in the correct box. But you will need to keep details of the separate investments to give your tax inspector if requested.

## Interest you receive without any tax deducted

However, if you received interest from an investment which was paid before tax was deducted (gross) and you made that investment before 6 April 1994, special transitional rules apply. Broadly, the investments covered by these rules include National Savings (Ordinary and Investment accounts, Income,

Deposit and Capital Bonds and the Pensioners' Guaranteed Income Bond), British Government stocks (those bought through the National Savings Stock Register available via the post office and $3^1/_2$ per cent War Loan) and some bank accounts.

In the tax year ending 5 April 1996, this interest was taxed on a preceding year basis, that is you were taxed on the interest you received in the year ending 5 April 1995. And in the tax year ending 5 April 1998, it will be taxed on a current year basis, that is you will be taxed on the amount of interest you received in that tax year.

The transitional period covers the interest you received in the two years ending 5 April 1997, which have not yet been taxed. You should add up the before-tax amount of interest you received in the two-year period and enter half that sum.

> ### EXAMPLE
> Brian Perry received £400 interest from his National Savings Investment Account in the tax year ending on 5 April 1996 and £300 for the year ending on 5 April 1997. He adds the two together (£700) and enters half that sum (£350) in box 10.1.

## Banks and building societies

- Interest from UK banks, building societies and deposit takers

Most saving income is now paid with tax deducted and the current rate of tax is 20 per cent. Common examples are building societies, banks, British Government stocks, local authority loans, National Savings First Option Bonds and annuities.

Income from accounts in UK banks, building societies, finance houses, organisations offering high-interest cheque accounts and other licensed deposit takers is paid after deduction of tax. There is no further tax bill to pay if you pay tax at the lower or basic rate only on your income, which applies to most taxpayers. If you pay tax at the higher rate, there will be extra tax to pay, at the rate of 20 per cent (see p. 65).

|  | Taxable amount |
| --- | --- |
| – where **no tax** has been deducted | 10.1 £ |

You may have received interest from your bank or building society paid gross, that is without tax deducted. If you received interest paid gross on an investment you made before 6 April 1994, see the special transitional rules on p. 83 for what to include here.

Add up all the interest you have received without tax deducted from your bank, building society or deposit taker in the tax year ending 5 April 1997 and enter it in box 10.1.

If you are a beneficiary of a trust and you are entitled to income as it arises, you should include in box 10.1 any untaxed interest paid direct to you because the trustee has authorised the payer to do so.

Don't include National Savings interest here.

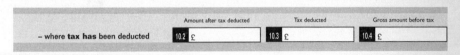

| | Amount after tax deducted | Tax deducted | Gross amount before tax |
|---|---|---|---|
| – where **tax has** been deducted | 10.2 £ | 10.3 £ | 10.4 £ |

You can get the information for these boxes from your pass books or ask your bank, building society or deposit taker direct to give you a tax deduction certificate. Enter the totals for all three figures in the boxes.

## Unit trusts

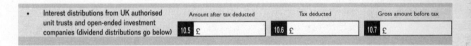

| | Amount after tax deducted | Tax deducted | Gross amount before tax |
|---|---|---|---|
| • Interest distributions from UK authorised unit trusts and open-ended investment companies (dividend distributions go below) | 10.5 £ | 10.6 £ | 10.7 £ |

Some types of unit trusts and open-ended investment companies pay interest rather than dividends. These include unit trusts which invest in British Government stocks and other fixed-interest distributions. In these cases, tax has been deducted from the income at the basic rate before you get it in the same way as for bank or building society interest (see left) and you will get a tax voucher telling you the amount paid. You may be able to claim some or all of it back, or you may have to pay more tax in the same way as for bank or building society interest.

The interest may not be paid out to you but automatically reinvested in accumulation or other units. However, you still have to enter the interest in your tax return.

Add up all the interest you receive after tax has been deducted and enter the total in box 10.5. Put the tax deducted in box 10.6. Then add together boxes 10.5 and 10.6 and enter the sum in box 10.7 (gross amount before tax). If you received interest without any tax deducted, enter nil in boxes 10.5 and 10.6 and enter the before-tax amount in box 10.7.

When you buy units in a unit trust, part of the purchase price includes an amount of income which the trust has received but not yet paid out. The first payment you receive will include an equalisation payment, which is not income, but is a refund of the original purchase price you paid. It is not taxable.

### National Savings

| National Savings (other than FIRST Option Bonds and the first £70 of interest from a National Savings Ordinary Account) | Taxable amount |
|---|---|
| | 10.8 £ |

You will receive interest paid before deduction of tax from the following National Savings investments:

- Ordinary Account
- Investment Account
- Deposit Bonds
- Income Bonds
- Capital Bonds
- Pensioners' Guaranteed Income Bonds

Tot up the before-tax interest you received in the tax year ending 5 April 1997. If you made the investment before 6 April 1994, you will need to apply the special transitional rules (see p. 83). You don't include the first £70 of interest on a National Savings Ordinary Account, as this is tax-free (as are many other National Savings investments – see box on p. 83).

Enter the total amount you received in box 10.8.

| | Amount after tax deducted | Tax deducted | Gross amount before tax |
|---|---|---|---|
| National Savings FIRST Option Bonds | 10.9 £ | 10.10 £ | 10.11 £ |

This investment is an exception among the range of National Savings investments. Interest is paid with tax deducted. Enter in box 10.9 the amount you received, in box 10.10 the amount of tax deducted and in box 10.11 the amount of interest before tax.

## British Government stock and other interest-paying investments

| | Amount after tax deducted | Tax deducted | Gross amount before tax |
|---|---|---|---|
| • Other income from UK savings and investments (except dividends) | 10.12 £ | 10.13 £ | 10.14 £ |

There is a hotch-potch of interest from other investments which should be entered here. Depending on the nature of the interest, it may be paid without tax being deducted or after tax is deducted. Tot up the relevant amounts and enter in boxes 10.12 to 10.14. If no tax has been deducted, put the interest in box 10.14 only and put nil in boxes 10.12 and 10.13. Remember the special transitional rules on p. 83 and use them to work out what you should enter in box 10.14. If tax has been deducted fill in all the boxes.

Here is a list of the investments to include here:

- certificates of tax deposit when the certificates is applied payment of a tax bill
- British Government stock (see below)
- other loan stocks (see below)
- loans to an individual or organisation
- income from credit unions or friendly societies
- interest from Enterprise Zone trusts
- discount on relevant discounted securities (enter in box 10.14)
- discount from gilt strips (enter in box 10.14)
- income from securities to which you have sold or transferred the right to the income, but not the security – even if you have not received the income (enter in box 10.14)
- purchased life annuities (see below).

You may have received cash or shares when two or more building societies have merged or a building society has converted to a company or been taken over by a company. You may have to pay either income or capital gains tax and your building society should be able to tell you this. If you have received a cash payment on which you should pay income tax, put the details on page 3 of the basic tax return. If you don't know if you have to pay income tax, put the details under Q13 on page 4. Any capital gain should be in the Capital gains supplementary pages. If you have received shares, you may need to supply details only when you dispose of the shares.

### British Government stock
Tax at the rate of 20 per cent for the tax year ending 5 April 1997 has already been deducted from the interest on most British Government stocks (or gilts) before you receive it. Your interest payment should be accompanied

by a tax voucher which lets you know how much tax has been deducted. If you are a non-taxpayer, you should be able to claim back the amount deducted. If you are a basic-rate taxpayer, there is no more tax to pay. Enter the appropriate amounts in the three boxes 10.12, 10.13 and 10.14.

There are a few examples where the interest is paid without any tax deducted. If you buy your British Goernment stocks through the Post Office (the National Savings Stock Register), the interest will be paid before tax. With $3^1/_2$ per cent War Loan, however it is purchased, the interest is before tax. And with small amounts of interest (£2.50 gross each half year) there is no tax deducted.

If you own fixed-interest securities with a nominal value in excess of £5,000, and you buy or sell them there are special tax rules designed to stop tax avoidance by turning income into capital gains. Ask your tax inspector to send you Inland Revenue leaflet *IR68 Accrued Income scheme.*

### Other loan stocks
There are other loan stocks, such as local authority loans and stocks, which you can buy as well as British Government stocks. These pay interest with tax deducted. If you are a non-taxpayer, you can reclaim the tax deducted and you can arrange for the interest to be paid before it is deducted.

### Annuities
An annuity is an investment made with a life insurance company. You invest a lump sum and in return the insurance company will pay you an income. Sometimes this could be for a particular period, say ten years, or it could be until you die. The income which you receive is considered to be in two parts: some of it is your original investment being returned to you. There is tax to pay on only the interest.

The annuity payment is made to you with tax at the rate of 20 per cent of the interest part already deducted. The tax voucher which accompanies the payment will tell you how much tax has been deducted. If you are a non-taxpayer you can claim back the tax deducted.

With an annuity which you buy as part of your pension, the tax treatment is different. Tax will be deducted from the whole payment through the PAYE system. Details of annuities bought under personal pension schemes or retirement annuity contracts should be entered on page 4 of the tax return under Q11.

# DIVIDENDS

You will receive share dividends from UK companies and distributions from authorised unit trusts with no more basic rate tax to pay because you also receive a tax credit. The payments are accompanied by a tax voucher which sets out the amount of the tax credit (and for the year ending 5 April 1997 the amount is 20 per cent, the same as on other forms of savings). You work out the gross amount of dividend by adding together the net dividend and the tax credit (see p. 64).

If you are a beneficiary of a trust and you are entitled to income as it arises, include in these boxes any dividends or distributions shown on your trust voucher.

## Shares in UK companies

| | Dividend/distribution | Tax credit | Dividend/distribution plus credit |
|---|---|---|---|
| • Dividends and other qualifying distributions from UK companies | 10.15 £ | 10.16 £ | 10.17 £ |

Your dividend voucher should show the amount of the dividend and the tax credit. Put these in boxes 10.15 and 10.16 and add them together to enter the sum in box 10.17. Note that foreign income dividends or scrip dividends are included below in boxes 10.21 to 10.26.

Companies can make other kinds of distributions as well as dividends, for example, payment in kind. A distinction is drawn between qualifying and non-qualifying distributions. A non-qualifying distribution is broadly one which gives a future rather than a current claim on the company's assets, such as a bonus issue of redeemable shares. Qualifying distributions should be entered in boxes 10.15 to 10.17 (non-qualifying distributions are entered below in boxes 10.30 to 10.32).

## Unit trusts

| | Dividend/distribution | Tax credit | Dividend/distribution plus credit |
|---|---|---|---|
| • Dividend distributions from UK authorised unit trusts and open-ended investment companies | 10.18 £ | 10.19 £ | 10.20 £ |

Distributions from most authorised unit trusts are treated in the same way as dividends (see previous page). If you have invested in an accumulation unit trust, you don't receive the income but the unit trust managers reinvest it for you in more units. However, for tax purposes this is treated in exactly the same way as if you received the cash. You will receive a tax voucher with a tax credit.

Your dividend vouchers show the amount of the dividend and the tax credit. If you own units in more than one unit trust, add up the distributions and tax credits enter the totals for each in boxes 10.18 and 10.19. Add them together to get the entry for box 10.20. Don't enter any equalisation payments (see p. 86).

## Scrip dividends

| | Dividend | Notional tax | Dividend plus notional tax |
|---|---|---|---|
| • Scrip dividends from UK companies | 10.21 £ | 10.22 £ | 10.23 £ |

If you receive new shares instead of cash as a dividend, this is known as a scrip dividend. The value of the scrip dividend is known as the cash equivalent and is the amount of cash dividend forgone. It should be shown on your dividend statement as the appropriate amount of cash. This is what you enter in the dividend box. You are treated as having received the cash equivalent grossed up at 20 per cent.

If you pay tax at the basic rate only, there is no further tax to pay. If you pay tax at the higher rate of 40 per cent, there will be extra tax to pay. But unlike a cash dividend you cannot claim back any tax credit if you are a non-taxpayer.

Enter in box 10.21 the appropriate amount of cash. In box 10.22 enter the notional tax. For the tax year ending 5 April 1997, this is found as follows:

$$\left( \text{cash equivalent} \times \frac{100}{80} \right) - 80$$

Or you can take 25 per cent of the cash equivalent.

Enter this figure in box 10.22. Add together boxes 10.21 and box 10.22, and enter the sum in box 10.23.

## Foreign income dividends

| | Dividend | Notional tax | Dividend plus notional tax |
|---|---|---|---|
| • Foreign income dividends from UK companies | 10.24 £ | 10.25 £ | 10.26 £ |

If a company pays share dividends out of profits from a foreign source, the company can pay dividends under the foreign income scheme. From the shareholder's point of view, these are the same as ordinary dividends, except that non-taxpayers cannot claim back the tax credit.

Your dividend voucher should show the dividend (put in box 10.24) and the notional tax (put in box 10.25). Add these together and put the sum in box 10.26.

| | Dividend | Notional tax | Dividend plus notional tax |
|---|---|---|---|
| • Foreign income dividend distributions from UK authorised unit trusts and open-ended investment companies | 10.27 £ | 10.28 £ | 10.29 £ |

Your dividend voucher should show the amount of the foreign income distribution (put in box 10.27) and the tax treated as paid or notional tax (put in box 10.28). Add boxes 10.27 and 10.28 together to get the figure to enter in box 10.29. Note that the notional tax cannot be reclaimed by a non-taxpayer.

If you are invested in an accumulation unit trust and don't actually receive the distribution because it is automatically reinvested, you should still show the distribution in your tax return.

Don't enter the amount of any equalisation payment (see p. 86).

## Non-qualifying distributions

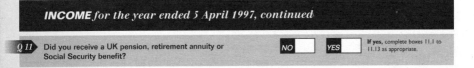

| | Notional tax | Taxable amount |
|---|---|---|
| • Non-qualifying distributions and loans written off | 10.30 £ | 10.31 £ | 10.32 £ |

A non-qualifying distribution is broadly one which gives a future rather than a current claim on the company's assets, such as a bonus issue of redeemable shares. The amount of the distribution is the nominal value of the securities you received less any consideration (for example, cash) you paid. If you pay tax at the lower or basic rate, there is no more tax to pay. If you pay tax at the higher rate, an amount of lower rate tax is treated as already paid by you and set against your tax bill.

Enter the amount of the distribution in box 10.32. Multiply box 10.32 by 20 per cent to get the amount of notional tax to enter in box 10.31. Leave box 10.30 blank.

For loans written off, contact your tax adviser or tax office.

## PENSIONS AND SOCIAL SECURITY BENEFITS

**INCOME** *for the year ended 5 April 1997, continued*

**Q11** Did you receive a UK pension, retirement annuity or Social Security benefit? | NO | YES | **If yes,** complete boxes 11.1 to 11.13 as appropriate.

If you received none of these, tick the NO box and go to Q12.

But if you received one or more of these, you will need to find out whether what you received should be entered here in your tax return. Some pensions and benefits are not taxable.

### What pensions and benefits should not be included in your tax return
If you received any of the following, you do not need to give details here in the tax return because they are tax-free:
• additions to your state pension or social security benefits which you get because you have a dependent child
• Christmas bonus for pensioners
• family credit and childcare allowance
• maternity allowance
• social fund maternity payments

- student grants
- school uniform grants
- child benefit
- child's special allowance (only payable to those already claiming before 6 April 1987)
- one-parent benefit
- war orphan's benefit
- guardian's allowance
- war widow's pension and some pensions paid to other dependants of deceased Forces and Merchant Navy personnel. Ask the Orderline for Help Sheet *IR310 War Widow's and Dependant's pensions*
- widow's payment
- severe disablement allowance
- war disablement benefits
- industrial disablement benefit
- incapacity benefit for the first 28 weeks (but not taxable after that time if you were receiving invalidity benefit before 13 April 1995 unless there is a break in your claim; incapacity benefit replaced invalidity benefit)
- disability living allowance
- disability working allowance
- attendance allowance
- housing benefit (rent rebates and allowances)
- council tax benefit
- most income support
- payments from the social fund
- jobfinder's grant, most YT training scheme allowances, employment rehabilitation and training allowances
- similar benefits paid by foreign governments.

Refunds of surplus additional voluntary contributions are not entered here. Details should be put in boxes 12.10 to 12.12.

**What pensions and benefits should be entered in your tax return**
Details of the following should be entered here:

- state retirement pension, the basic pension and state earnings related pension
- old person's pension for people aged 80 or over
- widow's pension
- widowed mother's allowance
- industrial death benefit
- unemployment benefit, income support and jobseeker's allowance
- invalid care allowance
- statutory sick pay and statutory maternity pay paid by the DSS

- taxable incapacity benefit
- pension from a former employer or a pension from your late husband or wife's employer
- pension from a personal pension scheme or retirement annuity contract or trust scheme
- pension from a free-standing additional voluntary contribution
- pension for injuries at work or for work-related illnesses
- pension from service in the armed forces
- income withdrawals from a personal pension plan where the purchase of an annuity has been delayed.

If you receive any of the above pensions or benefits, tick the YES box in answer to Q11.

## The documents you need

You will need to gather together certain information such as the details of your state pension and, your P60, which your pension payer may have given you, or any other certificate of pension paid and tax deducted. Details of any taxable amounts of social security benefits, such as unemployment benefit (until October 1996), jobseeker's allowance (from October 1996), income support, incapacity benefit or any other taxable state benefits will also be required.

## State pensions and benefits

■ *State pensions and benefits*

Enter the amount of pension or benefit you were entitled to for the tax year ending 5 April 1997, whether or not you actually received that amount in the year.

### State retirement pension

| | Taxable amount for 1996-97 |
|---|---|
| • State Retirement Pension | 11.1 £ |

The state retirement pension is taxable, although paid without tax deducted. So if you have other income you will find that tax on your state retirement pension might be collected from your other income.

In box 11.1, you should enter the amount you were entitled to receive in the tax year ending 5 April 1997, but excluding any amount paid for a dependent child and the Christmas bonus.

A married woman might receive a pension which is based on her husband's contributions and not her own (but not any dependency allowance which he receives for her before her 60th birthday). She can claim a personal allowance to deduct from her pension and the pension should be entered in her tax return, not her husband's.

## Widow's pension

| • Widow's Pension | 11.2 £ |
|---|---|

Enter the full amount you were entitled to receive in the tax year ending 5 April 1997, including any earnings-related additional pension, in box 11.2.

For more information on the benefits available to widows, ask for leaflet NP45 A guide to widow's benefits from your benefits agency.

## Widowed mother's allowance

| • Widowed Mother's Allowance | 11.3 £ |
|---|---|

You should include in box 11.3 the flat rate basic allowance which you were entitled to and any earnings-related increase. But don't include any child dependency increase.

## Industrial death benefit

| • Industrial Death Benefit pension | 11.4 £ |
|---|---|

In box 11.4 you should enter the yearly pension you are entitled to receive under the industrial death benefit scheme. But do not include industrial death benefit child allowance which is tax-free.

## Unemployment benefit, income support and jobseeker's allowance
Unemployment benefit, jobseeker's allowance and income support (in some circumstances) are taxable but paid without any tax deducted.

| • Unemployment Benefit, Income Support and Jobseeker's Allowance | 11.5 £ |
|---|---|

Income support is not taxable if you are 60 or over, a single parent living with a child under 16 or staying at home to look after a severely disabled person. Any amount you receive over the standard weekly amount of job-seeker's allowance (before October 1996 unemployment benefit) for a couple or single person is not taxable.

The benefit office will usually have given you a statement of the total unemployment benefit, income support and jobseeker's allowance paid and the taxable portions. You should enter the taxable amount in box 11.5. If you haven't received a statement, tell your tax office. You have 60 days to check your statement to see if it is correct.

### Invalid care allowance

| • Invalid Care Allowance | 11.6 £ |
|---|---|

Enter the amount you were entitled to receive in the tax year ending 5 April 1997. Include any addition for a dependent adult, but exclude any additional amount for a dependent child, because this is tax-free.

### Statutory sick pay and statutory maternity pay

| • Statutory Sick Pay and Statutory Maternity Pay paid by the Department of Social Security | 11.7 £ |
|---|---|

Generally, these are paid by your employer and taxed under the PAYE system (see p. 21). They will be included in your P60 or P45. Details should be entered in the Employment supplementary pages.

But if your employer didn't pay you, and the Department of Social Security did so instead, enter the total received here in box 11.7.

### Taxable incapacity benefit

| | Tax deducted | Gross amount before tax |
|---|---|---|
| • Taxable Incapacity Benefit | 11.8 £ | 11.9 £ |

Some incapacity benefit is tax-free. You will not pay tax on it when you receive it during your first 28 weeks of incapacity or you are receiving it for a period of incapacity which began before 13 April 1995, and for which invalidity benefit used to be payable.

The Department of Social Security will give you a form showing you whether your incapacity benefit is taxable or not. If it is taxable, enter the amount of the benefit in box 11.9 and any tax that has been deducted in box 11.8.

## Other pensions

- *Other pensions and retirement annuities*

| | Amount after tax deducted | Tax deducted | Gross amount before tax |
|---|---|---|---|
| • Pensions (other than State pensions) and retirement annuities | 11.10 £ | 11.11 £ | 11.12 £ |

You should enter here details of pensions paid to you by someone in the UK who is not paying on behalf of someone outside the UK. Pensions received from abroad will be entered in the Foreign pages (see p. 231).

You should total the amount you receive from all your pensions (excluding state pension) and put it in box 11.10. You should include in the total:

- annuity payments from a personal pension scheme
- if you have taken advantage of the ability to defer buying the annuity, perhaps because annuity rates were low, the income withdrawals which you receive during the deferred period
- any annual payments from a retirement contract or trusts scheme.

Put the amount of tax deducted in box 11.11. The information about an employer's pension should be on Form P60 and for other pensions from a certificate given to you by the pension payer. Adding up boxes 11.10 and 11.11 should give you the total for box 11.12, unless you have received some non-cash benefit. If you have, you'll need to ask your tax office what to do.

There are some special pensions which can be free of UK tax or entitled to a deduction so that only 90 per cent of the pension is taxed in the UK.

## Tax-free pensions

There are two examples. First a pension which is received for wounds or disability incurred while in military service or other war injuries is free of tax. Second is the extra amount of pension which you might receive as a former employee who was awarded a pension on retirement because you were disabled by injury on duty or a work-related illness. If that pension is more than the amount you would receive if you had retired at the same on the grounds of ordinary ill-health, the extra amount is free of tax.

## 10 per cent deduction

This applies to some UK pensions for service for certain overseas governments. Only 90 per cent of the pension is taxed.

Include any exemption or deduction in box 11.13.

# OTHER INCOME TO BE ENTERED HERE

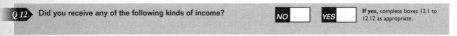

Q12 | Did you receive any of the following kinds of income? | NO [   ] YES [   ] | **If yes,** complete boxes 12.1 to 12.12 as appropriate.

The income includes taxable maintenance or alimony, gains on UK life insurance policies, life annuities or capital redemption policies or refunds of surplus additional voluntary contributions.

If you tick the NO box you should go to Q13.

## Maintenance income

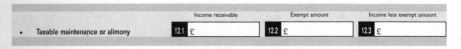

| | Income receivable | Exempt amount | Income less exempt amount |
|---|---|---|---|
| • Taxable maintenance or alimony | 12.1 £ | 12.2 £ | 12.3 £ |

Maintenance you receive could be taxable. It depends on whether your maintenance agreement was made under the old rules or the new rules.

If you receive maintenance under the new rules you do not pay tax and you do not need to enter the amount in your tax return. Even if you remarry and carry on receiving maintenance from your former husband or wife, for example, for your child, the maintenance received will be tax-free.

A maintenance agreement is made under the new rules if:

- it was made on or after 15 March 1988 (unless it merely alters or replaces an arrangement to which the old rules apply)
- it was made before 15 March 1988, but you didn't tell your tax inspector about it in writing by 30 June 1988
- it is a court order which was applied for after 15 March 1988
- it was a court order made after 30 June 1988 (unless it is merely altering or replacing an arrangement to which the old rules apply)
- it is assessed by the Child Support Agency
- the person paying the maintenance has opted for it to be taxed under the new rules.

If the maintenance you receive is made under a legally-binding agreement not in the list above, it will be taxed under the old rules. This means that you may have to pay income tax on it and will need to enter the details in boxes 12.1 to 12.30.

Under the old rules, the first £1,790 in the tax year ending 5 April 1997 is tax-free. Anything else you receive above this is taxed at your top rate of tax, except that, if what you receive in maintenance has increased since the tax year ending 5 April 1989, you pay no tax on this extra bit. If you remarry and you carry on receiving maintenance, the first £1,790 will no longer be tax-free.

If your child receives maintenance under the old rules paid direct to him or her, rather than to you for his or her benefit, there is no tax-free band. What he or she receives, up to the amount received in the tax year ending 5 April 1989, counts as taxable income, but the child can set his or her personal allowance against it (giving a tax-free band of £3,765 in the tax year ending 5 April 1997.

If you are receiving maintenance from your parents and are over 21, you do not have to pay tax on it.

If your maintenance is taxable, you have to pay tax on the lower of:

- the amount you were due to receive and did receive between 6 April 1988 and 5 April 1989, or
- the amount you were due to receive and did receive between 6 April 1995 and 5 April 1996.

In box 12.1 put in the lower of these two amounts. If you receive maintenance from more than one source under the old rules, treat each maintenance payment separately. Add together the amounts and put the total in box 12.1.

The first £1,790 for the tax year ending 5 April 1997 is tax-free if:

- you received it from your separated or former husband or wife; and
- it is for yourself or for the support of a child aged under 21 of whom you are both the parents, or whom you have treated as part of the family; and
- you have not remarried; and
- you did not, during the tax year ending 5 April 1997, live again with your separated husband or wife who pays the maintenance.

If all these apply to you, you can claim your tax-free bit of maintenance. In box 12.2 put the lower of the maintenance you received or £1,790.

Deduct box 12.2 from box 12.1 and enter the difference in box 12.3.

There is more information in Chapter 6.

---

### EXAMPLE

Patricia Smith receives maintenance from her ex-husband. The agreement was made in 1986 and is taxed under the old rules. The agreement was that she would receive £5,000 a year. This is what she was paid in the tax year ending 5 April 1989. For the tax year ending 5 April 1997 she received £4,500 as her former husband was having difficulty meeting the payments. In box 12.1 she puts the lower of the amounts she received in the tax years ending 5 April 1989 and 5 April 1997. This was the £4,500 she received in the tax year ending 5 April 1997. In box 12.2 she puts the lower of what she entered in box 12.1 or £1,790. She enters £1,790. She will be taxed on £4,500 less £1,790, that is £2,710.

---

## Life insurance policies

Gains on life insurance policies, contracts for life annuities or capital redemption policies are treated as investment income and may be taxable.

The tax treatment of life insurance policies depends on whether it is qualifying or non-qualifying. Most types of life insurance which involve you paying regular premiums are qualifying; if you pay just a single premium, it will almost certainly be a non-qualifying policy, which has less favourable tax treatment.

The Inland Revenue has issued a consultative document which would change the taxation of life insurance – this could cause particular problems for single-premium bonds.

## Taxation of qualifying policies

The life insurance company will have paid tax on the income and gains which its life fund makes as they arise. And so, with qualifying policies, there is not usually any income or capital gains tax to pay when the policy matures – that is, it comes to the end of its agreed period or the person insured by the policy dies.

The exception to this is if you cash in or make a policy paid up before the end of the agreed period. A policy might be treated as non-qualifying if this happens before ten years or, if this is less, three-quarters of its term.

## Taxation of non-qualifying policies

The tax treatment of non-qualifying policies is less favourable than for the qualifying ones and it is possible that income tax might be due when you receive the proceeds. Most insurance policies are treated as having already paid basic rate tax, but the basic rate tax is notional only and cannot be reclaimed by a non taxpayer or lower rate taxpayer.

But if you are a higher rate taxpayer, or become one when you add the proceeds of your policy to your other taxable income, there will be higher rate tax due on it.

The proceeds are treated as a chargeable gain and the amount of the gain is usually what you receive less what you have paid during the life of the policy. If the person insured has died and the policy pays out, the gain is taken as the cash-in value of the policy, if this is less than you receive.

You may be able to draw an income from your non-qualifying policy by cashing part of it. Under the current rules, these withdrawals won't be taxed at the time as long as you have not cashed in five per cent or more of what you paid for each year of the policy. But at the end of the policy, the amount you have withdrawn will be added to the gain to work out the tax due. If you don't cash the full five per cent each year, you can carry forward the unused amount, meaning that you might be able to cash more than five per cent in a later year without paying tax at the time. However, you will eventually be taxed on what you have received during the life of the policy, unless you are no longer a higher rate taxpayer when it comes to an end (see overleaf). Selling a non-qualifying policy is treated the same as a policy maturing or being cashed in.

The gain on a non-qualifying policy is added to your taxable income for the year. But there is no basic rate tax due. For the tax year ending 5 April 1997, there will be higher rate tax to pay if your taxable income and the gain come to £25,500 or more.

If the policy is treated as having had basic rate tax deducted, the rate of tax to pay is 40 – 24 = 16 per cent for the tax year ending 5 April 1997. This could still mean a large tax bill in the year of the gain. But you may be able to benefit from top-slicing relief which spreads the gain you make over the years of the policy. Broadly, you work out the average gain for each year you have held the policy. Calculate the amount of tax that would be due if the average gain was added to your income and multiply this by the number of years the policy was held. The tax return asks you to enter the number of years so that top-slicing relief can be worked out.

Although most gains from UK insurances are treated as having had basic rate tax deducted, gains from certain life annuities and friendly societies' tax exempt policies are not treated in this way, that is, there is no notional tax paid. Your insurance company should be able to tell you how your gain is treated. And you may have received a chargeable event certificate showing your gains and the other information you need to fill in your tax return.

If you have made a gain and it is not treated as having had basic rate tax deducted, put the amount of the gain in box 12.5 and the number of complete years since the insurance was made in box 12.4.

If you have made a gain and it is treated as having had basic rate tax deducted, put the amount of the gain in box 12.8 and the notional tax in box 12.7 (24 per cent of the amount in box 12.8). Enter the number of complete years in box 12.6.

Where you have made more than one sort of gain, or you hold a cluster of policies, things become complex. You will probably need to put additional information in the section on page 8 of the tax return. Ask the Orderline (see p. 75) for a copy of Help Sheet *IR320 Gains on UK life insurance policies.* Consult your tax office or tax adviser for more guidance.

If you had a life insurance policy on which you made a loss on final surrender, you may be able to claim a relief to ensure that the amount treated as income is not more than the total gain made under the policy. Ask for Help Sheet *IR320 Gains on UK life insurance policies.*

## Repayment of additional voluntary contributions

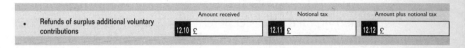

Additional voluntary contributions are extra payments you can make to your employer's or your own free-standing additional voluntary contribution scheme (see p. 69). A condition of the contributions is that they cannot buy you pension benefits greater than the maximum limits set by the Inland Revenue for approved schemes. If you inadvertently contribute so much in additional voluntary contributions that the benefits would exceed the limits, the excess will be paid back to you at retirement, with a deduction to cover the tax relief the contributions have enjoyed.

Your certificate from your pension scheme provider should show you the amount of surplus contributions and the tax refunded to you. Enter the total amount in box 12.12, the amount actually repaid to you in box 12.10 and the tax deducted in box 12.11.

## Any other income

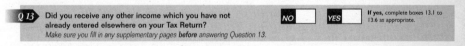

You should have already filled in the appropriate supplementary pages for income from employment, self-employment, trusts, abroad and so on. You may have other odd bits of income not yet entered. For example:

- freelance or casual income
- profits from the odd literary or artistic activity
- income received after you close a business (post-cessation receipts). This could include money which you have recovered from a bad debt or royalties arising after the business ceased from contracts made before it ceased. You can claim to have this treated as income for the year in which the business ceased (tick box 22.5 on page 8 of the tax return). Or you can enter the total here
- any recovery of expenses or debts for which you claimed relief as post-cessation expenses
- sale of patent rights if you received a capital sum

- receipts from covenants entered into for genuine commercial reasons which are in connection with the payer's trade, profession or vocation. Losses cannot be set against this income
- rental from leasing equipment you own
- income from guaranteeing loans, dealing in futures and some income from underwriting
- accrued income on the transfer of securities (but not if the nominal value of securites in the tax year ending 5 April 1997 was £5,000 or less)
- annual payments received in the year including annual payments received from UK unauthorised unit trusts, and annual payments paid by former employers which do not count as a pension. Expenses cannot be deducted from this income. Losses cannot be set against this income.

You should also enter in this section any cashbacks or other incentives which you received to take out a mortgage if there is tax to pay. Ask the person who gave you the incentive or check with your tax office to find out if it is taxable. Enter it in Box 13.3.

Some part of income received under a permanent health insurance policy may be taxable and should be entered here. This does not include income from a policy which you paid for yourself, as that is tax-free. Income from your employer for sickness and disability should go on the Employment pages. But if you have left your employer and you are still receiving benefits because you are covered by your former employer's scheme, you should enter that amount here (part might be tax-free if you contributed to the cost of the scheme – check with your tax office).

If you received any other income which should be taxed but which you have not put anywhere else, you should tick the YES box at Q13.
You need to keep careful records of the income and the expenses.

If you are self-employed and make losses in your business, one option available to you is to deduct the loss from any other income which you have in that year or the next year. You can deduct the losses from all the income listed above except from the covenant income received, the annual payments and benefits from a disability policy.

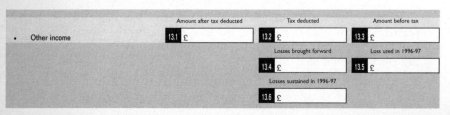

| | Amount after tax deducted | Tax deducted | Amount before tax |
|---|---|---|---|
| • Other income | 13.1 £ | 13.2 £ | 13.3 £ |
| | | Losses brought forward | Loss used in 1996-97 |
| | | 13.4 £ | 13.5 £ |
| | | Losses sustained in 1996-97 | |
| | | 13.6 £ | |

Enter the amount of income after any tax deducted and after any allowable expenses or capital allowances in box 13.1. If you made a loss put nil.
In box 13.2, put the amount of tax deducted from the payments you received. Add together boxes 13.1 and 13.2, to find the figure for box 13.3.

If you made a loss in box 13.3, you can deduct it from some other income in a future year. Put it in box 13.6.

If you have made losses in earlier years, either from your business or other income, enter the amount of unused allowable losses brought forward in box 13.4. If you have any income in box 13.3, and unused losses brought forward in box 13.4, you can deduct the losses from box 13.3, reducing it to nil (and thus cutting your tax bill). Put in box 13.5 the amount of losses you are using this year.

If you have several types of other income, the calculation can become complex. Help Sheet IR325 *Other income* has a worksheet to help you complete this task.

# RELIEFS

## CHAPTER 11

You can pay less tax by spending more money on things the government wants to encourage – and thus gives tax relief on – such as pensions and training. In some instances you can get tax relief at your highest rate of tax, which could be 40 per cent. Assuming that you want to spend the money, buying any of these things could be highly advantageous. You claim for them on page 5 of the basic tax return.

You get your tax relief in different ways. Frequently you get basic rate tax relief by deducting it from what you spend. Any higher rate tax relief that is due you will claim here in the tax return and give yourself the relief when you are working out your tax bill. Or you could get higher rate relief through your PAYE code. Non-taxpayers will not have to repay the tax deducted, except in the case of covenants and Gift Aid.

If you don't get basic rate relief by deducting it from what you pay, you will claim the relief here in the tax return and get it by deducting the amount from the tax you owe on 31 January or through your PAYE code.

### The documents you need
You must gather together all the supporting documents you need to be able to prove to your tax inspector that you are entitled to the relief you are claiming. These could include:

> ## TAX-SAVING IDEA
> You can go back six years to claim deductions which you forgot to claim at the time or didn't know you were able to. You will get tax relief at the rate you should have got it if you had claimed the deduction at the right time.

- certificates of premiums paid from your pension provider
- receipts of payments paid for vocational training
- certificates of interest paid on loans
- maintenance agreements, court order, Child Support Agency assessments
- share certificate in a venture capital trust
- Forms EIS3 or EIS5 (for Enterprise Investment Scheme)
- details of covenants paid or lump sums to charity under Gift Aid

# What deductions can you claim

There is no entry in this section of the tax return for payments for private medical insurance for people aged 60 or over. This is because you can get tax relief only at the basic rate and this is obtained by deducting the after-tax amount from what you pay the insurance company.

You can claim here for:

- pension contributions
- additional voluntary contributions to a pension scheme
- vocational training payments
- interest paid on qualifying loans
- maintenance payments
- investments in growing business (venture capital trusts or Enterprise Investment scheme)
- payments to charities (through covenants or Gift Aid)
- post-cessation expenses for a business and losses on relevant discounted securities
- payments to a trade union or friendly society.

## PENSIONS

You can get tax relief at your highest rate of tax on contributions to a pension scheme. If you are an employee, your employer can also make contributions to an approved pension scheme for you, and these would also get tax relief (and not count as a fringe benefit for you). There are more details about saving for your pension in Chapter 8.

> ## EXAMPLE
>
> Tony Jabot is wondering which is the best way to save for his retirement. He considers tax-free investments such as PEPs or TESSAs or taking out a personal pension plan. The tax treatment of PEPs, TESSAs or the pension fund is similar in that no tax is payable on any income or capital gains generated while your money is invested. But with a pension scheme, the government helps Tony to invest with tax relief on his contributions. He is a basic rate taxpayer. If he invested £1,000 in a personal pension plan, it would cost him just £770 in the year ending 5 April 1998.

**Q 14** **Do you want to claim relief for pension contributions?**
*Do not include contributions deducted from your pay by your employer because tax relief is given automatically.*

 NO  YES

If yes, complete boxes 14.1 to 14.17 as appropriate.

You can save for a pension through an employer's pension scheme or a personal pension scheme if you are an employee, and through a personal pension scheme if you are self-employed or a partner.

With an employer's pension scheme, you are likely to get tax relief on your contributions deducted at source (they will be deducted from your salary before your employer works out your income tax through the PAYE system). If this is the only way you are saving for a pension, you can tick the NO box and go on to Q15. Obviously, if you are not saving at all for a pension, you should also tick the NO box.

## What you should claim for

In the tax return you can claim tax relief for payments into two different types of pension scheme:

- retirement annuity contracts (new contracts not available from 1 July 1988)
- personal pension plans (not available before 1 July 1988)

If you started saving for a pension before 1 July 1988, unless you converted it into a personal pension, your scheme will be a retirement annuity contract. If you started saving for a pension on or after 1 July 1988, you will be saving in a personal pension plan. You could have started a personal pension plan in addition to a retirement annuity contract.

## How much tax relief?

The amount of tax relief you can get depends on three factors:

- your net relevant earnings (see below)
- your age
- whether you are saving in a personal pension plan or a retirement annuity contract.

Net relevant earnings are:

- your earnings from non-pensionable jobs, including the taxable value of fringe benefits, but after deduction of allowable expenses if you're an

employee (boxes 1.32 to 1.36 on the Employment pages)
- your taxable profits, less certain payments made by your business after deduction of tax, for example, patent royalties, covenant payments (box 3.89 on the Self-employment pages) if you're self-employed,
- your share of partnership profits (box 4.19 on the Partnership pages)
- profit from furnished holiday lettings (box 5.14 on the Land and property pages).

The amount of your net relevant earnings on which you can get tax relief is given below:

| Age at 6 April | Personal pension % | Retirement annuity % |
|---|---|---|
| 35 or less | 17.5 | 17.5 |
| 36-45 | 20.0 | 17.5 |
| 46-50 | 25.0 | 17.5 |
| 51-55 | 30.0 | 20.0 |
| 56-60 | 35.0 | 22.5 |
| 61-74 | 40.0 | 27.5 |

Any contributions made by your employer to your personal pension count towards the limits above. There is a limit set on what you can save in a personal pension scheme, known as the earnings cap. For the tax year ending 5 April 1997, you can work out the percentage you can invest on no more than £82,200 of your earnings. For the tax year ending 5 April 1998, the cap is £84,000.

There is no earnings cap on what you can save in a retirement annuity. If you're a high earner, you may be able to save more in a retirement annuity.

## EXAMPLE

Mark Fisher is aged 55 and has a retirement annuity contract. His net relevant earnings for the year ended 5 April 1997 are £100,000. Because it is a retirement annuity contract, there is no earnings cap. The limit on investment for his age is 20 per cent of net relevant earnings. Mark can invest up to £20,000 in his pension for the year.

## TAX-SAVING IDEA

If you're a high earner and you have both a retirement annuity contract and a personal pension scheme, you may find that because of the effect of the earnings cap on the personal pension scheme, you can make bigger contributions to the retirement annuity contract.

## TAX-SAVING IDEA

If your earnings are within the earnings cap for pension contributions and you are currently saving just in a retirement annuity contract, consider taking out a personal pension scheme as well. The limits on contributions are higher and you will find that you can save more for your pension.

## EXAMPLE

Philip Brampton is aged 55 and has a personal pension plan. His net relevant earnings for the year ended 5 April 1997 are £100,000, but as it is a personal pension plan there is an earnings cap of £82,200. The limit on contributions for his age is 30 per cent of net relevant earnings up to the cap. He can invest 30 per cent of £82,200 which is £24,660.

## EXAMPLE

Marion Mould is an employee. Her monthly contributions of £50 to an employer's pension scheme are deducted from her salary before tax is worked out under the PAYE scheme.

Margaret May is an employee. She doesn't contribute to her employer's pension scheme, but saves in a personal pension scheme instead. She saves £50 a month, but only hands over £38.50 to the pension provider, because she has deducted £11.50 (basic rate tax at 23 per cent for the year ending 5 April 1998). The pension provider claimes back the £11.50 from the Inland Revenue.

Marcia Mumps is self-employed, saving £50 a month in a personal pension scheme. She hands over £50 each month to the pension provider. She claims her basic rate tax relief in her tax return, deducting it from her income before working out how much tax she should pay on 31 January.

## EXAMPLE

Shelagh Fitzherbert has two pension schemes, a personal pension scheme and a retirement annuity contract. Her earnings for the year ending 5 April 1998 are likely to be £40,000. She likes investing in both her schemes because it gives her more flexibility in when she can start drawing her benefits and also gives a spread of risk, in case either of her policies should prove to be poor investment performers. She is aged 52. She can invest 20 per cent of £40,000, that is £8,000, in her retirement annuity contract. Or she could invest 30 per cent of £40,000, that is £12,000, in her personal pension scheme.

Tax relief is always given for the retirement annuity contract first and she chooses to invest £8,000. This means she has £12,000 less £8,000, that is £4,000 she can invest in her personal pension scheme.

While it is possible for you to have both a retirement annuity contract and a personal pension scheme, you cannot get double the tax relief. The tax relief for the retirement annuity contract is always given before the relief for the personal pension scheme. Relief for retirement annuity contract reduces the relief for the personal pension. The Inland Revenue has produced Help Sheet *IR330 Pension payments* which has an explanation and working sheets.

## How do you get tax relief?

If you are self-employed you get tax relief on either a personal pension scheme or a retirement annuity by claiming it here in your tax return. You make your payments gross to the pension provider (normally a life insurance company).

If you are an employee, you will normally get tax relief on contributions to an employer's scheme through the PAYE system. If you are saving in a personal pension scheme, you make your payment to the pension provider after deducting tax at the basic rate. If you are a higher rate taxpayer you will claim your higher rate relief though your tax return. If you save in a retirement annuity contract, you will make your payments to the pension provider without deducting any tax. You will get your tax relief by claiming it in your tax return or by having it in your PAYE code and thus getting it in your salary.

## Which year do you get tax relief?

Pensions are treated specially and you are allowed to make payments in one year and have them set against income for a different year – these rules are known as 'carry back', 'bring back' and 'carry forward'. The rules allow you to make the maximum use of your limits, even if you do not have sufficient cash to pay for the contributions in a particular tax year.

You can choose to carry back payments you make to a personal

> ## EXAMPLE
>
> Roger Cox, a circus proprietor, is aged 50. He has a personal pension scheme, which he started in 1992. But he has also been saving for a number of years starting in 1985 in a retirement annuity contract. His earnings for the year ended 5 April 1997 were £200,000.
>
> The amount of net relevant earnings which he can save in his retirement annuity contract is 17.5 per cent of £200,000, because there is no earnings cap. This comes to £35,000. The amount of net relevant earnings which he can save for this year ended 5 April 1997 in his personal pension scheme is 25 per cent of £82,200 (the earnings cap), which is £20,550. If his objective is to invest the maximum he can in a pension, he should choose to save for this tax year in the retirement annuity scheme.

pension scheme or retirement annuity contract in a tax year to the previous tax year. For example, you can choose to carry back payments made in the tax year ending on 5 April 1997 to the tax year ending on 5 April 1996. And if you had no relevant earnings in the year ending on 5 April 1996, you could carry back the payments to the year ending on 5 April 1995 – but no further. You might choose to carry back payments if your rate of tax in the previous year was higher than your current rate of tax, thus saving yourself money (see example on p. 113).

For example, if you could make personal pension contribution of £2,000 in the tax year ending 5 April 1997 but invested just £1,000. This leaves you with £1,000 of unused relief for that tax year. You could backdate contributions which you make during the tax year ending 5 April 1998. You might want to do this if your top rate of tax was higher in the earlier tax year. You need to claim before 31 January 1999 by completing Form PP43.

You can also use your tax return to bring back payments for the tax year not yet ended. If you make a pension payment before you submit your tax return, you can claim to deduct the payment from your income for the year ending 5 April 1997 (see example on p. 113).

Sometimes you may not use up all the limits for relief which are available. If this is the case, you can carry forward unused relief for up to six years. After

---

# EXAMPLE

James Loch has net relevant earnings as set out below. He is 36 and can make personal pension contributions of 20 per cent of those earnings and get tax relief.

| Tax year ending 5 April | Net relevant earnings £ | Maximum premiums £ | Premiums paid £ | Unused relief £ |
|---|---|---|---|---|
| 1992 | 20,000 | 4,000 | 2,000 | 2,000 |
| 1993 | 15,000 | 3,000 | 2,000 | 1,000 |
| 1994 | 20,000 | 4,000 | 2,000 | 2,000 |
| 1995 | 22,000 | 4,400 | 2,000 | 2,400 |
| 1996 | 24,000 | 4,800 | 2,000 | 2,800 |
| 1997 | 22,000 | 4,400 | 2,000 | 2,400 |

The total amount of unused relief is £12,600. If James uses up the maximum relief available to him on his earnings for the tax year ending 5 April 1998, he could also make a lump sum payment of £12,600. If he chooses to make a lower payment he will use up the unused relief starting with the tax year ending on 5 April 1992. On the lump sum payment he gets tax relief at the highest rate of tax he is paying in the tax year ending on 5 April 1998.

that the relief can't be used. You can use the relief in a later year, if you have used up all your relief for that year. Any relief you get will be at the tax rates for the year in which you use it up. Unused relief from the earliest years is used first, as the example on p. 112 shows.

## Retirement annuity contracts

■ *Retirement annuity contracts*

| | | |
|---|---|---|
| Payments made in 1996-97 **14.1** £ | 1996-97 payments used in an earlier year **14.2** £ | Relief claimed |
| | | box 14.1 *less* box 14.2 *less* box 14.3 |
| 1996-97 payments now to be carried back **14.3** £ | Payments brought back from 1997-98 **14.4** £ | **14.5** £ |

Under the heading of Retirement annuity contract you need to give the information about your payments in the tax year ending 5 April 1997, about any you wish to carry back to an earlier year, and about any payments you have made since 5 April 1997 which you want to bring back to get tax relief in this tax return.

In Box 14.1, enter the amount of payments which you have made to a retirement annuity (started before 1 July 1988) in the year before 5 April 1997. You will be entering gross figures (before deduction of tax).

You are allowed to carry back pension payments (see left). You may have already claimed tax relief on some of the amount in box 14.1, for example,

---

## EXAMPLE

Paul Taylor has a retirement annuity contract. For the year ended 5 April 1997, he earned £20,000 and is aged 37. He can save £3,500 within the limits of 17.5 per cent of his net relevant earnings. He made payments of £3,000 and enters this figure in box 14.1. However, £1,000 of his pension contributions were made before he returned his tax return for the last tax year and he had asked for them to be carried back to the year ending 5 April 1996. He enters that amount in box 14.2. He chooses now to carry back a further £1,000 to the last tax year as he was a higher-rate taxpayer and this would mean he would get more tax relief. The figure of £1,000 is entered in box 14.3.

    The amount of tax relief he is now claiming on his contributions in the year ended 5 April 1997 is box 14.1 less box 14.2 less box 14.3, that is £3,000 less £1,000 less £1,000. He is claiming relief on pension contributions of £1,000 for the year ended 5 April 1997.

for the year ending 5 April 1996. If you have done so, enter the amount used in an earlier year in box 14.2.

If you now want to carry back some of what you paid in the year ending 5 April 1997 to the previous tax year (or possibly the one before that, see p. 112), put this amount in box 14.3. On this amount you will get tax relief at the rate of tax you paid in the previous year.

Between 5 April 1997 and the date you are filling in your tax return, you may have made some pension payments. If you want these to be included in your tax return for the year ending 5 April 1997, enter the amount in box 14.4.

The amount of relief you are claiming for your retirement annuity contract payment for the tax year ending 5 April 1997 will be worked out in box 14.5 (box 14.1 less box 14.2 less box 14.3). If the amount you are claiming for this year is greater than the percentage limit (see p. 109), you may have unused relief from the previous six years which could be set against the excess.

You need to fill in Form PP42 to carry forward unused relief from earlier years. There is no place to claim on the tax return. You claim it and the Inland Revenue has to ask you for your workings. Use the working sheets which come with Help Sheet *IR330 Pension Payments.*

## Personal pension plans

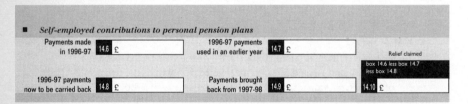

If you are self-employed and contributing to a personal pension plan (started after 1 July 1988), you claim your tax relief in boxes 14.6 to 14.10.

Under the heading of Personal pension plans, you need to give the information about your payments in the tax year ending 5 April 1997, about any you wish to carry back to an earlier year, and about any payments you have made since 5 April 1997 which you want to bring back to get tax relief in this tax return.

In Box 14.6, enter the amount of payments which you have made to a personal pension scheme (started on or after 1 July 1988) in the year before 5 April 1997. The self-employed pay before-tax amounts to the pension provider, so you will be entering gross figures (before deduction of tax).

You are allowed to carry back pension payments (see p. 111). You may have already claimed tax relief on some of the amount in box 14.6, for example, for the year ending 5 April 1996. If you have done so, enter that amount used in an earlier year in box 14.7.

If you now want to carry back some of what you paid in the year ending 5 April 1997 to the previous tax year (or possibly the one before that, see p. 112), put this amount in box 14.8. On this amount you will get tax relief at the rate of tax you paid in the previous year.

Between 5 April 1997 and the date you are filling in your tax return, you may have made some pension payments. If you want these to be included in your tax return for the tax year ending 5 April 1997, enter the amount in box 14.9.

The amount of relief you are claiming for your personal pension scheme will be worked out in box 14.10 (box 14.6 less box 14.7 less box 14.8). If the amount of relief you are claiming for this year is greater than the percentage limit (see p. 109), you may have unused relief from the previous six years which could be set against the excess. There is no place for this on the tax return. You claim it and the Inland Revenue has to ask you for your workings. Use Help Sheet *IR330 Pension Payments*.

| *Employee contributions to personal pension plans* (remember to include basic rate tax by dividing your payment by 76 and then multiplying by 100 - see note on box 14.11 in your Tax Return Guide) | | |
|---|---|---|
| Payments made in 1996-97 **14.11** £ | 1996-97 payments used in an earlier year **14.12** £ | Relief claimed |
| 1996-97 payments now to be carried back **14.13** £ | Payments brought back from 1997-98 **14.14** £ | box 14.11 *less* box 14.12 *less* box 14.13 **14.15** £ |

Employees pay their contributions into a personal pension plan after deducting basic rate tax. So you will need to adjust the figures you paid to enter the gross amount here. For the year ending 5 April 1997, multiply the amount you paid by 100 and divide it by 76. (Or multiply the amount you paid by 1.32.)

In Box 14.11, enter the gross amount of payments which you have made to a personal pension scheme (started on or after 1 July 1988) in the year before 5 April 1997.

You are allowed to carry back pension payments (see p. 111). You may have already claimed tax relief on some of the amount in box 14.11, for example, for the year ending 5 April 1996. If you have done so, enter that amount used in an earlier year in box 14.12.

If you now want to carry back some of what you paid in the year ending 5 April 1997 to the previous tax year (or possibly the one before that, see p. 111), put this amount in box 14.13. On this amount you will get tax relief at the rate of tax you paid in the previous year.

Between 5 April 1997 and the date you are filling in your tax return, you may have made some pension payments. If you want these to be included in your tax return for the tax year ending 5 April 1997, enter the amount in box 14.14.

> ## TAX-SAVING IDEA
> Make the most of the amount you are allowed to save in a pension scheme if you are an employee. You can save up to 15 per cent of your earnings including fringe benefits. Top up contributions to an employer's scheme if you can by making additional voluntary contributions either to your employer's scheme or to one of your own (known as a free-standing additional voluntary contributions scheme)

The amount of relief you are claiming for your personal pension scheme for the tax year ending 5 April 1997 will be worked out in box 14.15 (box 14.11 less box 14.12 less box 14.13). If the amount of relief you are claiming for this year is greater than the percentage limit (see p. 109), you may have unused relief from the previous six years which could be set against the excess. There is no place for this on the tax return. You claim it and the Inland Revenue has to ask you for your workings. Use Help Sheet *IR330 Pension Payments*.

### Additional voluntary contributions
If you are going to qualify for less than the maximum permitted amount of an employer's pension and want to improve the benefits you will get, you can

| | |
|---|---|
| • Amount of contributions to employer's schemes **not deducted** at source from pay | 14.16 £ |

get tax relief on additional voluntary contributions (see p. 69).

If you paid your contributions in a lump sum, it is possible that you did not get tax relief at the time. If that is the case, enter the amount you paid to your employer's scheme at box 14.16. Don't enter the amount of additional voluntary contributions on which you received tax relief through the PAYE system.

| | |
|---|---|
| • Gross amount of free-standing additional voluntary contributions paid in 1996-97 | 14.17 £ |

Instead of paying additional voluntary contributions into your employer's scheme, you can choose to invest in the fund of a pension provider, such as a life insurance company or unit trust manager. (free-standing additional voluntary contributions).

When you made your payment to the pension provider, you would have made it after basic rate tax was deducted. But in box 14.17, you have to enter the gross amount. Take the amount you paid, divide it by 76 and multiply it by 100 to give the gross figure. Using the tax return you will be able to claim higher-rate tax relief if you are entitled to it.

## OTHER RELIEFS YOU CAN CLAIM

| | | | |
|---|---|---|---|
| Q 15  Do you want to claim any of the following reliefs? | NO ☐ | YES ☐ | **If yes**, fill in boxes 15.1 to 15.12 below, as appropriate. |

Your tax return on page 5 lists out the possible reliefs you might be able to claim. If you are entitled to any of these deductions from your income, put a tick in the YES box. Otherwise tick the NO box and go to Q16.

### Vocational training

| | Amount of payment |
|---|---|
| • Payments you made for vocational training | 15.1 £ |

You can get tax relief at your highest rate of tax for fees paid for training which would count towards the National Vocational Qualifications and Scottish Vocational Qualifications up to level five. From 6 May 1996, if you are aged 30 or over you can also get tax relief on fees for full-time vocational courses lasting between four weeks and a year, whether or not they lead to the qualifications.

Relief at the basic rate is normally deducted from the payments you make so you can benefit even if unemployed. You can get higher-rate tax relief on vocational training if applicable, so you need to claim for it in your tax return.

Enter at box 15.1, the amount of the payment you have made for the tax year ending 5 April 1997, that is after the deduction of basic rate tax.

For the year ending 5 April 1997, you are only entitled to relief if you are not receiving or entitled to receive financial assistance for a course under a government scheme. The 1996 budget introduced changes for the year starting 6 April 1997.

**Loan interest**

- Interest on loans to purchase your main home (other than MIRAS)  | 15.2 | £

You can get tax relief on interest you pay on loans of £30,000 or less to buy your only or main home (or to improve it but only if the loans were taken out on or before 5 April 1988 – see p. 55).

The rate of tax relief is 15 per cent. So every £1 of interest you pay within the £30,000 limit will be reduced by tax relief to 85p.

Most taxpayers get their tax relief through MIRAS (mortgage interest relief at source). Under this system, you make reduced payments to your lender. Your lender receives the amount of tax relief direct from the Inland Revenue. And you get the relief whether you pay tax or not. If your mortgage is in MIRAS, put nothing in box 15.2.

If your mortgage is **NOT** in MIRAS, claim here for tax relief. You will need a certificate of interest from your lender. If your mortgage is for more than £30,000 or if your home is used partly for business, you will have to work out what proportion of the interest you can claim (see pp. 56 and 198).

## Interest on other qualifying loans

Claim here for tax relief on the interest for a variety of loans to buy:

- a share in or putting capital into a partnership (but not if you are a limited partner)
- plant or machinery for use in your job if you are an employee or partner (if you are self-employed you claim in the Self employment supplementary page)
- shares in a close company (see below). To be eligible you should own more than 5 per cent of the company or be a shareholder and work for most of your time in the business
- an annuity, if the loan is secured on your only or main home and the borrower or the person who receives the annuity was 65 or over when the loan was made.This is commonly known as a home income scheme (see p. 52).

A close company is one which is controlled by a small number of people. Broadly, it should have five or less 'participators', such as shareholders, or it should be controlled by shareholder directors.

Don't enter here to claim tax relief on the interest on a loan for a self-employed business (use box 3.47) or to buy a property you let (use box 5.4).

### Maintenance payments

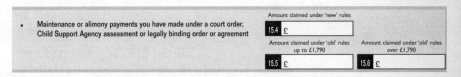

You are entitled to tax relief on payments you make to your former or separated spouse and your children, but not if these are voluntary payments (that is you can't be forced to make them). And you can't get tax relief on payments made to or for your children if they are 21 plus.

Payments on which you can get tax relief include those made under:

- a Court Order
- a Child Support Agency assessment
- a written agreement

- a verbal agreement made before 15 March 1988, if written details were received by your tax inspector by 30 June 1988.

There are different rules about tax relief on maintenance payments depending on when the agreement was made. Chapter 6 on p. 37 explains the distinctions between the old and new rules and gives tax-saving ideas.

### What to enter if your maintenance comes under the new rules

If your payments come under the new rules what you should enter in box 15.4 is the lower of £1,790, which is the maximum payments each year on which you can get tax relief under the new rules, and the amount you paid in the year ending 5 April 1997. If your former husband or wife has remarried during the tax year to 5 April 1997, you are not entitled to tax relief on any payments made after he or she remarried. If what you paid before marriage is less than £1,790, enter that amount.

You can get tax relief on maintenance payments only up to a total of £1,790, no matter how many ex- or separated husbands or wives you have.

You will need to give the dates of the court order, agreements or so on in the section headed Additional information on page 8 of the tax return.

You do not get tax relief at the rate of tax you pay. This is a fixed-rate relief and is 15 per cent for the year ending 5 April 1997 (and for the year ending 5 April 1998).

### What to enter if your maintenance comes under the old rules

You can get tax relief on the amount of maintenance payments which you paid and got tax relief on in the tax

## EXAMPLE

Peter Smith pays maintenance to his ex-wife and child. The agreement was made in 1992, so it comes under the new rules. In the year ending 5 April 1997 he paid £5,000. He is entitled to tax relief of the lower of what he paid (£5,000) or £1,790. He puts £1,790 in box 15.4.

He is entitled to tax relief on his maintenance payments at the rate of 15 per cent. On the £1,790 which he can claim under the new rules he will get tax relief of 15 per cent of £1,790, which is £268.50.

## EXAMPLE

Jane Spires was divorced from her husband in 1987. She pays him maintenance of £2,500 a year under a written agreement. In the year ending 5 April 1997, she paid him the amount he was entitled to. She can get tax relief on the full £2,500 a year because it is paid under the old rules. She enters £1,790 in box 15.5 and the difference (£2,500 less £1,790 equals £710) goes in box 15.6.

year ending 5 April 1989, unless you were due to pay less and did pay less in the tax year ending 5 April 1997. If the lower of these two amounts is less than or equal to £1,790, enter it in box 15.5. If it is more than £1,790, put £1,790 in box 15.5 and the excess in box 15.6.

You can get tax relief on maintenance payments to more than one former husband or wife under the old rules. Maintenance payments for two agreements under the old rules must be looked at separately. You can get tax relief on the sum of the lower of the two amounts for each agreement. If the sum of the two amounts is less than or equal to £1,790, enter it in box 15.5. If it is more than £1,790, put £1,790 in box 15.5 and the excess in box 15.6.

If you make two lots of maintenance payments, one under the old rules and one under the 'new rules', you may be able to get tax relief under both sets of rules. Work out the amount on which you can get tax relief under the old rules and put the figures in boxes 15.5 and 15.6 (as instructed above). If the figure in box 15.5 is less than £1,790 for the tax year ending 5 April 1997, you can claim under the new rules for maintenance payments which come within those rules.

Deduct the figure in box 15.5 from £1,790 and put in box 15.4 the lower of that figure and the amount of maintenance payments you made in the year ending 5 April 1997 under the new rules.

## Investing in growing businesses

The government is anxious to encourage investment into growing businesses which require risk capital. These types of investments can carry a high degree of risk and to compensate investors for carrying this extra risk element, there is a broad range of tax incentives. For more details, see Chapter 8.

### Venture capital trusts

| | | Amount on which relief claimed |
|---|---|---|
| • Subscriptions for Venture Capital Trust shares (up to £100,000) | | 15.7 £ |

If you invest in a venture capital trust, you are not investing directly in these companies but in a fund like an investment trust which is quoted on The Stock Exchange.

When you buy new ordinary shares in a venture capital trust, you can get income tax relief at 20 per cent on your investment up to £100,000 for the year ending 5 April 1997 (and the year ending 5 April 1998), as long as you hold your shares for five years. If you are reinvesting the gain made from selling some other asset, you can also claim capital gains tax reinvestment relief on that gain (that is, you can put off paying the capital gains tax until you dispose of your new asset, in this case the shares you hold in the venture capital trust).

Any dividends paid out by the venture capital trust and gains you make on the shares in the trust are all free of tax.

In box 15.7, put the amount you have invested in venture capital trusts, up to a maximum of £100,000.

*Enterprise Investment Scheme*

| • Subscriptions under the Enterprise Investment Scheme (up to £100,000) | 15.8 | £ |

You can get tax relief of 20 per cent on investments (not more than £100,000 in a tax year) made in the shares of unquoted trading companies. Any gain you make on the shares will be free of capital gains tax. There are a lot of detailed rules about which companies are eligible and whether you yourself are eligible.

If you have invested in shares eligible for the Enterprise Investment Scheme after 5 April, but before 6 October 1997, you can ask for half the investment up to a maximum of £15,000 to be deducted from your income for the year ending 5 April 1997.

You can claim here in this tax return for an investment only if you have received Form EIS3 from the company in which you invested. This form certifies that the company qualifies for the scheme.

Enter in box 15.8 the total investments (up to £100,000) for which you are claiming relief in the tax year ending 5 April 1997. If you have made an investment for which you have not yet received Form EIS3 (Form EIS5 for an investment made through a fund), don't enter it here. You can either claim before 31 January 1998 by asking your tax office to amend this tax return of you can claim using the form in EIS3 after 31 January 1998.

Enter details of each investment for which you are claiming relief in the section headed Additional information on page 8 of the tax return.

**Giving to charity**

As well as making donations in the street or in other ways, you can make more formal donations and use the tax system to reduce what it costs you to make the donation. With either a covenant or Gift Aid, you can get tax relief at your highest rate of tax.

**TAX-SAVING IDEA**
If you are giving to charity, try to arrange to do so either with a covenant or through the Gift Aid scheme. The charity you support can receive more by reclaiming the basic rate tax on what you give.

*Covenants*

| | | Amount of payment |
|---|---|---|
| • Charitable covenants or annuities | | 15.9 £ |

Enter in box 15.9 the amount you actually paid to the charity (not the gross amount which you agreed to pay). You can get tax relief at your highest rate of tax on payments you make to registered charities if you make them under a deed of covenant. This is a legally binding agreement to make a series of payments and to get the tax relief on payments to charity they should continue for more than three years. You won't get the tax relief if you get significant benefits from the payments, but you will get tax relief if you are allowed access to the charity's property as a benefit of membership. This includes subscriptions to charities such as the National Trust and those which conserve wildlife for the public benefit, even though you get free or reduced-price entry to the property.

When you make the payment to the charity, you will agree to pay a gross amount, for example, £100 a year. But when you make the payment, you pay only the net amount, because you deduct tax at the basic rate. For the tax year ending 5 April 1997, the basic rate tax is 24 per cent, so you would have handed over to the charity £76, not the £100 you

**TAX-SAVING IDEA**
If you are married and wanting to donate to charity using a covenant make sure that the covenant is made by whichever of you has the highest rate of tax.

agreed to pay. The charity reclaims the £24 of basic rate tax which you deducted from the Inland Revenue. So the charity receives £100, but it costs you £76. And you can get higher-rate tax relief if you pay tax at 40 per cent.

If you don't pay tax at the basic rate, but the lower rate of 20 per cent or if you are a non taxpayer, you may have to hand money back to the Inland Revenue. If you pay tax at the lower rate for the year ending 5 April 1997, and you had agreed to make a gross payment of £100, handing over £76 to the charity, you will have to repay £4 to the Inland Revenue.

It depends on the exact wording of the covenant, but unless you agreed to hand over a fixed net amount, you will need to alter how much you pay to the charity for the year ending 5 April 1998, as the basic rate of tax has been reduced to 23 per cent. For a gross amount of £100, you will need to pay £77.

EXAMPLE

Julia West is a higher rate taxpayer. She has agreed to donate to her favourite charity, the Cricketers Benevolent Foundation, £200 a year. This is the gross amount entered in the covenant. But before she pays over the donation each year she deducts basic rate tax. In the year ending 5 April 1997, she deducted £48 and sent £152 by standing order. The charity reclaimed the £48 from the Inland Revenue. Because she is a higher rate taxpayer, she is entitled to more tax relief and claims it through her tax return. In box 15.9, she enters the amount she actually paid, £152 (not the gross amount of £200 which she agreed to pay). She gets her higher rate tax relief when she works out her tax bill and the amount she has to pay or can claim as a refund on 31 January 1998.

You can get more information about charitable covenants from the Charities Aid Foundation, 48 Pembury Road, Tonbridge, Kent TN9 2JD.

EXAMPLE

Julia West (see above) has to alter her standing order for her covenant for the year ending 5 April 1998 because the basic rate of tax has changed. She cancels the standing order for £152 and amends it to £154.

Annuities and covenants entered into for full value, for genuine commercial reasons in connection with the payer's trade or profession are also eligible for tax relief at the highest rate, but covenants paid to individuals don't get any tax relief.

## Gift Aid

| | | Amount of payment |
|---|---|---|
| • Gift Aid | | 15.10 £ |

Enter in box 15.10 the amount you actually paid to the charity.

You can get tax relief at your highest rate of tax on single one-off gifts to a charity of £250 or more made during your lifetime. There is no upper limit. You make the payment by agreeing to pay a gross amount, for example, £1,000. You actually hand over to the charity £1,000 less the amount of basic rate tax. For the tax year ending 5 April 1997, this would be £1,000 less £240 giving a pay-

> **TAX-SAVING IDEA**
> If you are married and want to make a donation to charity under Gift Aid, make sure that whichever of you pays the highest rate of tax makes the donation.

ment of £760 (for the tax year ending 5 April 1998, this would be a payment of £770 after deducting basic rate tax at 23 per cent).

If you pay tax at less than the basic rate, you are a lower rate taxpayer or a non taxpayer, you will have to pay back to the Inland Revenue some of the tax you have deducted. For example, a lower rate taxpayer who had deducted £240 from a gross amount of £1,000 in the tax year ending 5 April 1997 will have to pay £40 to the Inland Revenue.

### Closing a business

| | | Amount of payment |
|---|---|---|
| • Post-cessation expenses, and losses on relevant discounted securities | | 15.11 £ |

Even after you have closed a business, you may find that there are certain obligations and expenses which you have to meet. For example, you made need to put right some defect in work which you carried out.

You can deduct some expenses from any other income and gains you have in the year in which the business expenses arises, if you have no income from your closed business. The relief is available for up to seven years after the business closure. You must claim for the relief by 31 January in the second year after the tax year in which you incurred the expense. So for an expense which you met in the tax year ending 5 April 1997, you must claim by 31 January 1999.

The expenses which qualify for this special relief are:

- costs of putting right defective work you did or fault goods or services which you supplied and the cost of paying any damages as a result
- premiums for insurance against claims due to defective work or faulty goods and services
- legal and other professional expenses you incur in defending yourself against accusations of defective work or providing faulty goods or services
- debts owed to the business which you included in your accounts but which have subsequently turned out to be bad debts
- cost of collecting debts owed to the business and included in its accounts.

Expenses which don't qualify for post-cessation relief can only be set against future income which comes from the closed business.

Enter in box 15.11 the amount of expenses which you want to deduct from your income in the tax year ending 5 April 1997 (and in box 8.5 of the Capital Gains pages the amount you want to deduct from your capital gains). There are some special rules about unpaid expenses. Ask your tax adviser or your tax office for help.

You also claim in box 15.11 for losses on relevant discounted securities (formerly deed discount bonds and deep gain securities) including a new investment called gilt strips (available early 1997). A loss incurred in the tax year ending 5 April 1997 can be deducted only from the income in the same tax year.

### Payments to a trade union or friendly society

| | Half amount of payment |
|---|---|
| • Payments to a trade union or friendly society for death benefits | 15.12 £ |

Friendly societies supported their members before the arrival of the welfare state by paying sickness benefit, unemployment benefit and widow's pensions. Some continue in existence and you can get tax relief on premiums you pay on certain combined sickness and life insurance policies they offer. The tax relief is at half your top rate of tax on the life part of the premium; you can also get the same tax relief on part of your trade union subscription if it includes pension, funeral or life insurance benefits. With the friendly society policy, to be eligible for tax relief.the premiums must be £25 or less a month and 40 per cent or less of the premium should be for the death benefit.

Ask your friendly society or trade union to tell you how much of the premium was for pension, life insurance, funeral or death benefit. Enter in box 15.12 half that amount.

# ALLOWANCES

## CHAPTER 12

Another way of reducing the amount of income tax you have to pay is to claim any allowances to which you are entitled. These are deducted from your income, along with reliefs (deductions), to make your taxable income smaller – and so also your tax bill.

**ALLOWANCES** *for the year ended 5 April 1997*

*Q 16* You get your personal allowance of £3,765 automatically. If you were born before 6 April 1932, enter your date of birth in box 21.4 to get age-related allowances. Fill in other boxes as appropriate.

Do you want to claim any of the following allowances?  NO  YES If yes, fill in boxes 16.1 to 16.28 as appropriate.

## Personal allowances
Everyone gets a personal allowance. It comes automatically; you don't have to claim it in the tax return.

## Age-related personal allowances
However, people aged 65 or over at the start of the tax year, 6 April 1996, can claim a higher allowance (see p. 38). There is one level of age-related allowance if you were 65 or over on 6 April 1996 and a still higher rate if you were 75 or over. On the tax return it says if you were born before 6 April 1932, enter your date of birth in box 21.4 to claim the age-related allowance. Box 21.4 is at the bottom of page 7 of the return.

> ### TAX-SAVING IDEA
> You can go back six years to claim an allowance which you forgot at the time or didn't know you were entitled to. You get tax relief at the rate of tax which would have applied if you claimed the deduction at the right time.

## Blind person's allowance
Anyone registered as blind with a local authority can claim blind person's allowance. The amount of the allowance for the tax year ending 5 April 1997 is £1,250 and for the tax year ending 5 April 1998 it is £1,280. A reg-

istered blind person must be unable to perform any work for which eyesight is essential. The partially sighted cannot claim the allowance.

In box 16.1, enter the date you were registered blind if this is the first year you are claiming, and enter the name of the local authority in box 16.2.

If you are not registered until after 5 April 1997 but before 6 April 1998, you can still get the allowance for the tax year ending 5 April 1997 if you can show that you were blind at that date, for example, with an opthalmologist's certificate.

The requirement for Scotland and Northern Ireland is different from England. You don't need to be registered. You can claim blind person's allowance if you are not able to perform any work for which eyesight was essential. To claim, write Scotland claim or Northern Ireland claim in box 16.2.

If your income is less than your allowances, including blind person's, and you are married and living with your husband or wife, you can transfer the unused part of this allowance to your partner (see p. 135). If both of you are blind, you can claim two allowances.

## Transitional allowance

■ **Transitional allowance** (for some wives with husbands on low income if claimed in earlier years)

• Tick to claim and give details in the 'Additional information' box on page 8 please
(see page 23 of your Tax Return Guide for what is needed)    16.3

• If you want to calculate your tax enter amount of transitional allowance you can have in box 16.4    16.4 £

Transitional allowance is for some wives with husbands on low income which was introduced to ease the changes to the allowances available for married men when independent taxation was introduced. To get this allowance for the year tax ending 5 April 1997 you must be:

• a married woman, and
• getting transitional allowance in the tax year ending 5 April 1996, and
• living with the same husband in the tax year ending 5 April 1997 as you were for the whole of the year ending 5 April 1996.

Your husband must have been resident in the UK for the year ending 5 April 1997, and have written to his tax office asking for the allowance to be given to you.

To claim the allowance tick box 16.3. You will need to enter details about your husband in the Additional information section on page 8 of the return – his name, address, tax reference, National Insurance number and tax office.

If you are working out your own tax bill, you will need to know the amount of the allowance and put it in box 16.4. You can ask either your husband or your tax office for the figure. It should be the lower of the transitional allowance you got in the tax year ending 5 April 1996 or the personal allowance (£3,765) less your husband's income for the tax year ending 5 April 1997.

## Married couple's allowance

This is an allowance which can be claimed when you marry. There are more details of it in Chapter 6.

The amount of the married couple's allowance for those aged under 65 for the tax year ending 5 April 1997 is £1,790 and higher levels can be claimed by the 65 or over and 75 or over age groups (see p. 38).

Married couple's allowance is automatically given to the husband but it can be split between the two of you or used 100 per cent by the wife.

### Splitting or transferring the married couple's allowance

If you want to do this, you have to plan ahead. You are too late to make these choices for the tax year ended 5 April 1997 and from 6 April 1997, too late to make the choice for the tax year ending 5 April 1998. Write to your tax inspector before 6 April 1998 if you want to share or transfer the allowance for the tax year ending on 5 April 1999.

The same time deadlines apply to altering the allocation.

If one of you is 65 or over at the start of a tax year, and entitled to a higher level of married couple's allowance, only the basic amount (£1,790 for the tax year ending 5 April 1997) can be allocated between the two of you. The extra bit always goes to the husband.

## Married men

**■ Married couple's allowance - if you are a married man** - see page 24 of your Tax Return Guide

- Wife's full name  [16.5]
- Wife's date of birth (if before 6 April 1932)  [16.7]  /  /
- Wife's tax reference (if known, please)  [16.9]

- Date of marriage (if after 5 April 1996)  [16.6]  /  /
- Tick box 16.8 if you and your wife have allocated half the allowance to her  [16.8]
- Tick box 16.10 if you and your wife have allocated all the allowance to her  [16.10]

A married man can claim married couple's allowance if he was married and living with his wife for at least part of the tax year. He can also claim it if he was separated from his wife before 6 April 1990 but maintaining her voluntarily (and not able to claim tax relief on the payments) from separation to 6 April 1996.

You should fill in boxes 16.5 to 16.10. Claim married couple's allowance by entering:

- your wife's full name in box 16.5
- her date of birth in box 16.7
- her tax reference (if known) in box 16.9.

Tick box 16.8 if you and your wife have decided to split the allowance equally between the two of you. Tick box 16.10 if you and your wife have decided to transfer the whole of the married couple's allowance to your wife.

If you married during the tax year ending 5 April 1997 and want to claim all or part of the married couple's allowance (see p. 40), put the date of your marriage in box 16.6.

However, there may be two other options open to you:

- if this is a second or later marriage, you may already be claiming married couple's allowance for a previous marriage. If you want to carry on doing this (because you would be able to claim more of the allowance), don't enter anything in box 16.6. And in boxes 16.5, 16.7 and 16.9 fill in the information about your former wife
- or if you have a child living with you, you can claim additional personal allowance instead of married couple's allowance. If you can claim only part of married couple's allowance, you would be better off doing this as

you could be entitled to the whole of additional personal allowance (unless you are sharing it). This would reduce your tax bill. If you make this choice don't enter anything in boxes 16.5 to 16.10, but fill in the additional personal allowance section instead.

## Married women

■ *Married couple's allowance - if you are a married woman* - see page 23 of your Tax Return Guide

Date of marriage (if after 5 April 1996) **16.11** / /

Husband's full name **16.12**

Tick box 16.13 if you and your husband have allocated half the allowance to you **16.13**

Husband's tax reference (if known, please) **16.14**

Tick box 16.15 if you and your husband have allocated all the allowance to you **16.15**

You should fill in boxes 16.11 to 16.15. You can claim married couple's allowance only if you and your husband have agreed to transfer it, but you can demand for it to be split equally between the two of you. You must have lived with your husband for all or part of the tax year ending 5 April 1997.

If you have agreed to split the allowance tick box 16.13. If you have agreed to transfer the whole allowance to you, tick box 16.15. Fill in your husband's full name (box 16.12) and his tax reference if you know it (box 16.14).

If you have married since 5 April 1996, enter the date of the marriage in box 16.11 if you want to claim married couple's allowance. If you are still receiving all or your share of the allowance for a previous marriage, don't enter anything.

If your husband died in the tax year ending 5 April 1997, you can use only the part of the married couple's allowance which is not used up against your husband's income. This applies even if you had agreed to allocate it differently. If this is the case, do not tick boxes 16.13 or 16.15. Tick instead box 16.26. And if you are filling in a tax return for your husband who has died, do not tick boxes 16.8 or 16.10 because the allowance has first to be deducted from your husband's income.

## Additional personal allowance

- **Additional personal allowance** (available in some circumstances if you have a child living with you - see page 24 of your Tax Return Guide

| | | |
|---|---|---|
| • Name of the child claimed for | 16.16 | |
| • Name of university etc/type of training if child 16 or over on 6 April 1996 and in full time education or training | 16.19 | |
| • Child's date of birth | 16.17 | / / |
| • Tick if child lives with you | 16.8 | |

**Shared claims**

Name and address of other person claiming

16.20

Postcode

- Enter your share as a percentage  16.21  %

- If share not agreed, enter number of days in year ended 5 April 1997 child lived with

  - you  16.22  days
  - other person  16.23  days

If you are a single parent, there is an allowance you may be able to claim if the child lives with you. This allowance is known as additional personal allowance. The amount of the allowance is the same as the married couple's allowance (£1,790 for the tax year ending 5 April 1997 and £1,830 for the tax year ending 5 April 1998). The amount of the relief is restricted to 15 per cent.

You may be able to claim this allowance if at some time in the tax year you are:

- single
- a widow or widower
- divorced
- married but separated (and so not entitled to the married couple's allowance if a man)
- a married man, but your wife is totally unable to look after herself throughout the tax year.

To get the allowance you must have a child (either your own or someone else's) living with you for the whole or part of the tax year. You can only claim for a child aged 16 or over at the start of the tax year, who is in full-time education at university, school or college or training full-time for at least two years for a trade or profession. If the child is not yours, you cannot claim if the child is 18 or over at the start of the tax year. Your child includes a step-child, adopted child or legitimated child.

It is possible that two people could claim the allowance for the same child because the child lives with each of them for part of the year (who has custody is not the deciding factor). If this applies to you, you can agree with the other what proportion each claims. If you cannot agree, the allowance will be divided up according to the amount of time the child lives with each of you during the tax year. If there are two or more children, you may be able to claim a full allowance each.

If you are living with someone as husband and wife, but are unmarried, you and your partner can claim only one additional personal allowance between the two of you and only for the youngest child. The allowance can be divided up as you wish. If you are not entitled to the allowance for the youngest child, you can't claim it at all.

---

## EXAMPLE

Nicky White is a single parent with two children living with her. Her income is £15,000. She can't claim the married couple's allowance, but she can claim the additional personal allowance (which is the same amount). The allowance is restricted to relief of 15 per cent of £1,790, that is £268.50 for the tax year ending 5 April 1997. Her tax bill is as follows:

| | |
|---|---:|
| Income | £15,000 |
| less personal allowance | £ 3,765 |
| | |
| Taxable income | £11,235 |

Tax bill:

| | | |
|---|---|---:|
| £3,900 | at 20 per cent | £780 |
| £7,335 | at 24 per cent | £1,760 |
| £11,235 | | £2,540 |

| | |
|---|---:|
| less tax relief on additional personal allowance | £268 |
| | |
| Tax for the year ended 5 April 1997 | £2,272 |

---

To claim the allowance, you need to give the name of the child claimed for in box 16.16 and the child's date of birth in box 16.17. Tick box 16.18 if the child lives with you. Fill in box 16.19 if you are claiming for a child over 16 years old.

If you and someone else want to share the allowance you will need to fill in boxes 16.20 to 16.23. Enter the name and address of the other person claiming the allowance in box 16.20 and the percentage of the allowance you are claiming in box 16.21. If you cannot agree the percentage for each of you, you will have to give the further information in boxes 16.22 and 16.23.

## Widow's bereavement allowance

| ■ *Widow's bereavement allowance* | • Date of your husband's death | 16.24 / / |
| --- | --- | --- |

You can claim widow's bereavement allowance in the tax year you are widowed and the following tax year (see p. 49). The allowance is £1,790 for the tax year ending 5 April 1997. This is restricted to 15 per cent, as it is with the married couple's and additional personal allowances. For the tax year ending 5 April 1998, the amount is £1,830.

To claim the allowance, enter the date your husband died in box 16.24.

## Transfer of surplus allowances

| ■ *Transfer of surplus allowances* - see page 25 of your Tax Return Guide before you fill in boxes 16.25 to 16.28 |
| --- |
| • Tick if you want your spouse to have your unused allowances 16.25 • Tick if you want to have your spouse's unused allowances 16.26 |
| Please give details in the 'Additional information' box on page 8 (see page 25 of your Tax Return Guide to see what is needed) If you want to calculate your tax enter the amount of the surplus allowance you can have. |
| • Blind person's **surplus** allowance 16.27 • Married couple's **surplus** allowance 16.28 |

You can transfer any unused amount of married couple's or blind person's allowance to your wife or your husband if you did not have enough income in the year to use up the allowance and you lived with your wife or husband for at least part of that year.

In certain limited circumstances, if a husband cannot use up all his personal allowance, his wife can receive a transitional allowance (see p. 129).

If you want your wife or husband to have the surplus of married couple's and blind person's allowances or transitional allowance, tick box 16.25. In the Additional information box on page 8 of your tax return, give your spouse's name, address, tax reference, National Insurance number and tax office.

If you want to claim and use your spouse's unused allowances, tick box 16.26. Give your spouse's name, address, tax reference, National Insurance number and tax office in the Additional information box on page 8.

If you are working out your own tax bill, enter in boxes 16.27 and 16.28 the amount of the surplus allowances. You can ask your tax office for help if you are not sure of the amount.

# OTHER INFORMATION

## CHAPTER 13

The last two pages of the basic tax return are where you give additional bits of information about your tax bill, repayments and refunds.

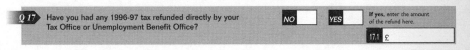

If NO, go direct to Q18.

If YES enter the amount you were refunded either through the PAYE system or from your unemployment benefit office. You might also have had tax refunded from dividend tax credits or other investments.

Enter the amount refunded for the tax year ending 5 April 1997 in box 17.1.

Tick YES if you intend to work out your own tax bill. While daunting, it really should not be a problem for most readers to work out your own tax bill. Chapter 24 will show you how to do it and what to enter in boxes 18.1 to 18.9 and boxes 19.1 to 19.11.

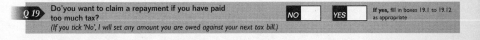

If you are not going to work out your own tax bill, tick NO and go to Q19.

If they are correct tick NO and go to Q21. If not correct, tick YES and make corrections on the front of the form.

**Q 21** Please give other personal details in boxes 21.1 to 21.4

Please give a daytime telephone number if convenient. It is often quicker to phone if we need to ask you about your Tax Return.

Your telephone number **21.1** [ ]

Say if you are single, married, widowed, divorced or separated **21.3** [ ]

or, if you prefer, your agent's telephone number **21.2** [ ]

(also give your agent's name and reference in the 'Additional information' box on page 8)

Date of birth **21.4** [ / / ]

If you were born before 6 April 1932, or you have ticked the 'Yes' box in Question 14, or you are claiming relief for Venture Capital Trust subscriptions

Fill in the details.

In box 21.4, you need to give your date of birth, so you can claim higher age-related personal and married couple's allowances, tax relief on investments in a venture capital trust or relief for pension contributions.

**Q 22** Please tick boxes 22.1 to 22.5 if they apply and provide any additional information in the box below

Tick box 22.1 if you expect to receive a new pension or Social Security benefit in 1997-98. **22.1** [ ]

Tick box 22.2 if you do **not** want any tax you owe collected through your tax code. **22.2** [ ]

Tick box 22.3 if this Tax Return contains figures which are provisional because you do not yet have final figures. Give details below. **22.3** [ ]

Tick box 22.4 if you have made payments of rent to someone outside the UK. Give their name and address below. **22.4** [ ]

Tick box 22.5 if you are claiming

- relief now for 1997-98 trading losses. Enter the amount and year in the 'Additional information' box below

- to have post cessation or other business receipts taxed as income of an earlier year. Enter the amount and year in the 'Additional information' box below

- backwards or forwards spreading of literary or artistic income. Enter in the 'Additional information' box details of any amounts spread back to last year and, if appropriate, the year before. **22.5** [ ]

*Additional information*

Give the information asked for.

In box 22.2, if you have completed your tax return and worked out your tax bill by 30 September, and the amount of tax you owe is £1,000 or less, you can ask to pay it through your PAYE code. Do this. It spreads out and delays the payment of your tax.

In box 22.3, you have to say whether any of the figures are provisional. If they are, don't delay sending in your tax return. In the Additional information box, explain which figures are provisional (including the box numbers), why they are provisional and when they will be finalised. If you know you are not going to be able to give reliable figures, because you have lost information, for example, explain what they are and how you have arrived at the estimates.

Be warned that if you negligently submit a provisional figure which is inaccurate or unnecessary, you may be liable to a penalty.

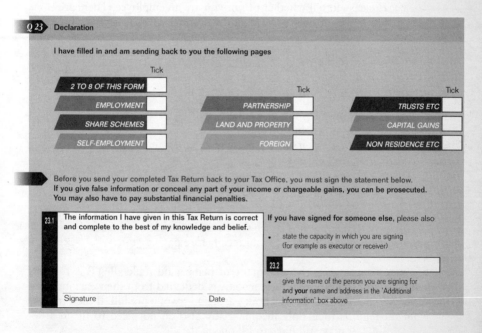

Tick any additional pages you are sending with the basic tax return and sign the declaration. If you are signing for someone else state in what capacity you are doing this.

# EMPLOYMENT

## CHAPTER 14

Q1 Were you an employee, or office holder, or director, or agency worker in the year ended 5 April 1997?   NO   YES   EMPLOYMENT YES

It is usually easy to tell whether or not you are an employee. There are some grey areas, however, where the Inland Revenue will seek to tax you as an employee even if you think of yourself as self-employed:

- if you are a company director (even if you own the company)
- if you work on a freelance or consultancy basis, but have to work closely under the control of your boss, working a set number of hours at an hourly rate, say, and at a particular location
- if you work on a casual, part-time basis
- if you work as a temp through an agency. This includes, for example, locum doctors; but it does not apply to entertainers or models working through an agency, or to people who work solely from home
- you have more than one job: you may be classed as an employee for one job, even if you are clearly self-employed in another.

The key significance of being an employee is that in most cases your employer will have to operate PAYE (see Chapter 3) on your earnings from that job and deduct tax and National Insurance before paying you.

For many employees, the advantage of being paid under PAYE is that the right amount of tax on all their income is deducted from their earnings and so they do not have to worry about paying a separate tax bill. If their income from their job is their only income many also do not need to fill in a tax return. But you may still have to fill one in if:

- you are a higher-rate taxpayer and get taxable perks such as a company car or receive investment income
- you have other income which is paid out before tax is deducted, such as some types of investment income
- your tax affairs are complex for any other reason.

If you are an employee and are sent a tax return, you need to tick the YES box at Q1 of the basic tax return and fill in a separate Employment page for each job you have. If you are not sure of your status, check with your tax office.

## Your employer

| Details of employer | |
|---|---|
| Employer's PAYE reference | Employer's name |
| 1.1 | 1.2 |
| Date employment started (only if between 6 April 1996 and 5 April 1997) | Employer's address |
| 1.3 / / | 1.5 |
| Date finished | |
| 1.4 / / | |
| Tick box 1.6 if you were a director of the company | and tick box 1.7 if it was a close company |
| 1.6 | 1.7 |
| | Postcode |

**TAX-SAVING IDEA**

A disadvantage of being an employee is that you cannot deduct as many expenses from your taxable income as you could if you were self-employed. So if you are setting up on your own, check that you will meet the Inland Revenue's conditions for self-employment.

So that your tax office can tie up the information on your tax return with that provided by your employer, give your employer's name, address and PAYE reference (shown on the P60). If the employment started or ended during the tax year ending 5 April 1997, you also need to give the start or end dates of the job, the length of time you worked there, whether or not you are a director (box 1.6) and if it is a close company (box 1.7). This may affect how much tax-free profit-related pay you are entitled to, and how your perks and benefits are taxed.

## What is taxed

Broadly speaking, the Inland Revenue seeks to tax any benefit you get from being employed, even if you get it from someone other than your employer. The tax return organises your remuneration into the following categories:

- money (including earnings from working abroad)

- benefits (taxable perks given by your employer) and expenses payments (either flat-rate allowances or reimbursement for expenses you have incurred)
- lump sums received on retirement, redundancy or death.

Not all of these will actually be taxable. But in general, you have to put it all down first, and the tax return then guides you to enter the various tax reliefs which you can deduct, for example, tax relief for expenses incurred in doing your job.

One thing you do not have to enter anywhere on your tax return is details of your National Insurance contributions as an employee. These should all be sorted out for you by your employer.

## The date income is taxable

As a general rule, you are counted as receiving income from employment from the earlier of:

- the date you get it
- the date you are entitled to it, even if you do not actually get it till later on.

So if, for example, you are entitled to payment on 15 March 1997, but do not actually receive it until 15 April, you must still include it in your tax return for the tax year ending 5 April 1997. If you receive payment early – on 15 March 1997, for work not completed until 15 April, for example – it is taxable from the date you received it, that is 15 March.

If you are a director, your earnings for a particular period may be decided on one date, credited to you in the company accounts on another date, but not paid out till much later. It is the earliest date that counts, unless the earnings for a particular period were decided before that period ended. In this case, you are treated as receiving them on the last day of the period to which the earnings relate.

## The documents you need

Most of the information you need will be on Forms P60, P11D or P9D.

Your P60 is a form your employer must give you by 31 May after the end of the tax year (that is, by 31 May 1997 for the tax year ending 5 April 1997). The P60 is a summary of how much you have been paid, and how much tax has been deducted. If you haven't got a P60, you should be able to find the information from your pay slips. If you left a job during a tax year, the information will be on your P45.

Your employer has to declare to the Revenue any taxable benefits or expenses you receive and the cash equivalent on form P11D or form P9D. Which form you get depends on how much you earn. You should get a copy from your employer by 6 July after the end of the tax year, that is by 6 July 1997 for the tax year ending 5 April 1997.

Note that if you leave a job, you will not automatically be given a form, but your ex-employer must give you one if you ask for it within three years after the end of the tax year in which you left. Your employer has 30 days from receiving your request in which to supply the form (if this is after the normal 6 July deadline).

Your P11D or P9D should be the starting point of all the expenses payments you have received. But you also need to keep receipts or documentation to back up your claim to deduct allowable expenses, particularly if they were not reimbursed by your employer and so did not appear on your P11D or P9D.

If you receive a lump sum from your employer, for example, when you left your job, it may be included on your P60, your P11D, or your P45, or you may just have a letter from your employer. Remember to include only payments that were made because of the change or job loss in the relevant tax year, even if they were actually paid in a different tax year. Your employer should be able to help you decide which category a payment falls within. If there is any doubt, employers can get advance decisions from their tax office, so it is worth talking about the tax consequences with your employer before any payment is made.

## MONEY FROM EMPLOYMENT

| Income from employment |
| --- |
| ■ *Money* - see Notes on page E2 |
| Before tax |
| ▪ payments from P60 (or P45 or pay slips) — 1.8 £ |

### You should enter as money:

- salaries, wages, fees, overtime, bonuses, commission and honoraria (after deducting money you have donated to a payroll giving scheme, or contributed to your employer's pension scheme, see p. 144)
- amounts voted to you as a director and credited to an account with the company, even if you cannot draw the money straight away
- voluntary payments and gifts, whether from your employer or anyone

else, such as tips and Christmas boxes (excluding some small gifts and personal gifts such as long-service awards, see Tax-free fringe benefits below)

- incentive awards (but see below)
- profit-related pay (excluding any tax-free amount – see opposite)
- sick pay, including statutory sick pay and statutory maternity pay (see opposite)
- holiday pay
- various payments to do with your employment which are not strictly pay. Examples are golden hellos paid to entice you to join the company; a loan written off because you satisfied or completed an employment condition; payments made to recognise changes in your conditions of service or employment; payments made if you leave a job and agree, in return for a lump sum, not to compete with your employer.

P60 forms vary slightly in design. The figure to look for is your pay 'for tax purposes' or 'this employment pay'. Enter the figure from Form P60 in box 1.8, but check that it does not include employer's contributions to a pension scheme or what you give under a payroll giving scheme (see below).

## Contributions to an employer's pension scheme
You can get tax relief on contributions you make to your employer's pension scheme, up to a maximum of 15 per cent of your taxable income from the job. This tax relief is given by deducting your contributions from your pay before tax is worked out on it, so giving you relief at your top rate of tax. The figure you enter as taxable pay in box 1.8 should be the figure after deducting pension contributions.

## Payroll giving schemes
You can get tax relief on charitable donations of up to £1,200 a year through the payroll giving scheme (sometimes called Give As You Earn, or GAYE) run by your employer. The money is deducted from your pay each week or month and passed straight to the charity by your employer. The donations are deducted from your pay before your tax is worked out on it, in the same way as contributions to an employer's pension scheme, so remember to check that what you enter in box 1.8. is your pay after payroll giving donations.

## Incentive awards
Broadly speaking, these are taxable whether you receive them from your employer or from someone else in connection with your job; for example, a car sales representative may receive prizes from the car manufacturer. However, the person paying the award may pay the tax for you, through a taxed award scheme. In this case, the award still counts as part of your

income, but the tax paid on your behalf will reduce your tax bill. Whoever makes the award should give you a Form P443 stating the value of the award and how much tax has been paid on it, unless the figures have been included on your P60. You should include the tax already paid in box 1.11.

Suggestion scheme awards are tax-free and need not be entered, provided that there is a formal scheme open to all employees, and the suggestion concerned is outside your normal job. If the suggestion is not taken up, the maximum award is £25; if is implemented, the maximum award is 50 per cent of the first year's expected net benefit, or 10 per cent of the benefit over five years, with an overall maximum of £5,000.

## Profit-related pay

If you are in a registered scheme, your profit-related pay is tax-free, up to a ceiling of £4,000, or (if lower) 20 per cent of your total pay in the profit period to which the profit-related pay relates. Any profit-related pay above the limit is taxable in the normal way. Your employer should take into account any tax relief when working out the taxable pay shown in your P60. You do not need to enter details of the scheme or tax relief itself in the tax return or the Employment page.

However, the tax relief on profit-related pay is being phased out. The 20 per cent of total pay limit will remain, but the ceiling is being reduced to:

- £2,000 between 1 January 1998 and 31 December 1998
- £1,000 between 1 January 1999 and 31 December 1999
- nil on or after 1 January 2000.

## Sick pay and maternity pay

If you are off work through illness or on maternity leave, any payment made to you by your employer, including statutory sick pay (SSP) or statutory maternity pay (SMP), is taxable. It will be taxed before you get it and shown on your P60 or P45 in the same way as other income, and you enter it with your other taxable pay in box 1.8. There are two exceptions to this rule:

- occasionally, SMP or SSP may be paid directly to you by the Department of Social Security. In this case, the benefit is still taxable, but tax is not deducted before it is paid to you and rather than enter it under Employment you should enter it in box 11.7 on page 4 of the basic tax return
- if you pay part or all of the premiums for an insurance policy taken out by your employer to meet the cost of employees' sick pay. In this case, the proportion of the sick pay which arises from your contributions is tax-free and need not be entered on the tax return. Any sick pay arising from your employer's contributions is taxable. Put it in box 1.8.

## Tips and other payments

<table>
<tr><td>•   payments not on P60 etc  -  tips</td><td>1.9  £</td></tr>
<tr><td>        -  other payments (excluding expenses shown below and lump<br>          sums and compensation payments or benefits shown overleaf)</td><td>1.10  £</td></tr>
</table>

Boxes 1.9 and 1.10 are there to catch any income which does not appear on your P60 (for example, because they are paid by people other than your employer) and for which there is no other place on the Employment page. For example, you should enter in box 1.10 pay from working overseas which you have actually sent to the UK – this may not all be taxable but any tax-free amounts are deducted later on (see p. 166). Also enter the taxable value of shares withdrawn early from an approved profit-sharing scheme (see Chapter 15).

## Tax deducted

<table>
<tr><td>•   tax deducted from payments in boxes 1.8 to 1.10</td><td>Tax deducted<br>1.11  £</td></tr>
</table>

The tax your employer has deducted under PAYE is set against your tax bill. Enter it in box 1.11, together with any other tax deducted (for example, under a taxed incentive scheme). Occasionally, your employer may have given you more tax back as a refund than was actually deducted. If so, remember to enter the amount in brackets.

## FRINGE BENEFITS AND EXPENSES

■   *Benefits and expenses* - see Notes on pages E2 to E6

Many employers give their employees non-cash fringe benefits, such as a company car or free medical insurance. Generally, you are taxed on the cash equivalent of these benefits (and the same applies, as for pay, if the benefit or expense is paid to you by someone other than your employer). Benefits for your family or household are regarded as a payment to you. However, some types of benefits are tax-free, and others are taxable only for higher-paid employees.

Expense payments you receive are yoked together with benefits in this section and sometimes the dividing line between them can be a fine one; for example, a company car may be a way of covering your travelling costs for work, as well as a perk of the job.

## Payments you do not need to enter
There are three sorts of payments which you can ignore when filling out the benefits and expenses section of the Employment supplementary page.

### Dispensations
You do not need to enter in your tax return expenses payments which are covered by a dispensation. A dispensation is a special permission from the Revenue which means that your employer does not have to include on your P11D or P9D expenses which would be tax-free anyway. Dispensations are usually given for things like travelling and subsistence expenses on an approved scale: they do not generally cover fringe benefits.

### PAYE Settlement Agreements
The tax on some of your expenses and benefits may already have been paid by your employer under a PAYE Settlement Agreement (PSA). This is a voluntary agreement between an employer and the Inland Revenue under which the employer undertakes to pay the tax due on some types of benefits and expenses. The advantage for your employer is the saving of paperwork; the advantage for you is that you do not need to enter the payments on your return and they are effectively tax-free in your hands. Only some types of benefits and expenses can be covered by this sort of agreement, for example, minor expenses such as taxi fares and one-off payments such as parties for employees.

### Tax-free fringe benefits
Your employer's own products or services provided to you at less than the price to the general public are tax-free as long as providing them does not cost your employer anything; for example, goods sold to you at the wholesale price, cheap conveyancing for solicitors which does not require the firm to take on extra staff, or free bus travel for bus company employees which does not displace fare-paying customers.

The following are also tax-free:
- free or subsidised meals at work, provided they are available to all employees and are not provided in a public restaurant
- luncheon vouchers (or equivalent) up to a maximum of 15p a day
- your employer's contributions to a pension, life insurance or sick pay insurance policy for you (but premiums to a private medical insurance policy for you do count as a taxable fringe benefit)
- routine medical check-ups or medical screening for you or your family

- the costs of medical treatment while you are working abroad (or insurance to cover it)
- nurseries and playschemes run by your employer (if the childcare is not on your employer's premises, then the employer must participate in financing and arranging the care)
- living accommodation provided it is either necessary for you to do your job, or beneficial and customary for someone in your line of work (for example, as a caretaker). This benefit is not tax-free if you are a director, unless you have no material interest in the company, and you are either a full-time working director, or director of a non-profit-making company or charity
- living accommodation provided as part of special security arrangements, and other security precautions, if there is a threat to your security because of your job
- if you live in accommodation which is tax-free for one of the two reasons above, any council tax paid by your employer is also a tax-free benefit
- the provision of a car-parking space at or near your work
- travelling expenses paid for your spouse if he or she has to accompany you on a business trip abroad because your health does not allow you to travel abroad alone
- reasonable extra travel or overnight subsistence expenses paid to you because of disruption to public transport by industrial action
- the cost of transport home if you are occasionally required to work late after public transport has shut down or cannot reasonably be used
- financial help with the cost of travelling between home and work if you are severely and permanently disabled and cannot use public transport
- some retraining and counselling costs paid for by your employer when you leave your job, providing you have worked for your employer for at least two years
- the cost of fees and books for further education or training courses paid for by your employer if the course is either necessary or directly beneficial for your work, or if you are under 21 when starting a general educational course. If you have to be away from your normal workplace for not more than 12 months, and will return to it after training, some travel and subsistence costs may be tax-free
- truly personal gifts from your employer of an appropriate size and nature (excluding cash), including gifts on marriage, and long-service awards of things or shares in the company. However, long-service awards are tax-free only if they are to mark service of 20 years or more, they do not cost more than £20 for each year of service, and you have received no similar award in the previous ten years
- suggestion scheme awards (see Incentive awards on p. 144)
- entertainment for you or your family provided by someone other than

your employer purely as a gesture of goodwill – but not if there are any strings attached, or if it counts as payment for your services
- small non-cash gifts from someone other than your employer. To qualify, the total cost of all gifts you received from the same donor must not be more than £150 in any tax year, and they must not be provided on any sort of condition, for example, that you will provide some particular service
- annual parties or similar functions, such as a Christmas dinner or summer party, which are open to staff generally and cost no more than £75 a head per year to provide
- sports facilities generally available to all staff and their families (and not available to the general public)
- incidental overnight expenses paid or reimbursed by your employer if you are away overnight on business, such as newspapers and phone calls home. The maximum payment is £5 a night (£10 outside the UK); if more is paid, the whole of the payment becomes taxable, not just the excess
- relocation expenses if you move house for your job, such as the costs of buying and selling homes, some travel and subsistence expenses, and bridging loan expenses. There is a maximum of £8,000 per move; you will be taxed on anything over this figure.

Note that there are conditions to meet before most of these benefits can be tax-free. Fuller information is given in Help Sheet *IR207 Non-taxable payments or benefits for employees.*

## Taxable benefits for all employees
There are four types of benefits which are always taxable. These are:
- assets transferred to you or payments made for you
- vouchers and any goods or services paid for by credit card
- living accommodation provided by your employer (apart from the few exceptions listed opposite)
- mileage allowances if you use your own car for work.

Other benefits are tax-free if you earn at a rate of less than £8,500 a year and are not a director. You cannot get around this by asking to be paid under £8,500 and getting substantial perks instead. To work out whether you earn at a rate of £8,500 a year, you need to take into account two rules:

### Rule 1
Your earnings for this purpose are any kind of pay you receive for the job – that is, including your expenses and the taxable value of any perks worked out as if you earned £8,500 or more. However, you can exclude any tax-free profit-related pay, your contributions to an employer's pension scheme,

and payroll giving donations.

*Rule 2*
The earnings are worked out assuming you work full-time for a whole year. So if you leave a job half-way through the year, having earned £5,000, you will still count as earning more than £8,500 – because in the second part of the year you would have earned another £5,000, that is, £10,000 in total.

If you are a director you are automatically counted as earning £8,500 or more unless all of the following three conditions apply:
- you are either a full-time working director or a director of a charity or non-profit-making concern
- you do not own or control more than 5 per cent of the share capital
- you earn under £8,500.

Your employer should take account of your rate of earnings when filling in your taxable benefits and their cash equivalent: you can tell what category you fall into depending on whether you get a form P11D (which is the form for people who earn at a rate of £8,500 or more) or P9D (the alternative form if you earn under £8,500).

*Assets transferred to you*

| | Amount |
|---|---|
| • assets transferred/ payments made for you | 1.12 £ |

This section is for payments in kind. For example, your employer may give you (or allow you to buy at a discount) a television set, furniture, groceries or your employer's own product. However, the section does not apply to assets which remain the property of your employer and which you merely have the use of, or to services supplied by your employer – these go in box 1.22, unless there is a more specific box. Payments in kind may be taxed in a number of ways, depending on how much you earn and whether you have the alternative of cash instead.

*If you earn less than £8,500*
The taxable value is the second-hand value of the payment in kind (whether or not you actually sell it). Since many assets have a much lower second-hand value than the cost of buying them new this can be advantageous to you.

*If you earn £8,500 or more*
The tax rules are tougher for those who earn at a rate of £8,500 or more, or

directors. They pay tax on the larger of:

- the second-hand value, or
- the cost to the employer of providing the asset, including ancillary costs such as installation or servicing. Remember, though, that if it is the employer's own product, you pay only the extra cost to the employer. So if it does not cost the employer anything (after taking into account anything you have paid for it) it should be tax-free, unless it has a second-hand value.

If you are being given something you have already had the use of (apart from a car, telephone or mobile phone), the taxable value is the larger of the following, less any amount you have paid:

- the market value when you are given it, or
- the market value of the asset when it was first loaned out (either to you or to anyone else), less the total amount on which tax has already been charged. This is because assets which have been on loan will already have had some tax paid on them. See Help Sheet *IR213 Payments in kind* for a calculator.

If you are given a car, telephone or mobile phone, for example on leaving a job, you are taxed on its second-hand value when you are given it, less anything you pay for it. If you buy your company car for a low price, you may have to pay tax on the difference between the price you paid and what your tax office reckons it would fetch on the open market.

### Cash or perks?
You may be given the alternative of either a particular payment in kind, such as free board and lodging, or cash. If you have a perk you can convert into money either immediately or at short notice, you have to pay tax on the value of the cash alternative, even if you opt for the perk. Enter the amount of the cash alternative in box 1.12. However note that there is a concession for some workers, including farm workers, and for cash alternatives to cars (see p. 158).

### Payments made for you
However much you earn, you pay tax on the full amount of any bill paid directly by your employer on your behalf, such as:

- your phone bill
- your personal credit card bill
- your council tax (unless it is tax-free because you live in tax-free accommodation, see p. 148)
- rent paid direct to your landlord
- a tax bill.

Note, though, that this normally applies only to payments settled directly by your employer, for example to the telephone company, the credit card company or your landlord. If you were given cash to settle the bill yourself, it should already have been added to your other pay on your payslip and taxed through PAYE (if it was not, of course, you need to include it here).

## Vouchers and credit cards

| | Amount |
|---|---|
| • vouchers/credit cards | 1.13 £ |

You may be given a voucher for a particular service (for example, a season ticket), a credit token or a company credit or charge card. If so, you are taxed on their cash equivalent unless they appear in the list of tax-free fringe benefits on p. 147 (for example, luncheon vouchers, gift vouchers which count as a small gift) or are provided to pay the cost of running a company car or van on which you are already taxed. However cash vouchers worth a specified amount of cash should already have been taxed under PAYE, so you will not usually have to enter them here as a benefit.

For vouchers and cards which do count as a taxable fringe benefit, broadly speaking you pay tax on the expense incurred by the person who provided them, less any amount that you have paid yourself. You will not have to pay tax on any annual card fee or interest paid by your employer.

Company credit cards and charge cards are often provided as a convenient way of paying business expenses. If so, you still have to enter the amount here; you can claim any allowable business expenses back in box 1.23. For more information see Help Sheet *IR201 Vouchers, credit cards and tokens*.

## Living accommodation

| | Amount |
|---|---|
| • living accommodation | 1.14 £ |

In some cases living accommodation may count as a tax-free fringe benefit – see the list on p. 148. But if it does not, it counts as a taxable perk however much you earn. It includes houses, flats, houseboats and holiday homes but not board and lodging or hotel-type accommodation where typically you get food and other services.

The taxable value of the accommodation is based on the higher of:

- the rateable value of the property, or
- if the property is let, the rent paid for it.

From the taxable value, you can deduct anything you pay for the accommodation, and also, if part of the property is used exclusively for your work, a proportion for that.

Rateable values are still used, although rates are no longer payable. However, for properties in Scotland, where rateable values were revalued more recently than elsewhere, only a percentage of the rateable value is used (found by multiplying the rateable value by 100 and dividing by 270). If there is no rateable value your employer will have to agree a value with your tax office.

If the tax is based on the rateable value, there may be an extra charge if the property cost more than £75,000, including the cost of any improvements made before the current tax year, but deducting anything you paid towards the cost. Broadly, you pay interest at the Inland Revenue's official rate at the start of the tax year (7.25 per cent at 6 April 1996) on the excess over £75,000, reduced in line with the number of days you do not have the property if it is provided for only part of the year. You can deduct any rent you pay not already deducted when working out the basic taxable value, and an amount for business use.

The basic taxable charge, and the extra charge if applicable, should be entered in box 1.14. However, if you have the alternative of getting cash instead of accommodation, and the cash alternative comes to more than the taxable value of the accommodation, you should enter the extra cash in box 1.12 as well as the taxable value in box 1.14. This applies even if you have decided to live in.

There is Help Sheet *IR 202 Living Accommodation* if you want to work out the taxable value in all these situations.

## Mileage allowances

If you use your own car for work, most employers pay you a mileage allowance of so many pence per mile. Quite often this is generous enough to allow you to make a profit on it. Any such profit needs to be entered as a benefit in box 1.15. Any loss should be entered in box 1.32.

There are three different methods of working out your profit. You can choose which suits you best. Note that:

- business mileage excludes travel between home and work
- motoring expenses are fuel, insurance, depreciation, servicing, road tax and tax relief on loan interest to buy the car (or capital allowances if you buy it outright).

## Method 1: Exact

You keep records of your business mileage, your overall mileage and your overall motoring expenses. At the end of the tax year, you divide your business mileage by your overall mileage to find what percentage of your mileage is down to your work. Then multiply your overall expenses by the same percentage to find out how much of these you can claim as business expenses. If your mileage allowances come to more than this, the excess is your profit (unless your employer has a dispensation).

## Method 2: Quick

You need only keep records of your business mileage. The Inland Revenue has a scale of pence per mile (the Fixed Profit Car Scheme scales) which they estimate to be the average cost of running a car of various engine sizes, including fuel, insurance, depreciation, servicing and road tax. You pay tax only on any mileage allowance you receive above this scale. At the end of the tax year you multiply your business mileage by the appropriate pence per mile. If your mileage allowances come to more than this, the excess is your profit.

## Scale charges under the Fixed Profit Car Scheme

| | Tax-free rate per mile | | | |
| | on the first 4,000 miles in the tax year | | on each mile over 4,000 miles in the tax year | |
| Size of car engine | 1996-97 | 1997-98 | 1996-97 | 1997-98 |
|---|---|---|---|---|
| up to 1,000 cc | 27p | 28p | 16p | 17p |
| 1,000 cc – 1,500 cc | 34p | 35p | 19p | 20p |
| 1,501 – 2,000 cc | 43p | 45p | 23p | 25p |
| over 2,000 cc | 61p | 63p | 33p | 36p |

*Method 3: Fixed Profit Car Scheme*
Your employer pays more than the scale above, but has agreed with your tax office that method 2 should apply when working out employees' profit. If so, the figures will not appear on your P11D, but your employer should give you the taxable figure, or the information you need to work it out.

*Which method?*
You do not have to stick with the Fixed Profit Car Scheme, even if your employer operates it, but using the scheme's scales is much simpler than keeping full records. Keep records for a few months to see how similar your actual cost per mile is to the Fixed Profit Car Scheme scale. Then:

- if your car happens to be more expensive to run than average, choose the exact method (but you must keep records of all your expenses)
- if its running costs are average, or cheaper than average, choose the Fixed Profit Car Scheme if your employer runs one, or the Quick method
- if you find that your mileage allowances come to less than the amount of your actual business expenses, do not enter anything in box 1.15 but remember to enter your loss in box 1.32.

*If you earn less than £8,500*
Only the taxable fringe benefits listed above are taxable for you. The remaining benefits listed in boxes 1.16 to 1.22 are taxable only if you earn £8,500 or more, or are a director. You can now enter your expenses in box 1.23. This means that benefits which are tax-free for you include:

- a company car or van
- a mobile phone
- private medical or dental insurance
- services without a second-hand value, such as hairdressing at work
- loans of things or money.

## Taxable benefits if you earn £8,500 or more

*Company cars*

The rules for taxing company cars have become less favourable over the years and many employers now give their staff the choice of whether to take a car or cash. If you only need a car for work occasionally, note that a 'pool car' is tax-free. To qualify it must not normally be kept overnight near your home, it must be used by more than one employee, and any private use must be a consequence of business use. But before you can work out which option is better for you, you need to be able to work out the taxable value of a company car and any free fuel you get.

The baseline for a car's taxable value is 35 per cent of its price. So a £15,000 new car has a basic taxable value of £5,250. The price is defined as the list price of the car at registration (not the dealer's price), including delivery charges, VAT and car tax (but not road tax). Any contribution you make towards the cost of the car is deducted from its price, up to a limit of £5,000, and the maximum price for tax purposes is capped at £80,000. For cars without a list price, your employer will have to reach agreement with the Revenue, usually on the basis of published car price guides. The market value is used for classic cars worth at least £15,000 and aged 15 years or more at the end of the tax year.

You cannot create an artificially low price by getting a basic model and adding accessories. The price includes any accessories fitted before the car was made available to you, and any accessories or set of accessories worth more than £100 which are fitted after that. Accessories needed because you are disabled are excluded.

This system of taxing company cars means that you are taxed on roughly the whole price of the car over three years. You are also taxed on free fuel you get (see p. 158), although other running costs borne by your employer, such tax, servicing and insurance, are tax-free. However, you can make various deductions from the basic taxable value if:

- you do at least 2,500 miles on business in the car each year – deduct one-third of the taxable value for 2,500 to 17,999 business miles each tax year, two-thirds of the taxable value for 18,000 or more business miles
- the car is more than four years old at the end of the tax year in question – deduct one-third of the taxable value you ended up with after any business mileage deduction
- you have to pay towards your private use of the car (as opposed to contributions you make towards the cost of buying it) – deduct the amount you pay. Note that you cannot deduct a contribution you make voluntarily, in order to get a better car, say.

If you qualify for more than one deduction, the taxable value is worked out on a cumulative basis – first you deduct one-third of the basic taxable value, then you deduct a further third (or two-thirds) from the result. The cash contribution towards your private use is deducted last.

# Example

Sanjay O'Hanlon got a new company car in March 1993 with a price of £15,000. From the tax year ending 5 April 1995 (when this system of taxing company cars was introduced) the basic taxable value for each tax year was 35 per cent of this, £5,250. But he does at least 2,500 miles on business in it each year, so he can claim a one-third deduction. One-third of £5,250 is £1,750, so the taxable value is £5,250 – £1,750 = £3,500. £3,500 is added to his pay for tax purposes each year, when working out his PAYE code.

However, in March 1997 the car had its fourth birthday. This means that he can claim a further one-third deduction for the whole of the tax year ending 5 April 1997. The deduction is one-third of £3,500, that is £1,167, so the car's taxable value for the tax year ending 5 April 1997 was £2,333. Had the car been registered just a month later, after 5 April 1993, he would have had to wait until the tax year ending 5 April 1998 for the further reduction.

## Changing, getting or losing a company car

At some point your company car is almost certain to be unavailable for part of a tax year, because you changed it, or you started or stopped getting one. The tax system recognises this by reducing the taxable value of the car in line with the number of days for which the car was unavailable. The same applies if you didn't have the car (or a replacement) for at least 30 days at a stretch during the tax year. The number of miles you need to do to qualify for the business mileage reductions is also reduced proportionately.

## Checking the figures

The form P11D you get from your employer should give you the appropri-

# Example

Sanjay changes his company car on 1 August 1997. He has had his old company car for only 111 days in the tax year, so the taxable value is $111/_{365}$ of the full year's value. But first he needs to check that he is still entitled to the business mileage deduction he usually gets. He multiplies the normal business mileage limit that applies (2,500 miles) by $111/_{365}$ to get 760 but his actual mileage is comfortably above this. The taxable value for a full tax year would be £2,333; the taxable value for the 111 days is £2,333 × $111/_{365}$ = £709.

Sanjay has to do a similar calculation for his brand new company car, using its price, but this time he cannot claim the reduction for a car aged four years or more. This time he adjusts all the figures by the number of days he had the new car: 365 – 111 = 254.

ate figures to put in box 1.16 and box 1.17 of your tax return. Help Sheet *IR203 Car benefits and car fuel benefits* gives a calculator. However, you may want to work out your own figures during the tax year in order to decide whether a company car will be beneficial for you. If so, beware of confusion if you have to adjust the figures to account for time when the car was unavailable. The method shown in the example above is the simplest but the Revenue tends to talk in terms of days unavailable, and then deducts a figure for those days from the full-year figure. So in the example above, Sanjay's tax office would probably work out the days for which the first car was unavailable (254) and then deduct $254/365$ths from the full-year figures.

## Two company cars?
If your employer provides you and your household with two company cars, you do not get a full business mileage reduction on the second (least-used) car. You have to do at least 18,000 business miles in the second car order to qualify for a reduction, and then it is only a one-third reduction.

## Giving up cars for cash
If you do decide that you would rather have cash than a company car, you will of course be taxed on the cash. Employees have to pay National Insurance contributions on extra cash but not on company cars. However, there is no employees' National Insurance to pay on earnings over £24,180 (in the tax year ending 5 April 1998) so if you are over this limit there would be no extra National Insurance to pay anyway.

---

# T AX - SAVING IDEAS
If you plan to keep a company car for some years, a car registered just before the end of the tax year (5 April) can get you the deduction for older cars nearly a year earlier than one registered at the beginning of the tax year. That is because you get the deduction for the whole tax year, but it is the age of the car at the end of the tax year which counts.

Keep an eye on your business mileage – if it is approaching 2,500 or 18,000 miles try to use the car for work enough to qualify for the business mileage deduction.

Be aware that if you want a large, luxurious company car, you will be taxed fairly heavily for the privilege.

If you have the option of a company car allowance which can be taken either as cash or as a car, consider taking a cheap, lightly-taxed company car and investing the rest of the cash in a tax-free investment, such as additional contributions to your pension plan.

---

## Fuel for company cars

If you get a company car, you may get free fuel for private use as well. This is taxed according to a fixed scale of charges added to your taxable income. The only reduction you get is if you have the car for only part of the year, in which case the scale charge is worked out in line with the number of days, in the same way as for cars. The only way in which you can avoid the scale charge is by being required by your employer to reimburse all the cost of fuel used for private purposes. However, fuel provided for the travel between home and work for disabled employees is tax-free.

### Car fuel scale charges

| | Engine size, cc | | |
| --- | --- | --- | --- |
| | 0-1,400 | 1,401-2,000 | 2,001+ |
| **Petrol** | | | |
| 1996-97 | £710 | £890 | £1,320[1] |
| 1997-98 | £800 | £1,010 | £1,490[1] |
| **Diesel** | | | |
| 1996-97 | £640 | £640 | £820 |
| 1997-98 | £740 | £740 | £940 |

[1]These figures also apply for cars without a cylinder capacity

### Vans

A van provided by your employer for your private use is lightly taxed, compared with a company car. The basic taxable value of a van is £500, and there is no tax charge for free fuel. You may also qualify for the following reductions:

- the taxable value is reduced to £350 if the van is aged four years or more at the end of the tax year
- if the van is shared with other employees and is not exclusively yours for any period of more than 30 days at a stretch, the taxable value is split between all the employees concerned
- the taxable value is reduced in line with the number of days within the tax year for which it is unavailable (in the same way as for company cars, above)
- any amount you have to pay for the use of the van is deducted from the taxable value.

## Cheap or free loans

The basic rule is that if your employer provides a cheap or interest-free loan, you have to pay tax on the difference between the interest you pay and the interest worked out at an official rate set from time to time by the Inland Revenue. You do not need to worry about any of this, however, if:

- your employer lends money as part of its normal business, comparable loans were available to members of the general public (a substantial proportion actually being sold to them), and the loan was made to you on the same terms as those comparable loans. Such loans are tax-free from 6 April 1994, even if they were first taken out before then
- the total loans you have outstanding are no more than £5,000 through-out the tax year. If you have several loans, one of which qualifies for tax relief, then the qualifying loan is ignored when deciding whether the other loans fall within the limit. If, for example, you have a £1,000 per-sonal loan and a £50,000 mortgage (on which you get tax relief), only the mortgage will be treated as a taxable loan.

To work out the tax on a loan, you take the average amount owing during the year (the whole amount, not just the amount above £5,000), adjusted if the loan was only outstanding for part of the year. You then multiply the average loan by the average official rate of interest for the period in the year during which the loan was outstanding (your tax office should be able to tell you this). Last, you deduct the interest you were actually liable to pay dur-ing the tax year, to find the amount on which you will be taxed.

If you think that you will lose out under this averaging method, you can choose to calculate the figures using the daily amounts of the loan and offi-

## EXAMPLE

Lene Mikkelsen has a £10,000 loan from her employer to help buy her flat, at a special low interest rate of 5 per cent (compared with the official interest rate of 7.5 per cent). She paid off £1,000 of the loan halfway through the year. The taxable value of the perk is £237.50, worked out as follows:

Amount outstanding:
At start of tax year                    £10,000
At end of tax year                      £9,000
Average:                                £19,000 ÷ 2 = £9,500.

Interest payable at official rate    £9,500 x 7.5% =    £712.50
Actual interest payable                                 £475.00
Difference (taxable value)                              £237.50

As the loan qualifies for tax relief, Lene can claim tax relief on both the actual interest payable (£475) and the difference between that and the interest payable at the official rate (£237.50) that is £712.50 in total. As the loan is to buy a home, the tax relief is 15 per cent of the total – a £107 saving.

cial rates of interest. However, you have to use the same method for all your taxable loans, and the calculations can get quite complex. If you want to make this choice, you have to tell your tax office within roughly 21 months of the end of the tax year in question.

Note that under either method, if the loan qualifies for tax relief, you get tax relief on both the interest you actually paid and the difference between that and the official rate of interest. Effectively, the tax relief is worked out assuming you paid the official rate of interest. Note that if it is a home loan, you may already have had relief on the interest you actually paid, under MIRAS (see Chapter 7). If so, claim the extra relief in box 15.2 on page 5 of the basic tax return. Claim tax relief on other qualifying loans in box 15.3.

If the loan is eventually written off, you pay tax on the amount written off. Include the amount with the taxable value of any other loans in box 1.19.

### Mobile phones

The taxable value of a mobile phone provided for you (or a member of your household) is a flat £200. The taxable value is reduced if the phone is unavailable for part of the year, in the same way as company cars above. You are not taxed, however, if you pay the full cost of any outgoing private calls.

In practice, many employers have arranged either a dispensation or a PAYE Settlement Agreement for mobile phones, which is why you may not see them on your P11D (and of course they are not taxable at all unless you earn at a rate of £8,500).

*Private medical or dental insurance*

| | Amount |
|---|---|
| • private medical or dental insurance | 1.21 £ |

If your employer pays premiums for a private medical expenses policy for you (for example, through a group scheme for all employees), the amount is a taxable benefit. The same applies to dental insurance schemes. You pay tax on the cost to your employer, less any amount you pay for the benefit. The amount should be shown on your P11D.

*Other benefits*

| | Amount |
|---|---|
| • other benefits | 1.22 £ |

This is a box to sweep up any other taxable perks which you have not already entered elsewhere. Remember, though, that it applies only if you earn at a rate of £8,500 or more. The figures should be shown on your P11D. The main types of benefits you may have to enter here are listed in the notes to the tax return. They include:

- relocation expenses which would normally be tax-free but which are above the £8,000 tax-free limit for each move. Remember to enter only the excess over £8,000
- childcare provided by your employer – workplace nurseries and playschemes should be tax-free, but if your employer just pays for you to arrange your own childcare, this will count as a taxable benefit
- services supplied, such as free hairdressing, holidays, gardening or a free chauffeur – but remember that you pay tax only on the

> **TAX-SAVING IDEA**
> Remember – you do not need to enter items covered by a dispensation or PAYE Settlement Agreement.

extra cost to your employer, so services that your employer provides as part of their normal business may be tax-free

- share schemes or share options which are not tax-free. You enter the taxable amount here only if it is shown on your P11D – otherwise, ask the Inland Revenue Orderline for the supplementary page on Share schemes. See Chapter 15 for more on these
- subscriptions and fees paid for by your employer for you to join professional bodies, societies, leisure or sports clubs etc. Note that if you pay for these yourself, you may be able to claim them against your tax if they are necessary for your work (see p. 172)
- any income tax paid for you by your employer, other than through PAYE – but only if you are a director (if you are not a director this goes in box 1.12). This may sometimes apply if PAYE was not deducted from your pay at the proper time, and the tax was later paid for you
- the value of anything provided for your use, except for cars, vans, mobile phones and living accommodation (for example, a television, furniture, a yacht or aircraft). The value is 20 per cent of the market value when it was first provided (to you or to anyone else), plus any expense of providing it met by your employer. If you are later given whatever it is, you should enter the value of the gift in box 1.12
- help with educating your children (unless this is nothing to do with your job, for example it is pure coincidence that your child gets one of the generally available scholarships your employer's firm provides).

### Expenses payments and balancing charges

| | | Amount |
|---|---|---|
| • | expenses payments received and balancing charges | 1.23 £ |

You should enter here all expenses payments and expense allowances you received, whether or not they are tax-free. You can deduct tax-free expense payments later on in boxes 1.32 to 1.35. The only expenses which you should not enter either here or later on are those for which your employer has a dispensation.

Your expenses payments should be shown in your P11D or P9D. In your P11D they will be broken down into the gross amount received, any contributions you made or amounts on which tax has already been deducted, and the taxable amount. Enter the taxable amount in box 1.23.

Balancing charges are not something you will see on your P11D or P9D. They apply only if you claimed capital allowances on something that you bought for your work and that you have now disposed of (see p. 172).

## LUMP SUMS AND COMPENSATION

You may have something to enter here if:

- you receive a lump sum when you leave a job, such as redundancy pay
- you retire and received a lump sum from a non-approved retirement scheme (that is, anything other than an Inland-Revenue approved, foreign government or other statutory pension scheme)
- your employer (or ex-employer) paid you a lump sum which you have not already entered as pay (for example, in box 1.8 or box 1.10).

You will need Help Sheet *IR204 Lump sums and compensation payments* in order to work out what to enter in each of the boxes. It is important to enter the right bit in the right category because each is taxed under different parts of tax legislation. You can get various types of tax relief on some categories, but not on others. One payment might be made up of several different types. They may also affect your overall tax calculation, and there is a special lump sums tax calculation guide if you are planning to work out your own tax.

|  | Tax deducted |
|---|---|
| • tax deducted from payments in boxes 1.27 to 1.29 | 1.30 £ |

Your employer may deduct tax from any taxable sums you get before paying you. If so, make sure you enter it in box 1.30, so that it is taken into account when working out your tax bill.

### Payment expected under the terms of your employment

**Taxable lump sums**

| • from working sheet, box H (from Help Sheet IR204) | 1.27 £ |
|---|---|

Lump sums that you should enter here include:

- any payment that you receive under the terms and conditions of your contract, or where the expectation that you would get it is firm enough

for it to be regarded as part of your contract – for example, a payment based on length of service which it is your employer's established policy to make when a job ends
- payments received in return for you undertaking not to carry out certain actions, sometimes called a restrictive covenant (if not already entered with other pay in box 1.8 or 1.10)
- bonuses on leaving a job (for example, for doing extra work in the period leading up to redundancy). Do not enter redundancy payments themselves in this category – they go in box 1.29, after deducting various reliefs.

All these payments are taxable in full. For tax purposes, they are treated just like the rest of your pay.

### Payments from non-approved retirement schemes

- retirement and death lump sums    1.26 £
- from working sheet, box Q (from Help Sheet IR204)    1.28 £

Most pension schemes are approved by the Inland Revenue or statutory schemes, and the lump sums you receive from them are tax-free (within limits). Payments from a non-approved scheme are also tax-free if:

- they arose because of an accident, or
- they were funded by a contribution from your employer on which you have already paid tax, or
- they arose from your own contributions.

If you have any tax-free payments, the total should go in box 1.26. Any taxable payments you receive should be entered in box 1.28.

### Other payments

- £30,000 exemption    1.24 £
- foreign service and disability    1.25 £
- from working sheet, box R (from Help Sheet IR204)    1.29 £

Some payments are tax-free altogether if:

- you get them as a result of accident or chronic illness which meant that you couldn't do your job (or they are payments to your family because of your death)
- 75 per cent of your service in the job was foreign service, or if you worked abroad for least ten out of the last 20 years (and 50 per cent of your time in the job, if longer than 20 years). If you can't meet these conditions, you may still get some relief – see Help Sheet *IR204 Lump sums and compensation payments.*

Enter these payments under reliefs in box 1.25.
The first £30,000 of the following payments are also tax-free:

- redundancy pay (either statutory or at the employer's discretion)
- pay in lieu of notice which is not included in your terms and conditions of employment
- any other payments on leaving a job which were not part of your terms and conditions, or 'expected' or received as payment for work done.

Enter the first £30,000 (or total received) under reliefs in box 1.24. Anything over £30,000 is taxable and should be entered in box 1.29.

## FOREIGN EARNINGS

The broad principle of the UK tax system is that you are taxed on foreign earnings if you are resident or ordinarily resident in this country, even if your permanent home (your domicile) is elsewhere. A full explanation of all these terms is included in Chapter 18. If you think you may be able to claim non-residence you should read that chapter first.

You should include foreign earnings in boxes 1.8 to 1.10 (your employer may already have included foreign earnings in your P60). But if you are a UK resident, or a British citizen, a Crown employee or a citizen of some other countries you can claim personal allowances to set against your income. You may also be able to claim deductions in boxes 1.31, 1.37 and 1.38 which make the possibility of tax on foreign earnings a less fearsome prospect.

### Foreign earnings not taxable in the UK

■ *Foreign earnings not taxable in the UK in year ended 5 April 1997* - see Notes on page E6     £

In some cases, foreign earnings can be free of UK tax if:

- you were prevented from bringing the earnings into the UK by law, government action, or shortage of foreign currency in the country where they

were earned, or

- you are resident but not ordinarily resident in the UK, or
- you are resident and ordinarily resident, but not domiciled in the UK, and the job is carried out wholly outside the country (except for incidental duties such as attending a directors' meeting in the UK).

This is called the remittance basis. You may be able to claim a deduction on these grounds even if you were non-resident for only part of the year, or if you have included in your tax return income for a different year (for example, if you have only just been able to bring into this country income earned in an earlier year). Help Sheet *IR211 Employment – Residence and Domicile issues* helps you through the calculations to see how much you should enter in box 1.31.

## Foreign earnings deduction

■ *Foreign Earnings Deduction*  £

Even if you are resident (and ordinarily resident) in the UK you can still receive all your foreign earnings free of UK tax if you spend at least 365 days abroad in a qualifying period. This is called the foreign earnings deduction and you claim it in box 1.37. Note, however, that you cannot claim the foreign earnings deduction if you are taxed on the remittance basis.

You do not need to work for the whole of your absence abroad, and you can make return visits to the UK during the qualifying period, as long as:

- no single visit back to the UK lasts for more than 62 consecutive days, and
- the total number of days you spend in the UK is not more than one-sixth of the total number of days in the visit itself, plus the stretches abroad on either side of the visit.

Whenever you break one of these conditions, a new qualifying period must begin. If you are in the UK at the end of a day (midnight) that day counts as a day spent in the UK. There are special rules for seafarers working on ships abroad (anyone who performs all or most of their duties on a ship, any other duties being merely incidental).

Help Sheet *IR205 Foreign earnings deduction* (or the separate version for seafarers) will help you keep track of your periods abroad and visits home, and tell you if you can claim the deduction.

# EXAMPLE

Chris Batty goes to work in Bahrain on a short-term contract, coming home every few months. His diary looks like this:

| | | | running total in each period |
|---|---|---|---|
| 3 July 1995 | to Bahrain | 40 days | 40 days |
| 12 August 1995 | to UK | 20 days | 60 days |
| | | (break in qualifying period) | |
| 1 September 1995 | to Bahrain | 40 days | 40 days |
| 11 October 1995 | to UK | 10 days | 50 days |
| 21 October 1995 | to Bahrain | 120 days | 170 days |
| 16 February 1996 | to UK | 50 days | 220 days |
| 6 April 1996 | to Bahrain | 160 days | 380 days |
| 13 September 1996 | to UK permanently | | |

His first visit home is within the 62-day limit, but it is more than one-sixth of the 100 days from when he first went to Bahrain on 3 July to when his second visit to Bahrain ended on 11 October (40 + 20 + 40 = 100). So the first 40 days do not count towards his qualifying period. That only starts at the beginning of his second period in Bahrain (1 September 1995).

His second Bahrain + UK + Bahrain stretch (1 September to 16 February) is 170 days, and the UK visit is comfortably within that. The third Bahrain + UK+ Bahrain stretch (21 October 1995 to 13 September 1996) is 120 + 50 + 160 = 330 days; one-sixth of 330 days is 55 days, so his third UK visit does not break his qualifying period either. By now, Chris has reached a qualifying period of 365 days, so all his Bahraini earnings between 1 September 1995 and 13 September 1996 are free of UK tax. He claims his tax-free earnings for the tax year ending 5 April 1997 (received between 6 April 1996 and 13 September 1996) as a foreign earnings deduction in box 1.37.

If you can claim the deduction, enter in box 1.37 the amount of earnings for the tax year ending 5 April 1997 arising from your work abroad during the qualifying period. Remember, though, that you should already have included this amount in your earnings in boxes 1.8 to 1.10. Also note that you should deduct from your qualifying foreign earnings any pension contributions or allowable expenses.

From the tax year ending 5 April 1997 onwards, you must claim the deduction by 31 January after the end of the tax year for which it applies (that is, by the final date for getting your tax return in for the year). However, if your tax position for earlier tax years has not yet been finalised, you may still be able to claim the deduction for those years.

## Foreign tax

If you work abroad, you may be liable to two lots of tax: tax charged by the country in which you earn the money and UK tax. You have two options for avoiding this double taxation:

- claiming tax credit relief (if you are a UK resident)
- deducting the foreign tax from your foreign earnings.

Because tax credit relief can wipe out all or part of the foreign tax, it is usually the best option. There are various Inland Revenue working sheets which may help you decide which is the best option for you (see Chapter 19 for more details). If you decide to claim tax credit relief, leave box 1.38 blank. Otherwise, enter the amount of foreign tax.

## EXPENSES INCURRED IN DOING YOUR JOB

*Income from employment* continued

■ *Expenses you incurred in doing your job* - see Notes on page E6

You should already have entered all the expenses payments and allowances you received in box 1.23. However, not all these expenses will be taxable, and there may be expenses for which you were not reimbursed and on which you can claim tax relief. So you should enter all your tax-allowable expenses, whether or not you were reimbursed, in boxes 1.32 to 1.36. The only exception is expenses for which your employer has a dispensation (see p. 147). These should not be entered anywhere on your tax return, unless your allowable expenses came to more than the amount covered by the dispensation (in which case you should enter the extra). Your employer should be able to tell you what dispensations exist.

The overall rule is that only those expenses which are expended wholly, exclusively and necessarily in doing your job are allowable, except for travel and related meal and accommodation expenses, which must be necessarily incurred. In both cases, necessarily means that it would be necessary for anybody doing the job, not just necessary for you.

There is no neat list of definitions in tax law, and much depends on previous court judgements. In practice, a lot comes down to agreement with your tax inspector and you should keep all the evidence you have (receipts, mileage details and so on) to back up your claims. However, the main tax-allowable expenses are listed below.

## Travel and subsistence costs

| • travel and subsistence costs |  1.32 £ |
| --- | --- |

These include:

- business travel costs, for example fares. If you use your own car for work, the taxable amount of any mileage allowance should already have been entered in box 1.15. However, if you do not get a mileage allowance, or your mileage allowance does not cover the full cost of your business travel, you can enter the costs you bear here. You can claim either the exact amount of your expenses in line with your business mileage (method 1 on p. 154) or a fixed number of pence per mile (method 2 on p. 154). You may also be able to claim capital allowances on the cost of the car, but enter these in box 1.35, not here
- meals and accommodation costs (subsistence) incurred in making the journey
- other business expenses arising because of the journey, for example telephone costs. You cannot deduct personal expenses, such as phone calls home, daily newspapers and personal laundry – but in practice, you may not have had to include these in box 1.23 in any case, since small amounts of personal expenses are tax-free (see p. 149).

A difficult area has long been deciding what is business travel. The cost of travel between your home and your normal place of work is not an allowable expense, but there are special rules for:

- directors who are directors of more than one company in the same group – they can claim the cost of travel between the companies
- a journey for work purposes between your home and somewhere other than your normal workplace (known to the Revenue as triangular travel). You can claim the costs of either the actual journey between your home and the temporary workplace, or a journey between the normal place of work and the

> ### TAX-SAVING IDEA
>
> If you often work away from home, and think you may be affected by changes in what expenses you can claim, start keeping a note now of your costs of normal commuting (for example expired season tickets). It may help you to establish what costs of travel you can claim.

temporary workplace, whichever is less. This would also apply if you are temporarily absent – that is required to work somewhere other than your normal workplace for not more than 12 months, and you return to your normal workplace afterwards

- people who are required by their employer to work at home (that is, not if it just a matter of personal choice). They may be able to claim the cost of travel from home to other places of work, but in practice few employees can do this
- travelling workers who are considered to be working the moment they leave home (for example, a commercial traveller). They can claim for journeys which start or finish at home. However, a commercial traveller who operated from a particular office each day, or a computer consultant who worked at a succession of places as part of the same employment (a site-based employee) would not qualify
- some workers in the building and related trades who are covered by working rule agreements between employers' federations and trade unions. The Inland Revenue has agreed that certain travel and lodging allowances paid under such agreements are tax-free
- employees who work outside the UK. The treatment differs depending on whether you work wholly or partly abroad.

If you are claiming home to work travel for one of these reasons, you should include the amount here, and also tick box 1.36. Be prepared to justify your claim.

There are many grey areas, and the record-keeping can be difficult for both employees and employees. A clearer system has been proposed to start from 6 April 1998. Under this system, if you:

- are a site-based employee working from a succession of different bases, or
- are required to travel from home to a temporary place of work

you will be allowed to claim the actual costs of travel to and from any workplace minus the costs of normal commuting which you have saved. If there is no saving – for example, you have a season ticket and cannot claim a refund – you will be able to claim the full cost of travel to the temporary workplace. In addition, the requirement for a temporary assignment to be expected to last for no more than 12 months is being extended to 24 months, with the requirement for you actually to return to your normal workplace being dropped.

## Fixed deductions for expenses

| | | |
|---|---|---|
| • fixed deductions for expenses | 1.33 £  | |

The Inland Revenue has agreed flat-rate expenses with various trade unions and other bodies to cover the costs of providing equipment and special clothing which is not provided by employers. For example, carpenters and joiners in the building trade can claim a flat-rate £105, uniformed bank employees can claim £40. Ask your union or other staff body if you are covered. You do not have to claim the flat-rate deduction – if you spend more, you can claim more, but if so, you should enter the amount in box 1.35, under other expenses, not here.

## Professional fees and subscriptions

| | | |
|---|---|---|
| • professional fees and subscriptions | 1.34 £ | |

You may pay for membership of a particular body or society which is relevant to your work. You can claim it in box 1.34 as an allowable expense provided that:

- membership of the organisation, or registration with it, is a condition of your job, for example, as a dentist, optician or solicitor
- the organisation is approved by the Revenue as being a non-profit body which exists for a worthy purpose such as to maintain professional standards, and membership is relevant to your work.

Any such organisation should be able to tell you whether it is on the Revenue's list of approved bodies.

## Other expenses and capital allowances

| | | |
|---|---|---|
| • other expenses and capital allowances | 1.35 £  | |

These must be wholly, necessarily and exclusively incurred for work. This means that you cannot claim expenses which merely put you in a position to do your job – for example, a journalist's expenditure on newspapers, employment agency fees, childcare. The expenses you should be allowed are:

- the costs of providing and maintaining tools and special clothing which you have not already claimed a fixed deduction for in box 1.33. Special clothing does not cover clothes which you could wear outside work, even

if you would never choose to do so
- the cost of special security needed because of your job – you can claim this only if your employer paid for the security or reimbursed you, and you have already entered the appropriate amount as a benefit
- costs and expenses if you are held liable for some wrongful act as an employee, or insurance premiums to cover you against such costs
- training expenses for which you are not reimbursed, providing that your employer requires or encourages you to attend the course and gives you paid time off to do so, it is full-time (or virtually so) and lasts for at least four weeks. The expenses allowed are fees (unless you have already had tax relief on these) and the cost of essential books. You may also be able to claim some accommodation or travel costs if you count as being temporarily absent from your normal workplace (see p. 170)
- if you are required to work at home (and do not do so merely from choice) a proportion of the heating and lighting costs, and, for a room used exclusively for work, council tax.

As well as expenses, you may be able to claim capital allowances here if:

- you buy equipment such as a computer which is necessary (as defined on p. 169) for your job. You cannot claim an allowance if your employer would have provided the equipment had you not chosen to do so
- you buy a car or other vehicle for use in your job. This does not have to be necessary (as defined on p. 169) and what's more, if you can claim allowances, you can also claim the interest on any loan to buy the car. However, you can claim only the proportion of your capital allowance and loan interest that arises from your use of the car for work.

When you finally dispose of an asset on which you claimed capital allowances there may be a balancing charge to add to your taxable income. (See Chapter 16 for how to work out capital allowances and balancing charges.)

# SHARE SCHEMES

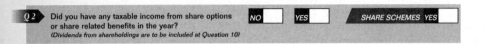

## CHAPTER 15

Q2 ▶ Did you have any taxable income from share options
or share related benefits in the year?
*(Dividends from shareholdings are to be included at Question 10)*    NO ☐   YES ☐        SHARE SCHEMES YES ☐

Part of your payment from a job may come in the form of shares (or share options – the right to buy shares at a set price at some point in the future) in your employer's company. However, there are special approved schemes under which you can get your shares or options tax-free. You only have to tick the YES box and complete the purple supplementary page, if your shares or share options are not received through an approved scheme, or if you are in a scheme but breach its rules in some respect. You have to complete the back of the supplementary page before the front and you need to fill in a separate page 2 (or a photocopy) for each taxable event arising from a share scheme.

The benefit you get from share schemes may come in the following forms:

- a gift of the shares themselves, or a discount on the purchase price
- an option to buy a set number of shares, at a set price, at a particular time in the future
- dividends from the shares once they become your property
- a capital gain (or loss) arising from movements in the share price once the shares become your property.

The share dividends are taxed like the dividends from any share you own and you enter them at Q10 of the basic tax return (see Chapter 10). The same is broadly true for the capital gains, except that some special rules may apply, for example when deciding what allowable expenditure can be deducted (see below). You give details of capital gains on the Capital gains supplementary pages. The Share scheme supplementary pages apply only on the gift (or discounted purchase) of the shares themselves, or an option to buy them, and to any associated advantages. Occasionally, with some unapproved schemes, they may also apply when you sell the shares themselves.

## DIFFERENT TYPES OF SHARE SCHEMES

For tax purposes, share schemes fall within three broad categories:

- approved profit-sharing schemes
- share option schemes – either approved savings-related schemes or discretionary share option schemes (that is, company share option plans and executive share option schemes), or unapproved schemes
- cheap or free gifts of shares through an unapproved scheme (sometimes called share incentive schemes).

You may have come across Employee Share Ownership Trusts (ESOTs) – these are a special type of trust set up to acquire shares in the company and distribute them to employees. For the employee, the shares are taxable in the same way as shares received through an unapproved scheme.

If you received shares or share options which are taxable in the tax year ending 5 April 1997, you will need to declare them on the Share

> **T**AX-SAVING IDEA
> As an employee, you do not often have a choice of scheme, since employers are likely to have either just one scheme, or to have one scheme that is open to all employees and another which is open to a select few. But if you know that your employer is considering a scheme, try to make your voice heard so that the scheme which is chosen is one which suits you.

schemes supplementary page, unless they have already been taxed under PAYE. If so, you should put the taxable value of the benefit in box 1.10 of the Employment page, and the tax in box 1.11. The types of scheme to which this might apply are:

- approved profit-sharing schemes
- shares or options through unapproved schemes, received after 25 November 1996 (those received before that date are taxed through your tax return).

### The documents you need

You should have some correspondence from your employer concerning your scheme, including (where relevant) a share option certificate and a copy of the exercise note. You will also need to know the market price of the shares at various dates – if your employer cannot help, ask your local reference library. If the company is not quoted on the Stock Exchange, the market value has to be agreed with the Inland Revenue.

## Approved profit-sharing schemes

These are a way of transferring free shares in a company to its employees via a special trust. As long as you stick to the rules, shares you receive under an approved profit-sharing scheme will be tax-free and you will not need to enter them on the Share scheme pages. However, they will be taxable if you sell them within three years of being allocated them.

There are two exceptions to this rule:

- shares disposed of before 29 April 1996 were tax-free only after five years; for disposals during the fourth year, you paid tax on 75 per cent of their value
- if the shares are sold before the three years (or five years) are up and the job ended because of an injury, disability, redundancy or death or reaching a specified age (between 60 and 75), tax is due on only 50 per cent of the market value of the shares when allocated.

### Working out the tax

If tax is due, the taxable value is the lesser of:

- the initial market value of the shares at the date when they were allocated to you (occasionally, an earlier date may be used) or
- the actual proceeds of selling them, minus your expenses of selling, for example, stockbrokers' commission. If you give them away, the market value at the time of the gift will be used.

Your employer should work out the taxable value for you and deduct the right amount of tax before passing on the proceeds. If you have left the company, the trustees will work out the taxable value and deduct basic-rate tax: enter the amount deducted at box 1.11 in the Employment supplementary page. For more information, see Inland Revenue leaflet IR 95.

### Share option schemes

There are three key events in the life of an option:

- when you are first granted the option
- when you exercise your right to buy (you may decide not to)
- if you cancel the option in return for some benefit.

If you receive your options through an approved scheme, you will never have to pay tax on the grant of the option. You have tax to pay on the exercise of the option only if you fail

> **TAX-SAVING IDEA**
> When you take your shares out of an approved profit-sharing scheme or savings-related share option scheme, you can transfer them into a single company personal equity plan (see p. 71), providing you do so within 90 days.

to meet various conditions. But you will always be taxed if you agree not to use your option in return for some benefit.

To work out the taxable amount (if any), you need to keep records of :

- the date on which each key event takes place
- the number of shares involved
- the share price – both the price you actually have to pay, and the market value at the time of each event
- any cash you contributed for the option, or any cash (or other benefit) you received for cancelling it.

You have to give this information on page 2 of the Share Scheme supplementary pages for each occasion on which your options are taxable.

*Approved savings-related share options*

| Income and expenses | | | | | |
|---|---|---|---|---|---|
| Read the notes on pages S1 to S4 **before** filling in the boxes | | | | | |
| ■ *Approved savings-related share options* | | | | | |
| | | Name of company | | Tick if shares unquoted | Taxable amount |
| • Exercise | 2.1 | | | 2.2 | 2.3 £ |
| • Cancellation or release | 2.4 | | | 2.5 | 2.6 £ |

These schemes give you the right (or 'option') to buy a set number of ordinary shares in your employer's company at some point in the future, at a price fixed now, but you must do so using savings in a Save-As-You-Earn plan (SAYE). If you meet the various conditions laid down by the Revenue, you will get your shares tax-free (see Inland Revenue leaflet IR 97).

Among other conditions you must agree to:

- save a set amount each month, with a minimum of £5 a month (£10 before 30 April 1996) and a maximum of £250
- save for a set period – either three years, five years or seven years (the three-year option applies only if you join the scheme on or after 30 April 1996).

The price of the shares (the subscription price) is fixed when you are granted the option, but cannot normally be less than 80 per cent of their market value at that time (or up to 30 days before). So if, for example, shares in Horridges' plc stand at 400 pence, the lowest subscription price is 320 pence.

You have no tax to pay when the option is granted to you. You will not have tax to pay when the option is used unless:

- you exercise your option when your company is taken over or sold, and you have not yet had them for three years. In this case, fill in the Exercise column on page 2 of the Share schemes supplementary page (boxes 2.32 to 2.40) and carry the taxable amount to boxes 2.1 to 2.3 on page 1 (see p. 180 for the calculation)
- you benefit from the option in any way other than using it to buy shares – for example, if you receive compensation for not using or agreeing not to use your option. Fill in the Cancellation/release column on page 2 (boxes 2.34, 2.38 and 2.41) and then carry the taxable amount to boxes 2.4 to 2.6 on page 1.

*Approved discretionary share options*

| ■ *Approved discretionary share options* | | | | | |
|---|---|---|---|---|---|
| | | Name of company | | | |
| • Exercise | 2.7 | | 2.8 | 2.9 | £ |
| • Cancellation or release | 2.10 | | 2.11 | 2.12 | £ |

Discretionary schemes may be restricted to groups of employees. Their original name was executive share option schemes, replaced in 1995 by company share option schemes. Broadly, options received under both these schemes are tax-free as long as you exercise them within strict time limits (see opposite).

Unlike savings-related share option schemes, the price at which you can buy the shares under your option must not be less than the market value of the shares when the option is granted (or up to 30 days before). However, you may have been granted a discount of up to 15 per cent of the market value if you:

- were granted options in an Executive Share Option Scheme after 1 January 1992 and before 17 July 1995, and
- your company already had an

---

**T AX - S A V I N G   I D E A**
Whether or not you will benefit from a savings-related share option scheme depends on the option price and the share price when you exercise your option.

You do not have to exercise your option if you would make a loss and the rate of return on five-year SAYE schemes (taken out on or after 30 April 1996) is equivalent to 5.7 per cent a year, tax-free. So if you are a higher-rate taxpayer, or are optimistic that you will make some profit on the shares, joining the scheme is worthwhile.

approved savings-related share option scheme or approved profit-sharing scheme.

If you did receive a discounted option after those dates, this is unapproved and you will be taxed on the grant of the option, as well as when it is exercised.

You only have to pay tax on other options if:

- you give up the right to exercise the option in return for some benefit, or
- the scheme had ceased to be approved by the time you exercised your options, or
- you exercise the option within three years of being granted it, or
- you exercise the option more than 10 years of being granted it, or
- it is less than three years since you last exercised an option under *any* Executive Share Option Scheme or Company Share Option Scheme.

If the first point applies, fill in the Cancellation/release column on page 2 of the Share schemes supplementary page (boxes 2.34, 2.38 and 2.41) and then fill in boxes 2.10 to 2.12 on page 1. If any of the other conditions apply, fill in the Exercise column on page 2 (boxes 2.34 to 2.40) and then fill in boxes 2.7 to 2.9 on page 1.

## Unapproved share options

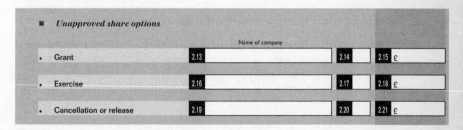

With unapproved schemes, income tax may be payable on both the grant and exercise of an option, or if it is given up in return for some benefit. However, there is no income tax to pay if the option is exercised by your legal representatives after your death, or if the option is not a long option.

**EXAMPLE**

In 1990 Edward Brough is granted an option which can be exercised at any time between 1 January 1995 and 1 January 2000. This counts as a long option, so he had to pay tax when it was granted. The market value of the shares in 1990 was £3. Edward has the option to buy 1,000 shares at £2. The market value of the shares over which he has the option is £3 x 1,000 = £3,000: he has the option to buy them at £2 x 1,000 = £2,000. The taxable amount is £3,000 – £2,000 = £1,000. As a higher-rate taxpayer, Edward paid £1,000 x 40 per cent = £400 tax on this.

In October 1996 Edward exercised his option. This cost him £2 x 1,000 = £2,000. Since the market price had risen to £3.50, the market value of the shares was £3.50 x 1,000 = £3,500. The taxable amount is £3,500 – £2,000 = £1,500, incurring tax at £1,500 x 40 per cent = £600. However, Edward can deduct the tax he has already paid, so he only actually has to pay £600 – £400 = £200.

A long option is one which can be exercised more than seven years after the date on which it was granted. You pay tax at the time it is granted on the market value of the shares at that time, less the price at which you can exercise the option, less anything you pay for the option. So, there will be no tax to pay if the option is to buy shares at the current market value. You may have further tax to pay when you finally exercise the option, but you can deduct any income tax you paid when the option was granted.

An option which must be exercised within seven years is not taxable at the time it is granted (except for some non-residents).

*How to work out the taxable amount*

Whatever type of share option scheme you have, and whether it is approved or unapproved, if the event (the grant, exercise or cancellation) is taxable, the taxable amount is worked out as in the box on the right. You enter the amounts in the right-hand column of page 1 headed Taxable and highlighted in purple.

### Free or cheap shares through an unapproved scheme

Employers have many reasons for offering cheap or free shares. These count as part of your payment from the job. The exact tax treatment depends on whether the shares count as your earnings (and so should be entered under Shares received from your employment in boxes 2.22 to 2.24), or whether

# TAX ON THE EXERCISE OF AN OPTION

Step 1: take the market value of the share at the date the option was exercised (which you should have entered in box 2.40) and multiply by the number of shares you actually bought (entered at box 2.36). This gives you the market value of all the shares you have bought.

Step 2: take the price at which you exercised the option (in box 2.37) and multiply by the number of shares you bought (at box 2.36). This is the actual price

Step 3: deduct the actual price (at Step 2) from the market value (at Step 1). If you paid anything for the option, you can deduct that too. The result is the taxable amount to enter on page 1 in box 2.3, 2.9, or 2.18 as appropriate.

## The grant of an option

This is taxable only for an unapproved share option which can be exercised more than seven years after it was granted. The method is the same as if you were exercising the option, except that you start with the market value at the time the option is granted. Fill in the 'Grant' column on page 2 of the column and carry the taxable amount to box 2.15 on page 1.

## The cancellation of an option

If you get anything in return for not exercising your option, the taxable amount is what you received, less anything you paid for your option. Fill in the 'Cancellation' column on page 2, and the boxes 2.19 to 2.21.

they are treated as a fringe benefit (and entered under Shares as benefits in boxes 2.25 to 2.27).

The distinction is fine, but significant: whereas with shares which count as earnings you are taxed on the difference between the market value of the shares and the price at which you acquired them, with shares which count as benefits you are taxed as if you received an interest-free loan from your employer (see p. 160). In some circumstances, this may mean no tax to pay.

You should enter under Shares as benefits:
- shares you are allowed to pay for in instalments (partly-paid shares)
- shares which you buy but where part of the purchase price is deferred, for example, when a particular profit target is met
- any other cheap or free shares which do not count as earnings.

All other free or cheap shares should go under Shares received from your employment (see below). Even after you have acquired the shares, you may be considered to receive further taxable benefits from them, for example, an increase in their value when a restriction is lifted. You should enter these under Post acquisition charges in boxes 2.28 to 2.30.

## Shares received from your employment

| Shares received from your employment | Name of company | | |
|---|---|---|---|
| | 2.22 | 2.23 | 2.24 £ |

You may get some benefit tax-free if the company for which you work decides to sell shares to the public and offers shares on special terms to its employees. You have to distinguish between:

- a discounted price offered to employees
- a priority allocation of the shares.

The discounted price is taxable: you pay tax on the difference between the price you pay and that paid by the general public. Enter the taxable amount under Shares received from your employment. However, the benefit of the priority allocation itself is tax-free and need not be entered unless:

- it is reserved for directors or higher-paid employees, or those who are entitled to it do not all get it on similar terms, and
- the shares reserved for employees in their priority allocation are more than a certain percentage of the overall shares on offer – normally, more than 10 per cent of the total shares on offer.

The calculation is very straightforward. Take the market value of the shares at the time you acquired them. Deduct anything you paid for them. The result is the taxable amount.

---

E XAMPLE

Linden works for Good Holdings, which has just been offered for sale to the public. Using the priority allocation for employees, Linden bought 500 £1 shares, at the discounted staff price of 80p. Linden is not taxed on the benefit of the priority allocation. However, the discounted price is taxable. The market value of the 500 shares was £1 x 500 = £500, but Linden only paid 80p x 500 = £400. She is taxed on £500 – £400 = £100.

---

## Shares as benefits

Anything entered under this category is treated as an interest-free loan. The loan is the difference between what you paid and the market value. The loan is taxable only if:

- you count as earning at a rate of £8,500 or more or are a director (see

| • Shares as benefit | 2.25 | | 2.26 | | 2.27 £ | |
|---|---|---|---|---|---|---|

p. 149 for how this is worked out)
- the total amount of all the cheap or interest-free loans from your employer outstanding in the tax year comes to more than £5,000 (see p. 160).

If tax is payable, it will be spread out over the whole life of the loan.

The taxable value of the loan is the theoretical interest you would have paid had you been charged interest at an official rate set down by the government.

*Post-acquisition charges*

| • Post acquisition charges | 2.28 | | 2.29 | | 2.30 £ | |
|---|---|---|---|---|---|---|

You are charged tax on any further benefit from cheap or free shares. This applies even if you have since left the company. There is no charge if the shares were on offer to the public generally (and you did not buy them through a special offer for employees). Otherwise, you may have further tax to pay on:
- an increase in value when rights or restrictions attached to the shares are changed – for example, if you gain the right to dividends
- an increase in value if the shares are in a subsidiary company. Tax is chargeable on the seventh anniversary of acquiring the shares, or when they are sold, if earlier
- other benefits reserved only for insiders (that is, which are not available to at least 90 per cent of all the shareholders), such as bonus or rights issues of shares, cash, vouchers or tokens.

You need to enter these in boxes 2.28 to 2.30 on page 1 of the Share schemes supplementary page, giving the details on page 2.

# SELF-EMPLOYMENT

## CHAPTER 16

*Q3*   Were you self-employed (but not in partnership)?    NO   YES     SELF-EMPLOYMENT YES

If any of your income for the tax year ending 5 April 1997 came from running your own business as a self-employed person, answer YES at question 3 on the basic tax return. You'll need to fill in the orange Self-employment supplementary pages.

Self-employed people are able to claim more income tax reliefs than employed people and they usually pay less in National Insurance, so you might need to prove to your tax office that you really are self-employed. In general, you'll count as self-employed provided you can answer yes to all of the following questions:

- do you control how your business is run? For example, do you decide what work you take on, where you do the work, what hours you keep?
- is your own money at risk in the business? For example, have you had to pay for your own premises, do you have to finance the lag between incurring costs and receiving payments?
- do you have to meet any losses as well as keeping any profits?
- do you provide the major equipment necessary for your work – for example computer and photocopier for office-based work or machinery for an engineering business? It's not enough that you provide your own small tools – many employees do this too
- are you free to employ other people to help you fulfil the contracts you take on? Do you pay your employees yourself?
- if a job doesn't come up to scratch, do you have to redo it or correct it in your own time and at your expense?

Usually, it will be obvious whether you are an employee or self-employed. But sometimes it's not so clear – for example, if you are newly in business doing work for just one client, perhaps working at a former employer's premises on a freelance basis. Beware if you work through an agency – for example as an agency carer or temporary secretary. Even if you choose whether or not to take on a particular job, you will almost certainly count as an employee rather than self-employed.

If you pay tax and National Insurance as if you are self-employed, but later either your tax office or the Contributions Agency decides you are really an employee, you could face a large bill for back taxes, so it is important to get your status straight right from the start. If you're in any doubt, you can ask your tax office or the Contributions Agency for a written decision about your employment status. If you don't agree with the decision, you can appeal.

## BUSINESS DETAILS

Name of business

3.1

Description of business

3.2

Address of business

3.3

• Tick this box if details in boxes 3.1 or 3.3 have changed since your last Tax Return    3.6

The first part of the supplement simply deals with basic details – the name and nature of your business and the address from which you trade.

### Your accounting year

Accounting period

Start

3.4    /    /

End

3.5    /    /

You also need to give the start and finish dates of the accounting period for which you are giving details. Normally, an accounting period is a year long, with the new accounting year starting immediately the previous year ends. But in the first and last year or two of your business, your accounting year might be longer or shorter (see p. 189).

## If you started in business on or after 6 April 1994

You will now be taxed on a current year basis. This means that your tax bill for the tax year ending 5 April 1997 will be based on the profits you made during the accounting period which ended during that tax year.

### Transitional rules for businesses started before 6 April 1994

If you had already been in business for a while on 6 April 1994, you switch to the current year basis only from the tax year ending 5 April 1998 onwards. Until the tax year ending 5 April 1996, you were taxed on the preceding year basis – that is your tax bill for that year was based on your profits for the accounting year ending in the previous tax year. To make the shift from one basis to another, the tax year ending 5 April 1997 is a transitional year when you are taxed on the average of your profits for the two accounting years ending in the tax years ending 5 April 1996 and 5 April 1997. In most cases, this means that you are taxed on only half the profits you made during those two accounting years.

---

### EXAMPLE

Frank Mills has been in business for ten years, running a take-away food shop. His accounting year runs from 1 August to the following 31 July. His profits for the last few years are as follows:

| Accounting year | Profits | Tax year in which taxed |
|---|---|---|
| 1.8.93-31.7.94 | £15,400 | Year ending 5 April 1996 |
| 1.8.94-31.7.95 | £17,800 | Year ending 5 April 1997 |
| 1.8.95-31.7.96 | £17,000 | Year ending 5 April 1997 |
| 1.8.96-31.7.97 | £17,200 | Year ending 5 April 1998 |

For the tax year ending 5 April 1997, Frank's taxable profits are worked out, taking the average of the two accounting years 1994-95 and 1995-96, as follows:

$$(£17,800 + £17,000) \times 365 \div (366 + 365) = £17,400$$

In the tax year ending 5 April 1998, his tax bill is based on profits for his accounting year to 31 July 1997. Out of that year, 248 days fall before 6 April 1997, so he has transitional overlap profits of:

$$248 \div 365 \times £17,200 = £11,687$$

---

If you did not send your tax office any accounts with your 1996 tax return, you should send in accounts for both these years with your 1997 return. This can be in the form of either two separate accounts, one for each year, or a single account covering a two-year period. If you are sending in a two-year account, the start date you enter in box 3.4 should be the beginning of the accounting year which ended in the tax year ending 5 April 1996 and the end date in box 3.5 should be the last day of the accounting period which ended in the tax year ending 5 April 1997. If you are sending in two separate one-year accounts, you'll need to ask for two Self-Employment supplements, filling in one for each set of accounts.

The transitional rules, in effect, mean that a whole accounting year's profits drop out of the tax assessment process. However, something of this sort would have happened anyway when you eventually closed your business. This is because, under the old tax system, when you opened for business, some profits were taxed twice or even three times. The record would have been set straight under the old closing year rules. Under the new closing year rules, you won't get full relief for this double or triple taxation. So that you don't lose out, the transitional rules identify part of your profits for the tax year ending 5 April 1998 as transitional overlap profits (see example opposite). These are the profits earned in the period from the start of your accounting year up to 5 April 1997. You will eventually get tax relief on these profits in the same way as for other overlap profits (see p. 193).

For more information see Help Sheets *IR230 Transitional Rules* and *IR222 Basis period for businesses starting after 6 April 1994.*

### Rules to stop you saving tax

Anyone who has been in business for some years has had an exceptional opportunity to save tax by making as much profit as possible during the two accounting years ending in 1995-96 and 1996-97, because of the transitional rules. Only half those profits are being taxed. The temptation is to shift as much income as possible into those years and allocate expenses to earlier or later years. There is also an advantage in boosting profits for 1997-98 in order maximise the transitional overlap profits. However, the government anticipated this and passed some stiff anti-avoidance laws designed to stop you saving tax by artificial means. The sorts of activities which might be regarded with suspicion include, for example:

- changing the intervals at which you normally buy in supplies
- altering the accounting treatment of long-term contracts
- bringing forward or deferring routine maintenance
- switching to a different way of calculating your business expenses
- changing the timing or way in which you invoice your customers
- altering your procedure for collecting and paying debts
- changing the date to which you make up your company accounts
- making a financial arrangement with a family member or trust fund, say, which results in profits or expenses being temporarily altered
- agreements to buy back supplies at some future date.

A change to your business or accounting practices or a transaction which, on the face of it, could be regarded as a tax-saving dodge will trigger a tax penalty, unless it passes one of the following tests:

- the motive test – it was made purely for commercial reasons
- the benefit test – the main benefit is not the tax advantage
- the too small to count test. If the increase in profit is less than a set amount or if the profits shifted from one year to another are less than a given percentage of the total profits for the year or if your turnover is less than a given amount, the change or transaction will be ignored. The Inland Revenue does not intend to announce the amounts at which the various limits have been set until just before tax returns are sent out in April – that is too late for you to exploit the rules.

> # TAX-SAVING IDEA
> Are you worried that some change which affects your profits might be interpreted as a measure to save tax during the transitional period? If so, tick box 3.8 on the tax return and work out your profits on the basis that the suspect amount is fully taxable.
>
> If applicable, attach a note explaining why you think the anti-avoidance rules should not apply. If the Inland Revenue agrees with you, your accounts will be re-adjusted and less tax demanded. If it disagrees, you'll have to pay the full tax due, but there will be no penalty because you have volunteered to pay tax on the profits.

# EXAMPLE

It turned out that Frank Mills (see p. 186) had boosted his profits in the transitional period by allowing an invoice for £1,000 from the previous year to be held over until the 1994-95 accounting year.

| Accounting year | Profits | Tax year in which taxed |
|---|---|---|
| 1.8.93-31.7.94 | £15,400 | Year ending 5 April 1996 |
| 1.8.94-31.7.95 | £17,800 | Year ending 5 April 1997 |
| 1.8.95-31.7.96 | £17,000 | Year ending 5 April 1997 |
| 1.8.96-31.7.97 | £17,200 | Year ending 5 April 1998 |

His tax office imposes a penalty by adding the following amount to his taxable profits for the tax year ending 5 April 1997:

$$50 \text{ per cent} \times £1,000 \times 1^1/_4 = £625$$

This means that instead of being taxed on just £500 of the shifted profits as Frank had intended, he in fact pays tax on £1,125. If he had voluntarily applied the anti-avoidance rules, he would have paid tax on the full £1,000 but would have escaped any penalty.

Tick box 3.8, if you have adjusted your accounts so that profits, which would otherwise have been shifted to produce a tax-saving, have been brought back into your calculation of taxable profit. If you fail to adjust your profits for any dubious changes or transactions, not only will the profits be taxed, but you'll also have to pay a penalty. In the case of profits being taxed in the tax year ending 5 April 1997, half the shifted profits will be taxed through the normal transitional rules. The half on which you had thought you would save tax is multiplied by $1^1/_4$ and then taxed.

## STARTING OR CLOSING A BUSINESS

If you start a business, special rules say how you will be taxed in the first two or three years.

### First tax year during which you're in business

You are taxed on your profits from the date your business started to the end of the tax year (that is the following 5 April). This is worked out by waiting until your first set of accounts is drawn up and then allocating a proportion of those profits to the period up to the end of the tax year. This is usually done on the basis of days. For example, suppose you started in business on 1 January 1997 and your first accounting period runs to 31 January 1998. Out of that first 396-day accounting period, 95 days fall between 1 January to 5 April, so your profits for the tax year ending 5 April 1997 are deemed to be $^{95}/_{396}$ths of the profit for the whole accounting period.

### Second tax year during which you're in business
In most cases, the end of an accounting period (not necessarily your first) will fall sometime during this second tax year. Provided you have been trading for at least 12 months, your tax bill will be based on profits for the 12 months up to that date. In the example above, there is an end accounting date falling within the tax year ending 5 April 1998. This is 31 January and, at that date, the business has been running for more than a year. Therefore, tax will be based on profits for the 12 months up to 31 January 1998 – that is $^{365}/_{396}$ths of the profits for the whole accounting period.

If there is an accounting date within the tax year, but you have been trading for less than 12 months, your tax is based on the first 12 months of trading, with a proportion of the profits from your next accounting period being used to make up the full 12 months. For example, suppose you started in business on 1 March 1996 and draw up your accounts to 30 June 1996 and then to each subsequent 30 June. Tax in your second year, the year ending 5 April 1997, would be based on the whole of the profits for the period 1 March to 30 June 1996 (122 days) and and $^{243}/_{365}$ths of the profits for the accounting year from 1 July 1996 to 30 June 1997.

If there is no accounting date at all during your second tax year, tax is based on the profits for the tax year itself – that is from 6 April to 5 April. For example, if you started in business on 1 March 1996 but did not draw up your first accounts until 30 June 1997, an accounting period of 482 days, you would be taxed on $^{365}/_{482}$nds of the profits for that whole period.

### Third tax year during which you're in business
If an accounting period at least 12 months after you started up finished during your second tax year, from the third year onwards, you are simply taxed on the profits for the accounting year ending during the tax year – that is normal current year basis.

Where the first accounting period to end at least 12 months after start-up comes to a close in your third tax year of trading, you are taxed on profits for the 12 months to the end of that period. From the fourth year onwards, you are taxed on the normal current year basis.

### Overlap profits
As you can see, the opening year rules described above mean that some profits may be taxed twice. For example, for the business which started on 1

January 1997, the profits for the first two years were as follows:

| Tax year | Profits on which your tax bill is based |
|---|---|
| Year ending 5 April 1997 | $^{95}/_{396}$ths **x** profit for accounting period from 1 January 1997 to 31 January 1998 |
| Year ending 5 April 1998 | $^{365}/_{396}$ths **x** profit for the period from 1 January 1997 to 31 January 1998 |

This means that (95 + 365) – 396 = 64 days' worth of profit have been taxed twice. This is called 'overlap profit' and the period over which it arose is called the overlap period'. One of the principles of the current year basis tax system is that, over the lifetime of your business, all your profits should be taxed, but only taxed once. Therefore, you are given overlap relief to compensate you for having paid tax on some profits twice in your opening year. But there is a snag: overlap relief is usually given only when you finally close the business down (see p. 192) and inflation in the meantime will reduce its value. You can get some of the relief earlier, if you change your accounting date to one which falls later in the tax year.

### Fiscal accounting
You can avoid all the problems of opening year rules and overlap relief, if you opt for fiscal accounting. This means using the tax year as your accounting year. By Inland Revenue concession, this includes having an accounting date of 31 March, rather than exactly on the tax year end of 5 April. For example, you might have started in business on 1 September 1996, drawing up your first accounts on 31 March 1997 and on each 31 March thereafter. Your tax for the tax year ending 5 April 1997 will be based on your profits from 1 September 1996 to 31 March 1997. Your tax for the next year will be based on profits for 1 April 1997 to 31 March 1998 and so on.

For further information see Help Sheet *IR221 New business starting after 6 April 1994.*

> ## TAX-SAVING IDEAS
>
> Fiscal accounting makes accounting for tax very simple, especially in your opening years, but it has drawbacks too: you don't have long to make up your accounts and there's only a short delay between making your profits and paying tax on them (see p. 15).
>
> If you don't choose fiscal accounting, try to keep your profits as low as possible during the first year or two, so that your overlap profit is small.

## EXAMPLE

Jim Newall started working as a freelance computer consultant on 1 July 1994 and drew up his first accounts on 30 April 1995. 30 April is his normal accounting year end. His profit and tax position for the first few years of business was as follows:

| Accounting period | Profit for the period |
|---|---|
| 1 July 1994 – 30 April 1995 | £ 4,000 |
| 1 May 1995 – 30 April 1996 | £ 8,500 |
| 1 May 1996 – 30 April 1997 | £18,500 |

| Tax year | Tax basis | Profits on which tax based |
|---|---|---|
| 1994-95 | Profits for tax year | 279 ÷ 304 x £4,000 = £3,671 |
| 1995-96 | First 12 months of trading | £4,000 + (61 ÷ 366 x £8,500) = £5,416 |
| 1996-97 | Profits for 12 months to 30 April 1996 | £8,500 |
| 1997-98 | Profits for accounting year ending on 30 April 1997 | £18,500 |

The profit for the period 1 July 1994 to 5 April 1995 is taxed twice, as is profit for the 61 days from 1 May to 30 June 1995. This gives Jim an overlap profit of £3,671 + (61 ÷ 366 x £8,500) = £3,671 + £1,416 = £5,087.

## Closing your business

### Closing before 6 April 1997 if you were already in business on 6 April 1994

If your business had been running for several years and closed down before 6 April 1997, you will be taxed completely under the old rules. Current year basis and transitional provisions will not apply to you. Under the old rules, your tax inspector chooses whether to tax you in the last two full years of your business on either a preceding year basis or on the basis of your actual profits for those tax years. For the tax year in which you close down, you are taxed on your actual profits. The tax inspector will choose the basis which produces the largest tax bill. If you closed down in the tax year ending 5 April 1997, the choice is as summarised in the table opposite:

Working out your actual profits for a tax year means taking a proportion of the profits for each accounting period which falls partly within the tax year.

| Tax year | Profits on which your tax bill is based | |
| | Option 1 | Option 2 |
| --- | --- | --- |
| Year ending 5 April 1996 | Profits for accounting year ending in 1994-95 | Actual profits for 1997-98 |
| Year ending 5 April 1997 | Profits for accounting year ending in 1995-96 | Actual profits for 1996-97 |
| Year ending 5 April 1998 | Actual profits for 1997-98 | Actual profits for 1997-98 |

If your accounting year ends on 30 September, 178 days of one accounting year and 187 days of the next accounting year fall within the tax year (ignoring leap years). Therefore, your actual profits for, say, the tax year ending 5 April 1997 would be 178 ÷ 365 x profits for the accounting year ending on 30 September 1996 and 187 ÷ 365 x profits for the accounting year ending on 30 September 1997. There is an example on the next page.

### Closing in other circumstances

If your business started on or after 6 April 1994, it is taxed completely under the new rules. And, in general, if you were an established business on that date but you close down on or after 6 April 1997, you will be taxed according to the new rules, but there is an exception. If you close down in the tax year ending 5 April 1998, your tax office can decide that you will be taxed under the old rules if that would mean a higher tax bill.

## TAX-SAVING IDEA

If you have transitional overlap profits, closing down under the new rules rather than the old rules can work to your advantage because you will then get tax relief on the overlap profits.

Delaying closure from 1996-97 to 1997-98 does not help you to benefit from the new rules, because your tax inspector can decide to apply the old rules if this means you pay higher tax. But, if you can put off closure until 1998-99, the new rules will apply.

The new rules are straightforward. In the tax years up to the one before closure, you are taxed on the normal current year basis. For the tax year in which you close down, you're taxed on profits from your last accounting date up to the date on which you close down less any overlap profits which you have been carrying forward (see p. 187 and 190). The position for a business taxed under the new rules and closing down in the tax year ending 5 April 1998 is summarised overleaf.

## Closing down under the new rules

| Tax year ending | Profits on which your tax bill is based |
|---|---|
| 5 April 1996 | Profits for accounting year ending in 1995-96 |
| 5 April 1997 | Profits for accounting year ending in 1996-97 |
| 5 April 1998 | Profits from day after end of accounting year ending 1996-97 up to date of closure less overlap profits |

For more information see Help Sheet *IR228 Cessation*.

---

# EXAMPLE

Jessie Parker had been running a small art gallery for 20 years but decided to close down in August 1996 so that she could spend more time travelling. Her normal accounting year ran from 1 May to the following 30 April and her profits and tax position for the last three years were as follows:

| Accounting period | Profits |
|---|---|
| 1 May 1993 to 30 April 1994 | £10,500 |
| 1 May 1994 to 30 April 1995 | £12,000 |
| 1 May 1995 to 30 April 1996 | £ 5,500 |
| 1 May 1996 to 31 August 1996 | £   900 |

| Tax year | Profits on which tax is based | |
|---|---|---|
| | *Option 1* | *Option 2* |
| 1994-95 | Preceding year basis = £10,500 | Actual profit for tax year = (25 ÷ 365 x £10,500) + (340 ÷ 365 x £12,000) = £11,897 |
| 1995-96 | Preceding year basis = £12,000 | Actual profit for tax year = (25 ÷ 365 x £12,000) + (341 ÷ 366 x £5,500) = £5,946 |
| 1996-97 | Actual profit for tax year = (25 ÷ 366 x £5,500) + £900 = £1,276 | Actual profit for tax year = (25 ÷ 366 x £5,500) + £900 = £1,276 |

Under option 1, in total, £23,776 of profit is taxed over the last three years of Jessie's business.
Under option 2, only £19,119 is taxed. The tax office will, therefore, stick with option 1.

# INCOME

## If your turnover is less than £15,000 a year

Complete boxes 3.11 to 3.13. You can get guidance on what expenses are allowable by reading pp. 197 to 204.

You do not need to give full details of your accounts. This does not mean that you can get away with preparing proper accounts – you must have these ready, in case your tax inspector asks to see them, together with all the background paperwork (see p. 12).

Do not complete page 2 of the Self employed supplement, but go straight to page 3. Turn to p. 204 for guidance on filling in boxes 3.58 and beyond.

## If your turnover is £15,000 a year or more

Sales/business
income (turnover)

3.16 £

You should complete the details asked for on page 2 of the Self-employed supplementary pages. You don't need to attach a copy of your accounts. If the headings do not tally with the headings you use in your own accounts, don't be tempted to leave any out. Instead, use your judgement to allocate them to boxes on page 2, but make sure that whatever method you adopt this year is followed consistently in future years.

If you're covered by the transitional rules and you have drawn up a single two-year account, give details about income and expenses for the whole two-year period. If you have drawn up two separate one-year accounts, you need to complete two Self-employment supplements.

If you produce a balance sheet, there is space for the entries on page 4 of the supplement. Enter the amounts in boxes 3.94 to 3.110. If you don't have a balance sheet, leave these boxes blank.

## Value added tax (VAT)

If your turnover is £48,000 a year or more from 26 November 1996 (£47,000 from 28 November 1995 until then), you must register for VAT. Below that threshold, you can choose whether or not to register. Registration means that you must normally charge your customers VAT on the goods and services that you sell, but you can usually reclaim VAT on the things that you buy to sell, or use, in your business. You must regularly hand over to the Customs & Excise department of the government the net amount of VAT you have collected (or claim a refund if what you are claiming comes to more than the VAT paid by your customers). This VAT does not form part of your profits and needs to be stripped out before your tax bill is calculated. For this reason, the tax office needs to know whether the figures you report in your tax return include VAT or have already had the VAT element stripped out.

If you are registered for VAT, you will need to enter the net amount of VAT paid over to Customs & Excise as other expenses in box 3.50 or the net refund you received over the year as other income/profits in box 3.17. However, the amount you enter in either of these boxes should be only the VAT paid or refunded on non-capital items. If you have bought any capital equipment (see p. 204) during the year, subtract the amount of VAT you paid on the equipment from the VAT figure you enter in box 3.50 or box 3.17.

If you are not registered for VAT, you do not charge your customers VAT and the VAT you pay to your suppliers counts as a legitimate business expense. Your figures should include the VAT you have been charged.

### Gross profits
Your taxable profits are the income of your business less all the allowable expenses – that is the expenses you are allowed to deduct under the tax rules.

The starting point for working out your taxable profits is your gross profits.

| | Any disallowable expenses included in boxes 3.33 to 3.50 | Total expenses |
|---|---|---|
| • Cost of sales | 3.17 £ | 3.33 £ |
| • Construction industry subcontractor costs | 3.18 £ | 3.34 £ |
| • Other direct costs | 3.19 £ | 3.35 £ |
| | | box 3.16 *less* (box 3.33 + box 3.34 + box 3.35) |
| | Gross profit/(loss) | 3.36 £ |
| | Other income/profits | 3.37 £ |

If you are in the business of selling something, this will be the income you get from sales less the cost of buying in the items you sell. If you sell your services, this will be the income you receive.

In your accounts, direct costs (for example, marketing, sales discounts) might include a figure for depreciation of equipment or machinery used in producing your goods. This is not an allowable expense (see Capital allowances on p. 204) and should be entered in box 3.19.

Other income or profits (box 3.37) includes things like income from renting out premises, interest on bank and building society accounts, discounts you get, and so on. If you receive any Enterprise Allowance, put this in box 3.88, not here.

## EXPENSES

| | | |
|---|---|---|
| • Employee costs | 3.20 £ | 3.38 £ |
| • Premises costs | 3.21 £ | 3.39 £ |
| • Repairs | 3.22 £ | 3.40 |
| • Depreciation and loss/ (profit) on sale | 3.31 £ | 3.49 £ |
| • Other expenses | 3.32 £ | 3.50 £ |
| | Put the total of boxes 3.17 to 3.32 in box 3.53 below | total boxes 3.38 3.50 |
| | Total expenses | 3.51 £ |

You don't need to complete page 2 of the self-employment supplement if your turnover is less than £15,000. If it is £15,000 or more you need to allocate your costs and expenses to boxes 3.17 to 3.50. In the boxes in the right hand column you should enter total expenses under each heading. In the left-hand column you should enter the amount of any expenses not allowed but which have been included in the right-hand column.

You total the amounts in boxes 3.17 to 3.32 and enter the total in box 3.53 below.

Deducting an expense from your business income has the effect of giving you tax relief at your top rate(s) of tax, so it is important to claim all the expenses you can. According to tax law, you get tax relief on an expense only if it is incurred wholly and exclusively for business. Strictly speaking, this means you can't get relief at all on expenditure which is partly for your private benefit. In practice, the Inland Revenue does allow you to claim a proportion of some costs where something – for example, your car or home – is used partly for business. However, your tax office may baulk at some expenses which arise because of a joint business and private purpose – for example, combining a trip abroad to see a client with a holiday.

---

# EXAMPLE

Hannah Brown has converted the garage at her home into an office which is used exclusively for her computer software business. She can claim part of her household expenses as allowable expenses for business purposes and, because she uses part of the home exclusively for business, she can also claim part of her mortgage interest. She makes the following calculation:

| | |
|---|---|
| add up total household expenses | £1,800 |
| add up the number of rooms in the house, ignoring separate toilets, halls and landings (unless large enough to be used as rooms) | 8 rooms |
| divide the expenses by the number of rooms to give a cost per room figure | £1,800 ÷ 8 = £225 per room |
| multiply the cost per room by the number of rooms used for business (or by the relevant fraction of a room, if a room is used only partly for business) | 1 x £225 = £225 |

She also claims one-eighth of her mortgage interest as a business expense. This comes to $^1/_8$ x £3,600 = £450. However, Hannah may become liable for business rates and capital gains tax on the garage when she sells her home.

---

It is hard to lay down hard and fast rules which apply to all businesses. Different types of businesses can claim different expenses and to a different extent. It is up to you to show that any claim is justified within the context of your own line of work.

You can claim expenses you incur before you open for business if they would have been allowable anyway. If your business started on or after 6 April 1995, treat them as expenditure incurred on the first day of business.

Expenses which you incur after you close down can be set against any late income which comes into the closed business. However, if there is

**TAX-SAVING IDEAS**
Claim all the allowable expenses you can. If you're not sure whether an expense is allowable, deduct it from your taxable profits but ask your tax office to confirm whether this is correct.

If you work from home, beware of allowing any part of it to be used exclusively for business. Although you might be able to claim more relief against income tax, you could become liable for business rates and, when you eventually come to sell the home, there could be capital gains tax to pay on part of the home (see p. 59).

no income, tax relief on the expenditure is usually lost. From 29 November 1994 onwards, with a few particular types of income, for up to seven years you can get tax relief by setting the expenses against any other income or gains you have (in box 15.11 of the basic tax return, see p. 125).

## Employee costs

| Employee costs | 3.20 £ | 3.38 £ |

### Normally allowed
Salaries, bonuses overtime, commissions etc paid to your employee, together with the on-costs, such as National Insurance contributions, pension and insurance benefits. The costs of hiring locums to stand in for you or fees paid to people to whom you subcontract work. Training. Council tax paid on behalf of employees if a genuine part of the pay package, taxed as normal through PAYE. Include the cost of employing your wife, husband or other family member in the business, provided their pay is reasonable for the work done. Costs of entertaining staff – for example, a Christmas party.

### Not allowed
Your own wages, National Insurance, income tax, pension costs (though you can get personal tax relief for these), your drawings from the business. Wages

to employees which remain unpaid nine months after the accounting date (although they can be deducted in the accounting period in which they are eventually paid). Payments to family members if excessive for the work done – be especially careful employing young children which might, in any case, be illegal.

## Premises costs

### *Normally allowed*
If you work from dedicated business premises, include any rent, business rates, water rates, cost of lighting, heating, power, insurance, cleaning, security, and so on. If you work from home, you can claim a proportion of your home related expenses – for example, heating, lighting, power, cleaning, maintenance. If part of the home is used exclusively for business, part of your mortgage interest. Also part of your council tax, though the tax rules are not clear on whether it's enough just to work from home or whether part of it must be dedicated exclusively to business use. The proportion you claim must relate to your business use of the home – for example, based on the number of rooms used or floor area. You should explain the basis used in the space for additional information at the end of the supplement.

### *Not allowed*
Cost of buying premises (see Capital allowances on p. 204), costs relating to any part of the premises not used for business.

## Repairs

### *Normally allowed*
General maintenance and repairs to your business premises and machinery, cost of replacing small tools.

### *Not allowed*
Costs of alterations and improvements (see Capital allowances on p. 204), costs relating to any part of the premises not used for business, general reserve for repairs.

# General administrative expenses

General administrative expenses    3.23 £    3.41 £

*Normally allowed*
Office expenses, such as postage, telephone, stationery, printing, subscriptions to trade journals, professional fees, cost of computer software (unless bought at the same time as hardware), accountancy and audit fees and regular expenses not included elsewhere.

*Not allowed*
Personal expenses, premiums for your own insurances, payments to political parties, most donations and fees to clubs, charities and churches. Any non-business part of a cost.

## Motor expenses

Motor expenses    3.24 £    3.42 £

*Normally allowed*
Costs of running a vehicle used in your business – for example, insurance, servicing, repairs, road tax, breakdown insurance, parking charges, fuel, hiring or leasing charges. A proportion of those costs if you also use the vehicle privately.

*Not allowed*
Travel between your home and business premises. Cost of buying a vehicle (see Capital allowances on p. 204). Parking fines, other fines.

## Travel and subsistence

Travel and subsistence    3.25 £    3.43 £

*Normally allowed*
Rail, air and taxi fares, hotel accommodation.

*Not allowed*
Cost of lunches.

## Advertising, promotion and entertainment

| • Advertising, promotion and entertainment | 3.26 £ | 3.44 £ |
|---|---|---|

### Normally allowed
Advertising, mail-shots, free samples, gifts up to £10 a year to clients provided they promote your firm or its products or services and are not food or drink.

### Not allowed
Entertaining clients, business associates etc (only entertaining staff is allowed), gifts except those specifically allowed (see above).

## Legal and professional costs

| • Legal and professional costs | 3.27 £ | 3.45 £ |
|---|---|---|

### Normally allowed
Fees charges by accountants, auditors, solicitors, surveyors, stocktakers and so on, professional indemnity fees.

### Not allowed
Legal costs of buying premises, equipment etc (treated as part of their cost – see Capital allowances on p. 204), legal expenses on setting up your business, cost of settling tax disputes, fines etc as a result of acting illegally.

## Bad debts

| • Bad debts | 3.28 £ | 3.46 £ |
|---|---|---|

### Normally allowed
Items you have sold or amounts you have invoiced but for which you no longer expect to be paid. A proportion of a bad debt given up under a voluntary arrangement. If in a later tax year you are paid, include the amount recovered in box 3.37 (other income/profits).

### Not allowed
General pool for bad debts.

# Interest

| | 3.29 £ | 3.47 £ |
| --- | --- | --- |
| Interest | | |

## Normally allowed
Interest and arrangement fees for a business loan or overdraft.

## Not allowed
The part of loan payments which represents capital repayments.

# Other finance charges

| | 3.30 £ | 3.48 £ |
| --- | --- | --- |
| Other finance charges | | |

## Normally allowed
Charges on your business current account, credit card interest and fees, the interest element of hire purchase charges, leasing payments.

## Not allowed
The part of any payment which represents capital repayment.

# Depreciation and loss/(profit) on sale

| | 3.31 £ | 3.49 £ |
| --- | --- | --- |
| Depreciation and loss/ (profit) on sale | | |

## Not allowed
None of these costs are allowable – instead you claim capital allowances (see p. 204). The figure you enter at 3.49 should exactly match the amount you put in box 3.31.

# Other expenses

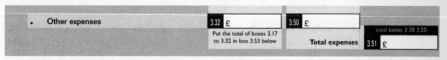

| | 3.32 £ | 3.50 £ | total boxes 3.38 3.50 |
| --- | --- | --- | --- |
| Other expenses | Put the total of boxes 3.17 to 3.32 in box 3.53 below | Total expenses | 3.51 £ |

## Normally allowed
Any expenses which you haven't found a place for in boxes 3.33 to 3.49. For example, any insurance premiums not included elsewhere, contributions (up to 30 March 2000) to Business Links, trade and part or all of professional

subscriptions which secure some benefit for your business or to societies which have an arrangement with the Inland Revenue.

## Not allowed

The non-business element of any expenses included in box 3.50. This includes, for example, ordinary clothing even if you bought it specially for business and would not normally wear it otherwise, buying a patent (see Capital allowances below), cost of computer hardware and any software bought at the same time (see Capital allowances below).

## Tax adjustments to net profit or loss

All the expenses which are not allowable are added together and the total entered in box 3.53. In the next box, you must enter the profit attributable to any goods which you took for personal use. These are added to your profits. You can reduce the profits for certain items, such as any overlap relief (see pp. 187 and 191) which you are claiming.

For more information see Help Sheet *IR225 Turnover, allowable expenses and taxable profit or loss.*

## CAPITAL ALLOWANCES

When you buy capital items for your business – that is things which will be in use for many years – you are not allowed to set the full cost against your business income in the year you buy the item. In your ordinary business accounts, you'll instead deduct an amount for depreciation each year which varies from business to business. Your figures for depreciation are not allowed as an expense. Instead you deduct capital allowances calculated

| | Capital allowances | Balancing charge |
|---|---|---|
| • Motor cars (separate calculations must be made for each motor car costing more than £12,000 and for cars used partly for private motoring.) | 3.58 £ | 3.59 £ |
| • Other business plant and machinery | 3.60 £ | 3.61 £ |
| • Agricultural or Industrial Buildings Allowance (A separate calculation must be made for each block of expenditure) | 3.62 £ | 3.63 £ |
| • Other capital allowances claimed (Separate calculations must be made) | 3.64 £ | 3.65 £ |
| | total of column above | total of column above |
| Total capital allowances/balancing charges | 3.66 £ | 3.67 £ |

according to standard rules which apply to everyone.

To be eligible for capital allowances, the item you have bought must generally be wholly and exclusively for business use. But, as with allowable expenses (see p. 198), in some cases, you can claim a proportion of the allowance if the item is used partly for business and, in part, privately.

## How much you can claim
The basic capital allowance is called a writing-down allowance and it is available for plant and machinery (which covers most of your ordinary business equipment), cars and vans, patents and know-how. In general, capital allowances are not given for what you spend on buying business premises (for example a shop or office), but industrial and agricultural buildings and hotels with ten or more bedrooms are exceptions. Expenditure which qualifies for allowances is lumped together in one or more pools and you can claim a certain proportion of the pool at the end of each tax year as a writing down allowance.

TAX-SAVING IDEAS
Do not claim more capital allowances than needed to reduce your taxable profits the level of your personal allowances.

Earmarking a capital item as a short-life asset means you can get full tax relief on the cost of the item in just five years.

If you buy software at the same time as you buy a computer, it will count as a capital item for which you claim capital allowances. Buy the software separately and it does not count as capital, so you can get immediate tax relief by claiming its cost as an allowable expense.

The maximum you can claim is:
- 25 per cent a year for machinery plant, vans, patents, know-how
- 25 per cent a year for cars but, for any car costing over £12,000, there is

also a cash limit of £3,000 a year
- 4 per cent a year for industrial and agricultural buildings and qualifying hotels, and an initial allowance in the first year of 100 per cent for industrial buildings in an enterprise zone. If part of this is not claimed, you can claim 25 per cent a year of the remaining cost.

You can claim less than the maximum. It would be worth restricting your claim if your taxable profits or income were so low that some of the maximum allowance would be wasted. The allowance is not lost. The effect is to carry forward a higher value of assets in your pool of expenditure. This increases the value of the maximum writing-down allowances you can claim in future years. For example, suppose your pool of expenditure is valued at £10,000. If you claimed the full writing-down allowance of 25 per cent, the allowance would be £2,500 and the value of the pool carried forward would be £7,500, so next year you could claim up to 25 per cent x £7,500 = £1,875. If instead, you claimed only a 10 per cent allowance in the first year, the pool carried forward would be £9,000 and the maximum allowance in the second year would be 25 per cent x £9,000 = £2,250.

Various categories of capital expenditure have to be allocated to their own separate pools. These are:
- any car costing more than £12,000 must be hived off to its own pool and the writing-down allowance is limited to the smaller of 25 per cent or £3,000 in each year. Cars costing £12,000 or less are in another pool. Vans, lorries and so on do not count as cars
- industrial and agricultural buildings
- an asset used partly for private use must have its own pool and you can claim only a proportion of the allowance reflecting the proportion of business use
- short-life assets. Capital equipment (other than cars) which you expect to have a useful life of no more than five years can be put in a separate pool. The advantage of doing this is that you get tax relief on the full cost of the item more rapidly than if it were in the general pool of expenditure (see Buying and selling capital items below).

You do not get capital allowances on items you lease rather than buy. Instead the leasing charge counts as an allowable expense (see pp. 201 and 203). If you buy something on hire purchase, the capital element of the charges can qualify for capital allowances but the interest element is treated as an allowable expense (see p. 203).

## Buying and selling capital items
When you buy an item of capital, its cost is added to the appropriate pool of

expenditure. This increases the year-end value of the pool on which the writing-down allowance is worked out.

When you first start in business, you might take into the business capital equipment you already own – for example a desk, shelving, a computer. Although no money changes hands, you are treated as having sold the item to your business and you can claim capital allowances in the normal way. Value each item at its second-hand market value given its age, state of repair and so on.

When you sell a capital item, the amount you get for it (up to its original cost) is deducted from the expenditure pool. Occasionally, this may be more than the total value of the pool, in which case, the excess (called a balancing charge) is added to your profits or (taxable income) for the year, increasing your tax bill. These are entered in boxes 3.59, 3.61, 3.63 and 3.65.

If you sell the item for less than its written-down value – at the extreme, you might scrap it for nothing – the shortfall remains in your pool of expenditure and continues to be written down. So you could be claiming allowances on an item for many years after you have sold it. Only when you finally close

---

# EXAMPLE

Joe Morris has been running a dairy since 1978. He makes up his accounts to 31 December each year. For him, the tax year ending 5 April 1997 is a transitional year based on a two-year accounting period running from 1 January 1995 to 31 December 1996. During that period, he made the following purchases and sales of capital items:

| Date | Capital item | Purchase/sale price |
|---|---|---|
| 10 March 1995 | New van bought | £17,000 |
| 5 May 1995 | Old van sold (cost £12,000 when new) | £ 5,000 |
| 2 February 1996 | Secondhand cream separator bought | £38,000 |

On 31 December 1994, after claiming writing-down allowances, Joe's general pool of capital expenditure stood at £158,000. To this he now adds the new expenditure during the two years of £17,000 + £38,000 = £55,000 and deducts the £5,000 from selling the old van. This gives him a general pool at 31 December 1996 of £208,000. He can claim a maximum writing-down allowance of 25 per cent x £208,000 = £52,000 to set against his taxable income for the year. In fact, he has only enough profits and other income to use up £37,000 of the allowance. His capital pool at 1 January 1997 becomes £208,000 – £37,000 = £171,000.

down the business can you claim a balancing allowance for any remaining value of the pool. This is where short-life assets come into their own.

If you scrap a short-life asset within five years, you can claim tax relief on the difference between what you get (if anything) for the asset and its written-down value. The relief is given in the tax year in which you scrap it – you don't have to wait until the business closes down. If, having declared an asset as short life, you actually go on using it beyond five years, it is transferred into your general pool of expenditure and treated like any other capital item.

If you are registered for VAT, the amount you put in your expenditure pools should not include VAT. If you are not registered for VAT, you claim capital allowances on the cost including VAT.

## Claiming capital allowances
If you started in business on or after 6 April 1994, capital allowances are given as a deduction in working out your taxable profits for the year. From the tax year ending 5 April 1998 onwards, all other businesses will claim capital allowances in this way too. Tick the NO box and complete the right-hand column of page 3.

| Adjustments to arrive at taxable profit or loss | | |
| --- | --- | --- |
| **Income tax basis period begins**<br>*See notes on page SE2* | 3.68 / / | and ends 3.69 / / |

| Did your business start before 6 April 1994? - *Important: tick either the 'Yes' box or the 'No' box below* | |
| --- | --- |
| Yes | No |

If you were already in business on 6 April 1994 and the tax year ending 5 April 1997 is a transitional year, your capital allowances are worked out separately from your profits and deducted from your taxable income for the tax year. (This is because deducting the allowance from your profits which are then averaged would mean that you could lose some allowance.) The period on which your tax bill is based is the two years running from the start of the accounting year ending in 1996-97 to the end of the accounting year ending in 1997-98.

Take the value of your pools at the start of that two-year period, adjust for any purchases or sales of assets, and base your written-down allowances on the value of the pools at the end of the two-year period. If you have drawn up two separate one-year accounts and, as a result, you are completing two sets of tax return supplements, leave the capital allowance section for one set blank. Just make one calculation for capital allowances, based on the whole two-year period. Tick the YES box and complete the left-hand column of page 3.

## LOSSES

If you make a loss, you can get tax relief on it. There are several ways in which tax relief can be given.

### Other income or gains for this year

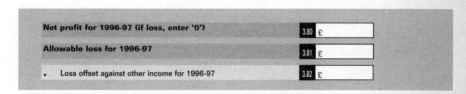

| Net profit for 1996-97 (if loss, enter '0') | 3.80 £ |
| Allowable loss for 1996-97 | 3.81 £ |
| • Loss offset against other income for 1996-97 | 3.82 £ |

Complete box 3.82 to set the loss against other income you have during 1996-97 – for example from working for an employer or from your savings. If this does not use up all the loss, you can ask for the rest to be set against any taxable capital gains for tax year ending 5 April 1997. If any loss still remains, you can ask for relief on it to be given in some other way. The time limit for making this choice with respect to losses made in the accounting period being declared for tax year ending 5 April 1997 is 31 January 1999.

### Other income and gains for the previous year

| • Loss to carry back | 3.83 £ |

Complete box 3.83 to carry back the loss to the tax year ending 5 April 1996 to set against your income from any source for that year. If this does not use up the full loss, you can ask for the rest to be set against any capital gains for the tax year ending 5 April 1996. If some loss still remains, you can ask for relief on it to be given in some other way. The time limit for making this choice is 31 January 1999.

#### Other income for earlier years

You can ask for a loss made in the first four years of the business to be carried back and set against income (but not gains) for the previous three tax years – that is, those ending 5 April 1994, 1995 and 1996. The loss is set against the earliest year first. The time limit for this choice is also 31 January 1999.

## EXAMPLE

Sonja Frisk has been an antiques dealer for the last ten years. Normally, she makes a reasonable living but, in 1995, the sale of some expensive artifacts fell through and Sonja made a loss for the tax year. Her tax position in the transitional year is as follows:

| Accounting year | Profit/(loss) |
|---|---|
| 1 May 1994 to 30 April 1995 | (£15,000) |
| 1 May 1995 to 30 April 1996 | £26,000 |

Transitional period: 1 May 1994 to 30 April 1996

Profits for the transitional period = (£15,000) + £26,000) x 365 ÷ (366 + 365)
= £5,500

Repeat calculation setting losses to zero = (£0 + £26,000) x 365 ÷ (366+365)
= £13,000

Loss which has already been relieved through the averaging process = £13,000 – £5,500 = £7,500

Loss which remains to be relieved in another way = £15,000 – £7,500 = £7,500

Sonja decides to set the remaining loss against other income which she had in the tax year ending 5 April 1997 from a part-time job lecturing in art history at the local university.

## Future profits

- **Loss to carry forward**
  **(that is allowable loss not claimed in any other way)** | 3.84 | £ |

Complete box 3.84 to carry the loss forward to set against your future profits from the same business. It will be set against the next profits you make with any remaining loss being rolled forward to set against the next profits and so on until the loss is completely used up. You have until 31 January 2003 to make this choice.

## Closing down

If your business closed down during the tax year ending 5 April 1997, you have a further option. A loss you made during your last 12 months of trading can be set against your profits for the three previous tax years – that is you can go back to the tax year ending 5 April 1994. The time limit for this choice is also 31 January 2003.

## Special rules if you were in business on 6 April 1994

If this applies to you, the tax year ending 5 April 1997 is your transitional year when tax is based on your results for two accounting periods. Applying the normal averaging rules (see p. 186) would mean you did not get full relief for your losses, so special rules apply:

- if you make a loss in both of the accounting years on which tax bills for the tax year ending 5 April 1997 are based, you get full relief for both losses – they are not averaged
- if you make a loss in one of the usual accounting years, find your average profits for the tax year ending 5 April 1997 (see p. 186).

TAX-SAVING IDEAS
If you are a basic rate taxpayer, carrying back losses to the tax year ending 5 April 1997 when the basic rate of income tax was 25 per cent will give you higher relief than setting losses against income or gains for the tax year ending 5 April 1997 when the basic tax rate is 24 per cent.

You do not have to make up your mind about how to get tax relief for your losses straightaway. You have a while to wait and see how your business affairs turn out. But the time limits for each option are strict, so don't delay so long that you miss them.

Then you repeat the calculation, substituting 0 for any losses. Subtracting the first answer from the second tells you what proportion of the loss has already been relieved through the averaging process. Deduct that amount from the actual loss made. What remains is the unrelieved loss which you can claim relief on through any of the methods already outlined.

For more information see Help Sheets *IR227 Losses*, *IR228 Cessation* and *IR230 Transitional Rules for 1996/97*.

## NATIONAL INSURANCE

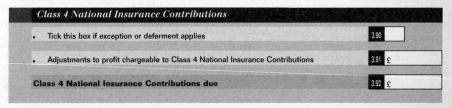

| Class 4 National Insurance Contributions | | |
|---|---|---|
| • Tick this box if exception or deferment applies | 3.90 | |
| • Adjustments to profit chargeable to Class 4 National Insurance Contributions | 3.91 | £ |
| Class 4 National Insurance Contributions due | 3.92 | £ |

Running your own business, you will usually have to pay National Insurance contributions (NICs) both for yourself and for any people you employ. You will have to pay:

- Class 2 contributions at a flat-rate of £6.05 a week in the tax year ending 5 April 1997 and £6.15 a week in the tax year ending 5 April 1998. If your profits are less than £3,430 in the tax year ending 5 April 1997 or £3,480 in the tax year ending 5 April 1998, you can opt not to pay. However, Class 2 NICs help you to qualify for certain state benefits, such as unemployment and incapacity benefit, so it might be better to carry on paying even if your profits are low. Class 2 contributions are paid direct to the Contributions Agency, usually by direct debit.

You may also have to pay Class 4 contributions. Unlike other types of National Insurance, Class 4 contributions do not entitle you to any state benefits – they are simply a tax on profits which is collected along with your income tax. In the tax year ending 5 April 1997, Class 4 NICs were payable at a rate of 6 per cent on profits over £6,860 up to £23,660. For the tax year ending 5 April 1998, the rate is unchanged, but the lower and upper profit limits are increased to £7,010 and £24,180, respectively. There are no Class 4 NICs to pay on profits below the lower limit and above the upper limit. If your profits are less than the lower limit, you do not pay any Class 4 NICs at all.

A few groups of people are excluded from having to pay Class 4 NICs. They include people over state pension age (currently 60 for women and 65 for men), people under age 16 if they have been granted an exemption by the Contributions Agency (ask for leaflet CA03 at your local Contributions Agency) and people who are not resident in the UK.

## EXAMPLE

Jim Newall has profits for income tax purposes of £8,500 for the tax year ending 5 April 1997. These are also the profits on which his Class 4 NICs are based. They are calculated as follows:

| | |
|---|---|
| Profit for Class 4 NICs purposes | = £8,500 |
| Less lower profit limit | = £6,860 |
| Amount chargeable (£8,500 - £6,860) | = £1,640 |
| Class 4 NICs at 6 per cent x £1,640 | = £98.40 |

In some circumstances, you might have earnings which count as profits of your business and on which Class 4 NICs might be payable, but which have already had Class 1 NICs deducted – for example, where part of your income derives from fees for teaching in a school. There is a cap on the overall amount you have to pay in National Insurance, so it may be that Class 4 NICs won't be payable after all. However, you usually don't know whether this is the case until after part of the Class 4 NICs would have become payable, so you can ask to have payment deferred until the position is known.

If you are either excluded from paying Class 4 NICs or your Contributions Agency has agreed that you can defer paying them, you should tick the box at 3.90 and put 0 in boxes 3.91 and 3.92. In all other cases, leave box 3.90 blank. If you have any losses which have been carried forward to set against your profits for the tax year ending 5 April 1997, enter them in box 3.91 because they can also reduce your profits used for working out Class 4 NICs. If you have paid interest for business purposes but it has not been deducted in working out your profits for income tax purposes, you might be able to deduct it for Class 4 NICs purposes. If this applies enter the amount of interest also in box 3.91.

Box 3.92 invites you to write down the amount you owe in Class 4 NICs. You don't have to do this sum yourself. Provided you send in your tax return by the 30 September deadline, you can leave the box blank and let your tax office do the sums. If you prefer to work out your Class 4 NICs yourself, there is a calculator included in the notes accompanying your Self-employment supplement. (The calculator is not suitable if you run more than one business, see Help Sheet *IR220 More than one business*.)

Class 2 and Class 4 contributions are not allowable expenses and can't be deducted when working out your profits for income tax purposes. If you have employees, you have to pay employer's Class 1 NICs for them if they earn more than the lower earnings limit (£61 a week for the tax year ending 5 April 1997 and £62 a week for the tax year ending 5 April 1998). In this case, the amount you pay counts as an allowable expense (see p. 199).

# PARTNERSHIP

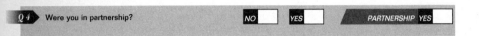

## CHAPTER 17

Q4 ▶ Were you in partnership?   NO ☐   YES ☐      PARTNERSHIP YES ☐

If you are in business with one or more partners, you should answer YES to Q4 in the basic tax return and fill in the turquoise Partnership supplement. There are two versions:

- short version. Use this if the partnership income is from trading profits or interest from bank or building society accounts which has already been taxed at the savings rate
- full version. If your partnership earnings are more complex because you have untaxed investment income, foreign income or income from land and property, for example, you'll need to complete this longer supplement.

The partnership should already have provided you with a Partnership Statement summarising your share of the profits, losses and other income. If you received the full statement, you need the full version of the supplementary pages; if you received a short statement, you need only the short supplement. If you haven't received a Partnership supplement or you need the full version, phone the Inland Revenue Orderline (see p. 75). This guide cannot take you in detail through completing the pages, so here we give guidelines on how partnerships are taxed.

You and your fellow partners are jointly responsible for the partnership tax return. The Partnership Statement is a section in the Partnership supplementary pages. Profits are calculated as if the partnership were a single person using largely the same rules as for a self-employed person (see Chapter 16). How profits are shared between partners depends on your partnership agreement. For the tax year ending 5 April 1997, how your share is taxed depends on when the partnership started.

# Becoming a partner

If the partnership was formed on or after 6 April 1994, each partner is treated as if they were carrying on a business on their own. This means that when you join a partnership, the normal opening rules described on pp. 189 to 192 apply. The period on which your tax is based is likely to be different from the accounting year for the partnership. The dates you put in boxes 4.5 and 4.6 should reflect how the opening year rules apply to you. The opening year rules may result in overlap profits (see p. 191) on which you can eventually claim tax relief either when you leave the partnership or, possibly, if the partnership accounting date is changed. Once the special opening year rules have worked through, you are taxed on the normal current year basis. The period on which your tax is based will then be the same as the accounting year of the partnership, so you put the start date of the partnership year in box 4.5 and the end-year in box 4.6.

From the tax year ending 5 April 1998 onwards, the rules described above apply to all partnerships whenever they were first set up. However, if, during the tax year ending 5 April 1997, you joined a partnership that had already been going for some time on 6 April 1994 (an old partnership), different rules apply (see below). If you were a partner in an old partnership during the tax year ending 5 April 1997, leave boxes 4.5 and 4.6 blank.

## Ceasing to be a partner

If you leave a partnership which was formed on or after 6 April 1994, you are treated as if you are closing down your own business. The normal closing rules apply (see p. 192), including the claiming of tax relief on any overlap profits carried forward from the opening years. From the tax year ending 5 April 1998 onwards, these rules will apply to all partners whenever the partnership was set up. But, if during the tax year ending 5 April 1997, you left a partnership that had already been running some time on 6 April 1994, different rules apply (see overleaf).

## New partnership for old

Partnerships set up before 6 April 1994 are in the tax year ending 5 April

1997 still covered by the old system for taxing partnerships. This worked in a different way.

## How partnerships are taxed in the tax year ending 5 April 1997

|  | New partnerships (set up on or after 6 April 1994) | Old partnerships (set up before 6 April 1994) |
|---|---|---|
| *Which profits are taxed?* | Current-year basis applies – that is tax is normally based on profits for the accounting year ending in the tax year ending 5 April 1997 (see p. 186) | Transitional rules apply – that is tax is normally based on the average of profits for the two accounting years ending in the tax years ending 5 April 1996 and 5 April 1997 (see p. 186) |
| *How are the profits shared between the partners for tax purposes?* | According to the way the profits for 1996-97 are actually shared out | According to the agreement for sharing profits in 1996-97, even if the profits were actually shared in a different way in the previous year |
| *How is tax worked out?* | For each partner individually | Each partner's bill is added together to find the tax bill for the partnership |
| *Whose tax bill is it?* | Each partner treated as if they run their own separate business | The partnership as a whole |
| *Whose tax are you responsible for?* | Just tax on your own share of the partnership profits | The whole partnership tax bill – if a partner doesn't pay up, the others have to pick up the tab |

If a new partner joins or an existing partner leaves an old partnership, the partnership is initially treated as having come to an end. The closing rules under the old tax system apply (see p. 192). The new line up of partners are treated as having started a new partnership which, being set up after 5 April 1994, is immediately covered by the new tax system as outlined above.

> ## TAX-SAVING IDEA
> If you belong to a partnership set up before 6 April 1994 and, in the two years up to 5 April 1997, you have had a change of partners, consider whether making a continuation election would save you tax. Whether or not it would depends on the pattern of profits and losses for your particular firm, so ask your accountant for advice.

However, the partners can make a continuation election. In that case, the partnership is not deemed to have closed down and reopened. Instead, it's treated as having continued without any interruption – that is, the transitional rules continue to apply to the tax year ending 5 April 1997 with transitional overlap relief to be carried forward (see p. 187) and the preceding-year basis applying to earlier years. The partners have two years from the date of the change in the partners to make this election. Once the election has been made, it can't be reversed.

From the tax year ending 5 April 1998 onwards, all partnerships are taxed under the new system. Under the new rules, changing partners does not affect the partnership itself for tax purposes. The continuation election ceases to be relevant and will no longer be available.

# LAND AND PROPERTY

 Did you receive any rent or other income from land and property in the UK?    NO    YES   LAND & PROPERTY YES

If you ticked the YES box against question 5 on page 2 of the tax return, you will need the red Land and property supplementary pages. Many people renting out the odd room in their home may have to do little more than tick one box on the first page. But there is also space for details of more substantial lettings businesses and for income from holiday homes.

If you take in lodgers in your home, providing meals and other services, this may amount to a form of business and details should be entered on the Self-employment supplementary pages (see Chapter 16). Income from property abroad is entered on the Foreign pages (see Chapter 19).

## The documents you need
You will need details of the rents you have received and any receipts or invoices for expenses. With furnished holiday lettings, you will also need records of the periods the properties were available for letting out.

If any of these properties is jointly owned, remember to enter only your share from these documents when filling in the tax return.

## THE RENT A ROOM SCHEME

Are you claiming Rent a Room relief for gross rents of £3,250 or less? (or £1,625 if the claim is shared)    NO    YES   If 'Yes', and this is your only income from UK property, you have finished these pages

The rent a room scheme means that a modest rent from letting out furnished accommodation in your home is tax-free. The scheme applies whether you own your home or are yourself a tenant. But it must be your only or main home (see p. 50) and in the UK.

For the tax year ending 5 April 1997, you could have rent before deduction of any expenses of up to £3,250 tax-free – or £1,625 if you were jointly letting the rooms with your husband, wife or partner. If this applies to you, tick the YES box. If this is your only letting income, there is nothing more to enter – you don't even need to bother claiming expenses.

For the tax year beginning 6 April 1997, the amount of rent before deduction of any expenses you can have tax-free rises to £4,250 – or £2,125 if you are jointly letting the rooms.

If you are married or share your home, the income is treated as belonging to the person who actually rents out the room.

### Rent just above the rent a room scheme level?

If your gross letting income – that is rent before deduction of expenses – is higher than the maximum for the rent a room scheme, you have two options:

- you can choose to pay tax on the amount by which the gross rent exceeds the maximum (that is, £3,250 for the tax year ending 5 April 1997)
- you pay tax on the letting income in the same way as any other property income – you pay tax on the net income (the rent after deduction of various expenses and allowances).

If your gross letting income is just over the rent a room maximum, you will almost certainly be better off with the first option. For example, if your gross letting income was £3,500 in the tax year ending 5 April 1997, you could choose to pay tax on £3,500 – £3,250 = £250.

> ### TAX-SAVING IDEA
> If your income from renting out rooms in your home is expected to be somewhat over £4,250 in the tax year which began on 6 April 1997, think about claiming rent a room relief. It will pay you to claim if the amount by which the gross rent exceeds £4,250 is less than your net income after deductions.

> ### EXAMPLE
> Natalie Lean lets out three rooms in her house, bringing in a total of £150 a week in rent. This means her gross rental income for the tax year beginning 6 April 1997 will be £7,800, on which she could claim expenses and alowances of £2,350.
>
> If the rental income is taxed as normal property income, she will pay tax on £7,800 – £2,350 = £5,450. But if she claims the rent a room relief, she will pay tax on the excess of the gross rental income of £7,800 over £4,250 – that is, on £3,550.
>
> Rent a room relief means Natalie will pay tax on £900 less income.

If you want to choose the first option, tick the NO Box and put the rent before deduction of expenses in box 5.20 on the second page. Don't enter any expenses in boxes 5.24 to 5.30, or claim any capital allowances in box 5.36 (or wear and tear allowance in box 5.37). Enter the tax-free amount you are claiming under the rent a room scheme in box 5.35 (either £3,250 or £1,625) and don't enter any claim for losses.

If you want to choose the second option (that is the income taxed as other property income), tick the NO box and follow the instructions for Other property income see p. 225).

## FURNISHED HOLIDAY LETTINGS

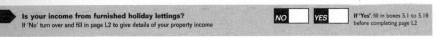

**Is your income from furnished holiday lettings?**
If 'No' turn over and fill in page L2 to give details of your property income

NO   YES

If 'Yes', fill in boxes 5.1 to 5.18 before completing page L2

If you have no income from short-term furnished lettings, tick the NO box and turn over to page L2 and to p. 225.

### Tax benefits of furnished holiday lettings

Income from furnished holiday lettings is treated differently from other forms of property income, to reflect the fact that it is a form of business for many owners. This offer several tax benefits:

- you can claim capital allowances on plant and equipment (see p. 204)
- losses can be set off against other income for the same or next tax year and losses in the first four years of the business can be deducted from other income from the previous three years (see p. 209)
- it counts as relevant earnings for tax relief on pension contributions (p. 108)
- you can claim the special business reliefs for capital gains tax (p. 274).

To count as furnished holiday lettings, the property must meet all the following conditions for the year ending 5 April 1997:

- be available for letting to the general public on a commercial basis (that is, with a view to a profit) for at least 140 days
- actually let for at least 70 of those days
- not let for more than 31 days in a row to the same person in a period of at least seven months.

If you first started letting the property during the tax year which ended 5 April 1997, these conditions must be satisfied for the first 12 months of letting. If you finished letting the property during that tax year, the conditions must have been met for the 12 months ending with the last letting. If you

## WHAT INCOME IS TAXED?

Income from land and property is now taxed in the same way – irrespective of its type. All income from land and property in the UK is added together. You pay tax on the total after deduction of allowable expenses, interest paid on loans to buy or improve the properties and losses from letting out property in the past. You can also claim allowances for some equipment you buy.

The tax you pay in a tax year is based on the property income and expenditure during that year. If you make up accounts for your property business for the year ending on 31 March or 5 April, the figures in your accounts will be the ones to use in filling in your tax return.

But if your accounting year runs to different dates, you will have to use two sets of accounts to work out what your property income and expenditure was for the tax year (see p. 185).

own more than one furnished holiday letting, you can average out the letting and occupancy periods between all of them.

### Income

| *Furnished holiday lettings* | | |
| --- | --- | --- |
| • Income from furnished holiday lettings | 5.1 | £ |

Enter the total income from all your furnished holiday lettings in the UK for the tax year ending 5 April 1997 – before any deductions such as agents' commission. Include any income for services provided to tenants, such as cleaning, linen hire and use of additional facilities. Also include any money received from insurance policies for loss of rent.

### Expenses

| ■ *Expenses* (furnished holiday lettings only) |
| --- |

If your total property income is less than £15,000, enter your total expenses in box 5.8 (you don't need to give details of individual expenses). If your total property income is over this limit, you need to list expenses separately:

## Rent, rates, insurance, ground rents etc

| | | |
|---|---|---|
| • Rent, rates, insurance, ground rents etc | 5.2 | £ |

Enter the amount of rent, business rates, council tax, ground rent and insurance premiums on the furnished holiday lettings (including for insurance against loss of rents) in box 5.2.

## Repairs, maintenance and renewals

| | | |
|---|---|---|
| • Repairs, maintenance and renewals | 5.3 | £ |

Claim in box 5.3. Any work that prevents the property deteriorating is a repair – such as painting and damp treatment. You can't claim here the cost of improvements, additions or extensive alterations, though part of the cost might be allowable if it makes repairs unnecessary.

If you aren't claiming capital allowances for the furniture, fixtures and fittings, you can claim a renewals deduction for the cost of replacing them. If the new items are better, you cannot claim the full cost. And if any of the old items are sold, the proceeds should be deducted from the amount you claim.

## Finance charges

| | | |
|---|---|---|
| • Finance charges, including interest | 5.4 | £ |

Enter the cost of any loan you took out to buy the property – including interest paid and charges for setting up the loan.

## Legal and professional costs

| | | |
|---|---|---|
| • Legal and professional costs | 5.5 | £ |

You can claim legal and professional expenses for a letting of less than a year, including fees for agents, surveyors and accountants and commission. You can also claim such costs when renewing the lease for a longer letting provided it is for less than 50 years. But you cannot claim expenses incurred in the first letting of a property for more than a year. Nor can you claim costs of registering title to land, getting planning permission or in connection with the payment of a premium on renewal of a lease.

## Cost of services provided

Cost of services provided, including wages    5.6 £

You can claim as an expense the cost of services such as gardening, cleaning and porterage. You can't claim the cost of your own time, but you can claim the cost of paying other people such as one of the family.

## Other expenses

Other expenses    5.7 £     total of boxes 5.2 to 5.7   5.8 £

Other expenses include advertising costs, stationery, telephone calls, rent collection and travel to the property when solely for the letting.

Add together the figures in boxes 5.2 to 5.7 and enter the total in box 5.8.

## Net profit

**Net profit** (put figures in brackets if a loss)    box 5.1 less box 5.8   5.9 £

Net profit is income less expenses. Deduct the figure in box 5.8 from that in box 5.1 and put the amount in box 5.9, in brackets if it is a loss.

## Tax adjustments

■ *Tax adjustments*

• Private use    5.10 £

### Private use

If a furnished holiday letting is partly used for your own enjoyment or that of friends staying rent-free, this counts as private use. Part of the costs must be apportioned to this private use, and cannot be claimed as an expense. If it was available for letting for nine months of the year and used by you for the rest of the time, you can claim only three-quarters of the costs of owning it. (You can still claim the full costs of letting it out as expenses.)

There are two ways to make an adjustment to reflect private use. You can enter the appropriate share of the costs in boxes 5.2 to 5.7. Or, better, you enter the costs in full in these boxes and enter in box 5.10 a figure for private use which is deducted from the total.

## Capital allowances and balancing charges

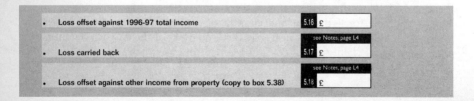

| | | box 5.10 + box 5.11 |
|---|---|---|
| • Balancing charges | 5.11 £ | 5.12 £ |
| • Capital allowances | 5.13 £ | |

You can claim capital allowances for the cost of buying furniture, machinery such as a lawnmower or equipment such as a water pump. If you get rid of an item you have claimed capital allowances on, a balancing charge may be added to your profits to reflect its second-hand value. There's more on p. 204 about capital allowances and balancing charges. You might also find it useful to get Help Sheet *IR250 Capital allowances and balancing charges in a rental business* from the Orderline.

Enter the amount of any capital allowances you are claiming for the tax year ending 5 April 1997 in box 5.13 and the amount of any balancing charge in box 5.11. Add the figures in boxes 5.10 and 5.11 together and enter the total in box 5.12. Total boxes 5.9 and 5.12 and subtract the amount in box 5.13.

| | boxes 5.9 + 5.12 less box 5.13 |
|---|---|
| **Profit for the period** (copy to box 5.19). If loss enter '0' and put the loss in box 5.15 | 5.14 £ |
| **Loss for the period** (If '0' in box 5.14) | boxes 5.9 + 5.12 less box 5.13 |
| | 5.15 £ |

If the answer is a negative number, you have made a tax loss on your furnished holiday lettings. Enter 0 in box 5.14 and put the amount of the loss in box 5.15. If you have made a profit, enter it in box 5.14.

## Losses

| | | |
|---|---|---|
| • Loss offset against 1996-97 total income | 5.16 £ | |
| | | see Notes, page L4 |
| • Loss carried back | 5.17 £ | |
| | | see Notes, page L4 |
| • Loss offset against other income from property (copy to box 5.38) | 5.18 £ | |

Any loss in box 5.15 can be used to reduce the amount of tax you pay on other income or capital gains in the tax year ending 5 April 1997 or earlier tax years:

- other income for the tax year ending 5 April 1997 (enter the amount you wish to claim in box 5.16)
- capital gains for the same tax year – include the amount you wish to claim in the total you enter in box 8.5 of the Capital gains supplementary pages (see p. 254)
- income and gains for earlier tax years – enter the amount you wish to claim in box 5.17.

If you haven't used all the loss in box 5.15, you can set what remains off against other property income for the tax year ending 5 April 1997. Enter what is left in box 5.18 and copy it into box 5.38 on page L2 of the Land and property supplementary pages.

## OTHER PROPERTY INCOME

Income

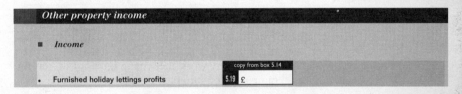

Copy the figure for profits on furnished holiday lettings from box 5.14 to box 5.19.

*Rents and other income from land and property*

Enter in box 5.20 the total income from all your lettings in the UK except furnished holiday lettings for the tax year ending 5 April 1997 – before any deductions such as agents' commission. Include the following:

- rent you will receive after 5 April 1997 which is payment in arrears for the tax year ending 5 April 1997 (equally, leave out any rent received on or before 5 April 1997 which is payment in advance for rent for periods after 5 April 1997)
- any income for services provided to tenants, such as cleaning, gardening

or porterage
- any money received from insurance policies for loss of rent
- ground rent and feu duties
- grants from local authorities for repairs (you can claim the cost of repairs as an expense)
- payments for using your land – for example, to shoot or graze.

If any tax has been deducted from the income before you get it, enter the total in box 5.21. The figure you enter in box 5.20 should be the before-tax amounts – so should include the amount in box 5.21.

If you own and let the property jointly with someone else, enter only your share of the income in box 5.21, and your share of the expenses lower down. If you only know your share of the profit after expenses, enter this in box 5.20 or any loss in box 5.29.

## Chargeable premiums

If you receive a premium from a tenant in return for granting a lease, you will have to pay income tax on part of it if the lease lasts less than 50 years (and capital gains tax on the rest). Any work the tenant agrees to do for you on being granted a lease counts as a premium.

If you are paid the premium in instalments, the total premium is still taxable in the year the lease is granted. But if paying in one go would cause you hardship, you can ask your tax inspector to allow you to pay by yearly instalments. The maximum number of instalments is eight (or the number of years you are getting the premium over, if less).

The proportion on which you will have to pay income tax is calculated as follows:

$$\frac{51 - \text{number of years of the lease}}{50}$$

So if the lease is a 20-year one, the proportion of the premium which is taxable is:

$$\frac{51 - 20}{50} = \frac{31}{50}$$

Enter the amount of the premium which is taxable in box 5.22. Add the figures in boxes 5.19, 5.20 and 5.22 together and put it in box 5.23.

# Expenses

| | | |
|---|---|---|
| ■ *Expenses* (do not include figures you have already put in boxes 5.2 to 5.7 on page L1) | | |
| • Rent, rates, insurance, ground rents etc | 5.24 £ | |
| • Repairs, maintenance and renewals | 5.25 £ | |
| • Finance charges, including interest | 5.26 £ | |
| • Legal and professional costs | 5.27 £ | |
| • Cost of services provided, including wages | 5.28 £ | total boxes 5.24 to 5.29 |
| • Other expenses | 5.29 £ | 5.30 £ |

If your total property income for the tax year ending 5 April 1997 is less than £15,000, go straight to box 5.30 and enter your total expenses in it. If your total property income is over this limit, you need to list the expenses incurred in the tax year ending 5 April 1997 separately.

The details of what expenses you can claim in boxes 5.24 to 5.29 are given under Furnished holiday lettings on p. 221. Note that with furnished property, you can claim a renewals deduction here for the cost of replacing furniture, fixtures and fittings, but not if you are already claiming a wear and tear allowance on the property (see below).

Don't include any expenses you have already claimed in boxes 5.2 to 5.7.

Add together the figures in boxes 5.24 to 5.29 and enter the total in box 5.30.

| | box 5.23 less box 5.30 |
|---|---|
| **Net profit (loss)** | 5.31 £ |

Subtract the figure in box 5.30 from that in box 5.23 to find the net profit or loss on the letting. Enter the figure in box 5.31, in brackets if it is a loss.

## Tax adjustments

| | | |
|---|---|---|
| ■ *Tax adjustments* | | |
| • Private use | 5.32 £ | box 5.32 + box 5.33 |
| • Balancing charges | 5.33 £ | 5.34 £ |

## EXAMPLE

Miriam Patel has divided most of her house into furnished rooms which she lets out, providing cleaning. The total yearly income is £9,640 but she can deduct these expenses:

- a proportion of the outgoings on the house (council tax, water rates, gas, electricity and insurance) which add up to £2,400 a year. Miriam is letting out three-quarters of the house and claim this proportion
- the cost of cleaning (cleaner's wages plus materials) – £1,300 a year
- an allowance for wear and tear of the furniture and furnishings – Miriam claims the actual cost of replacement (£300 for this year).

Thus Miriam's tax bill would be calculated as follows:

| | | |
|---|---|---|
| Total rent received | | £9,640 |
| Less expenses | | |
| Three-quarters of the outgoings of £2,400 a year | £1,800 | |
| Cost of cleaning | £1,300 | |
| Cost of replacing furniture and furnishings | £300 | |
| Total allowable expenses | | £3,400 |
| Taxable rental income | | £6,240 |

If Miriam does the cleaning, no allowance can be made for her time. But if she pays someone else to do the work (her mum, say), she can claim this cost as an allowable expense.

In box 5.32 (see previous page) you need to enter a figure for private use (if any) and this is explained under Furnished holiday lettings (see p. 223).

Any balancing charges (see p. 224) should be put in box 5.33. And now you should total the amounts in boxes 5.32 and 5.33 and put the sum in box 5.34.

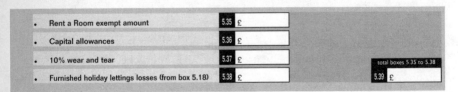

Enter any tax-free amount you are claiming under the rent a room scheme (see p. 218) in box 5.35. Otherwise leave it empty.

If you want to claim capital allowances (see p. 224), enter the amount in box

5.36. You can't claim capital allowances if you let a furnished home (other than as furnished holiday lettings). You can instead claim a renewals deduction for the cost of replacing such items (see box 5.25 above). Or you can claim a wear and tear allowance in box 5.37 of 10 per cent of the rent less service charges and local taxes. Once you have chosen a method, you can't switch. And if you have been using a different method of allowing for wear and tear agreed with your tax inspector before 6 April 1976, you can carry on using it.

You should already have filled in box 5.38 if you wish to set off a loss on furnished holiday lettings against other property income (see box 5.18).

In box 5.39 enter the total of boxes 5.35, 5.36, 5.37 and 5.38.

| | | |
|---|---|---|
| Adjusted profit (if loss enter'0' here and put the loss in box 5.41) | | boxes 5.31 + 5.34 less box 5.39 **5.40** £ |
| Adjusted loss (if '0' in box 5.40) | boxes 5.31 + 5.34 less box 5.39 **5.41** £ | |
| • Loss brought forward from previous year | | **5.42** £ |
| **Profit for year** | | box 5.40 less box 5.42 **5.43** £ |

Add the figures in boxes 5.31 and 5.34 together and subtract the figure in box 5.39. If the answer is a negative number, you have made a tax loss on your property interests. Enter 0 in box 5.40 and put the amount of the loss in box 5.41. There are several ways that a tax loss on property income can be used to reduce your tax bill (see boxes 5.44 to 5.46, below).

If you have made a profit, enter it in box 5.40. You can reduce this – and the amount of tax you pay on your property income – if you made a loss on property income from the tax year ending 5 April 1996. Enter the total loss from that year in box 5.42, and subtract it from the figure in box 5.40.

If the answer is a negative number, enter 0 in box 5.43 and put the balance in box 5.43. If the answer is more than zero, you have made a taxable profit on your property income for the tax year ending 5 April 1997.

## Losses

| | | |
|---|---|---|
| • Loss offset against total income for 1996-97 | 5.44 | £ |
| • Loss to carry forward to following year | 5.45 | £ |
| • Pooled expenses from 'one estate election' | 5.46 | £ |

You can deduct a property income loss from other forms of income for the tax year ending 5 April 1997. However, you can set off some of the loss in box 5.41 against other income only if you have claimed capital allowances in box 5.36. Even then, the maximum loss you can set off in this way is the amount of capital allowances minus any balancing charge – box 5.36 minus box 5.33.

If this is what you want to do, enter the amount you wish to deduct in this way in box 5.44. Alternatively, a loss which reflects an excess of capital allowances over balancing charges can be carried over to next year and set against your income for the tax year ending 5 April 1998. If this is what you would like to do, make a note of the figure to enter in the 1998 tax return.

Finally, any other unused losses can be carried over to deduct from future profits from property – enter these in box 5.45. If the figure in box 5.43 is 0 you will have already entered the right figure in box 5.45. If the figure in box 5.40 is 0, you find the figure to enter in box 5.45 by adding together the figures in boxes 5.41 and 5.42 and subtracting the figure in box 5.44.

Ignore box 5.46 unless you own an agricultural estate. If you think it might apply to you, ask for Help Sheet *IR251 Agricultural estates and land managed as one estate* to see what you should enter.

| | |
|---|---|
| Tick box 5.47 if these pages include details of property let jointly | 5.47 |

Tick box 5.47 if you own and let property jointly with someone else – and give the name and address of the person who keeps the records in the space for 'Additional information' on page 8 of the basic tax return (see Chapter 13).

# FOREIGN

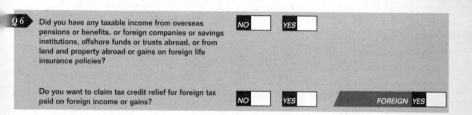

## CHAPTER 19

**Q6** Did you have any taxable income from overseas pensions or benefits, or foreign companies or savings institutions, offshore funds or trusts abroad, or from land and property abroad or gains on foreign life insurance policies?

NO ☐   YES ☐

Do you want to claim tax credit relief for foreign tax paid on foreign income or gains?

NO ☐   YES ☐   FOREIGN YES ☐

If you ticked either YES boxes at Q6 on page 2 of the basic tax return, you will need the olive supplementary pages called Foreign. These have space to give details about your foreign savings, pensions and benefits, property income and other investment income from abroad. Earnings from work abroad should be entered in the Employment, Self-Employment or Partnership pages of the tax return as appropriate. Similarly, details of capital gains on overseas transactions should be entered in that supplement.

This chapter tells you how to fill in the Foreign pages, and about the expenses and allowances you can claim. But the tax treatment of people who live abroad is beyond the scope of this guide. If this applies to you, seek professional advice from your bank or accountant.

## How foreign income is taxed
Income from abroad is taxable in the UK, even if you have already paid foreign tax on it. You can deduct any foreign tax paid from the income before working out your UK tax bill – so you pay UK tax only on what you get after paying foreign tax.

But in most cases, you can instead claim a deduction from your UK tax bill to reflect the foreign tax paid, known as tax credit relief. This is likely to mean paying less in UK tax than if you simply deduct the foreign tax from the gross income before working out the tax bill.

However, working out the amount of tax credit relief can be complicated. You can work it out for yourself, but this guide assumes you are leaving the calculations to your tax inspector. If you feel up to the calculations, you can use the guidance notes sent out by the Inland Revenue to calculate your tax credit relief and thus your UK tax bill on such income.

## What income is taxed

The instructions below are for people who are domiciled in the UK and ordinarily resident here. Their foreign income is taxed on an arising basis – when they get it or it is credited to them, not when it is brought back to the UK. You should enter the amounts you got in sterling, using the exchange rate at the time the income arose.

---

### EXAMPLE

Bill Livingstone made £2,500 after expenses last year letting out his villa in Freedonia. He paid the equivalent of £400 tax on this to the Freedonian tax authorities.

In calculating his UK tax, he could have simply deducted the £400 of Freedonian tax from the £2,500 and paid tax on £2,100. Since he paid tax on the income at the basic rate of 24 per cent for the tax year which ended on 5 April 1997, the tax bill would have been £504.

But he claimed tax credit relief, so the full £2,500 was taxable at 24 per cent – £600 in tax. But he could then deduct the £400 of Freedonian tax, making his UK tax bill just £200.

---

For the tax year ending 5 April 1997, there are special rules for calculating your tax bill on foreign income. This is because the taxation of these types of income is changing with the introduction of self-assessment and there are transitional arrangements to bridge the two systems. This means the figures you enter on the tax return depend on when you first got income from this type of investment:

- if you first got the income on or after 6 April 1994, the figures to enter are those for the tax year ending 5 April 1997
- if you first got the income before 6 April 1994, the figures to be entered are half the total for the two tax years between 6 April 1995 and 5 April 1997

There are different rules for people who are not domiciled or ordinarily resident in the UK. The latter is likely to apply to you only if you don't visit the UK regularly and either have no home here or spend less than 91 days on average here in a tax year.

### Tax-free foreign income

The following types of foreign income are tax-free in the UK:

- pensions paid by Germany or Austria to the victims of Nazi persecution and to pensioners who have fled from persecution
- the extra foreign pension paid to you if you have been retired because you were disabled by injury on duty or by a work-related illness
- any part of a pension from overseas that reduces the amount of tax-free UK war widows' and dependants' pensions
- social security benefits which are similar to UK benefits that are tax-free – child benefit, maternity allowance, guardian's allowance, child's special allowance, widow's payments, sickness benefits, incapacity benefit, attendance allowance, mobility allowance, disability living allowance and severe disablement allowance.

A tenth of overseas pensions funded by an overseas employer or pension fund is tax-free in the UK.

## Income stuck in a foreign country
In some cases, you will be unable to remit foreign income to the UK because it arises in a country which has exchange controls or is short of foreign exchange. If income is unremittable, give details of the amount of income and foreign tax in the currency of the country concerned – you will be unable to give other information asked for.

## The documents you need
You will need to gather together dividend vouchers for overseas shares, bank statements for overseas bank accounts, pension advice notes, foreign property bills – as well as details of any foreign tax paid.

# FOREIGN INCOME
## Savings and pensions

### Foreign savings

Fill in columns A to E, and tick the box in column E to claim tax credit relief.

| Country<br>tick box if income<br>is unremittable ▼<br>A | Amount<br>before tax<br>B | UK tax<br>C | Foreign tax<br>D | Amount chargeable<br>tick box to claim<br>tax credit relief ▼<br>E |
|---|---|---|---|---|
| **Interest, dividends and other savings income** - see Notes, page F4 | £ | £ | £ | £ |
| | £ | £ | £ | £ |
| | £ | £ | £ | £ |

On page F1 give details of foreign interest, dividends and other savings income. On page F2 give details of foreign pensions, social security benefits and property income. Enter each source of income on a separate line. If any of these types of income is from joint holdings, enter your share only.

The following types of such income should not be included:

- foreign income dividends received from a UK company – you should enter details of these on page 3 of the basic tax return
- distributions by a foreign company in the form of its shares (but enter details of any cash alternative you took instead)
- stock dividends from foreign companies
- bonus shares from a scrip issue by a foreign company
- capital distributions – for example, the return of your capital or distributions in the course of a liquidation.

In column A give the name of the country where the income arose and tick the box if the income cannot be remitted to the UK. In columns B, C, D give the amount of income before tax, the amount of any UK income tax deducted and the amount of foreign tax paid.

Remember that with income that first arose on or before 5 April 1994, you need to enter averages for the two tax years between 6 April 1995 and 5 April 1997 (see p. 232). But if you receive foreign dividends through a UK collecting or paying agent, enter the amount received in the tax year ending 5 April 1997 – whenever the income first arose.

Under double taxation agreements signed between the UK and more than 100 countries, tax should be deducted from investment income by the foreign country at a reduced rate which is then taken into account in calculating your UK tax bill. If the figure in column D is more than you should have paid under such an agreement, ask the foreign tax authority for a refund.

The amount you enter in column E depends on whether you wish to claim tax credit relief:

- if you intend to claim it, enter the amount in column B and tick the box
- if you are not claiming tax credit relief, enter the figure in column B less any foreign tax in column D.

Add up the figures in column C and enter the total in box 6.1. Put the total for column E in box 6.2.

## Income from foreign land and property

Income from overseas property is taxed in much the same way as for UK property (see p. 222). You can deduct expenses including the cost of managing the property and collecting the income (for example, paying an agent). If you buy equipment, you may be able to claim a capital allowance or some other form of deduction (see p. 228). And can you can deduct loan interest on the property.

As for UK property, there are certain expenses you cannot claim. These include personal expenses – such as the costs incurred while the property is not let. Nor can you claim any loss you make when you sell the property.

There is space on page F2 of the Foreign supplement for details of the income and tax paid on overseas property and land. But before you fill this in, you must turn to page F4 and complete a copy of it for each property, giving details of the income, expenses and other deductions for the tax year ending 5 April 1997.

If the income first arose from the property on or before 5 April 1994, you will have to fill in two copies of page F4 for the property – because of the transitional arrangements during the change in the taxation of this income. On one, give the details for the tax year ending on 5 April 1996; on the other, for the tax year ending 5 April 1997.

## Offshore funds

| · Income from offshore funds, income received by trusts or companies abroad | 6.5 £ |
| --- | --- |

Gains on selling offshore fund investments are taxed as income unless the fund qualifies as a distributor fund – one which distributes most of its income as dividends. This is to stop investors rolling up income in offshore funds to create capital gains and reduce their income tax bills. If the fund does not count as a distributor fund, enter any gain made on cashing in part or all of your investment in box 6.5.

If you have received an equalisation payment from a distributor fund, you should enter the part of the gain taxable as income in box 6.5. The taxable amount will be shown on the voucher given to you by the fund manager.

Also enter the value of any payment or benefit such as a loan received from other sorts of offshore funds such as offshore bonds. You must include the amount of any unexpended income from such sources – income held in trust or by a company on your behalf. Give the full name of the trust in the Additional information box at the foot of the page, or the name and address of the company receiving the income. If you have these complex types of investments, you should take specialised tax advice.

## Foreign life insurance policies

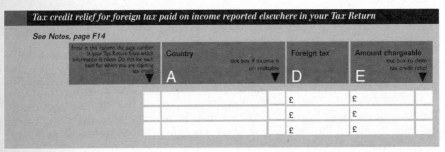

| | Number of years | Notional income tax | Gains |
|---|---|---|---|
| **Gains on foreign life insurance policies etc** | 6.6 | 6.7 £ | 6.8 £ |

Give details here of any gains you have made on foreign life insurance policies – whether because the policy has come to an end or because you have drawn some benefit from it. Enter the number of years you have held the policy in box 6.6 and the gain in box 6.8.

Most such gains are simply added to your taxable income because no foreign tax has been paid on them. If foreign tax has been deducted, you may be able to get a 'credit for notional basic rate tax' which means the gain will be taxed only at the difference between the basic and higher rate in the same way as a UK life insurance policy gain (see p. 100). Enter the amount of any notional income tax credit in box 6.7.

## TAX CREDIT RELIEF

**Tax credit relief for foreign tax paid on income reported elsewhere in your Tax Return**

See Notes, page F14

| Enter in this column the page number in your Tax Return from which information is taken. Do this for each item for which you are claiming tax credit ▼ | Country   tick box if income is unremittable ▼ A | Foreign tax D | Amount chargeable   tick box to claim tax credit relief E ▼ |
|---|---|---|---|
| | | £ | £ |
| | | £ | £ |
| | | £ | £ |

With all types of foreign income, you can simply deduct any foreign tax already paid from the income before working out the UK tax bill. But you are likely to pay less UK tax if you claim tax credit relief which reduces the UK tax bill to reflect the foreign tax already paid.

This section is for calculating tax credit relief on all your foreign income. This includes foreign income from investments, pensions, benefits and property already entered above. But you can also claim the relief on foreign income from employment, self-employment and partnerships which you will have entered elsewhere on the tax return.

First you must enter details of these other forms of foreign income. Give the country the income arose in, the amount of foreign tax paid on it and the gross amount of the income before deduction of foreign tax. In the first column, give the page number of the tax return where the income is fully reported.

Next, there is room to enter the amount of tax credit relief you wish to claim on any of your foreign income. This is only for people who want to do the sums themselves – if you don't want to get involved in the calculations, go on to the next section.

If you want to work out your tax credit relief, you need to use the Tax Credit Relief Working Sheet on page F17 of the Tax Return Guide. There are full instructions on the facing page F16, and all the data you need to complete it on the following pages. You won't be able to complete the working sheet until you have completed most of the rest of the tax return. Some of the figures you have to enter on it are drawn from the Tax Calculation Guide which you use to work out your overall tax bill.

| | |
|---|---|
| • If you are calculating your tax, enter the total tax credit relief on your income in box 6.9 | 6.9 £ |

Fill in a separate working sheet for each item of foreign income you wish to claim relief for. Enter the total amount you wish to claim in box 6.9.

*Tax credit relief for foreign tax paid on chargeable gains reported on your Capital gains pages*

See Notes, page F15

| Amount of gain under UK rules | Period UK gain accrued over | Amount of gain under foreign tax rules | Period foreign gain accrued over | Foreign tax paid | |
|---|---|---|---|---|---|
| | | | | D | tick box to claim tax credit relief ▼ |
| £ | days | £ | days | £ | |
| £ | days | £ | days | £ | |
| £ | days | £ | days | £ | |

The bottom half of the page is for details of capital gains you wish to claim tax credit relief on. Help Sheet *IR261 Tax Credit Relief: Capital Gains* tells you what to enter and how to do the sums if you wish to calculate the tax credit relief on your foreign gains.

If you are calculating your tax, enter the total tax credit relief on your gains in box 6.10   6.10 £

If you have calculated the tax credit relief on your capital gains, enter the total in box 6.10.

# TRUSTS

 **Did you receive any income from trusts, settlements or estates of deceased persons?**  NO [ ]  YES [ ]    TRUSTS ETC YES [ ]

If you ticked the YES box at Q 7 on page 2 of the basic tax return, you will need the brown supplementary page called Trusts etc. You should give details about taxable income from trusts and other forms of settlement such as a transfer of assets, and from the estates of people who have died. In some cases, you may have to give details of income from trusts you have set up. Even though the money has been paid to someone else, it may be treated as yours.

### The documents you need
You require details of any income received. With a payment from a discretionary trust, the trustees should have given you a certificate R185 setting out the details; personal representatives handling the estates of people who have died should give similar statements when handing over income.

If you have directly or indirectly provided funds for a settlement and are not sure whether the income will be treated as yours, Help Sheet *IR270: Trusts and settlements – income treated as the settlor's* should help. Ask the Orderline (p. 75).

## INCOME FROM TRUSTS AND SETTLEMENTS

Income from trusts and other forms of settlement comes with a tax credit which reflects the amount of tax already deducted from it or deemed to have been paid on it. What you receive is the net (after-tax) amount of income. To find the gross (before-tax) amount, you need to add back the tax credit. You can find out the amount of the tax credit from certificate R185 or similar statement the trustees should give you.

## How trust income is taxed

The amount of the tax credit depends on the type of trust:

- trust with an interest in possession where you have the 'absolute right' to the income from the trust. The tax credit will be at the rate of 20 per cent of the grossed-up amount of savings income, such as interest and share dividends; for other sorts of income, such as rents or royalties, it will be at the basic rate of tax – 24 per cent for the tax year ending 5 April 1997
- a discretionary trust where the trustees have discretion about paying out the income. The tax credit will be 34 per cent of the grossed-up income.

If the tax credit is more than the amount of tax you would have paid if the grossed-up income had come direct to you, you can claim a rebate. For example, if you get interest or share dividends from a trust and your income – including the grossed-up trust income – is too low to pay tax, you could reclaim all the tax credit which comes with it.

With a discretionary trust, anyone not liable to higher rate tax can reclaim part of the tax credit. Any payment you receive from the trust will come with a tax credit of 34 per cent of the grossed-up amount. But if you pay tax at no more than the basic rate – even after the grossed-up trust payment is added to your income – you should have paid tax on the payment at 24 per cent in the year ending 5 April 1997. You can thus reclaim the difference of 34 – 24 = 10 per cent of the grossed-up amount.

Higher rate taxpayers will have to pay extra tax on income from either sort of trust. With a discretionary trust, this would be an extra 6 per cent of the grossed-up amount (the difference between the 40 per cent higher rate and the 34 per cent tax credit that comes from the trust).

## Trust income that might be treated as yours

If you have directly or indirectly provided funds for a settlement, the income from those funds may be treated as yours – even though you haven't received it.

> **TAX-SAVING IDEA**
> Reclaim some or all of the tax credit that comes with income from trusts if it is more than you would have paid if the income had come straight to you. Unless you pay tax at the higher rate, you will always be entitled to a rebate on income from a discretionary trust.

The most likely way of finding yourself in this position would be if you make some investments on behalf of your children when they are under the age of 16 – for example, opening a savings account in their names. Any income from such investments is treated as yours unless it is £100 a year or less

## EXAMPLE

Gerry Hall received £250 from a discretionary trust in the tax year ending 5 April 1997, which comes with a tax credit of £128.79. He pays tax at no more than the basic rate (even when the grossed-up trust payment of £378.79 is added to his income). So he should have paid tax on the payment at the basic rate of 24 per cent only – a tax bill of 24 per cent of £378.79, or £90.91. He is thus entitled to a rebate of:

£128.79 – £90.91 = £37.88

before tax. This exception applies to gifts from each parent, so a child can have up to £200 a year before tax in income from gifts from both parents without a problem.

You can't get round this by giving the funds to someone else who passes them on to your child. You would still have indirectly provided the funds and the income would be yours. The same would be true if you settled some money on a friend's child in return for him doing the same for you.

Other sorts of trust which might produce an income that would be treated as yours include:

- a trust you set up for your husband or wife
- a trust that has lent money to you or your spouse
- a trust where the capital would come back to you if the beneficiaries died before becoming entitled to it.

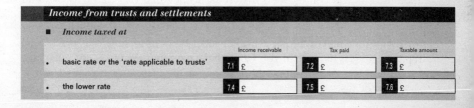

| Income from trusts and settlements | | | |
|---|---|---|---|
| ■ Income taxed at | Income receivable | Tax paid | Taxable amount |
| • basic rate or the 'rate applicable to trusts' | 7.1 £ | 7.2 £ | 7.3 £ |
| • the lower rate | 7.4 £ | 7.5 £ | 7.6 £ |

Enter the income from trusts in the tax year ending 5 April 1997 in these boxes. For discretionary trusts, put the actual amount received in box 7.1, the tax credit in box 7.2 and the gross income in box 7.3 (this should be the sum of boxes 7.1 and 7.2). Also include here any income from trusts or settlements which is treated as yours even though you haven't received it.

For income from a trust with an interest in possession on which the tax credit is at the 24 per cent basic rate, give the same details in boxes 7.1, 7.2 and 7.3. For savings income on which the tax credit is at the 20 per cent lower rate, enter the details in boxes 7.4, 7.5 and 7.6.

You don't need to enter the following here:

- scrip dividends or foreign income dividends received from a trust with an interest in possession and paid by UK companies, authorised unit trusts or open-ended investment companies – give details of these on page 3 of the basic tax return (see p. 90)
- income from foreign sources paid to you by a trust with an interest in possession – give details on the Foreign supplementary pages (see p. 233)
- income from a discretionary trust where the trustees are not resident in the UK for income tax purposes – this should also go on the Foreign pages (see p. 233).

## INCOME FROM ESTATES

You do not pay income tax on anything you inherit from a dead person. And if you inherit something that produces an income, such as money in a bank savings account, you should enter the interest in the appropriate part of the main tax return.

However, you should give details in this section of the tax return of income you receive from the estate while it is being wound up by the personal representatives – the executors or administrators. You would be entitled to this income if you were a residuary beneficiary – the person or one of the people who gets what is left after all the specific bequests and legacies have been made.

Such income will come with a tax credit in the same way as a trust with an interest in possession. Some of this income will have been taxed at the basic rate (24 per cent for the tax year ending 5 April 1997) some at the lower rate for savings income of 20 per cent. For most types of income, this tax will be repayable if it is more than you would have paid; but the tax is not repayable for some types of income such as gains on life insurance policies and UK stock dividends.

The statement supplied by the personal representatives – tax certificate R185E – will show you the rate the income has been taxed at and whether it is repayable or not. Enter the details given on the statement for the tax year ending 5 April 1997 in boxes 7.7 to 7.18. Give the name of the estate and the total amount paid to you in the Additional information box at the bottom of the page.

■ *Income bearing*

| | Income receivable | Tax paid | Taxable amount |
|---|---|---|---|
| • basic rate tax | 7.7 £ | 7.8 £ | 7.9 £ |
| • lower rate tax | 7.10 £ | 7.11 £ | 7.12 £ |
| • non-repayable lower rate tax | 7.13 £ | 7.14 £ | 7.15 £ |
| • non-repayable basic rate tax | 7.16 £ | 7.17 £ | 7.18 £ |

In some cases, income accrued during the life of the dead person and paid into the estate after their death will come to you after being taken into account in calculating the inheritance tax bill on the estate. There is a special tax relief that stops you having to pay higher rate tax on such income – ask your tax inspector for details.

## Income from foreign estates
If you get income from a foreign estate, it will not have borne full UK tax – either because the personal representatives are outside the UK tax net or because the estate is that of someone who died while domiciled outside the UK and has income from non-UK sources. In this case, enter the full amount of such income in boxes 7.7 and 7.9. Don't enter anything in box 7.8, even if some foreign tax has been deducted.

If the foreign estate has some income from UK sources, it will have paid some UK tax. In this case, you can reduce the amount entered in boxes 7.7 and 7.9 by the following amount:

$$\frac{\text{net amount of income subject to UK tax}}{\text{total estate income less UK tax}} \times \text{total estate income before UK tax}$$

### Foreign tax paid
If you have been paid income from an estate which has already been taxed in a foreign country, you may end up paying two lots of tax on it: tax in the foreign country and tax in the UK. You may be able to reduce the amount of UK tax you pay on the income to reflect the foreign tax paid – this is known as tax credit relief. You claim this on the Foreign supplementary pages (see p. 236).

If you don't want to claim tax credit relief – which can be quite complicated – you can instead deduct the foreign tax you have paid from the income. Enter the amount in box 7.19.

| • | Total foreign tax for which tax credit relief not claimed | 7.19 | £ |

Leave box 7.19 blank if you are claiming tax credit relief.

# CAPITAL GAINS TAX

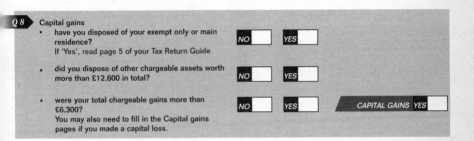

## CHAPTER 21

Q 8   Capital gains
- have you disposed of your exempt only or main residence?
  If 'Yes', read page 5 of your Tax Return Guide   NO ☐   YES ☐
- did you dispose of other chargeable assets worth more than £12,600 in total?   NO ☐   YES ☐
- were your total chargeable gains more than £6,300?
  You may also need to fill in the Capital gains pages if you made a capital loss.   NO ☐   YES ☐   CAPITAL GAINS YES ☐

If you have ticked any of the three YES boxes to Q 8 on page 2 of the basic tax return, you will need the blue supplementary pages called Capital gains.

You need to give details of gains you have made on buying and selling assets such as shares, unit trusts and property. You may also have to report a taxable gain even though you haven't sold something – if you give it away, for example. And if you have made a loss on such assets, you should give details here also, since it might reduce your overall tax bill now or in the future.

This chapter begins with a brief introduction to capital gains tax. It then tells you how to fill in the Capital gains supplementary pages. The rest of the chapter contains detailed information to guide you through the sometimes complex calculations needed to fill in the tax return and help you claim all the relief and allowances that can reduce your capital gains tax bill.

## Did you sell your home in the tax year ending 5 April 1997?
You may not need to fill in anything on these Capital gains pages if the only reason you have been sent them is because you have sold your only or main home. There is likely to be no capital gains tax to pay unless any of the following applies:

- you have a large garden (more than half a hectare)
- part or all of it has not been used as your home – for work, for example
- you have been living away from it for lengthy periods.

Even if one of these applies to you, there may be little or no tax to pay. For more about capital gains tax and homes, see p. 57.

## AN INTRODUCTION TO CAPITAL GAINS TAX

If you own items which increase in value, you may find yourself paying capital gains tax. For example, shares, unit trusts, land, property and antiques can increase in price, giving you a capital gain. If you sell them – or even give them away – you may be faced with a tax bill on the gain.

The average taxpayer is unlikely to pay capital gains tax because there are a number of ways in which the gain can be reduced. There is also a long list of assets on which gains are tax-free (see opposite).

### When do you have to pay capital gains tax?
You may have to pay this tax whenever you dispose of an asset. What is meant by dispose is not defined by law. But if you sell an asset, swap or give something away, this will normally count as a disposal. So will the loss or destruction of an asset (although not if you replace or restore it by claiming on an insurance policy, or by using some types of compensation from an overseas government).

T AX-SAVING IDEA
If you are thinking of making a gift to charity of an asset which is showing a loss, think again. You won't be able to claim the loss to reduce other taxable gains.

Ideally, find something which is showing a taxable gain to give – there will be no tax to pay on the disposal. Alternatively, sell the asset which is showing a loss and give the proceeds to the charity. That would create an allowable loss which could reduce your tax bill on other disposals.

There are some occasions when there is no capital gains tax to pay, regardless of what is being disposed of or how much it is worth:

- assets passed on when someone dies
- gifts to a husband or wife, unless separated (p. 48)
- gifts to charity.

But nor are there any allowable losses on these occasions (see p. 263).

### Tax-free gains
There is no capital gains tax to pay on a gain you make on any of the following assets:

- your home (although not a second home in most cases – see p. 57)
- private cars
- personal belongings – known as chattels – sold for less than £6,000 (see p. 262)
- wasting assets with a useful life of 50 years or less (for example, a boat or caravan), so long as you could not have claimed a capital allowance on it
- British money, including sovereigns dated after 1837
- foreign currency for your personal spending abroad (including what you spend on maintaining a home abroad), but not foreign currency accounts
- gains on insurance policies, unless you bought them and were not the original holder (although you may have to pay part of the insurance company's capital gains tax bill – see p. 67)
- betting, pools or lottery winnings
- National Savings investments such as National Savings Certificates and Capital Bonds
- personal equity plans (PEPs) – see p. 71
- Business Expansion Scheme (BES) shares bought after 18 March 1986, provided you have owned them for at least five years and they carried on their qualifying activity for at least three years (see p. 73)
- Enterprise Investment Scheme (EIS) shares, provided you have owned them for at least five years and they carried on their qualifying activity for at least three years (see p. 72)
- shares in venture capital trusts (see p. 73)
- terminal bonuses on save as you earn (SAYE) contracts
- British Government stock and any options to buy and sell such stock
- certain corporate bonds such as company loan stock and debentures issued after 13 March 1984 and options to buy and sell such bonds
- interests in trusts or settlements, unless you bought them
- decorations for bravery, unless you bought them
- some gifts for public benefit (p. 347)

> ### EXAMPLE
> Leonie Dale wants to give a house she used to let out to students to a charity for the homeless. It has become badly run-down, and would produce a capital loss of £40,000 if sold on the open market.
>
> However, she also owns shares which are showing a chargeable gain of much more than £40,000. She decides to sell the house to produce an allowable loss and at the same time sells some shares to produce a similar gain – saving around £10,000 in capital gains tax. She gives the proceeds of the house sale to the charity together with a donation of £5,000 towards the expense of buying another house for their purposes.

- damages or compensation for a personal injury or wrong to yourself or in your personal capacity (for example, libel)
- compensation for being given bad investment advice that left you worse off after being persuaded to buy a personal pension between 29 April 1988 and 30 June 1994.

Disposals of land to housing associations may also be free of capital gains tax.

If an asset can be disposed of tax-free, any loss you make on it cannot normally be used to reduce your overall tax bill. But if you dispose of a chattel worth £6,000 or less at a loss, you may be able to use this to reduce your tax bill (see p. 262).

## Who has to pay?

Capital gains tax applies to you as an individual in your private life or in your business, whether you are self-employed or in partnership. Trustees may also have to pay capital gains tax on the assets that are held in trust (see p. 250).

Any capital gains tax for the tax year ending 5 April 1997 will have to be paid by 31 January 1998. Capital gains tax for the tax year beginning 6 April 1997 will have to be paid by 31 January 1999.

## How to work out the gain or loss

Broadly, the gain or loss on an asset is worked out as follows:

*Step 1:* Find the final value of the asset – what you get for selling it or its market value if given away.

*Step 2:* Find its initial value – normally what you paid for it or its market value (see p. 257).

*Step 3:* Deduct the initial value from the final value to find the gross capital gain or gross capital loss.

*Step 4:* If you incurred any allowable expenses in acquiring, owning or disposing of the asset, these can be deducted from the gross capital gain or loss to give the net capital gain or net capital loss. (See p. 257 for more about expenses.)

*Step 5:* If you have made a net capital gain, you can reduce this by claiming indexation allowance which reflects the impact of inflation on the figures

(p. 259). You may also be able to claim special reliefs – for example, when disposing of your only or main home (p. 57) or retiring from your business (p. 274).

*Step 6:* The figure you end up with after all these deductions is the chargeable gain on the asset. Add together all your chargeable gains for the tax year and subtract any net capital losses to get your net chargeable gain. If your losses outweigh the gains, there will be no capital gains tax to pay for this tax year – and the net allowable loss can be used to reduce your tax bill elsewhere in various ways (see p. 263).

*Step 7:* If you have made a net chargeable gain, subtract the tax-free capital gains allowance for the tax year from it – this was £6,300 for the tax year ending 5 April 1997. You can also subtract any losses carried over from previous tax years (see p. 264 for details).

*Step 8:* If there is anything left after all these deductions, it is added to your taxable income for the year and income tax is charged on it at the lower rate, basic rate or higher rate as appropriate.

There are special rules for calculating the gains on assets owned before 1 April 1982 (see p. 260). And the detailed rules for working out the gains on shares and unit trusts – including what happens when you buy and sell batches of the same shares or unit trusts – are on p. 268.

## How to reduce or delay your capital gains tax bill

There are a number of ways to reduce or delay a capital gains tax bill:

- claim all the allowable expenses you can (p. 257), and your indexation allowance (p. 259)
- take advantage of the special rules for disposing of assets owned before 31 March 1982 (p. 260)
- use the tax-free capital gains allowance you can make each year (see p. 262) – and that of your husband or wife
- don't overlook losses which you can deduct from gains (see p. 263)
- pass the tax bill for gifts of business assets and certain other gifts on to the recipient if possible, or pay it in instalments if not (p. 266)
- if you don't need the proceeds of a disposal immediately, consider investing the money in growing businesses – you may be able to defer the tax bill by claiming reinvestment relief on buying shares in small companies (p. 267)
- if you are disposing of a business, take advantage of the special reliefs which can reduce your tax bill (see p. 274).

## EXAMPLE

Ben Barber bought a painting for £2,000 in April 1985, paying a buyer's fee to the auction house of £200. In the same week, he spent £500 having the painting cleaned. The painting was sold in May 1996 for £20,000, with a seller's fee of £3,000 for the auction house. Ben calculates the tax due as follows:

*Step 1:* The final value of the painting is what he sold it for – £20,000.

*Step 2:* The initial value is what he paid for it – £2,000.

*Step 3:* He deducts the initial value from the final value to find the gross capital gain of £18,000.

*Step 4:* He incurred allowable expenses of £3,700: the £200 fee paid when buying the painting, the £500 spent on cleaning it and the £3,000 fee paid when selling it. He deducts this from the £18,000 gross capital gain to get the net capital gain of £14,300.

*Step 5:* He can claim indexation allowance for the £2,000 cost of buying the painting, the £200 buyer's fee and the £500 cleaning charge. The allowance is £1,655 (for calculation, see p. 260). The indexation allowance of £14,300 is deducted from the net capital gain to get the chargeable gain of £12,645.

*Step 6:* This is his only chargeable gain for the tax year which ended on 5 April 1997, and he has no allowable losses for that tax year. So Ben has net chargeable gains of £12,645 for the tax year.

*Step 7:* The tax-free allowance for the tax year ending 5 April 1997 is £6,300. He subtracts this from the net chargeable gain to get his taxable chargeable gain for the year of £6,345. He has no losses carried over from previous tax years to reduce this figure further.

*Step 8:* The £6,345 is added to Ben's taxable income for the tax year ending 5 April 1997 and income tax is charged on it. His income is already high enough for him to be paying tax at the higher rate of 40 per cent, so that is the rate he pays on the gain.

Ben must pay 40 per cent of £6,345 – a capital gains tax bill of £2,538.

---

Minimising your capital gains tax bills means taking advantage of all these deductions and allowances. It will help in claiming these if you keep a record of the assets you have acquired which may fall into the capital gains tax net, together with relevant receipts (for example, for allowable expenses).

## Trusts

Where assets are held in trust, the trustees are liable for capital gains tax on disposals of the assets in the trust, in much the same way as individuals. However, the slice of net taxable gains that is free of capital gains tax in any tax year is half the figure that applies to individuals. So for the tax year ending 5 April 1997, the first £3,150 of net chargeable gains is free of tax for a trust; for the tax year beginning 6 April 1997, the tax-free allowance for trusts is £3,500.

The rate of capital gains tax for trustees is equivalent to the basic rate of income tax (24 per cent for the tax year ending 5 April 1997 and 23 per cent for the tax year beginning 6 April 1997). For a discretionary trust (including accumulation trusts), there is a single flat rate of tax on gains of 34 per cent.

## FILLING IN THE SUPPLEMENTARY PAGES

You must start by filling in the second page, CG2, giving details of your disposals in the tax year ending 5 April 1997. This will provide you with the information you need to complete the first page, CG1.

### The documents you need
You will need details of anything you have spent on buying or selling or maintaining the value of assets. With shares and unit trusts, you need any paperwork relating to share issues while you owned them or company reorganisations.

With assets owned on 31 March 1982, you may also need details of their value on that date (see p. 260). Use catalogues, press advertisements or stock market share price records to value them.

### Married couples
A husband and wife are treated as two single people for capital gains tax purposes, and are responsible for paying their own capital gains tax bills. With assets jointly owned by husband and wife – second homes, shares, valuables and so on – the gain or loss should be split 50:50 between you unless you have told your tax inspector that they are not owned equally.

To divide the gains or losses on assets held in your joint names unequally, you need to complete a declaration of beneficial interests using Form 17. If the asset produces income, you may already have filled in Form 17 to allocate the income other than 50:50 (see p. 41). There is no need to fill in another one for capital gains tax purposes.

### Filling in page CG2
This page is for giving details of each taxable disposal made during the tax year ending 5 April 1997. Include anything you have been given as a result of the reconstruction or takeover of a company, building society or mutual insurance company (see p. 272).

You don't need to enter any details of disposals of assets on which gains are tax-free. Thus you should leave out possessions which are worth £6,000 or less when you disposed of them. However, if you made a loss on the disposal of such an asset, you should give details since it can be used to reduce your tax bill. (See p. 262 for how to calculate the gain or loss on these chattels.)

In some circumstances, you may need to give details of capital gains or losses on this page even though you haven't disposed of the assets they relate to in the tax year ending 5 April 1997. For example, if you have been given something and agreed to take over the gain from its previous owner (holdover relief), you have to pay tax on that gain if you become non-resident within six years of the end of the tax year in which the gift was made (see p. 266).

| 1 Description of asset | tick box if shares are unquoted ▼ | 3 Disposal proceeds | 4 Net gain (loss) | tick box if estimate used ▼ | 6 Assets held at 31 March 1982 | tick box if relief claimed ▼ | 8 Further information |
|---|---|---|---|---|---|---|---|
| | | | | | | | |
| | | | | | | | |

*Column 1:* Give details to identify the asset – the address of property, for example. With shares or unit trusts, give the name of the company or unit trust fund manager, type of shares or units and the number disposed of.
*Column 2:* Tick if the shares were unquoted – that is, not listed on The Stock Exchange, the Unlisted Securities Market or the Alternative Investment Market.

*Column 3:* Enter the total disposal proceeds, including any cash or other asset to be received in the future. But you should enter the market value of the asset if the disposal was a gift or a sale to a connected person. For capital gains tax, a connected person includes your husband or wife, your business partner and their spouse, a relative of yours or these others (brother, sister, parents, child, grandchild) and the spouse of one of these relatives.

If you have been given the right to something in the future in return for the disposal, this should also be included unless it would be taxed as income (for example, dividends or royalties). If it is not clear what you will get in the future – for example, it is a share of any profits – include an estimate in the disposal proceeds. When that uncertain part is finally paid, this will count as another disposal – the right to the share of the profits will have been exchanged for real cash. There will then be another capital gain or loss to report at that time.

*Column 4:* Enter the chargeable gain or allowable loss after all allowances and reliefs. Put losses in brackets. If claiming reliefs, such as reinvestment relief, enter the amount after deduction of the relief and give the reason in column 8. You don't have to submit the calculations done to reach these figures, but you can if you want to.

*Column 5:* Tick this box if your figures include any estimates – of market value, for example, or future payments in return for the disposal.

*Column 6:* If you owned the asset on 31 March 1982, tick this box – there are special rules for calculating the gains and losses (see p. 260).

You should also tick the box if you will be treated as if you owned the asset on that date. This would apply, for example, if the asset had been given to you by someone who owned it on that date and you agreed to take over that person's gain on it (hold-over relief – see p. 266).

*Column 7:* Tick this box if you have claimed any one of the many reliefs which reduces the chargeable gain on disposing of an asset. These include private residence relief for your only or main home (p. 57), retirement relief when you retire from your business (p. 274), roll-over relief when you replace business assets (p. 275) and reinvestment relief when you invest in certain types of small companies (p. 267).

*Column 8:* Give any other relevant details on the disposal, including which reliefs have been claimed and why you have used estimates.

### Filling in page CG1
Use the information you have entered on page CG2 to complete the first page of the Capital gains supplement.

Add up all the chargeable gains for the tax year ending 5 April 1997 and enter the total in box 8.1.

| *less* | Total allowable losses for 1996-97 | 8.2 | £ |
| --- | --- | --- | --- |

Add up all the allowable losses for the tax year ending 5 April 1997 and enter the total in box 8.2.

| *equals* | Net chargeable gains for 1996-97 | 8.3 | £ |
| --- | --- | --- | --- |
| *or equals* | Net allowable losses for 1996-97 | 8.4 | £ |

Subtract box 8.2 from box 8.1. What you do next depends on the answer:

- if the answer is less than zero, you have made a net allowable loss for the tax year ending 5 April 1997. Enter this net loss in box 8.4, put 0 in box 8.8 and go to box 8.10 (see p. 256)
- if the answer is between zero and £6,300, you have made a net chargeable gain for the tax year ending 5 April 1997. Enter this in box 8.3. Since you can have chargeable gains of up to £6,300 tax-free in that tax year, there will be no capital gains tax to pay. Put 0 in box 8.8 and go to box 8.10 (see p. 256)
- if the answer is more than £6,300, enter it in box 8.3 and go on to box 8.5.

| *less* | Trading losses, losses from furnished holiday lettings, post-cessation expenditure, or post-employment deductions deductible from chargeable gains | 8.5 | £ |
| --- | --- | --- | --- |

There are losses on several types of income you can claim against net chargeable gains if you haven't enough income to set them off against:

- any trading losses from self-employment (p. 209) or a partnership
- losses from furnished holiday lettings (p. 224)
- certain expenses incurred in the seven years after you have closed a business which would have been allowable against business income (post-cessation expenditure) – for example, bad debts, the costs of rectifying faulty work (p. 125)
- certain expenses incurred by employees up to six years after they have left their jobs (post-employment deductions) – for example, insurance premiums for policies that pay out against claims of faulty work.

If you have such losses you can enter up to the amount you have put in box 8.3.

| *less* | Allowable losses brought forward | 8.6 | £ |

You can use allowable losses from previous tax years to reduce your net chargeable gains. If you have enough losses held over, you can reduce your net chargeable gains to £6,300, the amount that is tax-free for the tax year ending 5 April 1997.

If your losses from previous years are not big enough to reduce your net chargeable gains to £6,300, enter the full amount carried over in box 8.6. Then put 0 in box 8.10 and go to box 8.7, below.

If your losses from previous years are more than enough to reduce your net chargeable gains to £6,300, enter in box 8.6 the amount that, combined with any figure in box 8.5, will bring net chargeable gains down to £6,300 exactly. Then go to box 8.7.

box 8.3 *less* box 8.5 *less* box 8.6

| *equals* | Chargeable gains for 1996-97 | 8.7 | £ |

Subtract the figures in boxes 8.5 and 8.6 from the figure in box 8.3 and enter the result in box 8.7.

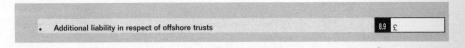

box 8.7 *less* £6,300

| Taxable chargeable gains for 1996-97 | 8.8 | £ |

You can have up to £6,300 of chargeable gains free of capital gains tax in the tax year ending 5 April 1997. So subtract £6,300 from the figure in box 8.7 to find your taxable chargeable gain for the tax year. Enter the result in box 8.8.

| • | Additional liability in respect of offshore trusts | 8.9 | £ |

If you are the beneficiary of a trust that is not resident in the UK or is also resident in another country (a dual resident trust), you may be liable to capital gains tax on anything you receive from the trust – whether it be cash, a loan or an asset. You need to give details here of the amount of tax due on what you have received in the tax year ending 5 April 1997. To work this out, use the calculator on Help Sheet *IR301 Capital gains on benefits from non-resident and dual resident trusts.*

## Capital losses

Use this part of the page as a permanent record of your allowable losses

■ *Earlier years' losses*

| | | |
|---|---|---|
| • unused losses of earlier years | 8.10 | £ |
| | | from box 8.6 |
| • used this year | 8.11 | £ |
| | | box 8.10 *less* box 8.11 |
| • carried forward losses of 1995-96 and earlier years | 8.12 | £ |

Here you can keep track of your allowable losses from previous years and this year – it will be useful when you come to fill in next year's tax return. The first three boxes are for losses carried over from previous years. Put the total unused losses you carried over from last year and earlier years in box 8.10. In box 8.11 enter the amount of those losses used this year – the same figure as in box 8.6. Finally subtract box 8.11 from box 8.10 and put the figure in box 8.12. The result is the amount of losses from earlier years still available to carry forward to the tax year beginning 6 April 1997.

■ *This years' losses*

| | | from box 8.2 |
|---|---|---|
| • total | 8.13 | £ |

This is where you can keep track of your allowable losses for the tax year ending 5 April 1997. Put the total allowable losses for the year in box 8.13 (the figure is in box 8.2).

| | | |
|---|---|---|
| • used against gains | 8.14 | £ |

Enter the amount of those losses used this year – the figure is in box 8.4.

| | | |
|---|---|---|
| • used against earlier years' gains (personal representatives only) | 8.15 | £ |

Personal representatives clearing up the estate of someone who has died can carry unused losses back to earlier tax years and effectively claim a tax rebate for the estate (see p. 264). Enter any amount this applies to in box 8.15.

| | | |
|---|---|---|
| • used against income | 8.16 | £ |

If you have made losses on shares in unquoted trading companies, you can set them off against income from the same tax year. For more information, see Help Sheet *IR286 Income tax losses for new shares you have subscribed for in unlisted trading companies*. If you make such a claim for the tax year ending 5 April 1997, enter the amount in box 8.16.

| | box 8.13 *less* box 8.14 *less* box 8.15 *less* box 8.16 | |
|---|---|---|
| • carried forward losses of 1996-97 | 8.17 | £ |

Subtract boxes 8.14, 8.15 and 8.16 from box 8.13 and put the figure you get in box 8.17. This is the amount of losses you can carry over from the tax year ending 5 April 1997 to reduce tax bills in future tax years.

## CAPITAL GAINS TAX – THE DETAILS

This section contains the details you will need to work out your capital gains tax bill.

### Working out your capital gains

*Valuing assets*
In most cases, the value of an asset when you acquire it is what it cost you to acquire it, or what you get on selling it. If you acquired something by inheritance, its initial value is its probate value.

With a gift, the value is its market value: what anyone selling it at the time of the gift would get for it on the open market. However, in certain circumstances, the initial value of a gift may be what the giver acquired it for if you agreed at the time of the gift to take over the giver's capital gain (see p. 266).

The market value is also the final value if you dispose of an asset to a connected person, however much you sell it for. For capital gains tax, a connected person includes your husband or wife, your business partner and their spouse, a relative of yours or these others (brother, sister, parents, child, grandchild) and the spouse of one of these relatives.

There are special rules for valuing assets owned before April 1982 (p. 260).

*Allowable expenses*
Deducting the initial value of an asset from its final value gives you the gross capital gain or gross capital loss. However, you can then deduct certain allowable expenses in computing the gain on an asset for capital gains tax. These include:

> # EXAMPLE
> When Melanie Hill sold her holiday cottage in September 1996 for £108,000, she feared an enormous capital gains tax bill – she had bought it in August 1988 for £52,000. But she soon realised there were a lot of expenses she could claim to reduce the capital gain:
>
> - acquisition costs of £1,735 – the £790 legal bill incurred in buying it, the £520 stamp duty and the £425 surveyor's fee for inspecting and valuing it
> - improvement costs of £18,750 – the cost of installing modern plumbing and central heating, rewiring and building an extension, which were all paid for in May 1989
> - disposal costs of £3,575 – legal bills for the sale of £1,725 and £1,850 commission paid to the estate agent.
>
> The net capital gain is worked out as follows:
>
> | | | |
> |---|---|---|
> | Final value | | £108,000 |
> | Less allowable expenses: | | |
> | original cost | £52,000 | |
> | acquisition costs | £1,735 | |
> | improvement costs | £18,750 | |
> | disposal costs | £3,575 | |
> | Total allowable expenses | | £76,060 |
> | Net capital gain | | £31,940 |
>
> However, Melanie won't pay capital gains tax even on this net capital gain of £31,940. – she can claim indexation allowance (see opposite).

- acquisition costs, such as payments to a professional adviser (for example, surveyor, accountant, solicitor), conveyancing costs and stamp duty, and advertising to find a seller
- what you spend improving the asset (although not your own time)
- what you spend establishing or defending your rights or title to the asset
- disposal costs, similar to acquisition costs, but including the cost of valuing it for capital gains tax.

Deducting these expenses gives you the net capital gain or net allowable loss.

## Part disposals
If you dispose of part of an asset, you will need to allocate expenses between the part you are getting rid of and the part you have kept.

Any expense connected only with the part being disposed of can be fully deducted from the proceeds in working out the gain. Anything connected only with the part you are keeping cannot be deducted. But some of the expenditure will be impossible to allocate in this way, and will thus have to be divided between the two parts, in proportion to their value. The proportion of such a cost that you can deduct from the gain is as follows:

$$\frac{\text{Disposal proceeds}}{\text{Disposal proceeds} + \text{Value of the part retained}}$$

There are special rules for allocating costs to shares and unit trusts where holdings are divided or added to (see p. 268).

---

### EXAMPLE

Martin Thompson buys a house which he converts into a pair of flats. He spends £5,000 converting one into a weekend retreat for himself and £3,000 on doing up the other one to sell.

Each of the flats is given identical valuations at the time of the sale. So any money spent on the whole house can be divided equally between the two flats. He can claim the following expenses to reduce the gain on the flat he sells:

- the £3,000 spent improving the flat he sells
- the expenses of selling the flat
- half the expenses of buying the house including the purchase price.

---

### Indexation allowance

If you end up with a net capital gain after deducting allowable expenses from the gross capital gain, you can claim indexation allowance to remove increases in value caused by inflation. If there is a net capital loss, you can't claim indexation allowance, however – indexation allowance cannot be used to create or increase a loss.

To calculate indexation allowance, multiply the initial value and each allowable expense by the following:

$$\frac{\text{RPI in disposal month} - \text{RPI in expenditure month}}{\text{RPI in expenditure month}}$$

RPI stands for Retail Prices Index (figures for the RPI since March 1982 are given in the Tax Return Guide sent to you by the Inland Revenue). The expenditure month is the month in which the payment of the initial value or the allowable expense became due.

Work out this sum for the initial value and each allowable expense to three decimal places, and add together the answers. Subtract this from the net capital gain to produce the chargeable gain. If the indexation allowance is bigger than the net capital gain, it reduces the gain to zero – it cannot be used to create a loss.

---

### EXAMPLE

Ben Barber works out the indexation allowance he can claim on the painting he disposed of in May 1996 (see p. 250). He can claim the allowance for the original cost of £2,000, the buyer's fee of £200 and the cleaning costs of £500 – all of this £2,700 was spent in April 1985.

The RPI in April 1985 was 94.78
The RPI in May 1996 was 152.9

The indexation allowance is as follows:

$$£2,700 \times \left( \frac{\text{RPI May 1996} - \text{RPI April 1985}}{\text{RPI April 1985}} \right)$$

$$= £2,700 \times \left( \frac{152.9 - 94.78}{94.78} \right)$$

$$= £2,700 \times 0.613$$

$$= £1,655$$

Ben's taxable gain is therefore £14,300 – £1,655 = £12,645

---

### Special rules for assets owned on or before 1 April 1982

If you owned an asset on or before 31 March 1982, only the gain since that date is liable to capital gains tax. Any gain made before 1 April 1982 is effectively tax-free. With such assets, the initial value is normally its market value on 31 March 1982. You cannot deduct expenses incurred on or before that date. Indexation allowance runs from March 1982.

In some circumstances, using the 31 March 1982 value could artificially inflate your gain or loss. Suppose, for example, you bought something in 1978 which fell in value before 31 March 1982, and has risen in value since. Basing the gain on the 31 March 1982 value would make it larger than the gain you've actually made. Similarly, if you dispose of something which rose in value while you owned it before 1 April 1982 and fell in value afterwards, this could produce a bigger loss than you actually made.

Thus when calculating the gain or loss on assets owned before 1 April 1982, you need to work out the sums using two different methods:

- the rebased chargeable gain – using the value on 31 March 1982 and ignoring costs incurred on or before that date
- the actual gain – using the original cost you paid for it and allowing for allowable expenses incurred on or before 31 March 1982 (with indexation allowance on them running from that date).

The two answers are then compared in what the Inland Revenue calls the kink test:

- if both methods produce a gain, the smaller gain is used to calculate your tax bill
- if both methods produce a loss, the smaller loss is allowable
- if one produces a gain and the other a loss, the disposal is assumed to produce no gain or loss.

To avoid all this palaver, you can make a rebasing election, which means all your gains and losses on assets owned on or before 31 March 1982 will be based on their market value on that date. This will avoid having to keep complicated records (although it could mean paying more tax if you have assets which fell in value before 31 March 1982 and have risen in value since).

If you want to make a rebasing election, tell your tax inspector in writing within two years of the first disposal of such an asset on or after 6 April 1988. This is likely to be the first disposal to which the rebasing rules apply. The election is irrevocable – so make sure it will pay for you. For more details, see Help Sheet *IR280 Rebasing – assets held at 31 March 1982*.

---

### EXAMPLE

Jim Brooke carries out the kink test on the home he rents out which he sold for £120,000 in December 1996.

He bought it in June 1979 when he paid £20,000 for it, with acquisition costs and other allowable expenses before 1 April 1982 of £2,000. Its value at 31 March 1982 was £16,300.

The net capital gain using the 31 March 1982 value as the initial value would be £120,000 – £16,300 = £103,700. The net capital gain based on what he paid for it in June 1979 and expenses before 1 April 1982 would be £120,000 – £20,000 – £2,000 = £98,000.

Both methods produce a gain, so the capital gains tax bill will be based on what Jim paid for it in June 1979, since that produces the smaller gain. If Jim had already opted for all his pre-1 April 1982 assets to be treated as if they were acquired on that date, his tax bill would be based on the larger figure produced by using the market value on 31 March 1982.

### Special rules for personal belongings – chattels

If personal belongings, known as chattels by the Inland Revenue, are sold for less than £6,000, the gain is tax-free. Chattels are defined as tangible, movable property and include furniture, silver, paintings and so on. A set (for example, a silver tea-set) counts as one chattel.

If a chattel is sold for more than the tax-free limit, the taxable gain is restricted to $5/_3$ of the amount of the disposal over the limit. So when the limit is £6,000 the maximum gain on a chattel sold for £8,100 would be $5/_3$ of £8,100 – £6,000 = $5/_3$ of £2,100 = £3,500.

---

EXAMPLE

William Baxter bought a piece of furniture for £4,000 and sold it for £7,500 in the tax year ending 5 April 1997. This produces a gain of £7,500 – £4,000 = £3,500. The sale price is over the £6,000 chattels limit so the gain is not tax-free. But for capital gains tax purposes, the gain cannot be more than $5/_3$ of £7,500 – £6,000. This is $5/_3$ of £1,500 = £2,500, thus reducing William's taxable gain by £1,000.

---

In most cases, disposing of an asset that would produce a tax-free gain means that you cannot claim any allowable loss made on such an asset. With chattels, relief for losses is restricted. If the chattel was disposed of for less than £6,000, the loss is calculated as if it had fetched £6,000.

---

EXAMPLE

William Baxter sold another piece of furniture for £4,500 which he had bought for £9,500. His gross loss would be calculated as if he had sold it for £6,000: it would therefore be £9,500 – £6,000 = £3,500 rather than the £5,000 loss William actually made.

---

For more about chattels, ask for Help Sheet *IR295 Chattels and capital gains tax*.

### The tax-free capital gains tax allowance

The first slice of chargeable gains in any tax year is free of capital gains tax. For the tax year ending 5 April 1997, the tax-free allowance is £6,300. For the tax year beginning 6 April 1997, the tax-free allowance has risen to £6,500.

If you don't use all your allowance in one year, you can't carry the unused part over to another year. So if you have assets showing big gains, try to spread the disposal of them over several years to take advantage of the tax-free amount.

## Married couples and capital gains tax

Husbands and wives are treated as separate individuals for capital gains tax. They pay tax on their own gains and can deduct their losses only from their own gains. They have their own tax-free allowances to deduct from their own chargeable gains.

### TAX-SAVING IDEA

If you own some shares which are showing a gain, consider selling enough to use up the tax-free capital gains tax allowance each year. With the allowance at £6,500, it could save you up to 40 per cent of that amount in capital gains tax – £2,600.

If you want to go on owning the shares, you can buy them back a few days later (this is sometimes known as bed and breakfasting). The costs of buying and selling are more than outweighed by the tax saved.

But if a married couple living together dispose of assets to each other, this is ignored for the purposes of capital gains tax. For example, if a husband buys shares worth £10,000 in June 1997 and gives them to his wife at a later date, her gain or loss when she sells them will be calculated as if she had bought them for £10,000 in June 1997. Anything they pay each other on such transfers is ignored.

A married couple is treated as living together unless legally separated or where the separation looks to be permanent. Gifts between husband and wife in the year of separation are free of capital gains tax, but after this, tax may be payable. For more about marriage and capital gains tax, see the Help Sheet *IR 281 Husband and wife, divorce and separation.*

## Losses

Losses you make on disposing of assets are deducted from gains before working out the taxable gain on which you pay capital gains tax. But having too much in the way of losses may not be helpful. You have to deduct losses from gains made in the same tax year, even if this reduces your net gains below the tax-free level.

### TAX-SAVING IDEA

Since there is no capital gains tax on gifts between husband and wife, you can effectively double your tax-free band if you are married by giving assets to your spouse to dispose of. So in the tax year beginning 6 April 1997, a married couple can effectively make £13,000 of gains tax-free.

A loss made when you dispose of an asset to a connected person (p. 257) can be set off only against a gain made to a connected person. This applies even if the loss was made when you disposed of the asset for a genuine commercial value.

### Carrying losses over

If your losses are greater than your gains, the excess can be carried over to the next tax year and beyond. The same is true if you make losses and no gains – the losses can be set against gains in future tax years. And carried-over losses do not have to be used to reduce chargeable gains below the tax-free allowance.

Losses can never be carried back to an earlier tax year, except in the year when you die. Your executors will be able to carry back these losses to set against gains you made in the three previous tax years – starting with the gains in the most recent year. There is further information in Help Sheet *IR 282 Death, personal representatives and legatees*.

### Claiming losses

You have to claim losses within five

## EXAMPLE

Elizabeth Ong made chargeable gains of £4,500 in the tax year ending 5 April 1997 and allowable losses of £8,000. She has to set off £4,500 of losses against her gains, even though the gains are less than the tax-free allowance for the year of £6,300. So there is no capital gains tax to pay for that tax year.

This leaves her with unused losses of £8,000 – £4,500 = £3,500 which she can carry forward to set against chargeable gains in subsequent tax years. In the tax year beginning 6 April 1997, she makes chargeable gains of £9,400 and losses of £1,500. Her net chargeable gains for that tax year are £9,400 – £1,500 = £7,900.

She can use some of the £3,500 of unused losses from earlier years to reduce these net chargeable gains to the tax-free allowance and pay no capital gains tax for the year. For the tax year beginning 6 April 1997, the tax-free allowance is £6,500, so she uses £7,900 – £6,500 = £1,400 of unused losses getting down to the tax-free allowance.

This still leaves her with £3,500 – £1,400 = £2,100 of unused allowances. These can be carried forward.

years and ten months of the end of the tax year in which they were made. So for losses made in the tax year ending 5 April 1997, you must claim losses by 31 January 2003.

You can claim the losses by giving details on the tax return – enter the amount in box 8.2 and give details in column 8 on page CG2 when entering the asset that made the loss. Alternatively, if you don't need to fill in the Capital gains supplement, you can write and tell your tax inspector.

### Calculating your capital gains tax bill

If there is anything left after deduction of expenses, indexation allowance, the tax-free allowance and losses, it is added to your taxable income for the year and income tax is charged on it.

If you are a basic rate taxpayer, you'll pay tax on the gain at the basic rate, unless your taxable income and gains added together take you over the limit for paying tax at the higher rate. For example, in the tax year ending 5 April 1997, your gains would be taxed at the basic rate of 24 per cent as long as your taxable income and gains didn't add up to more than £25,500. For the tax year beginning 6 April 1997, the basic rate of tax is 23 per cent on taxable income and gains up to £26,100

If your taxable income and gains add up to more than £25,500 for the tax year ending 5 April 1997, you'll pay tax on the excess at 40 per cent. The same applies for the tax year beginning 6 April 1997 if the total comes to more than £26,100.

If your taxable income was less than £3,900 in the tax year ending 5 April 1997, you'll pay tax on your taxable gains at the lower rate of 20 per cent until your combined taxable income and gains exceed this limit, when the excess will be taxed at the basic rate. For the tax year beginning 6 April 1997, taxable income and gains are taxed at 20 per cent until they exceed £4,100.

As well as these general rules, there are special rules for calculating the tax bill in some circumstances. For example, if you reinvest the proceeds in some kinds of shares, you can defer the tax bill, rather than paying it straightaway (see opposite). And there are also allowances to reduce the bill when you make gifts of business assets, retire from a business or sell it (p. 274).

*Gifts*
You can avoid paying capital gains tax if you give away certain assets or sell them for less than their market value by claiming hold-over relief. The gain is passed on to the recipient who is treated as having acquired the assets when you did and having paid the costs you paid (less anything paid to you). Since this effectively passes on your capital gains tax bill to the recipient, their agreement is necessary.

Hold-over relief is available only for the following gifts, however:
- business assets (see p. 275)
- heritage property
- gifts to political parties
- gifts which result in an immediate inheritance tax bill (mainly gifts to certain trusts and companies).

There is no point in claiming hold-over relief if your net taxable gains for the year, including the gift, will be within the tax-free band (£6,300 for the tax year ending 5 April 1997, £6,500 for the tax year beginning 6 April 1997). If the recipient of a gift on which hold-over relief was claimed becomes non-resident without having sold or given away the gift, the giver could have to pay a capital gains tax bill.

If you make a gift of land or certain types of shareholdings which doesn't qualify for hold-over relief, you may be able to pay the capital gains tax in ten annual instalments. The shareholdings which qualify are a controlling shareholding in a company or minority holdings in unquoted companies. Interest is charged on the unpaid tax, except with agricultural property. For more about hold-over relief, see Help Sheet *IR295 Relief for gifts and similar transactions*.

### Gifts received before 14 March 1989

People making almost any sort of gift before 14 March 1989 could pass the gain on to the recipient. Hold-over relief could be claimed providing both the giver and the recipient told the giver's tax inspector within six years of the tax year in which the gift was made.

If you now dispose of something you were given on which hold-over relief was claimed, you will need to take this into account in working out the gain. The initial value of the asset is what the giver acquired it for, not its market value when you were given it. You can also claim any allowable expenses incurred by the giver.

### Reinvestment relief

If you're facing a capital gains tax bill that you can't reduce by claiming losses or other reliefs, consider claiming reinvestment relief. This allows you to defer the tax bill if you invest the gain in the shares of certain types of small companies.

To get the relief you have to invest in the ordinary shares of unquoted companies – companies which are not listed on the UK Stock Exchange or any other recognised stock exchange. Investments in companies quoted on the Alternative Investment Market (AIM) are eligible, provided they meet the other requirements for reinvestment relief. The main one is that the company must be trading in certain qualifying sectors or be a holding company for such trading companies. There are more details in Help Sheet *IR291 Reinvestment relief*.

To get reinvestment relief, you must make the investment any time between one year before and three years after the disposal that produces the gain. The amount of the gain that you reinvest will be taxed only when you eventually sell the shares – although you could then defer the tax bill again by reinvesting any gain in more qualifying shares and claiming further reinvestment relief. Otherwise, the deferred gain will be taxed only if you emigrate or the company ceases to be a qualifying one during the three years after you acquired the shares.

To claim reinvestment relief, you must tell your tax inspector within five years after 31 January in the year following the tax year in which you make the disposal or acquire the shares. So if you made the disposal and bought the shares in the tax year ending 5 April 1997, you have until 31 January

2003 to make the claim. You can use the form at the end of Help Sheet *IR291 Reinvestment relief* to make the claim.

## Shares and unit trusts

Shares and unit trusts are treated in the same way as other assets for capital gains tax purposes. But if you buy and sell shares in a particular company, or units in a particular unit trust, how do you decide which you have bought or sold when working out the gain. And there are further complications when companies merge, are taken over or otherwise reorganise their capital. This section explains the special rules for working out the gains and losses on share transactions. There are also two Help Sheets – *IR284 Shares and capital gains tax*, and *IR 285 Share reorganisations, company takeovers and capital gains tax*.

### Valuing shares

The market value of shares bought and sold on one of the Stock Exchange markets is normally the amount you paid for them or got for selling them.

But you should use the market value when valuing gifts or disposals to a connected person (see p. 257) – use the prices recorded in the *Official Daily List* (which can be supplied by a stockbroker or bank). The market value is the lower of the following two figures, calculated using prices on the date of the gift or disposal:

- the selling price, plus a quarter of the difference between the selling price and the (higher) buying price – the quarter-up rule
- the half-way point between the highest and lowest prices of recorded bargains for the day.

With any disposal of unquoted shares, the market value must be agreed with the Share Valuation Division of the Inland Revenue. This cannot be negotiated in advance and reaching agreement can be a lengthy business. For more about the Share Valuation Division, see Inland Revenue leaflet SVD1.

### Unit trusts and investment trusts

The gain on disposing of unit trusts and investment trusts is worked out in the same way as for shares. If you receive an equalisation payment with your first distribution from a unit trust, this is a return of part of your original investment and it should be deducted from the acquisition price in working out your gain or loss.

### Which shares or unit trusts have you sold?

If you buy one batch of shares in a company and later sell it without any other dealings in the shares, it is quite simple to calculate the gain or loss.

But if you buy shares in the same company on different occasions and then sell them – together or in parcels – it is not so easy to identify which you have sold and what they cost you.

For this reason, shares of the same class in the same company are normally pooled. This means they are treated as a single asset, even if they were acquired at different times. If one share from a pool of ten is disposed of, the gain is taken to be one-tenth of the gain of the whole pool. A similar procedure applies to unit trusts.

The gain made on the whole pool is worked out by comparing its value at the time of the sale with the indexed cost of buying the shares or units that went into it. The example overleaf shows how pooling works.

### Shares bought on or before 5 April 1982

Shares owned on or before 5 April 1982 and on or after 6 April 1965 are kept in a separate pool, and treated like other assets owned before 1 April 1982:

- the gain is based on their value on 31 March 1982, unless it is to your advantage to base it on their cost when you bought them (see p. 260)
- indexation allowance runs only from March 1982.

If you have shares in a company bought after 5 April 1982 and some bought on or before that date, any shares you sell come from the pool of those acquired after 5 April 1982 first. Only when all those have been sold do you start to sell shares acquired on or before 5 April 1982.

### Shares bought before 6 April 1965

Shares acquired before 6 April 1965 are kept completely separate. They are the last to be sold if you have bought batches since that date – all shares bought after that date are sold first. When you come to sell pre-April 1965 quoted shares, it is assumed the last to be bought are the first to be sold.

However, you can elect for shares acquired before 6 April 1965 to be added to your pre-April 1982 pool. This is usually to your advantage, as their value on 31 March 1982 is likely to be more than what you paid for them more than 17 years before.

### Selling shares within ten days of buying them

If you sell shares in a company within ten days of buying shares in the same company, the shares you sell are assumed to be the most recently acquired ones, in the following order:

- any bought on the same day as the sale are sold first

## EXAMPLE

Diana Nichols bought 2,000 ordinary shares in United Enterprises plc in June 1983 for £7,000. In December 1988, she added another 2,000 United Enterprises shares for £10,000. That gave her a pool of 4,000 such shares. She sold 1,000 of them in July 1996 for £7,500.

Since she has sold one-quarter of her pool of United Enterprises shares, Diana's taxable gain will be quarter of the taxable gain she would have made if she had sold the lot in July 1996. She works out the taxable gain on the whole pool at July 1996 using the following figures for the Retail Price Index (RPI) on the dates of transactions:

- June 1983: 84.84
- December 1988: 110.3
- July 1996: 152.4

First Diana calculates the indexed cost of the pool at each stage in buying and selling the shares by adding indexation allowance to the value of the pool at each transaction. The first purchase in June 1983 started off the pool with a value of £7,000. By the date of the second purchase in December 1988, the value of the first batch had increased by the amount of indexation allowance due since June 1983. This is:

$$£7,000 \times \left( \frac{\text{RPI December 1988} - \text{RPI June 1983}}{\text{RPI June 1983}} \right)$$

$$= £7,000 \times \left( \frac{110.3 - 84.84}{84.84} \right)$$

$$= £7,000 \times 0.300$$

$$= £2,100$$

- any others bought in the ten days before the sale go next
- only if you sell more than you have bought in the previous ten days do you sell shares from the pool.

There is no indexation allowance if you sell shares within ten days of buying them.

### Employee share schemes

Employee share schemes allow employees to acquire shares in the companies free or cheaply – and if they are certain types approved by the Inland Revenue, without an income tax bill. However, there could be a capital gains tax bill when the shares are disposed of. The initial cost of the shares and when you are deemed to have received them depends on the type of scheme:

- approved savings-related share option schemes – you acquire the shares at the market value on the day you opted to buy them

By December 1988, the indexed cost of the June 1983 shares was £7,000 + £2,100 = £9,100. The second purchase of shares at £10,000 took the indexed value of the pool to £9,100 + £10,000 = £19,100.

No more United Enterprises shares had been bought by the first sale in July 1995. So the indexation allowance due on the pool since December 1988 was as follows:

$$£19,100 \times \left(\frac{\text{RPI July 1996} - \text{RPI December 1988}}{\text{RPI December 1988}}\right)$$

$$= £19,100 \times \left(\frac{152.4 - 110.3}{110.3}\right)$$
$$= £19,100 \times 0.382$$
$$= £7,296$$

The indexed cost of the pool was £19,100 + £7,296 = £26,396 in July 1996. However, Diana sold only 1,000 of the 4,000 shares in July 1996, that is one-quarter of the pool. So the indexed cost of the shares she sold was one-quarter of £26,396 = £6,599.

Since she sold the shares for £7,500, her taxable gain is:
$$£7,500 - £6,599 = £901$$

The indexed cost of the remaining 3,000 shares in Diana's pool in July 1996 is:
$$£26,396 - £6,599 = £19,797$$

- approved profit-sharing schemes – you acquire the shares at the market value on the day they are allocated to you, even though you can't sell them for three years
- approved discretionary share option schemes – you acquire the shares at the price you pay for them on the day you exercise the option. If you paid anything for the option, this is an allowable expense.

You can transfer up to £3,000 of shares into a single company personal equity plan (PEP) direct from approved profit-sharing and savings-related share option schemes (see p. 71). The shares transferred in this way will be free of capital gains tax on the transfer or when they are eventually sold.

Help Sheet *IR287 Employee share schemes and capital gains tax* has more details.

### Rights issues

If you get extra shares through a rights issue or a bonus issue, they are allocated to the relevant pool. So if half your shares are in the post-April 1982 pool and half in a pre-April 1982 pool, the rights issue is split 50:50 between the two pools. Whatever you pay for the rights issue is added to the initial costs of the two pools, with indexation allowance from the time the payment is made.

### Stock dividends and accumulation unit trusts

If you get extra shares instead of dividends, this is known as a stock dividend (or scrip dividend). The value of the new shares is the amount of dividend foregone excluding the value of the tax credit – the cash equivalent. Indexation allowance runs from the date of the dividend.

Accumulation unit trusts work in a similar way, with extra units allocated to the appropriate pool.

### Takeovers and mergers

If you own shares in a company which is taken over, you may get shares in the new parent company in exchange for your old shares. This exchange does not count as a disposal. The new shares are assumed to have been acquired at the cost of the old ones and on the same dates.

If part of the price for the old shares is cash, this is a disposal. For example, if you get half cash, half shares, you have disposed of half the old shares.

### Conversions or reorganisations of building societies and insurance companies

Some building societies and mutual insurance companies are converting to companies or are involved in other organisational changes that may produce benefits for their members. If you receive shares or cash – or both – in such circumstances, there may be a bill for income tax or capital gains tax. Ask the building society or insurance company for guidance.

### Payment by instalments

When you buy newly issued shares, you may be able to pay for them in instalments. Indexation allowance on the full purchase price runs from when the shares were acquired only if all the instalments were paid within 12 months of acquisition. If instalments are paid more than 12 months after the shares were acquired, indexation allowance on those instalments runs from when they were made.

However, if you paid in instalments when buying newly issued shares in a privatised state enterprise, indexation allowance runs from the date you acquired the shares (even though you handed over some of the money months or even years later).

*Monthly savings schemes*
If you have invested in unit trusts or investment trusts through a monthly savings scheme, working out your gains and losses could be very complicated. You would have to work out the gain and indexation allowance for each instalment you invested when making a disposal. You can opt for a simplified way of working out the initial costs and indexation allowances. This assumes all 12 monthly instalments for a year are made in the seventh month of the year (the year is the accounting year of the fund).

So if you invested £100 a month in a fund with an accounting year that runs from 1 January to 31 December, you could assume that you invested 12 x £100 = £1,200 in July, the seventh month.

You may have to add in or deduct extra amounts:

- any distribution or dividend reinvested during the year is added to your investment. So if there was a £50 dividend added to your fund in the above example, you would be treated as having invested £1,200 + £50 = £1,250 in July
- extra savings over the regular instalments are included, provided you don't add more than twice the monthly instalment in any month – a bigger payment is treated as a separate investment
- if you increase the monthly instalments, the extra is added to the year's investment as long as it is in or before the seventh month (if later, it is added to next year's fund)
- small withdrawals are deducted if they are less than one-quarter of the amount invested in the year by regular instalments (if withdrawals exceed this amount, the simplified calculation cannot be used).

To opt for this simplified method of calculating gains write to your tax office within two years of the end of the first tax year after 6 April 1988 in which you dispose of the units or shares and any of the following applies:

- you face a capital gains tax bill
- the disposal proceeds are more than twice the amount of the tax-free band for the year (£6,300 for the tax year ending 5 April 1997, £6,500 for the tax year ending 5 April 1996)
- your other disposals in the year create net losses.

## Special reliefs to reduce capital gains tax

If you are disposing of a business or farm, you could face an enormous tax bill on the gain. There are two important reliefs to reduce the impact of capital gains tax on entrepreneurs and others who create small businesses:

- retirement relief when you retire from your business (below)
- roll-over relief if you replace business assets (opposite).

What follows is a brief introduction to indicate their scope. But with large sums at stake, it would pay to seek professional advice on these reliefs to ensure you meet the complex requirements.

### Retirement relief

If you are disposing of a successful business you have built up, capital gains tax could eat into the proceeds which you hoped to live on in retirement. Retirement relief reduces the tax bill if you dispose of a business when aged 50 or more, or less if retiring due to ill-health. (For disposals before 28 November 1995, the qualifying age was 55.)

The amount of relief depends on how long you have owned the business:

- if you have owned it for at least ten years, up to £250,000 of capital gain can be tax-free. And only half the gain between £250,000 and £1,000,000 is taxable
- if you have owned the business for less than ten years, the amount on which you can get relief is reduced by ten per cent for each year less than ten – the example opposite shows how this works.

A husband and wife can each claim retirement relief if they are eligible – doubling the limits for a married couple who share ownership of a business.

Although this relief is called retirement relief, you do not have to retire to claim it – unless you wish to claim it before reaching 50. If you are selling or disposing of your business before 50, you must be retiring because of your ill-health (which is strictly defined) to claim the relief. If you wish to claim this relief because of ill-health, you must do so within two years of the end of the tax year in which you dispose of the business.

The relief applies to business assets, and to shares in a company in which you have at least 5 per cent of the voting rights, providing you have been a full-time director or an employee of the company for the past ten years.

You can still get retirement relief if you have owned several different businesses in the last ten years. Providing that each business qualifies for the relief, and the gap between each is not more than two years, you can add

# EXAMPLE

Harry Singh, aged 65, started a business 30 years ago and sold it in May 1996. The gain after indexation allowance was £500,000. He is entitled to the maximum retirement relief as he had owned the business for more than ten years.

Harry can claim full relief on the first £250,000 plus relief on half the gain between £250,000 and £1,000,000:

$$£250,000 + 50 \text{ per cent of } (£500,000 - £250,000)$$
$$= £250,000 + 50 \text{ per cent of } £250,000$$
$$= £250,000 + £125,000$$
$$= £375,000$$

Harry's taxable gain is:
$$£500,000 - £375,000 = £125,000$$
The first £6,300 of taxable gains in the tax year ending 5 April 1997 is free of capital gains tax, so tax is charged on:
$$£125,000 - £6,300 = £118,700$$
Harry's taxable income is £45,000 on which he pays tax at the higher rate of 40 per cent. His tax bill is therefore:
$$40 \text{ per cent of } £118,700 = £47,480$$

together the separate periods of business activity over the past ten years to calculate the total period that counts for the relief.

## Roll-over relief

If you sell or otherwise dispose of assets from your business, there could be capital gains tax to pay on any gain you make. But you can defer the bill with certain types of business assets if you replace them in the three years after the sale or the one year before it. You can claim this roll-over relief even if you do not buy an identical replacement as long as you use the proceeds to buy another qualifying business asset. Assets which qualify include land or buildings used by the business, goodwill, and fixed plant and machinery.

You usually get the relief by deducting the gain for the old asset from the acquisition cost of the new one. So when you come to sell the new asset, the gain on it has been increased by the gain on the old asset. However, when you sell the new asset, you can claim further roll-over relief, and currently capital gains tax will not have to be paid until you fail to replace the business asset.

# NON-RESIDENCE

## CHAPTER 22

Q9 Are you claiming that you were not resident, or not ordinarily resident, or not domiciled, in the UK for all or part of the year?

NO   YES      NON RESIDENCE ETC YES

If you are a resident of the UK, you are liable for UK tax on all your income whether it comes from within the UK or abroad. But, if you count as a non-resident, there is no UK tax on your income from abroad, only on any income which originates in the UK.

If you want to claim non-residence (or non-domicile) for the tax year ending 5 April 1997, you need to fill in the green Non-residence Supplement which you can get through the Orderline (see p. 75). You are likely to need this if:

- you are normally a UK resident but you are working abroad for an extended period
- you have been a UK resident but you are going to live abroad permanently or indefinitely – for example because you are retiring abroad
- you have been resident elsewhere but you are based in the UK for now.

This guide cannot give you all the detail you may need so you should consult a professional adviser.

Residency is not defined in the tax laws, but broadly it means the place where you usually live. Because different countries use different criteria to decide who is resident, it is possible to count as a resident of more than one country at the same time, in which case you could pay two lots of tax on the same income. However, the UK has double taxation agreements with many countries to avoid this situation.

In general, payment of UK taxes depends on whether or not you were resident during the particular tax year in question. Occasionally, it may hinge on where you are ordinarily resident. Again, there is no hard and fast definition, but basically your ordinary residence is the country you are resident in year after year, which you use as your base, returning to it for extended periods, and probably where you have an established home.

Your domicile can be the key to whether or not there is tax on foreign income and gains you receive and any inheritance tax to pay on your estate when you die. Your country of domicile is the place which you consider to be your permanent home and where you would intend to end your days. You can have only one country of domicile and it is not necessarily the country in which you are resident or ordinarily resident.

Note that even if you are non-resident for tax purposes, you might still be able to claim the UK personal tax allowances to set against your income from UK sources, for example, if you are a citizen of a Commonwealth country or a European country within the European Economic Area (this includes the UK), a Crown employee (or a widow or widower of someone who was a Crown employee) or employed by a UK missionary service.

If your intention is to be out of the country for less than four years, you can continue to pay any mortgage on your UK home through MIRAS and so claim the 15 per cent tax relief on it (see p. 55).

A word of warning: there are Inland Revenue concessions which might apply to you. You can claim the concessions, providing you don't use them simply as a means of avoiding tax. If the Inland Revenue suspects that tax avoidance is your main motive, it will refuse you the concession.

## How do you count as being non-resident?

If you have generally been considered as a UK resident, to count as non-resident for tax purposes, you need to pass all four of the following tests:

- the motive test
- the absent for a whole tax year test
- the 183 days test
- the 91 days test.

The notes which accompany the Non-residence supplement include a calculator which will help you to work out whether you pass all these tests.

### The motive test

You will pass this test if you go abroad to work full-time, providing the other tests are also met. Whether or not your job is full time is judged, first, by comparing your hours with the norm in the UK, but if your job is less structured it will be assessed on its own merits and in the light of what's normal for your type of work and the country you are going to. You could also count as working full time if you have two or more part-time jobs.

By concession, if you count as non-resident because of your work abroad, your wife or husband, if they go with you, will also count as non-resident, providing they pass the other tests.

Another way to pass the test is if you go abroad to live permanently or at least indefinitely. The Inland Revenue will want evidence that this is your intention – for example, that you have bought a home abroad or you are going to marry someone in another country. If you still have a UK home, it wants to know how that fits with your plans to live overseas. Once you've lived abroad for three years, it will be accepted that you are non-resident.

If you can't pass this test at the time you go away, the situation can be reviewed later on, if new evidence of your motive becomes available or once you have been abroad for three years.

### The absent for a whole tax year test
To count as non-resident for a tax year, if you work abroad, your job must last for at least a whole tax year and you must be out of the country for the whole tax year or longer, except for visits within the other rules (see below). Similarly, if you go to live abroad permanently or indefinitely, you must be out of the country for at least a whole tax year.

By concession, in the year you leave and the year you return, you can count as non-resident for just part of the year, provided that year is part of a longer period of non-residency. If you want to claim this split year treatment, you must give details of your date of arrival in or departure from the UK in box 9.25 or box 9.26 of the supplementary pages.

### The 183 days test
You will always count as resident for the tax year if you spend 183 days or more in the UK. There are no exceptions to this rule. For example, if you make visits back home during a period working abroad, the total of your visits during any tax year must come to less than 183 days if you are not to lose your status as a non-resident.

For the purposes of this rule and the next, the days on which you travel do not count as days spent in the UK.

### The 91 days test
In addition to the 183 days test, the average time you spend in the UK must come to less than 91 days in a tax year. This is worked out over the period

since you left until you have been away for four tax years. After that it is worked out over the most recent four tax years. You are allowed to ignore periods you had to spend in the UK for reasons beyond your control – for example because someone in your family was ill.

## How do you count as being non-domiciled in the UK?

Your domicile is relevant only if it will affect the tax you must pay, so unless you fall into one of the following categories, you do not need to fill in boxes 9.27 to 9.31, and you should also leave box 9.5 blank. The tax areas which might be affected are where:

- you have income or gains from foreign investments which you will not be bringing in full into the UK
- you are claiming UK tax relief on contrtibutions to a foreign pension scheme made out of earnings from a non-UK resident employer
- the costs of travelling between the UK and your normal home have been paid by your employer
- you worked abroad for a non-UK employer and have not brought all the earnings into the UK.

You can have only one domicile at a time and there are three ways in which it can be established: by birth, by dependency or by choice. From birth, you normally have the domicile of your father – that is not necessarily the same as the country in which you were born. If the domicile of the person on whom you are dependant changes, so will yours. Similarly, if you become dependant on someone else of a different domicile, your own domicile will fall into line with that. Women no longer acquire their husbands' domicile on marriage. Once you reach age 16, you have the right to choose a new domicile but the change is not easily made. You would need to show that you had settled in the new country of domicile with a view to staying there permanently. Your home, business interests, social and family ties, and the form of any will would all be relevant, but other factors could also be just as important.

> ## TAX-SAVING IDEAS
> If you go to work or live abroad, make sure your trips back home average less than 91 days a year and come to less than 183 days in any single tax year to avoid paying UK taxes on your overseas income.
>
> Taking a long lease of three years on a home abroad would help to show that you intended to live abroad permanently.
>
> If you are returning permanently to the UK after a period of non-residence abroad and you have been saving through an offshore roll-up fund (see p. 235), make sure you sell your investment before you become a UK resident again. If you don't, you will become liable for tax on the rolled-up income.

# KEEPING AN EYE ON YOUR TAX AFFAIRS

**CHAPTER 23**

The introduction of self-assessment means you can take much more control of your tax affairs, and make sure you don't pay a penny more than you should. But there are still several forms the Inland Revenue will send you that you need to check to make sure you aren't paying too much.

This chapter tells you how to check two of the most important forms:

- the PAYE Coding Notice sent to people who work for someone else – this tells your employer how much tax to deduct from your pay packet or salary cheque
- the Statement of Account sent to taxpayers who have income from being self-employed, rent from letting out property or income from investments paid without deduction of tax.

Other forms that will also need checking are the Revenue Calculation Slip, which will be sent to you if you ask your tax inspector to work out your tax bill. And if you have done your own calculations and your tax inspector spots an error, you will receive a Correction Notice. Neither of these was available at the time we went to press. You can use the leaflets which accompany them to check them, or ask us for a guide to checking them by writing to the address on p. ix.

## PAYE CODING NOTICE

This form sets out the calculations your Tax Inspector has made in setting your PAYE code for the tax year. Your employer will use the code to work out how much tax should be deducted from your pay before you get it. People with two jobs should have two PAYE codes – and Coding Notices.

If you have retired, any pensions you get from an employer's pension scheme or personal pension will also have tax deducted from them before you receive the money. Again, you should have a PAYE code for each one if you have more than one substantial pension.

Your PAYE code reflects the amount of allowances your tax inspector estimates you can set against your earnings in the current tax year. It may also be adjusted to collect tax on fringe benefits and income such as freelance earnings, odd pensions and savings interest. The amounts are based on information given in your tax return, by your employer and by other organisations that send details of payments to the Inland Revenue.

If you have been given the right code or codes, you will have paid the right amount of tax on your income by the end of the tax year. But if there has been a mistake, you may pay too much – and have to wait for a rebate. And while paying too little tax may seem attractive, you will have to make up any underpayment in the following tax year – often in one go if it is more than £1,000. So it makes sense to check your PAYE code carefully whenever you receive a Coding Notice.

## Checking a Coding Notice

The main figures on a PAYE Coding Notice are in two columns. The first lists the allowances that are to be set off against this income to reduce the tax bill on it. If this is your main source of income, the Coding Notice should normally list all your allowances unless they are specifically to be set off against other types of income (for example, against rents or freelance income). See p. 284 for the details of what might appear in this column.

The second column lists amounts that will be deducted from your allowances in order to collect extra tax. For example, if you have taxable fringe benefits, their taxable value will normally be in this column. So will other sources of untaxed income, such as freelance earnings, taxable state pensions and benefits and income from savings that have not been taxed. See p. 287 for how to check this column.

Total deductions are subtracted from total allowances to find the amount of income covered by this PAYE code which can be tax-free during the tax year. This is then converted into a PAYE code – normally by knocking off the last figure and adding one of the following letters:

- L – you have been given the personal allowance for those aged under 65
- H – you have also been given the married couple's allowance for those aged under 65 or the additional personal allowance
- P – you have been given the personal allowance for those aged 65 to 74
- V – you have also been given the married couple's allowance for those aged 65 to 74.

So if your only tax allowance is the single person's allowance of £4,045 and you have £160 deductions for fringe benefits, your total tax-free amount for the year will be £4,045 – £160 = £3,885. Your code is found by knocking off the last figure to give you 388, and adding L because you get only the single person's allowance. Your PAYE code will be 388L.

When it comes to deducting tax from your pay, the employer's tax tables will say that an employee with a code of 388 was entitled to tax-free pay during the tax year of £3,889 – divided equally over the year.

The letters after the number mean that if the main allowances change, your PAYE code can be adjusted by your employer or pension provider. So if the single person's allowance is increased from £4,045 to £4,545 in the budget, everyone with an L code will automatically get an extra £500 of tax-free pay.

If the code ends in the letter T, your tax position is more complicated – you may be getting other allowances, for example, blind person's allowance or allowances for people aged 75 and over. You could also get it if you have fringe benefits such as a company car, or have asked for it because you don't want your employer to know what allowances you are entitled to. Changes cannot be made automatically if you have this sort of code and you will have to wait longer for the tax office to make the adjustments.

---

## EXAMPLE

Harold Svensen checks his Coding Notice for the 1997-98 tax year – the one beginning 6 April 1997. This is the code for his main job with Viking Shipbuilders.

He first sees that he has been given the right tax allowances for the year:

- £60 a year for his subscription to his professional body
- £4,045 personal allowance
- £1,830 married couple's allowance.

That makes total allowances of £5,935. The following amounts are deducted from this:

- £150 for Harold's membership of a local sports club paid by the company
- £2,146 for the benefit of his company car
- £637 allowance restriction, to keep the tax relief a basic rate taxpayer such as Harold gets on the married couple's allowance to 15 per cent (see p.287).

Thus Harold has total deductions of £2,933. Harold's tax-free amount for the year is £5,935 – £2,933 = £3,002. His tax code is found by dropping the last digit to get 300; the letter to be added is T, because he has a company car. So Harold's code is 300T.

**Inland Revenue**

## PAYE Coding Notice

This form shows your
tax code for the tax year  | 1997-98 |

> *Please keep all your coding notices. You may need to refer to them if you have to fill in a Tax Return.*

846

MR H SVENSEN
143 WENDOVER ROAD
LONDON

SW14 5NJ

HM INSPECTOR OF TAXES
LONDON PROVINCIAL 24
GRAYFIELD HOUSE
5 BANKHEAD AVENUE
SIGHTHILL
EDINBURGH         EH11 4AE

| Tax Office telephone ☎ | Date of issue |
|---|---|
| 0131 453 7200 | 12 JAN 1997 |

*Please quote your Tax reference and National Insurance number if you contact us*

| Tax reference | National Insurance number |
|---|---|
| 976/52425 | YR 61 53 51 C |

Your tax code for the year shown above is | 300T |

This tax code is used to deduct tax payable on your income from

**VIKING SHIPBUILDERS**

If you move to another job, your new employer will normally continue to use this tax code.
The tax code is made up as follows:

The *'See note'* columns below refer to the numbered notes in the guidance leaflet P3 *Understanding Your Tax Code*. Leaflet P3 also tells you about the **letter part** of your tax code.

Check that the details are correct. If you think they are wrong, or you have any queries, contact your Tax Office (details above).

This coding notice replaces any previous notice for the year. You should pass it to your agent if you have one.

| See note | Your tax allowances | £ | See note | Amounts taken away from your total allowances | £ |
|---|---|---|---|---|---|
| 10 | PROFESSIONAL SUBSCRIPTIONS | 60 | 30 | BENEFITS IN KIND | 150 |
| 01 | PERSONAL ALLOWANCE | 4045 | 30 | CAR BENEFIT | 2146 |
| 02 | MARRIED ALLOWANCE | 1830 | 25 | ALLOWANCE RESTRICTION | 637 |
| | Total allowances | 5935 | | Total deductions | 2933 |

 Your tax free amount for the year is £ 3002 , making your Tax Code 300T  *See example overleaf*

The **Tax free amount** is the difference between your **Total allowances** and **Total deductions**.

*If necessary we will use this box to give you further information about your tax code*

## K codes

If the amount of deductions is more than your allowances, you will have a PAYE code that begins with a K. This is calculated as follows:

- subtract the deductions from the allowances – the answer will be a negative number
- take the last figure off the number
- reduce that number by one
- put a K in front of the answer to give a PAYE code.

K codes have to be recalculated every time the tax allowances change or there is some alteration in your circumstances.

---

### EXAMPLE

Sanjay Patel is a single man, and his only tax allowance is the personal allowance of £4,045. However, he has a company car with a taxable value of £4,650, so his tax-free amount for the year is £4,045 – £4,650 = – £605.

His PAYE code is therefore found by dropping the last digit to get 60. Then he subtracts 1 to get 59 – giving a code of K59. With a PAYE code of K59, Sanjay would have £599 added to his pay for the year before the tax was worked out (instead of having some allowances deducted).

---

## PAYE codes with more than one source of income

There are special PAYE codes which don't have numbers or which have numbers which don't stand for tax allowances. These are mainly used for deducting tax from second or third sources of income:

- BR – this income is all to be taxed at the basic rate. This is where other sources of income have had all your allowances set against them and used up the amount of income which is taxed at the lower rate
- D – this income is all to be taxed at the higher rate. This is where other sources of income have had all your allowances set against them and used up the amount of income which is taxed at the lower and basic rates
- DT – you are not entitled to any tax-free pay, but this source of income is to be taxed first at the lower rate, then the basic rate and perhaps eventually the higher rate
- NT – this income should be paid without any tax being deducted, perhaps because it is less than your tax-free allowances.

## Your tax allowances

In checking your PAYE Coding Notice, make sure you have all the allowances and deductions you're entitled to.

## Personal allowance

This will give the amount you are entitled to for your age (see p. 128).

If you are 65 or over, you are entitled to a higher rate, but this is reduced if your total income is over a set limit – £15,600 for the tax year beginning 6 April 1997. If your tax inspector thinks you are over this limit, you will find an estimate of your total income against Estimated income. If you think this is wrong – because you have stopped getting some income, for example tell your tax inspector.

## Married allowance

This will give the amount of married couple's allowance you are getting (see p. 37).

Again, there is a higher amount if you are 65 or over, which is reduced if your total income is over a set limit (see p. 38 for the exact rules).

## Other allowances

Any other allowances you are entitled to should be listed, including widow's bereavement allowance (p. 49), additional personal allowance (p. 133) and blind person's allowance (p. 129).

## Expenses

Deductions for job expenses (either the amount paid or the flat-rate amount for your job – see p. 172) and subscriptions to professional bodies (p. 172).

## Pensions, retirement annuities and superannuation

There should also be entries for deductions which you are allowed to claim on death and superannuation payments (p. 126) and retirement annuity payments (p. 113).

If you make contributions to a personal pension scheme, you get tax relief at the basic rate automatically, by paying lower premiums (see p. 111). But if

---

E XAMPLE

Gerry Walker makes £500 gross (before tax relief) in personal pension payments in the tax year beginning 6 April 1997. Since the basic rate of tax for the tax year is 23 per cent, he gets basic rate tax relief of 23 per cent of £500 = £115. So he actually hands over £500 – £115 = £385.

But Gerry pays tax at the higher rate, so he is entitled to tax relief of 40 per cent of £500 = £200. The extra £85 (£200 – £115) is given by increasing his tax allowances by £212.50, since 40 per cent of £212.40 is £85.

you pay tax at the higher rates, there will be a entry on your Coding Notice to give you the extra relief.

### Charity gifts relief and taxed annual payment
You can get tax relief on single gifts to charity of £250 or more – Gift Aid (see p. 125). You get tax relief at the basic rate by deducting the amount before handing over the gift; if there is higher rate tax relief due, this is given here as Charity gifts relief which operates in the same way as for personal pension payments.

Likewise, higher rate tax relief on gifts made by covenant to charity (see p. 123) is given under Taxed annual payment.

### Maintenance payments
If you are entitled to tax relief on maintenance payments you are required to make to a former spouse or child, this is where you get it. (See p. 42 for the complicated rules about the amount.)

### Building society interest and loan interest
If you are entitled to tax relief for interest paid on mortgages or other loans which are not in the MIRAS system (see p. 50), this is where the amount you can claim is entered.

There may also be an entry for Beneficial loan interest if you get a cheap or interest-free loan from your employer for a purpose that would entitle you to tax relief on interest paid – for example, a mortgage on your only or main home. There will be tax on the benefit which will be collected elsewhere on the Coding Notice – this entry gives you the tax relief.

### Lower rate tax allowance
If this is a PAYE code for a second source of income, it will normally be a BR code which means all this income is taxed at the basic rate (see p. 284). But if your first source of income isn't big enough to use up all the amount of income taxable at the lower rate (£4,100 in the tax year beginning 6 April 1997), you will get an allowance here to reduce the amount of tax paid on the second source of income.

### Balance of allowances
There may be an allowance here in the code for a second source of income where the first source isn't big enough to use up all your allowances.

### Other items
Lots of other less common tax allowances and deductions can be included in

this column – including losses from self-employment (p. 209) or letting property (p. 230), vocational training tuition fees (p. 117), tax relief on Enterprise Investment Scheme investments (p. 122) and wife's transitional relief (p. 129).

## Amounts to be taken away from your tax allowances

These amounts reduce the amount of your tax-free pay and thus increase the amount of tax deducted from your earnings or pension.

### Allowance restriction

Several tax allowances are restricted to tax relief at 15 per cent only – for example, married couple's allowance and additional personal allowance. You will have been given these allowances in the first column, but the PAYE system would then give you tax relief at your top rate of tax:

- 20 per cent if it is the lower rate
- 23 per cent if it is the basic rate in the tax year beginning 6 April 1997
- 40 per cent if it is the higher rate.

Allowance restriction will recover the extra tax relief you would get if this happened.

### EXAMPLE

Betty Pinder gets additional personal allowance – £1,830 at 15 per cent only for the tax year beginning 6 April 1997. This means she should get tax relief of 15 per cent of £1,830 = £274.50. But Betty pays tax at the higher rate of 40 per cent – so if the allowance of £1,830 is set against her income, the PAYE system would give her tax relief of 40 per cent of £1,830 = £732. This is £732 – £274.50 = £457.50 more tax relief than she should receive.

Betty's tax inspector corrects this with an Allowance restriction of £1,143.75. By deducting this amount from her allowances, the Inland Revenue recoups 40 per cent of £1,143.75 = £458.

For basic rate taxpayers, the amount of the restriction in the tax year beginning 6 April 1997 should be £637 for the married couple's allowance (or any other allowance worth £1,830 for the tax year). For lower rate taxpayers, the allowance restriction should be £458.

If you expect your top rate of tax to have changed in this tax year, this restriction might be too large or too small. If so, tell your tax inspector so the right amount of tax is deducted through PAYE.

### Married allowance to wife
This is for married men where the wife is to receive half or all the married couple's allowance given in the allowances column.

### State pension and state benefits
If you receive taxable state pension or other benefits, these are paid without deduction of tax. The amount you will receive during the tax year will be entered here, reducing your tax-free allowances to be set against any other earnings or pensions.

If you are a married man, the amount will not include any state pension based on your National Insurance contributions paid to your wife if 60 or over. This will be treated as your wife's and she can set her own personal allowance against it (see p. 95).

Small amounts of other pensions may be included here to collect tax on them. For example, armed forces pensions, other occupational pensions or income from personal pension schemes. If these are larger sources of income, they may be taxed under PAYE with their own PAYE code by the organisation making the payments.

### Unemployment benefit and incapacity benefit
This is the taxable amount of jobseeker's allowance or incapacity benefit you are due to get in the tax year.

### Car benefit, van benefit and car fuel benefit
If you have a company car or van available for private motoring, the taxable benefit will be included here (see p. 155 for how it is worked out). Likewise, if your employer pays for fuel for private use, there will be an entry here (see p. 158).

Check the amount of car benefit has been reduced if you do more than 2,500 miles a year on business trips or the car is four years old or more during the tax year. Any contributions for private mileage should be deducted from the benefit. And there are special rules to reduce the tax paid on vans that are not available to you all the time (see p. 159).

### Employer's loan benefit
This amount is the taxable benefit of any interest-free or low-interest loans from your employer (see p. 160). If you are entitled to tax relief on some of the interest paid (for example, on the first £30,000 of a loan to buy your home), this will have been entered in the first column under Beneficial loan interest.

## Other fringe benefits

There will be special entries if your employer pays for private medical insurance (p. 162), provides you with a mobile phone (p. 161), pays your home telephone expenses or provides any other benefits in kind (see p. 146).

If you get a taxable allowance for work expenses – for using your home or car, for example – this will be entered as Taxable expenses payments. Some of these costs may be claimed as expenses against tax and should then be entered in the first column against Job expenses.

## Part-time earnings, tips and commission

Tax on small amounts of earnings can be collected here – for example, on small amounts of part-time earnings, tips (p. 146), commission (p. 143) and other types of income from employment.

## Maintenance payments received

If you receive maintenance payments which are taxable, the taxable amount will be here (see p. 98).

## Property income

If you receive small amounts from letting out rooms or other property, the tax can be collected here from your earnings under PAYE.

## Untaxed interest

This amount collects tax on interest you are expected to get during the tax year which will not have tax deducted from it first – for example, from National Savings Investment Accounts (see p. 86).

This income is taxed at 20 per cent only (see p. 63). So if you pay tax at no more than the lower rate of 20 per cent the actual amount you are expected to receive will be entered here. But if you pay tax at the basic rate on your income – 23 per cent for the tax year beginning 6 April 1997 – the amount entered here will be less than you actually get. This is to avoid too much tax being collected on it.

---

E X A M P L E

Gerry Walker gets £200 of interest from his National Savings Investment Account in the tax year beginning 6 April 1997. He should pay tax of 20 per cent of £200 = £40. But he is a basic rate taxpayer, so adding £200 to his taxable income would collect too much – 23 per cent of £200 = £46.

Gerry's tax inspector adds £174 to Gerry's income with an Untaxed interest deduction from his PAYE code. This will collect the right amount, since 23 per cent of £174 = £40.

---

## Taxed annual payment

If you have deducted tax relief at the basic rate from covenant payments, but are entitled to tax relief at the lower rate only, this amount will take back the extra tax relief you have given yourself.

## Loan interest restriction

You are entitled to tax relief on mortgage interest on loans of up to £30,000 at 15 per cent only (see p. 50). The MIRAS system automatically gives you the right amount of tax relief, but if the loan is not in the MIRAS scheme, you will have claimed the tax relief direct from the Inland Revenue. The deduction for this interest should have been in the first column; this amount is what is needed to restrict your tax relief to 15 per cent.

## Lower rate tax adjustment

This adjustment is made if you are paying tax at the lower rate on more than one source of income and too much of your income is being taxed at this rate (that is, more than £4,100 in the tax year beginning 6 April 1997).

## Basic rate tax restriction

This is a similar adjustment if you have income from more than one source and too much has been taxed at the basic rate (more than £22,000 in the tax year beginning 6 April 1997).

## Higher rate tax adjustment

Higher rate taxpayers receive interest, dividends and some other sorts of income after deduction of tax which covers any basic rate tax due. This adjustment collects any extra higher rate tax due on such income.

---

### EXAMPLE

Betty Pinder pays tax at the higher rate and receives £1,000 of interest and dividends. This is paid after deduction of tax at 20 per cent: 20 per cent of £1,000 is £200, so she receives £1,000 − £200 = £800 of savings income net.

But Betty should have paid tax at 40 per cent on the gross amount − 40 per cent of £1,000 = £400. So she owes another £400 − £200 = £200. To collect this £200, a higher rate tax adjustment of £500 is made. By adding £500 to Betty's taxable income, she will pay 40 per cent of £500 = £200 on her income taxed under PAYE.

---

## Tax underpaid

If you have underpaid up to £1,000 of tax in a previous tax year, the Inland Revenue will normally try to collect this by an adjustment to your PAYE code.

> ## E X A M P L E
>
> Gerry Walker owes £450 in tax unpaid from the tax year ending 5 April 1997 and pays tax in the tax year beginning 6 April 1997 at the basic rate of 23 per cent only. His tax inspector adds the following amount to his taxable income for the tax year to collect the £450:
>
> $$£450 \times \frac{100}{23} = £1,957$$

### Allowances allocated elsewhere

If your allowances listed in the first column are more than the amount of income covered by this Coding Notice, the surplus may be allocated to other sources of income (and thus other Coding Notices). This entry in the second column is for any allowances thus allocated to other sources of income.

### Other items

Lots of other less common types of income and adjustments can be included in this column. For example, if you have a balancing charge to add to your income because you claimed capital allowances in an earlier year (see p. 173).

## STATEMENT OF ACCOUNT

If you have income of £500 or more in a tax year from being self-employed, from letting out property, or from investments which pay out income without deduction of tax, you will normally have to make two payments of tax on account against your final tax bill for the year. However, there will be no need to make such payments if most of your tax – 80 per cent or more – is deducted from your income at source.

If you do have to make payments on account, the first is due on 31 January during the tax year, the second by 31 July after it has finished. The amounts are based on the income you got in the previous tax year.

If you are calculating your own tax bill (see p. 295), it is up to you to calculate the amounts. But if you ask your tax inspector to do the calculations, the amounts will be notified to you in two Statements of Account sent out by the Inland Revenue: one around December during the tax year; the other around June after the end of the tax year. Note that for the tax year ending 5 April 1997, self-assessment had not been fully introduced, so all payments on account were calculated by the Inland Revenue.

Unless you appeal against a Statement of Account, you must pay the tax

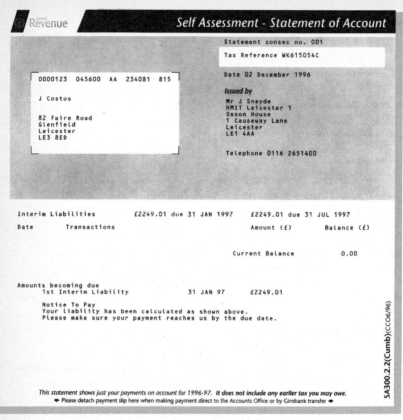

requested on it by the right date – paying late could mean an interest charge (see p. 17). So it is vital to check the statement. If it demands more than you should pay in the current tax year, you can ask for the payments to be reduced. But you must do this before the date the payment is due. This section of the guide tells you how to check a statement and how to claim a reduction.

## Payments on account for the tax year ending 5 April 1997

For the tax year ending 5 April 1997, the first payment on account was due by 31 January 1997 and asked for the following:

- half the income tax and Class 4 National Insurance paid on your profits from self-employment in the tax year ending 5 April 1996
- all the income tax paid on your income from property in the tax year ending 5 April 1996 (in some cases, only half)
- all the income tax paid on investments where the income is paid without

deduction of tax in the tax year ending 5 April 1996.

The second payment on account for this tax year is due by 31 July 1997, and is made up of the other half of the income tax and Class 4 National Insurance on your profits from self-employment paid in the tax year ending 5 April 1996 (plus the rest of any tax on property income).

Some pensioners have been able to pay tax on their pensions and earnings in four quarterly instalments instead of by deduction through PAYE. This ended with the introduction of self-assessment, and they will pay their tax in two instalments which will also be requested with the Statement of Account.

## Payments on account for the tax year beginning 6 April 1997
For the tax year beginning 6 April 1997, the first payment on account is due by 31 January 1998 and will ask for half the following:

- income tax and Class 4 National Insurance paid on your profits from self-employment for the tax year ending 5 April 1997
- the income tax paid on your income from property in the tax year ending 5 April 1997
- the income tax paid on investments where the income is paid without deduction of tax in the tax year ending 5 April 1997
- the higher-rate tax due for the tax year ending 5 April 1997 on any other income not already collected through PAYE.

This first payment on account will be made at the same time as your third and final payment for the tax year ending 5 April 1997. This latter will also include any capital gains tax due for the tax year ending 5 April 1997 and any higher rate tax due on income for that year.

The second payment on account for the tax year beginning 6 April 1997 will be due on 31 July 1998, and will be the other half of the amounts in the first payment on account.

The final payment for the year, due by 31 January 1999, will include any capital gains tax due for the tax year beginning 6 April 1997.

## Checking a Statement of Account
Since the amount of a payment on account is based on your tax bill for the previous tax year, it is relatively simple to check that you have been asked for the right amount. Simply add up the amounts from the previous year to check the totals on your Statement of Account.

## How to reduce your payments on account

If you think your tax bills for the types of income covered by a Statement of Account will be lower than the previous year, you can claim to make a lower payment on account than the Inland Revenue is asking for. This might happen if your income has dropped off – for example, you have received less in rent, profits from your business or on the investment income which is received without deduction of tax. Or your tax bill might be less because you are entitled to claim higher allowances and deductions against your income – if you have married, for example, or made a large investment in the Enterprise Investment Scheme (see p. 72).

If this is the case, work out your expected tax bill for this tax year carefully. Then calculate how this should be divided between the two payments on account. If you should be paying less than the Inland Revenue is asking for, make your claim to pay less on Inland Revenue form SA303. A copy is sent out with every Statement of Account – if you have lost yours, ask your tax office for another copy. You must send this back before the payment on account is due.

If later you realise you could pay still less, you can make a further claim – as long as it is before the payment is due. If you discover after making the first payment that it was too much, you can reduce the second payment on account to compensate.

It is probably better to pay slightly more rather than too little in your payments on account. If you pay too much, you will get interest on it; if you pay too little, you will pay interest. There are penalties in the form of fines if you are caught trying to hoodwink your tax inspector in the amounts you pay. And if you make the payments on account demanded on time, there is normally no interest to pay even if your tax bill turns out to have been much higher.

# ILLING IN THE TAX CALCULATOR

**CHAPTER 24**

**Q18** Do you want to calculate your tax? NO ☐ YES ☐ **If yes,** do it now then fill in boxes 18.1 to 18.9 below. Your Tax Calculation Guide will help

The objective of the new self-assessment system of tax collection is that you, the taxpayer, should calculate your own tax bill. If you prefer to leave it to your tax inspector, you can do so – provided you send the tax return back in time for this to be done (see p. 14). And in the first year of the new system, the Inland Revenue says it would prefer you to leave it to them to do the calculations.

There is nothing to stop you doing the calculations yourself. The Inland Revenue sends out a green Tax Calculation Guide with the tax return which is relatively easy to complete for most people. So if you are prepared to seize control of your tax affairs, tick the box against Q 18 on page 7 of the tax return and open the Tax Calculation Guide on page 5. There you will find the tax calculation working sheet you need to fill in – and this chapter takes you through the calculations step by step. The next chapter has examples of how two typical taxpayers might do the sums.

## Have you made a chargeable capital gain?
If you have made a chargeable capital gain in the tax year ending 5 April 1997 there is a special Tax Calculation Guide. If you entered a figure in box 8.8 on page CG1 of the Capital gains supplementary pages, ask the Orderline for the Tax Calculation Guide (Capital gains).

This version of the tax calculator – which is likely to be largely the same as the standard one – was not finalised at the time we went to press. If you need help filling it in, send for our extra guide (see p. ix).

## When you might not want to work out your own tax
Anyone with enough determination can calculate their own tax. But some

people's tax affairs are quite complicated that it will need a great deal of determination:

- foreign income from savings, pensions, benefits or property – you may be able to claim tax credit relief against any foreign tax you have paid on the income. If you want to claim tax credit relief, you can calculate your tax bill only if you have worked out the amount (see p. 236)
- non-resident – the tax treatment of people who live abroad is beyond the scope of this guide
- Lloyd's underwriters – you have your own tax return to fill in to reflect the special rules for taxing your income
- ministers of religion – you also have your own tax return
- farmers – special rules in various parts of the tax system.

See also the box below on special tax circumstances.

If you want the Inland Revenue to calculate your tax, remember to send your tax return back on time – normally by 30 September (see p. 14).

---

### SPECIAL TAX CIRCUMSTANCES

There is a special Tax Calculation Guide if in the tax year ending 5 April 1997 you received certain lump sums or income that comes with a notional tax credit for basic rate tax. Ask the Orderline for the Tax Calculation Guide (Lump sums etc) if you entered figures (other than zeros) in any of the following boxes elsewhere in the tax return:

- box 6.8 on page F2 of the olive Foreign section of the tax return, or boxes 12.5 or 12.8 on page 4 of the Income section – a chargeable gain on a life insurance policy
- box 1.29 on page E2 of the pink Employment section – a lump sum or compensation payment on leaving a job
- box 7.18 on page T1 of the brown Trusts etc section – income from the estate of someone who died which came with a notional tax credit at the basic rate
- box 12.12 on page 4 in the Income section – a refund of surplus additional voluntary contributions from a pension scheme.

This special Tax Calculation Guide spreads a chargeable life insurance gain over several years to reduce the tax bill on it (see p. 102). It also steers you through the complicated rules for deducting your various tax allowances and reliefs from other sorts of income.

# FILLING IN THE TAX CALCULATION WORKING SHEET

The working sheet begins on page 5 of the Tax Calculation Guide by asking you to bring together all your income for the tax year ending 5 April 1997 to find your total taxable income. You will need to draw figures from your tax return, so have it handy.

> **Total income from**

The first 11 boxes ask you to enter details of your income by drawing on figures you have entered in various parts of the tax return. Most people will not have to enter an amount in every box – only in the boxes that relate to the sort of income they receive.

- **Employment** *including* benefits and *less* expenses for **each** employment

|  | First employment | Other employments |
|---|---|---|
| **Add** income in boxes 1.8 to 1.10, 1.12 to 1.23 and 1.27 to 1.29 | £ | £ |
| **Deduct** any figures in boxes 1.31 to 1.38 | £ | £ |
| Total taxable income | £ | + £    = W1 £ |

Start with your employment income from working for someone else or a company – you will need amounts from the pink Employment section of the tax return.

First enter the total of earnings, expenses and the value of fringe benefits from your main job in the top box in the first column. Your earnings are in boxes 1.8, 1.9, 1.10 on page E1 of the Employment section; expenses and fringe benefits are in boxes 1.12 to 1.23 inclusive. You must also include in this total any amounts for taxable lump sums in boxes 1.27, 1.28 and 1.29 on page E2.

Then enter the amount of the above income which is not taxable in the second box down in the first column – boxes 1.31 to 1.38 in the Employment section inclusive. Subtract the total in the second box from that in the first box to get the total taxable income from your main job and enter this in the third box in the first column.

If you have employment income from more than one job, put the same totals for all the other jobs added together in the three boxes in the second column. The third box in the second column will then have your total taxable income from all jobs other than your main one.

Add the totals in the two boxes in the third row to get your total taxable income from employment, and enter this in box W1.

*   *Share Schemes* (from box 2.31)  W2 £

If you received any taxable income from share options or share-related fringe benefits in the tax year ending 5 April 1997, enter the total in box W2. This is the amount in box 2.31 on page S1 of the purple Share schemes supplementary pages.

*   *Self-employment* (from box 3.89)  W3 £

If you received income from being self-employed in the tax year ending 5 April 1997, enter the total taxable profits in box W3. This is the amount in box 3.89 on page SE3 of the orange Self-employment supplementary pages.

If you have more than one lot of income from self-employment, add together the total taxable profits from each and enter the grand total in box W3.

*   *Partnerships* (from boxes 4.32, 4.65 and 4.68)  W4 £

If you received income from partnerships in the tax year ending 5 April 1997, enter your share of the partnership's taxable income in box W4. This is found by adding the amounts in boxes 4.32, 4.65 and 4.68 on the turquoise Partnership supplement. (If you have had to complete only the short version, there is no box 4.32 to worry about.)

If you have more than one lot of income from partnerships, add together the amounts for each and enter the grand total in box W4.

*   *Land and property* (from box 5.43) W5 £

If you received income from letting out rooms, homes, land or other property in the tax year ending 5 April 1997, enter your total profit in box W5. This is the amount in box 5.43 on page L2 of the red Land and property supplementary pages.

- *Foreign income* (from boxes 6.2, 6.4, 6.5 and 6.8)  £

If you received income from abroad from investments, pensions, benefits or property, enter the amount chargeable to tax for the tax year ending 5 April 1997 in box W6. This is found by adding the amounts in boxes 6.2, 6.4, 6.5 and 6.8 on pages F1 and F2 of the olive Foreign income supplementary pages.

- *Trusts, settlements or estates of deceased persons*
  (add together any figures in taxable amount column and deduct any figure in box 7.19)  £

If you received taxable income from trusts, other forms of settlement such as a transfer of assets or the estates of people who have died, enter the amount for the tax year ending 5 April 1997 in box W7. This is found by adding the amounts in boxes 7.3, 7.6, 7.9, 7.12, 7.15 and 7.18 on page T1 of the brown Trusts etc supplement and subtracting any amount in box 7.19.

- *UK savings and investments* (total any figures in taxable amount column on page 3 of your Tax Return)  £

If you received any income from UK savings and investments in the tax year ending 5 April 1997, enter the total taxable amount in box W8. This is found by adding the taxable amounts entered in the Income section on page 3 of the tax return: boxes 10.1, 10.4, 10.7, 10.8, 10.11, 10.14, 10.17, 10.20, 10.23, 10.26, 10.29 and 10.32.

- *UK pensions, retirement annuities and benefits* (add together any figures in taxable amount column on page 4 of your Tax Return and deduct any exemption in box 11.13)  £

If you received any UK pension, social security benefit or income from a retirement annuity in the tax year ending 5 April 1997, enter the total taxable amount in box W9.

This is found by adding the following amounts in the third Taxable amount column in the Income section on page 4 of the tax return: boxes 11.1, 11.2, 11.3, 11.4, 11.5, 11.6, 11.7, 11.9, 11.12. Then subtract any amount in box 11.13.

- *Maintenance and alimony received* (from box 12.3)  W10 £

If you received taxable maintenance or alimony in the tax year ending 5 April 1997, enter the amount in box W10. This is the amount in box 12.3 in the Income section on page 4 of the tax return.

• **Other income** (copy the figure in box 13.3 less any figure in box 13.5)

Box W11 is for any other income you received in the tax year ending 5 April 1997 that was not entered somewhere else on the tax return. The figure to enter is the amount in box 13.3 in the Income section on page 4 of the tax return, less the amount in box 13.5.

Add the amounts in boxes W1 to W11 and enter the total in box W12. This is your total taxable income for the tax year ending 5 April 1997.

## Deductions for

This is where you enter the various deductions you are allowed to set against your total taxable income in the tax year ending 5 April 1997. You won't be asked here to give details of deductions which lead to a fixed reduction in the amount of tax you pay since these are entered later in boxes W40 to W46.

• **Personal pension** (add together any figures in boxes 14.5, 14.10, 14.15, 14.16 and 14.17)

If you are claiming tax relief for contributions to a personal pension or retirement annuity for the tax year ending 5 April 1997, enter the total contributions claimed in box W13. You can find this amount by adding the amounts in boxes 14.5, 14.10, 14.15, 14.16 and 14.17 in the Reliefs section on page 5 of the tax return.

• **Vocational training** (multiply any figure in box 15.1 by $^{100}/_{76}$)

If you are paying for certain types of vocational training, you can get tax relief on the cost (see p. 117). You get tax relief at the basic rate automatically by paying reduced fees. But you need to enter here the before-tax-relief amount you paid in the tax year ending 5 April 1997 in case you are due some tax relief at the higher rate.

To find the before-tax-relief amount, take the amount you entered in box 15.1 in the Reliefs section on page 5 of the tax return and multiply it by $^{100}/_{76}$. Enter the answer in box W14.

- **Interest on qualifying loans** (from box 15.3)   W15 £ [                    ]

Enter the amount of interest you paid in the tax year ending 5 April 1997 on which you can get tax relief in box W15. The amount to enter is in box 15.3 in the Reliefs section on page 5 of the tax return. Note that this amount excludes interest on loans to buy your only or main home – the tax relief on this is given automatically in the form of lower mortgage payments, through MIRAS (see p. 50).

- **Maintenance or alimony paid** (see notes on page 2)   W16 £ [                    ]

The amount of tax relief you get on maintenance or alimony paid depends on whether they are dealt with under the new rules for payments since 1988 or the old rules that previously applied (see p. 43). You will already have had to decide whether the new or the old rules applied in filling in boxes 15.4, 15.5 and 15.6 in the Reliefs section on page 5 of the tax return.

This is what you fill in here for the tax year ending 5 April 1997:

- if the payments are made under the new rules, leave box W16 blank. Then enter the amount from box 15.4 in box W42.6 on page 6 of the Tax Calculation Guide
- if the payments are made under the old rules, enter the amount from box 15.6 in box W16 and the amount from box 15.5 in box W42.6
- if the payments are made under both sets of rules, leave box W16 blank. Then add together any amounts in boxes 15.4 and 15.5 (one of them may be blank), and enter the total in box W42.6.

- **Charitable covenants, annuities and Gift Aid payments**
  (multiply any figures in boxes 15.9 and 15.10 by $^{100}/_{76}$)   W17 £ [                    ]

You can get tax relief on regular gifts made to charity by covenant and on larger one-off gifts under the Gift Aid scheme (see p. 125). You get tax relief at the basic rate automatically by handing over the gifts after deducting tax at the basic rate. But you need to enter here the before-tax-relief amount of such gifts in the tax year ending 5 April 1997 in case you are due some tax relief at the higher rate (or have had too much tax relief and must pay some back).

To find the before-tax-relief amount, add the amounts you entered in boxes 15.9 and 15.10 in the Reliefs section on page 5 of the tax return and multiply the total by $^{100}/_{76}$. Enter the answer in box W17.

- **Losses and post-cessation expenses** (from boxes 3.82, 4.12, 4.58, 5.16, 5.44, 8.16 and 15.11)  W18 £

If you have made losses from being self-employed, working in a partnership or letting property, you can set them off against other income. The same is true of capital losses on disposing of assets and – in certain circumstances – expenses incurred after you wind up a business or leave a job. This is where you enter such amounts in the tax calculation working sheet.

To claim such losses, add the following amounts:

- box 3.82 on page SE4 of the orange Self-employment supplement
- box 4.12 on page P1 of the turquoise Partnership supplement – plus, if you get the full four-page version of this section, box 4.58 on page P3
- box 5.16 on page L1 and box 5.44 on page L2 of the red Land and property supplement
- box 8.16 on page CG1 of the blue Capital gains supplement
- box 15.11 on page 5 in the Reliefs section of the basic tax return.

Enter the total in box W18.

- **Trade union and friendly society death benefit payments** (from box 15.12) W19 £

Enter the amount from box 15.12 in the Reliefs section on page 5 of the tax return in box W19.

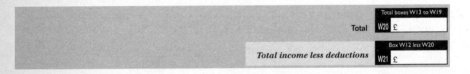

Total | Total boxes W13 to W19 <br> W20 £

Total income less deductions | Box W12 less W20 <br> W21 £

Add the amounts in boxes W13 to W19 and enter the total in box W20. This is your total deductions that can be set against total taxable income for the tax year ending 5 April 1997.

Subtract the amount in box W20 from the amount in box W12 and enter the answer in box W21. This is your total income less deductions for the tax year ending 5 April 1997.

# CALCULATING THE TAX DUE

Turn to pages 6 and 7 of the Tax Calculation Guide to work out the amount of income tax due on your total income less deductions. The working sheets will now calculate the income tax due on your total income after taking account of all the allowances and reliefs you can claim for the tax year ending 5 April 1997 – including personal allowances.

This involves some complications because there are different tax rates for different types of income. For example, up to £25,500 of savings income is taxed at 20 per cent for the tax year ending 5 April 1997. But only £3,900 of other sorts of income is taxed at 20 per cent, and the next £21,600 is taxed at the basic rate which was 24 per cent for that tax year.

The tax calculation working sheets therefore go through a four-step process to work out your tax bill. You don't need to understand it to do the sums – so if you want to get on with it, just jump on down to Reliefs, below. But for those who want to understand the calculation, the four steps are:

1. Work out how much tax you would pay if your total income after all allowances and reliefs was taxed at the lower rate of 20 per cent.
2. If your total income after all allowances and reliefs is more than £3,900, 4 per cent of the excess apart from any savings income is added to your tax bill. This 4 per cent means non-savings income over £3,900 is taxed at 24 per cent.
3. If your total income after all allowances and reliefs is more than £25,500, higher rate tax is due on the excess at 40 per cent. So 16 per cent of the excess is added to your tax bill. This means that non-savings income over the £25,500 limit has been taxed at 40 per cent (20 + 4 +16 per cent). But savings income has been taxed at only 36 per cent (20 + 16 per cent).
4. This step adds 4 per cent of savings income over £25,500 to your tax bill, bringing it up to the 40 per cent higher rate (36 + 4 per cent).

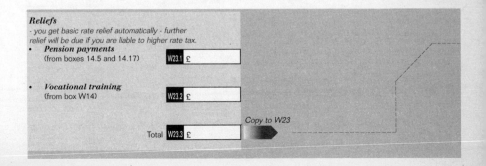

*Reliefs*
*- you get basic rate relief automatically - further*
*relief will be due if you are liable to higher rate tax.*
- *Pension payments*
  (from boxes 14.5 and 14.17)    W23.1 £

- *Vocational training*
  (from box W14)    W23.2 £

Total W23.3 £    *Copy to W23*

If you have made payments on which you have already had tax relief at the basic rate of 24 per cent, these payments must be added back here if you are not to get a second lot of tax relief:

**NEGATIVE ANSWERS?**

If any of the sums you are asked to do in filling in pages 6 and 7 of the Tax Calculation Guide produce a negative number, enter 0 as the answer.

- if you made contributions to a personal pension or free-standing additional voluntary contribution plan, add the amounts in boxes 14.15 and 14.17 in the Reliefs section on page 5 of the tax return and enter the total in box W23.1
- if you made payments for vocational training, enter the amount in box W14 on the previous page of the Tax Calculation Guide in box W23.2.

Add the amounts in boxes W23.1 and W23.2 and enter the total in box W23.3. Now follow the dashed line to box W23.

Complete this as follows:

- box W22 – enter the amount in box W21 on page 5 of the Tax Calculation Guide

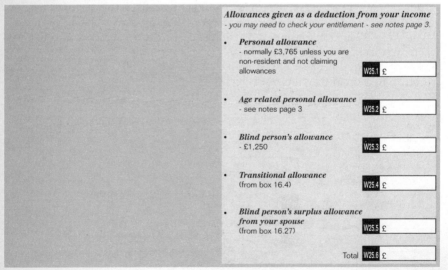

- box W23 – enter the amount in box W23.3, along the dashed line on the opposite page
- box W24 – enter the total of boxes W22 and W23.

Now go to Allowances given as a deduction from your income on the opposite page of the tax calculation working sheet.

This section (see below left) is to enter allowances that can be deducted from your income before tax is calculated. Enter the following allowances only if you have claimed them in the Allowances section on page 6 of the tax return:

- box W25.1 – your personal allowance. Enter £3,765
- box W25.2 – any extra personal allowance you are entitled to if born on or before 5 April 1932. Enter 0 if born on or after 6 April 1932; otherwise see box on p. 307 for what to enter
- box W25.3 – blind person's allowance. Enter £1,250
- box W25.4 – transitional allowance for some wives whose husbands have a low income (see p. 129) Enter the amount in box 16.4 in the Allowances section on page 6 of the tax return
- box W25.5 – blind person's surplus allowance your spouse cannot use up. Enter the amount in box 16.27 in the Allowances section on page 6 of the tax return.

Add boxes W25.1 to W25.5 and enter the total in box W25.6. Now follow the dashed line to box W25.

Enter the amount in box W25.6 in box W25. Subtract the amount in box W25 from the amount in box W24 and enter the result in box W26.

Multiply the amount in box W26 by 20 per cent ($^{20}/_{100}$), and enter the answer in box W27.

If box W26 is £3,900 or less, leave boxes W28 to W38 blank and go to box W39, on p. 308. Otherwise go to Savings income taxed at the lower (20%) rate on the opposite page of the tax calculation working sheet (see over).

*Savings income taxed at the lower (20%) rate*

- **Partnership savings**
  (from boxes 4.32 and 4.65)　W28.1 £

- **UK savings**
  (from box W8)　W28.2 £

- **Foreign savings**
  (from box 6.2)　W28.3 £

- **Trusts, settlements and estate income**
  (from boxes 7.6, 7.12
  and 7.15)　W20.4 £

*Copy to W28*

Total　W28.5 £

This part of the tax calculator works out how much of your income should have been taxed at the 20 per cent rate for savings:

- box W28.1 – your share of partnership savings income. Add the amounts in boxes 4.32 and 4.65 in the turquoise Partnership supplementary pages (if you have filled in the short version, there is no box 4.32)
- box W28.2 – UK savings income. Enter the amount in box W8 on the first page of the tax calculation working sheet
- box W28.3 – foreign savings income. Enter the amount in box 6.2 on page F1 of the olive Foreign supplementary pages
- box W28.4 – income from trusts, settlements and the estates of deceased persons. Enter the total of boxes 7.6, 7.12 and 7.15 on page T1 of the brown Trusts supplementary pages.

Add the amounts in boxes W28.1 to W28.4 and enter the total in box W28.5. Now follow the dashed line to box W28.

W28 £

box W26 *less* box W28
W29 £

W30 £ 3,900　box W29 *less* box W30 W31 £　box W31 x 4% W32 £

Enter the amount in box W28.5 in box W28. Subtract the amount in box W28 from the amount in box W26 and enter the result in box W29.

# BORN ON OR BEFORE 5 APRIL 1932?

If you were born on or before 5 April 1932, you qualify for extra personal allowance for the tax year ending 5 April 1997 – provided your total income is below £15,200 (see p. 10). This box helps you work out how much you are entitled to.

First add the amount in box W21 to the amount in box W19. Enter the amount here – this is your total income:

_____ **Amount A**

Then enter the following maximum amount of extra personal allowance for people of 65 and over as Amount B:

- if you were born on or after 6 April 1922 and on or before 5 April 1932 – £1,145
- if you were born on or before 5 April 1922 – £1,325.

_____ **Amount B**

If Amount A is £15,200 or less, enter Amount B in box W25.2.

If Amount A is more than £15,200, subtract £15,200 from Amount A and enter the answer as Amount C:

_____ **Amount C**

Multiply Amount C by $^1/_2$          _____ **Amount D**

If Amount D is more than Amount B, enter 0 in box W25.2.

If Amount D is less than Amount B, subtract Amount D from Amount B and enter the answer in box W25.2.

Subtract the amount in box W30 (£3,900) from box W29 and enter the result in box W31.

Multiply the amount in box W31 by 4 per cent ($^4/_{100}$) and enter the answer in box W32.

Add the amount in box W23 to the amount in box 12.9 in the Income section on page 4 of the tax return. Subtract the total from the amount in box W26 and enter the answer in box W33.

If the amount in box W33 is £25,500 or less, leave boxes W35 to W38 blank and go straight to box W39, below.

If the amount in box W33 is more than £25,500, subtract the amount in box W34 – £25,500 – from it and enter the answer in box W35. Multiply the amount in box W35 by 16 per cent ($^{16}/_{100}$), and enter the answer in box W36.

Look at boxes W28 and W35 to see which is the lower. Enter the lower of the two in box W37. Multiply the amount in box W37 by 4 per cent ($^4/_{100}$), and enter the answer in box W38.

Add boxes W27, W32, W36 and W38 and enter the total in box W39 to find the income tax due for the tax year ending 5 April 1997. There are still some further adjustments to be made, however.

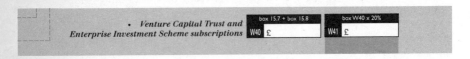

Add the amounts in boxes 15.7 and 15.8 in the Reliefs section on page 5 of the tax return, and enter the total Venture Capital Trust and Enterprise Investment Scheme subscriptions in box W40.

Multiply the amount in box W40 by 20 per cent (20/100), and enter the answer in box W41. Now go to Allowances and reliefs given in terms of tax on the opposite page of the tax calculation working sheet. This section is to enter allowances that have to be used to reduce your tax bill rather than the amount of your taxable income – because the tax relief is restricted to 15 per cent.

> **Allowances and reliefs given in terms of tax**
> these reduce your tax bill - you may need to use the Question 16 Notes on pages 23 to 26 of the Tax Return Guide and on pages 3 and 4 of this guide.
>
> • **Married couple's allowance**
>   - see notes on pages 3 and 4        W42.1  £

The first such allowance is the married couple's allowance. If both of you were born on or after 6 April 1932, the allowance for the tax year ending 5 April 1997 was £1,790 – though this is reduced if you were married for only part of the tax year (see p. 40). The married couple's allowance goes to the husband unless the wife has asked for half of it to be set off against her income (£895 each) or both have agreed the whole £1,790 goes to the wife. Enter the amount you are entitled to in box W42.1.

If either husband or wife was born on or before 5 April 1932, the husband may be entitled to a higher married couple's allowance – see box below for how to calculate the amounts both husband and wife should enter in box W42.1.

---

# WERE EITHER OF YOU BORN ON OR BEFORE 5 APRIL 1932?

If you or your spouse were born on or before 5 April 1932, you may be entitled to a higher rate of married couple's allowance for the tax year ending 5 April 1997. There are two parts of your married couple's allowance:

• the basic £1,790 married couple's allowance which goes to under-65s – you can allocate this between you in the same way as they can
• an extra amount which goes only to the husband – but this may be reduced if the husband's total income for the tax year ending 5 April 1997 was more than £15,200.

The calculator on the next pages will help you both work out how much you are entitled to. There is a worked example on p. 335.

# MARRIED COUPLE'S ALLOWANCE – CALCULATOR FOR THE 65S AND OVER

|  | Husband | Wife |
|---|---|---|
| Basic married couple's allowance | £_____ J | £_____ K |

**Extra married couple's allowance:**

| | | |
|---|---|---|
| Husband's total income: | £ | **L** |
| Subtract from Amount L: | £15,200 | |
| Total income over £15,200: | £_____ | **M** |
| Maximum extra allowances: | £_____ | **N** |
| Multiply M by 1/2 | £_____ | **P** |
| Subtract P from N | £_____ | **Q** |
| Maximum extra married couple's allowance: | £_____ | **R** |

Enter the smaller of
Amount Q or Amount R:               £_____ S

**Total married couple's allowance:**       £_____ T (J + S) £_____ K

## The basic married couple's allowance

The basic married couple's allowance of £1,790 goes to the husband unless arrangements have been made to split it between you or allocate it to the wife:

- if the basic married couple's allowance is all to go to the husband, enter £1,790 as Amount J and enter a 0 as Amount K
- if the basic married couple's allowance is to be divided between you, enter £895 as both Amounts J and K
- if the basic married couple's allowance is all to go to the wife, enter 0 as Amount J and £1,790 as Amount K.

Amount K is the figure to enter in box W42.1 of the wife's tax calculation working sheet for the tax year ending 5 April 1997.

## The extra married couple's allowance

The next step is to calculate how much extra married couple's allowance the couple is entitled to – all of this goes to the husband.

First find the husband's total income by adding the amount in Box W21 of his tax calculation working sheet to the amount in Box W19. Enter the answer in the calculator above as Amount L.

Then subtract £15,200 from Amount L and enter the answer as Amount M – the amount of husband's total income over £15,200. If Amount L is less than £15,200, enter 0 as Amount M.

Now enter the maximum extra allowances – personal and married couple's – the husband is entitled to for a couple of your ages as Amount N in the calculator above. You can find the figure to enter in the third column of the table below.

**Maximum extra allowances for the tax year ending 5 April 1997**

| Husband born | Wife born | Amount N | Amount R |
|---|---|---|---|
| On or after 6 April 1932 | Before 6 April 1932 but after 5 April 1922 | £1,325 | £1,325 |
| | On or before 5 April 1922 | £1,365 | £1,365 |
| Before 6 April 1932 but after 5 April 1922 | Before 6 April 1932 but after 5 April 1922 | £2,470 | £1,325 |
| | On or before 5 April 1922 | £2,510 | £1,365 |
| On or before 5 April 1922 | Any time | £2,690 | £1,365 |

If Amount M is 0, copy Amount N into Amount Q – you are entitled to the maximum extra allowances.

If Amount M is more than zero, halve it and enter the answer as Amount P. Subtract Amount P from Amount N and enter the answer as Amount Q. Then enter as Amount R the maximum extra married couple's allowance you are entitled to – you can find the figure in the fourth column of the Table.

Finally compare Amount Q with Amount R and enter the lower of the two as Amount S. This is the extra amount of married couple's allowance the husband is entitled to.

### Total husband's married couple's allowance

Add Amount S to Amount J and enter the total as Amount T – the amount of married couple's allowance the husband gets for the tax year ending 5 April 1997. Amount T is the figure to enter in box W42.1 of the husband's tax calculation working sheet.

**Married couple's surplus allowance**
(from box 16.28)

| W42.2 | £ |

**Additional personal allowance**
- usually £1,790, may be split with
another person - see the notes

| W42.3 | £ |

**Widow's bereavement allowance - £1,790**
(if your husband died this year or
last year and you have not
remarried)

| W42.4 | £ |

**Interest on loans**
(from box 15.2)

| W42.5 | £ |

**Maintenance and alimony**
(boxes 15.4 and 15.5 and the
notes for box W16)

| W42.6 | £ |

Total | W42.7 | £ |

Enter the following amounts:

- box W42.2 – married couple's surplus allowance unused by your spouse (see p. 135). Enter the amount in box 16.28 in the Allowances section of page 6 of the tax return
- box W42.3 – additional personal allowance. Enter your share of the £1,790 (see p. 133)
- box W42.4 – widow's bereavement allowance. If you are a widow whose husband died during the tax year ending 5 April 1997 or the previous tax year, enter £1,790 unless you have remarried
- box W42.5 – interest on loans to buy your only or main home. Enter the amount in box 15.2 in the Reliefs section on page 5 of the tax return
- box W42.6 – maintenance and alimony payments you make. You should have completed this box when filling in box W16 on the previous page of the tax calculation working sheet.

Add the amounts in boxes W42.1 to W42.6 and enter the total in box W42.7. Now follow the dashed line to box W42.

box W42 x 15%

| W42 | £ |   | W43 | £ |

Enter the amount in box W42.7 in box W42. Multiply this amount by 15 per cent ($^{15}/_{100}$), and enter the answer in box W43. Then go to Notional tax on the opposite page of the tax calculation working sheet.

- **Partnership notional tax**
  (from boxes 4.73 and 4.74)  W44.1 £

- **UK scrip dividends**
  (from boxes 10.22, 10.25, 10.28 and 10.31)  W44.2 £

- **Trusts, settlements and estate income** (from box 7.14)  W44.3 £

Total  W44.4 £  Copy to W44

Some types of income come with a notional tax credit – which reduces the amount of tax you have to pay on it but cannot be repaid if it is more than you should have paid. This section stops this notional tax being repaid if it is more than your tax bill for the year:

- box W44.1 – your share of a partnership's notional tax. Enter the total of boxes 4.73 and 4.74 on the turquoise Partnership supplementary pages (there is no box 4.73 on the short version)
- box W44.2 – notional tax on UK scrip dividends and other dividend income. Enter the total of boxes 10.22, 10.25, 10.28 and 10.31 from the Income section on page 3 of the tax return
- box W44.3 – notional income from trusts, settlements and the estates of dead persons. Enter the amount in box 7.14 on page T1 of the brown Trusts etc supplementary pages.

Add the amounts in these three boxes and enter the total in box W44.4. Now follow the dashed line to box W44.

W44 £

Enter the amount in box W44.4 in box W44.

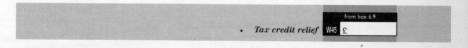

from box 6.9

- **Tax credit relief**  W45 £

If you have foreign income from savings, investments, pensions, benefits or property and have paid tax on it in another country, you can claim tax

credit relief to reduce your UK tax bill. If you are claiming tax credit relief –
and you have been able to work out the amount – enter it in box W45. The
amount to enter is in box 6.9 on page F3 of the olive Foreign supplement.

boxes W41, W43, W44 and W45

W46 £

Add the amounts in boxes W41, W43, W44 and W45 and enter the total in
box W46.

**Income tax due, after allowances and reliefs**   If the figure in box W46 is more
than the figure in box W39,
enter a zero   box W39 less box W46   W47 £

Subtract the amount in box W46 from the amount in box W39 and enter the
result in box W47.

Remember that if the answer is a negative number, enter 0 in box W47.

• **Recoverable tax on charitable covenants, annuities and
Gift Aid payments** (box W17 x 24%)   W48 £

Take the amount you entered in box W17 on page 5 of the Tax Calculation
Guide and multiply it by 24 per cent ($^{24}/_{100}$). Enter the answer in box W48.
This stops you getting two lots of basic-rate tax relief on gifts to charity
made by covenant or through the Gift Aid scheme.

• **Class 4 National Insurance Contributions**
(from box 3.92 or (box 4.22 less box 4.75))   W49 £

If you have income from being self-employed, enter the amount of Class 4
National Insurance contributions you must pay in box W49. The figure to
enter is in box 3.92 on page SE4 of the orange Self-employment supplement.
If you have income from a partnership, the figure to enter can be found from
the turquoise Partnership pages: subtract the amount in box 4.75 from the
amount in box 4.22 and enter the result in box W49.

If you have more than one source of income on which Class 4 National
Insurance contributions are due, you need Help Sheet *IR220 More than one
business* to calculate the amount.

| | boxes W47 + W48 + W49 |
|---|---|
| *Income tax and Class 4 National Insurance Contributions* | W50 £ |

Add the amounts in boxes W47, W48 and W49 and enter the total in box W50. This is the total amount of income tax and Class 4 National Insurance contributions due on your income for the tax year ending 5 April 1997.

## TAX ALREADY PAID OR ACCOUNTED FOR

The next page of the tax calculation working sheet covers the last leg of the calculation: working out how much tax you need still to pay – or the rebate you are entitled to.

First you must add up the tax you have paid already on your income for the tax year ending 5 April 1997.

Copy the amount in box W50 at the foot of the previous page into box W50.

Next look for your PAYE Coding Notice for the 1996-97 tax year and see if there is an adjustment to collect unpaid tax from previous tax years. If there is, copy the figure for the amount of tax being collected into box W51. Add the amounts in boxes W50 and W51 and enter the total in box W52.

Then enter the same amount in box 18.1 on the Other information section on page 7 of the tax return.

If you can't find your PAYE Coding Notice for 1996-97, ask your tax inspector whether there was any such tax collected, and the amount.

| *Tax paid at source* | |
|---|---|
| • *Employment* (from boxes 1.11 and 1.30) | W53.1 £ |

Enter in box W53.1 the amount of tax deducted from your earnings from jobs in the tax year ending 5 April 1997. You can find this by adding the amount in box 1.11 on page E1 of the pink Employment supplementary pages and the amount in box 1.30 on page E2. If you have more than one job, add together the amounts from each of them.

- **Self-employment** (from box 3.93) `W53.2` £ [                    ]

Most self-employed people have no tax deducted from their earnings before they receive them. But self-employed sub-contractors in the construction industry receive payment after tax has been deducted. Enter in box W53.2 the amount of tax deducted in the tax year ending 5 April 1997. You can find the amount in box 3.93 on page SE4 of the orange Self-employment supplement.

- **Partnerships** (from box 4.72) `W53.3` £ [                    ]

If you have income from a partnership, enter in box W53.3 your share of any income tax paid at source on its income in the tax year ending 5 April 1997. The amount is in box 4.72 on the back page of the turquoise Partnership supplementary pages.

- **Land and property** (from box 5.21) `W53.4` £ [                    ]

Enter in box W53.4 any income tax deducted from income from letting out property in the tax year ending 5 April 1997. The amount is in box 5.21 on page L2 of the red Land and property supplementary pages.

- **Foreign income** (from boxes 6.1 and 6.3) `W53.5` £ [                    ]

If any UK tax has been deducted from foreign income, enter in box W53.5 the amount deducted in the tax year ending 5 April 1997. The amount can be found by adding any amount in box 6.1 on page F1 of the olive Foreign supplementary pages to any amount in box 6.3 on page F2.

- **Trusts, settlements or estate income** (from boxes 7.2, 7.5, 7.8 and 7.11) `W53.6` £ [                    ]

Tax deducted from trusts, other forms of settlement such as a transfer of assets or the estates of people who have died should have been entered in the following boxes on page T1 of the brown Trusts etc supplementary pages: 7.2, 7.5, 7.8 and 7.11. Enter the total in box W53.6.

**UK savings** (from boxes 10.3, 10.6, 10.10, 10.13, 10.16 and 10.19)    W53.7 £

If you received any income from UK savings and investments in the tax year ending 5 April 1997, enter the total tax deducted from it in box W53.7 . This is found by adding the tax deducted from the following boxes in the Income section on page 3 of the tax return: 10.3, 10.6, 10.10, 10.13, 10.16 and 10.19.

**UK Pensions and benefits** (from boxes 11.8 and 11.11)    W53.8 £

If tax was deducted from a UK pension, social security benefit or income from a retirement annuity in the tax year ending 5 April 1997, enter the total in box W53.8. The amount should be the total of boxes 11.8 and 11.11 in the Income section on page 4 of the tax return.

**Other income** (from box 13.2)    W53.9 £

Box W53.9 is for the tax deducted from any other income you received in the tax year ending 5 April 1997 that was not entered somewhere else on the tax return. Enter the amount in box 13.2 in the Income section on page 4 of the tax return.

W53.10 £
Copy to box W53

W53 £

W54 £

Add boxes W53.1 to W53.9 and enter the total in box W53.10. Then copy this total to box W53.

W53 £

**Tax due for 1996-97 included in next year's PAYE tax code**    W54 £
Copy to box 18.2 in your Tax Return

box W53 + box W54
W55 £

If your PAYE tax code was reduced during the tax year ending 5 April 1997, it is possible that too little tax was deducted from your income. Your tax inspector will normally adjust your PAYE code for the following year to collect this underpayment. Since the inspector has made these arrangements, there is no need for you to make good the underpayment in calculating the amount you need to pay. So you add the amount that is to be collected in the tax year beginning 6 April 1997 back in here as tax that is accounted for.

To see if you need to enter anything here, find the last PAYE Coding Notice sent to you for 1996-97 – the tax year ending 5 April 1997. If your PAYE code was reduced, there will be a figure described as 'estimated underpayment' at the bottom of the notice. Enter the amount of the underpayment in box W54.

If you can't find a PAYE Coding Notice for the year or are unsure what to enter, ask your tax inspector.

Then copy the amount in box W54 into box 18.2 on page 7 of the tax return.

Finally, add box W53 and box W54 and enter the total in box W55.

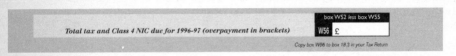

*Total tax and Class 4 NIC due for 1996-97 (overpayment in brackets)*    box W52 *less* box W55  W56 £

Copy box W56 to box 18.3 in your Tax Return

Subtract box W55 from box W52 and enter the answer in box W56. This is the amount of income tax and Class 4 National Insurance contributions due for the tax year ending 5 April 1997.

If the answer is a negative amount, you have paid too much – enter the figure for the overpayment in brackets.

Now copy the amount in box W56 into box 18.3 on page 7 of the tax return.

**Do you owe tax or are you due a rebate?**

*Tax owed or overpaid in 1996-97*

*1996-97 tax already refunded*
(from box 17.1)    W57A £

This part of the tax calculation working sheet works out whether you owe tax for the tax year ending 5 April 1997, or whether you are due a rebate.

If you ticked the YES box to Q 17 on page 7 of the tax return, you have already received a tax rebate for the tax year ending 5 April 1997. This would happen, for example, if you had claimed back tax deducted from savings income because you expected it to be more than your overall tax bill (see p. 64).

Enter in box W57A the amount of any such repayment – the amount you have already entered in box 17.1 on page 7 of the tax return. But do not include any repayment which was made against income from on or before 5 April 1996 – for example, if you have had trading losses carried back to set against income from earlier tax years.

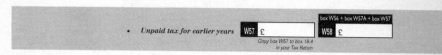

Have you paid too little tax for the tax year ending 5 April 1996 – or earlier tax years? It is unlikely, but it could happen if you have closed down a business and have since received some income from it (post-cessation receipts) which you want added to the year the business ceased (see p. 125). You need to recalculate your tax bill for the tax year you backdate the receipts to and enter any extra tax and Class 4 National Insurance contributions here.

You could also find yourself owing tax from earlier years if you are in one of the narrow range of professions that allows you to spread your income over several tax years – a farmer, writer or artist, for example. If this raises your income for earlier years, you need to recalculate your tax bill for those earlier years and enter the extra amount here.

If there is unpaid tax for earlier years, enter the amount in box W57 and copy it into box 18.4 on page 7 of the tax return. If you are unsure about this, ask your tax inspector for help.

Then add boxes W56, W57A and W57 and enter the total in box W58.

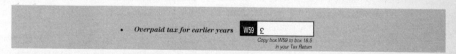

Have you paid too much tax for the tax year ending 5 April 1996 – or earlier tax years? This could happen if you want to set losses against income from such earlier years, or to carry back personal pension or retirement annuity payments (see p. 111). Farmers can also reduce their tax on earlier years if they are averaging their income.

Again you need to recalculate your tax bill for the tax year you have carried the losses or payments back to. Do not include losses or payments you have already claimed relief on.

Enter the tax and Class 4 National Insurance contributions you now think were overpaid in box W59, and copy the amount to box 18.5 on page 7 of the tax return. If you are unsure about this, ask your tax inspector for help.

Payments already made
(from your Statement of Account)
W60 £

box W59 + box W60
W61 £

You may already have made payments on account of tax and Class 4 National Insurance contributions for the tax year ending 5 April 1997. The two payments on account were due on 31 January 1997 and 31 July 1997 (some taxpayers may have been asked for only one payment this year).

Add the payments made and enter the total in box W60. Don't include interest charged for late payment, penalties for making late returns or other surcharges. If in doubt about what to enter, ask your tax inspector.

Then add the amount in box W60 to the amount in box W59 and enter the total in box W61.

If the amount in box W61 is smaller than the amount in box W58, you owe tax for the tax year ending 5 April 1997. If the amount in box W61 is larger than the amount in box W58, you have paid too much tax for that tax year.

Tax you owe for 1996-97

box W58 less box W61
W62 £

If you owe tax for the tax year ending 5 April 1997, subtract the amount in box W61 from the amount in box W58 and enter the answer in box W62. If the amount you owe is less than £1,000, you can choose to have it collected from your income through PAYE in the tax year beginning 6 April 1998. If it is more than £1,000 – or you want to pay it off sooner – you must pay it by 31 January 1998 with your first payment on account for the tax year beginning 6 April 1997. See opposite for how to calculate the amount of the payment on account.

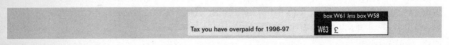

Tax you have overpaid for 1996-97

box W61 less box W58
W63 £

If you have overpaid tax for the tax year ending 5 April 1997, subtract the amount in box W58 from the amount in box W61 and enter the answer in box W63. You may be able to get a rebate now, depending on the amount of the payment on account you have to make for that tax year which began on 6 April 1997 – see below.

## WORKING OUT YOUR PAYMENTS ON ACCOUNT

The next stage in calculating your tax is to work out what payments on account you need to make for the tax year beginning 6 April 1997. How any underpayment for the previous tax year is collected – and whether you can claim a rebate of overpaid tax – depends on the amount of these payments.

*Payments on account for 1997-98*

Your payments on account for the tax year beginning 6 April 1997 are based on your income tax and Class 4 National Insurance contributions due for the tax year ending 5 April 1997 – the figure you entered in box W56. Normally you will be asked for two payments, each of half this total, one due on 31 January 1998, the other on 31 July 1998.

However, you will not have to make payments on account for the tax year which began on 6 April 1997 if the total is less than £500 or less than 20 per cent of your total tax including what is deducted at source. This next part of tax calculation working sheet checks whether you have to make payments on account – and if so, how much.

• *Your share of partnership tax and Class 4 NIC* (from boxes 4.74, 4.75)  £

If you are a partner, you may also have to pay a share of the partnership's tax and Class 4 National Insurance contributions. If you entered any amounts in boxes 4.74 and 4.75 on the back page of the turquoise Partnership supplementary pages, add these together and enter the total in box W64A.

Copy W62 to W64B if it is less than £1,000 and you would like the amount you owe collected through your 1998-99 tax code. Otherwise enter zero  £

If the tax you owe for the tax year ending 5 April 1997 – the amount in box W62 – is less than £1,000, you can choose to have it collected from your income through PAYE in the tax year beginning 6 April 1998. If this is what you want to do, enter the amount in box W62 in box W64B.

If the amount in box W62 is £1,000 or more – or you do not want your underpayment collected through PAYE – enter 0 in box W64B.

| If W65 is less than £500 you do not need to make payments on account. Leave 18.6 blank and tick 18.8. If W65 is equal to or more than £500 carry on | box W56 +box W64A less box W64B W65 £ |
| --- | --- |

Add the amounts in boxes W56 and W64A and subtract the amount in box W64B. Enter the answer in box W65.

If the amount in box W65 is less than £500, you do not need to make payments on account for the tax year beginning 6 April 1997. Tick box 18.8 on page 7 of the tax return and leave box 18.6 blank. If the amount in box W65 is £500 or more, move on to the next line.

| • Income tax due after allowances and reliefs | from box W47 W66 £ | | |
| --- | --- | --- | --- |
| • Class 4 National Insurance Contributions | from box W49 W67 £ | box W64A + W66 + W67 W68 £ | box W68 x 20% W69 £ |

If W65 is less than W69 you do not need to make payments on account. Leave box 18.6 blank and tick 18.8. If it is equal to or more than W69 you do have to make payments on account. Fill in box W70.

Enter in box W66 the amount of income tax due after allowances and reliefs from box W47. Then enter in box W67 the amount of Class 4 National Insurance contributions due from box W49.

Add boxes W64A, W66 and W67, and enter the total in box W68. Multiply box W68 by 20 per cent ($^{20}/_{100}$) and enter the answer in box W69.

If the amount in box W65 is less than the amount in box W69, you do not need to make payments on account for the tax year beginning 6 April 1997. Turn to box 18.6 on page 7 of the tax return and tick box 18.8. Leave box 18.6 blank.

If the amount in box W65 is equal to or larger than the amount in box W69, you will have to make payments on account for the tax year beginning 6 April 1997. Move on to the next line.

| This is the amount of each payment on account for 1997-98 | box W65 x 50% W70 £ | Copy box W70 to box 18.6 in your Tax Return |
| --- | --- | --- |

Halve the amount in box W65 and enter the answer in box W70. This is the amount of each of your payments on account for the tax year beginning 6 April 1997.

The amount in box W70 is normally the amount you should now enter in box 18.6 on page 7 of the tax return as your first payment on account for the tax year. However, you are entitled to pay less than this amount if you think smaller payments will cover your tax bill for the tax year beginning 6 April 1997. There are two reasons why you might feel it appropriate to make lower payments on account:

- your income for the tax year beginning 6 April 1997 will be lower than the previous year's
- you expect to be able to claim higher allowances and reliefs for this year than for last year.

No payments on account are needed if you expect your tax bill for the tax year beginning 6 April 1997 to be less than £500 or 80 per cent or more of the tax will be collected at source. For example, if more of your income is to be taxed under PAYE or comes from savings where tax is deducted at source, you might need to make no payments on account.

If you think that lower payments on account are needed, work out carefully how much you think should be paid. Put this estimate in box 18.6 on page 7 of the tax return and tick box 18.7. Then explain your reasons in the Additional information box on page 8 of the tax return.

It is probably better to pay slightly more rather than too little in your payments on account. If you pay too much, you will get interest on it; if you pay too little, you will pay interest. There are penalties in the form of fines if you are caught trying to hoodwink your tax inspector in setting payments on account. And remember, if you make the payments on account calculated in the Tax Calculation Guide on time, there is normally no interest to pay even if your tax bill turns out to have been much higher.

| . 1997-98 tax you are reclaiming now | 18.9 £ |
|---|---|

Enter here details of tax you wish to claim back from the tax year ending 5 April 1997 for either of the following:

- trading losses in the tax year beginning 6 April 1997 – give details in the Additional Information box on page 8 of the tax return
- pension payments you want to bring back from the tax year beginning 6 April 1997 – you entered these in boxes 14.4, 14.9 or 14.14 in the Reliefs section on page 5 of the tax return.

You will need to recalculate your tax bill for the tax year ending 5 April 1997 to take account of these backdated reliefs using the tax calculation working sheet. The amount to enter in box 18.9 is the difference between the figure you entered in box W56 on page 8 of the Tax Calculation Guide without backdating the reliefs and then after backdating the reliefs.

## Working out your payment due on 31 January 1998

You have now worked out what your payments on account should be for the tax year beginning 6 April 1997. But if you owe tax for the tax year ending 5 April 1997, this must also be paid with the first payment of account by 31 January 1998. And if you are entitled to a rebate, this can reduce your first payment on account. This last part of the Tax Calculation Guide on page 10 tells you how much you have to pay by 31 January 1998.

If you owe tax for the tax year ending 5 April 1997 – that is, if you have entered a figure in box W62 – complete the top half of this working sheet. If you have overpaid tax for the tax year – you have entered a figure in box W63 – complete the bottom half.

---

**If you have paid too little tax for 1996-97** the amount due on 31 January 1998 is:

- the figure in box W62 - the amount you owe for 1996-97 - **unless** it is less than £1,000 and is to be collected through your tax code (see page 26 in your Tax Return Guide)　　W62 £ _____

  **plus**

plus

- any figure in box 18.6 - the first payment on account for 1997-98　　18.6 £ _____

less　　　　　　　　　　　　　　　　　　　　　　　　　　　　　　　　　　　　**minus**

- any figure in box 18.9 - a 1997-98 repayment　　18.9 £ _____

equals　　　　　　　　　　　　　　　　　　　　　　　　　　　　　　　　　　　**equals**

- the amount due on 31 January 1998 (or, if negative, the amount we owe you)　　£ _____

---

If you paid too little tax in the tax year ending 5 April 1997, enter in the top line the amount you owe from box W62 on page 8 of the Tax Calculation Guide. But if it is less than £1,000 and you want it collected through PAYE, enter 0.

Then enter the amount of your payment on account for the tax year beginning 6 April 1997 – from box 18.6 on page 7 of the tax return. If you are claiming any repayment of tax for losses or pension payments made in the tax year beginning 6 April 1977, enter the amount from box 18.9.

Add the amount in box W62 to the amount in box 18.6 and subtract the amount in box 18.9. The answer is the amount you must pay by 31 January 1998 – enter it in the box on the bottom line.

**If you have paid too much tax for 1996-97**

- the figure in box W63 - the amount we owe you for 1996-97

  W63 £ [            ]

plus

plus

- any figure in box 18.9 - a 1997-98 repayment

  18.9 £ [            ]

less

minus

- any figure in box 18.6 - the first payment on account for 1997-98

  18.6 £ [            ]

equals

equals

- the amount we owe you (or, if negative, the amount due on 31 January 1998)

  £ [            ]

If you paid too much tax in the tax year ending 5 April 1997, enter in the top line the amount overpaid from box W63 on page 8 of the Tax Calculation Guide.

If you are claiming any repayment of tax for losses or pension payments made in the tax year beginning 6 April 1997, enter the amount from box 18.9 on page 7 of the tax return.

Then enter the amount of your payment on account for the tax year beginning 6 April 1997 – from box 18.6.

Add the amount in box W63 to the amount in box 18.9 and subtract the amount in box 18.6. The answer is the amount the Inland Revenue owes you – enter it in the box on the bottom line.

You can claim your rebate by ticking the YES box by Q 19 on page 7 of the tax return.

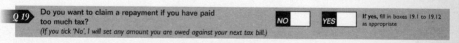

Q 19   Do you want to claim a repayment if you have paid too much tax?
(If you tick 'No', I will set any amount you are owed against your next tax bill.)

NO [   ]   YES [   ]   If yes, fill in boxes 19.1 to 19.12 as appropriate

If you owe the Inland Revenue any amounts from previous years, your tax inspector will deduct these from any rebate. If you tick the NO box the rebate will be used to reduce your next tax bill.

Should the repayment/payment be sent

- to you? *(tick box and go to Question 20)* 19.1 [ ]

or

- your bank or building society account or other nominee *(tick box and fill in boxes 19.3 to 19.7 or boxes 19.3 to 19.12 as appropriate)?* 19.2 [ ]

If you want the rebate to be sent to you, tick box 19.1. If you would prefer it to be paid into your bank or building society account or to someone else you nominate, tick box 19.2.

Give the details of the bank or building society account in boxes 19.3 to 19.7.

If you want the rebate to go to someone else, give details of your nominee in boxes 19.8 to 19.12.

# CASE STUDIES IN FILLING IN THE TAX CALCULATOR

## CHAPTER 25

In this chapter, we follow a simple case study to show how easy it is for most people to calculate their own tax bills. We run through the tax calculation working sheet for Mary Emmanuel – a company executive with a range of fringe benefits and income from a portfolio of savings and investments.

On page 333, we also follow through the calculations for Gerard Mallory – a pensioner with income from pensions and investments.

## MARY EMMANUEL WORKS OUT HER TAX

Mary Emmanuel earned £34,500 from her job in the tax year ending 5 April 1997. She has a company car, which has a taxable value of £3,715. And she gets free private medical insurance at work for herself and her family. This is worth £560 in the tax year ending 5 April 1997.

She also has freelance earnings from writing, which earned her £6,750 in the tax year ending 5 April 1997.

She has the following types of investment income – all in the UK:

- interest on her bank and building society accounts – her 1997 tax return gives a total of £107 after deduction of tax at 20 per cent (a gross amount of £134)
- interest from a National Savings Investment Account – £525 paid gross, without deduction of tax
- dividends from various shares she owns – the 1997 tax return gives a total of £287, with tax credits of £72 (a gross amount of £359)
- distributions from unit trusts – £150 with £37 of tax credits (£187 gross).

She can claim as an expense of her main job the £120 a year subscription she pays to her professional association. In the tax year ending 5 April 1997, she paid £180 after tax relief under a covenant to charity. She paid £2,736 into her personal pension scheme in the tax year ending 5 April 1997: this is after deduction of tax at the basic rate of 24 per cent – a gross amount of £3,600 for the year. And she and her husband jointly pay £4,800 a year in mortgage interest, paid net of tax relief under MIRAS (see p. 50).

Mary has been married for several years, and the married couple's allowance is split between her and her husband. Both are in their 30s.

Mary has no chargeable capital gains, so she completes the standard tax calculation working sheet.

## Total income from
Mary starts on the first page of the tax calculation working sheet, adding together her total income.

Her income from her first employment is her salary of £34,500 (from box 1.8 in the pink Employment supplementary pages), plus the value of her fringe benefits: £3,715 for her company car (box 1.16) and £560 for free medical insurance (box 1.21). That makes total income from her first job of £34,500 + £3,715 + £560 = £38,775. Mary enters £38,775 in the top line under First employment.

In the second line, she enters the £120 subscription to her professional association she can claim as an expense – from box 1.34 in the pink Employment supplementary pages.

She deducts the £120 in the second line from the £38,775 in the first line and enters £38,655 as her total taxable income from her first job in the third line.

She has no other employment, so she leaves the second column blank. She therefore copies the £38,655 in the third line of the first column into box W1.

The freelance earnings from writing count as income from self-employment. So Mary enters £6,750 in box W3 – she gets this figure from box 3.89 on page SE3 of the orange Self-employment supplement.

The only other income Mary has is from her UK savings and investments: £134 in interest from her bank and building society accounts (in box 10.4 on page 3 of the tax return); £525 in interest from her National Savings Investment Account (box 10.8); £359 from share dividends (box 10.17); £187 from unit trust distributions (box 10.20). This gives a total taxable amount of £134 + £525 + £359 + £187 = £1,205 – which she enters in box W8.

She adds the £38,655 in box W1, the £6,750 in box W3 and the £1,205 in box W8 to get a total of £46,610. She enters £46,610 in box W12.

## Deductions for

Mary now enters details of her deductions in the tax calculation working sheet.

She starts with her gross personal pension payments of £3,600 from box 14.15 on page 5 of the tax return. She enters £3,600 in box W13.

Then she turns to the £180 a year of payments she makes net under covenant to charity (box 15.9 on page 5 of the tax return). She multiplies this by $^{100}/_{76}$ to get £237 – the gross amount which she enters in box W17.

Although she gets tax relief on her mortgage interest payments, she does not claim any deduction in calculating her tax. She gets the tax relief through MIRAS by making payments net of tax relief.

She adds the £3,600 in box W13 to the £237 in box W17 to get total deductions of £3,837. She enters this amount in box W20. Then she deducts the amount in box W20 from the amount in box W12: £46,610 – £3,837 = £42,773. She enters £42,773 in box W21 as her total income less deductions.

## Reliefs

Mary turns to the next page of the tax calculation working sheet. She copies the figure of £42,773 into box W22 at the top of the page.

She now has to add back the personal pension payments, since she will already have had the tax relief on them by paying them net of basic rate tax relief. So she enters £3,600 (box 14.15 on page 5 of the tax return) in box W23.1. There is no figure to enter in box W23.2, so she enters £3,600 in box W23.3, and copies this into box W23.

She adds the amounts in boxes W22 and W23: £42,773 + £3,600 = £46,373. She enters £46,373 in box W24.

## Allowances given as a deduction from your income

Mary's only allowance given as a deduction against her income is her personal allowance of £3,765. She enters £3,765 in box W25.1 and as the total in box W25.6. She then copies it into box W25.

She deducts the amount in box W25 from the amount in box W24; £46,373 – £3,765 = £42,608. She enters £42,608 in box W26.

Mary then multiplies £42,608 by 20 per cent: £42,608 x $^{20}/_{100}$ = £8,522. She enters £8,522 in box W27.

## Savings income taxed at the lower (20%) rate
Mary's only income which is taxed at the lower rate of 20 per cent is her £1,205 from UK savings and investments (already entered in box W8). She enters £1,205 in box W28.2 and as the total for this section in box W28.5.

She then copies £1,205 into box W28. She subtracts this from the amount in box W26: £42,608 – £1,205 = £41,403. She enters £41,403 in box W29.

Mary subtracts box W30 from box W29: £41,403 – £3,900 = £37,503. She enters £37,503 in box W31.

She multiplies the amount in box W31 by 4 per cent: £37,503 x $^{4}/_{100}$ = £1,500. She enters £1,500 in box W32.

Next she calculates the figure to enter in box W33. There is no amount in box 12.9 of the Income section of the tax return, so she subtracts the amount in box W23 – £3,600 – from the amount in box W26 – £42,608. She enters the answer in box W33: £42,608 – £3,600 = £39,008.

The amount in box W33 is more than £25,500, so Mary subtracts the £25,500 in box W34 from the £39,008 in box W33: £39,008 – £25,500 = £13,508. She enters this in box W35 and then multiplies it by 16 per cent: £13,508 x $^{16}/_{100}$ = £2,161. She enters £2,161 in box W36.

Then Mary compares the amounts in boxes W28 (£1,205)and W35 (£13,508) to see which is the lower. She enters £1,205 in box W37 and then multiplies it by 4 per cent: £1,205 x $^{4}/_{100}$ = £48. She enters £48 in box W38.

Box W39 is the total of boxes W27, W32, W36 and W38: £8,522 + £1,500 + £2,161 + £48 = £12,231.

Mary has not invested in a venture capital trust or Enterprise Investment Scheme, so she leaves boxes W40 and W41 blank.

## Allowances and reliefs given in terms of tax
Mary enters her half of the married couple's allowance in box W42.1 – £895. Although she gets tax relief on mortgage interest, this is not entered here – she gets it direct from the lender by making payments net of tax relief through MIRAS.

So the total for allowances and reliefs given in terms of tax is £895 – she enters this in box W42.7, and copies it across to box W42. She multiplies £895 by 15 per cent: £895 x $^{15}/_{100}$ = £134. She enters £134 in box W43.

Mary has received no income with notional tax credits, so she leaves W44 blank. And she has no tax credit relief to claim from foreign investments – she leaves box W45 blank also.

Box W46 is found by adding boxes W41, W43, W44 and W45: in Mary's case, this is 0 + £134 + 0 + 0 = £134. She deducts this from the amount in box W39: £12,231 – £134 = £12,097 and enters £12,097 in box W47.

Mary has given herself tax relief on her covenant payments which must now be allowed for. She takes the £237 she entered in box W17 and multiplies it by 24 per cent: £237 x $^{24}/_{100}$ = £57. She enters £57 in box W48.

She does not have to pay any Class 4 National Insurance contributions, so she leaves box W49 blank. Her total tax bill for the year is therefore the total of boxes W47, W48 and W49: £12,097 + £57 + 0 = £12,154. She enters £12,154 in box W50, and copies it over to box W50 at the top of the next page of the tax calculation working sheet.

### Income tax and Class 4 NIC due
Mary has had no adjustment to her PAYE code for the tax year ending 5 April 1997 to collect unpaid tax from earlier tax years. So she leaves box W51 blank and copies £12,154 in to box W52.

She now finds out how much tax has been paid at source on her income. For her earnings from her main job, she finds she has paid £9,008 through PAYE (from box 1.11 on page E1 of the pink Employment supplementary pages for her main job). She enters £9,008 in box W53.1.

No tax has been paid on her earnings from her freelance writing, so she enters 0 in box W53.2.

On her savings income, she finds the amounts of tax deducted or credited from the following boxes on page 3 of the tax return:
- bank and building society interest – box 10.3 shows £26
- share dividends – box 10.16 shows £71
- unit trust distributions – box 10.19 shows £37

Interest on National Savings Investment Accounts is paid gross, so no tax has been deducted.

Mary adds these amounts of tax together: £26 + £71 + £37 = £134. She enters £134 in box W53.7.

She then adds the amounts in boxes W53.1, W53.2 and W53.7: £9,008 + £0 + £134 = £9,142. She enters £9,142 in box W53.10, and copies it into box W53.

No tax for the tax year ending 5 April 1997 has been included in the next year's PAYE code, so Mary enters 0 in box W54 and enters £9,142 in box W55.

She subtracts this amount from box W52: £12,154 – £9,142 = £3,012. She enters £3,012 in box W56 – her income tax and Class 4 National Insurance contributions due for the tax year ending 5 April 1997.

### Tax owed or overpaid in 1996-97
No tax for the tax year ending 5 April 1997 has already been refunded, nor is there any unpaid tax for earlier years, so she enters 0 in boxes W57A and W57. Box W58 is thus the same as box W56 – £3,012.

Mary did not overpay tax in earlier years, so she enters 0 in box W59. She has, however, made two payments on account of £830 each for the tax year ending 5 April 1997: one due on 31 January 1997; the other due on 31 July 1997. So she enters twice £830 = £1,660 in box W60. This is also the amount to enter in box W61.

Box W62 tells Mary the tax she still owes: box W58 – box W61: £3,012 – £1,660 = £1,352. This will be collected with Mary's first payment on account for the tax year beginning 6 April 1997. She now goes on to calculate how much the payment will be.

### Payments on account for 1997-98
There is nothing to enter in box W64A. And since the amount in box W62 is more than £1,000, Mary enters 0 in box W64B. Box W65 is therefore the same as box W56 – £3,012.

Box W56 is the amount of tax and Class 4 National Insurance due for the tax year ending 5 April 1997. But no payments on account will be needed if it is less than £500 (which it isn't) or less than 20 per cent of Mary's overall tax bill including tax collected at source. The next bit of the working sheet checks this second condition.

First it asks for Mary's total tax from box W47: she enters £12,097 in box

W66. No Class 4 National Insurance contributions are due, so Mary enters 0 in box W67 and £12,097 in box W68. She enters 20 per cent of £12,097 = £2,419 in box W69. Since the amount in box W56 is more than this, payments on account will be needed for the tax year beginning 6 April 1997.

Each payment on account is half the figure in box W65: half of £3,012 = £1,506. Mary enters £1,506 in box W70, and copies it into box 18.6 on page 7 of the tax return.

### Payment due on 31 January 1998
Lastly Mary turns to page 10 of the Tax Calculation Guide to work out how much is due on 31 January 1998. This will be:

- the amount of tax owed from the tax year ending 5 April 1997 from box W62 – £1,352
- plus the amount in box 18.6 – £1,506
- minus any figure in box 18.9 – £0 for Mary.

This gives an answer of £1,352 + £1,506 + £0 = £2,858, which is the amount due on 31 January 1998.

The second payment on account for the tax year beginning 6 April 1997 will be due by 31 July 1998 – this is £1,506.

## GERARD MALLORY WORKS OUT HIS TAX

Gerard Mallory, 67, has retired and lives with his wife Eva, 66. His main income is from pensions:

- the state retirement pension – he received £3,180 in the tax year ending 5 April 1997
- his pension from his former job – £11,650 in that tax year.

In addition, Gerard has income from savings and investments, most of which is paid after deduction of tax at 20 per cent. His 1997 tax return shows a gross amount of £4,429, with tax of £713 having been paid on £3,566 of this.

All their married couple's allowance is deducted from Gerard's income. Since he has no chargeable capital gains, he completes the standard tax calculation working sheet.

### Total income from
Gerard starts by entering his income totals on the first page of the tax calculation working sheet. He enters 0 in each of boxes W1 to W7, since he has

none of those sorts of income.

Box W8 is for the total taxable amount of income from savings and investments shown on page 3 of his tax return. This comes to £4,429.

Box W9 is for his total taxable amount of pension income, from page 4 of the tax return. He adds the £3,180 state retirement pension in box 11.1 to the £11,650 occupational pension in box 11.12: £3,180 + £11,650 = £14,830. He enters £14,830 in box W9.

He enters 0 in boxes W10 and W11. He adds the amounts in boxes W1 to W11: £4,429 + £14,830 = £19,259. He enters £19,259 as the total in box W12.

## Deductions for
Gerard has no deductions to enter in boxes W13 to W19. So he enters 0 for total deductions in box W20, and enters £19,259 in box W21 as his total income less deductions.

## Reliefs
Gerard copies the £19,259 to box W22 at the top of the next page of the tax calculation working sheet. He makes no payments for personal pensions or vocational training, so there is nothing to enter in the Reliefs boxes at the top of page 6. He enters 0 in box W23, and enters £19,259 in box W24.

## Allowances given as a deduction from your income
Gerard enters the £3,765 personal allowance in box W25.1.

Since he was born on or before 5 April 1932, he may be entitled to an extra amount of personal allowance on account of his age. Gerard was born on or after 6 April 1922, so the maximum extra he is entitled to is £1,145.

However, Gerard's total income is more than £15,200, so the amount of extra allowance is reduced by £1 for each £2 over this limit. Gerard uses the calculator on p. 307 of this guide to work out whether he is entitled to any extra allowance.

First, he works out his total income – the amount in box W21 plus the amount in box W19: £19,259 + £0 = £19,259. This is Amount A.

Then he enters the maximum amount of extra personal allowance for someone of his age as Amount B: £1,145.

Since Amount A is more than £15,200, he subtracts £15,200 from Amount A: £19,259 – £15,200 = £4,059. This is Amount C.

Gerard multiplies Amount C by $^1/_2$: £4,059 x $^1/_2$ = £2,029. This is amount D. Since Amount D is more than Amount B, Gerard is not entitled to any extra personal allowance on account of his age, so he enters 0 in box W25.2.

Gerard is not entitled to any of the other allowances in this section, so the total is box W25.1 + box W25.2: £3,765 + £0 = £3,765. He enters £3,765 in box W25.6 and copies it across to box W25.

He then deducts the amount in box W25 from the amount in box W24: £19,259 – £3,765 = £15,494. He enters £15,494 in box W26.

Gerard then multiplies £15,494 by 20 per cent: £15,494 x $^{20}/_{100}$ = £3,099. He enters £3,099 in box W27.

## Savings income taxed at the lower (20%) rate

Gerard's only income which is taxed at the lower rate of 20 per cent is his £4,429 from UK savings and investments (already entered in box W8). He enters £4,429 in box W28.2 and as the total for this section in box W28.5.

He copies £4,429 into box W28 and subtracts this from the amount in box W26: £15,494 – £4,429 = £11,065. He enters £11,065 in box W29.

Gerard subtracts box W30 from box W29: £11,065 – £3,900 = £7,165. He enters £7,165 in box W31.

He multiplies the amount in box W31 by 4 per cent: £7,165 x $^4/_{100}$ = £287. He enters £287 in box W32.

There is no amount in box 12.9 of the Income section of the tax return or in box W23. So he enters the £15,494 in box W26 in box W33.

Since the amount in box W33 is less than £25,500, Gerard leaves boxes W35 to W38 blank and moves on to box W39. He adds the amounts in boxes W27, W32, W36 and W38: £3,099 + £287 + £0 + £0 = £3,386.

Since he has not invested in a venture capital trust or Enterprise Investment Scheme, Gerard leaves boxes W40 and W41 blank.

## Allowances and reliefs given in terms of tax

Gerard and his wife were born on or before 5 April 1932, so he may be entitled to a higher married couple's allowance on account of his age. Gerard was born on or after 6 April 1922, so the maximum extra he is entitled to is £1,325. Gerard uses the calculator on p. 309 to work out whether he is entitled to a higher married couple's allowance – and if so, how much.

First he enters the basic married couple's allowance of £1,790 as Amount J, since it is all to be set against his income. He enters 0 as Amount K – Eva gets none of the married couple's allowance.

The next step is to calculate how much extra married couple's allowance the couple is entitled to – all of this goes to the husband. This depends on his total income, which he had already calculated above when working out his personal allowance. It is the amount in box W21 plus the amount in box W19: £19,259 + £0 = £19,259. He enters this as Amount L.

Then he subtracts £15,200 from Amount L: £19,259 – £15,200 = £4,059. He enters £4,059 as Amount M – the amount of his total income over £15,200.

Gerard looks at the table on p. 311 to find the maximum extra allowances – personal and married couple's – for a couple aged 67 and 66. This is £2,470 so he enters this as Amount N.

He halves Amount M: $^1/_2$ x £4,059 = £2,029. He enters £2,029 as Amount P. He subtracts Amount P from Amount N: £2,470 – £2,029 = £441. He enters £441 as Amount Q.

Then Gerard enters as Amount R the maximum extra married couple's allowance he is entitled to, which is £1,325, according to the table on p. 311. The lower of Amount Q (£441) and Amount R (£1,325) is Amount Q. So he enters £441 as Amount S – the extra married couple's allowance he is entitled to.

Gerard adds Amount S to Amount J: £441 + £1,790 = £2,231. He enters £2,231 as Amount T – the amount of married couple's allowance he gets for the tax year ending 5 April 1997. It is also the amount to enter in box W42.1 on Gerard's tax calculation working sheet.

Gerard is entitled to none of the other allowances and reliefs given in terms of tax, so he enters £2,231 in box W42.7 and copies it across to box W42. He then multiplies box W42 by 15 per cent: £2,231 x $^{15}/_{100}$ = £335. He enters £335 in box W43.

Gerard has received no income with notional tax credits, so he leaves W44 blank. And he has no tax credit relief to claim from foreign investments, so he leaves box W45 blank also.

Box W46 is found by adding boxes W41, W43, W44 and W45: £0 + £335 + £0 + £0 = £335. Gerard deducts this from the amount in box W39: £3,386 – £335 = £3,051 and enters £3,051 in box W47.

There is nothing for Gerard to enter in boxes W48 and W49. So he enters £3,051 in box W50, and copies it over to box W50 at the top of the next page of the tax calculation working sheet.

### Income tax and Class 4 NIC due

Gerard has had no adjustment to his PAYE code for the tax year ending 5 April 1997 to collect unpaid tax from earlier tax years. So he leaves box W51 blank and copies £3,051 to box W52.

He now finds out how much tax has been paid at source on his income. For his savings income, he finds the amounts of tax deducted or credited from the boxes in the second column of page 3 of the tax return – £713. He enters £713 in box W53.7.

Box W53.8 is for the tax deducted from his pension income. Although the state retirement pension is taxable, it is paid without deduction of tax; instead his pension from his job comes with tax on both pensions having been deducted under PAYE. He entered the figure for tax deducted from his occupational pension in box 11.11 on page 4 of the tax return. He enters this figure, £2,165, in box W53.8.

Gerard adds the amounts in boxes W53.7 and W53.8: £713 + £2,165 = £2,878. He enters £2,878 in box W53.10, and copies it into box W53.

No tax for the tax year ending 5 April 1997 has been included in the next year's PAYE code, so Gerard enters 0 in box W54 and enters £2,878 in box W55.

He subtracts this amount from box W52: £3,051 – £2,878 = £173. He enters £173 in box W56 – his income tax and Class 4 National Insurance contributions due for the tax year ending 5 April 1997.

The £173 is, in fact, the tax due on the £863 of investment income that was paid without deduction of tax. His tax inspector will probably try to collect this from his occupational pension in future years by making an adjustment to his PAYE code for Untaxed interest (see p. 289).

## Tax owed or overpaid in 1996-97

No tax for the tax year ending 5 April 1997 has already been refunded, nor is there any unpaid tax for earlier years – so Gerard enters 0 in boxes W57A and W57. Box W58 is thus the same as box W56 – £173.

Gerard did not overpay tax in earlier years, nor was he asked to make any payments on account for the tax year ending 5 April 1997, so he enters 0 in boxes W59, W60 and W61.

Box W62 is the tax Gerard still owes: box W58 – box W61: £173 – £0 = £173. This is will be collected through PAYE in the tax year beginning 6 April 1988. And since Gerard's tax bill for the tax year ending 5 April 1997 was less than £500, he will not have to make payments on account for the tax year beginning 6 April 1997.

# TAX-FREE INCOME

## Income from a job

Check with your employer if you are uncertain about whether any of these forms of income is taxable

- up to £4,000 a year of pay received under a registered profit-related pay scheme (see p. 145); this will be phased out after 1 January 1998
- earnings from working abroad for prolonged periods (see p. 166)
- work-related expenses you are reimbursed for by your employer covered by an agreement with the Inland Revenue that they do not need to be declared (see p. 147)
- some fringe benefits, such as canteen meals and Christmas parties provided for all staff, special clothes for the job and subscriptions to approved professional societies (see p. 147)
- foreign service allowances paid to diplomats and other servants of the Crown
- the first 15p a day of luncheon vouchers
- goods and services your employer lets you have cheaply (see p. 147)
- miners' free coal or cash allowances in lieu of coal
- long-service awards so long as they are not in cash and are within set limits (see p. 148)
- awards from approved suggestions schemes (see p. 148)
- payments for moving to higher-cost housing areas, within set limits (see p. 149)
- genuine personal gifts – for example, wedding presents

## Income on leaving a job

Check with your ex-employer

- statutory redundancy payments
- wages in lieu of notice
- gratuities from the armed forces
- lump-sum compensation for an injury or disability that means you can no longer do the job
- tax-free lump sum instead of part of a pension and certain other ex

gratia payments on retirement or death
- up to £30,000 of other compensation on leaving a job, including counselling and outplacement services (see p. 166)

## Pensions and benefits
Check with the organisation paying the pension or benefit

- state pension Christmas bonus
- war widows' and orphans' pensions and equivalent overseas pensions
- widow's payment
- certain compensation payments and pensions paid to victims of Nazi persecution
- war disablement pensions
- additional pensions paid to holders of some bravery awards such as the Victoria Cross
- the part of a pension paid to a former employee who retires because of a disability caused by injury at work or a work-related illness which is in excess of the pension paid to an employee who retires on normal ill-health grounds
- income support paid to people aged 60 or over, single parents with a child under 16 and those staying at home to look after a severely disabled person. Part of income support paid to unemployed people may be tax-free – see your statement of taxable benefits (p. 96)
- jobfinder's grant, most youth training scheme allowances, employment rehabilitation and training allowances
- family credit
- housing benefit and council tax benefit
- improvement and renovation grants for your home
- payments from the social fund
- maternity allowance (but statutory maternity pay is taxable)
- child benefit, one-parent benefit, school uniform grants
- additions for dependent children paid with a state pension or social security benefit
- guardian's allowance
- student grants
- incapacity benefit for first 28 weeks (and if paid to replace invalidity benefit)
- industrial disablement benefits
- disability living allowance, disability working allowance
- attendance allowance

## Investment income
If in doubt, check with the organisation paying the income

- interest on National Savings Certificates (and Ulster Savings Certificates

if you normally live in Northern Ireland), National Savings Children's Bonus Bonds
- interest and terminal bonuses on bank and building society Save-As-You-Earn (SAYE) schemes
- first £70 of interest each year from National Savings Ordinary Account (£140 for married couples with a joint account)
- dividends and other income from a personal equity plan (PEP), so long as no more than £180 is drawn out in interest (see p. 71)
- interest on a tax-exempt special savings account (TESSA) kept open for the full five years – provided some of it is reinvested for the term of the account (see p. 72)
- dividends on ordinary shares in a venture capital trust (see p. 73)
- part of the income paid by an annuity
- amount paid out by a regular-premium life insurance policy such as an endowment policy or a unit-linked one – including money paid out on the death of the policyholder (see p. 100)
- loan interest paid to members of a credit union

## Other tax-free income
If in doubt, check with the organisation paying out the money

- what you receive under maintenance agreements made on or after 15 March 1988 and any increases in maintenance paid on agreements made before that date (see p. 43)
- up to £4,250 a year of income from letting out a furnished room in your only or main home (£3,250 a year for the tax year ending 5 April 1997) – the rent a room scheme (p. 218)
- gambling winnings (as long as it is not your business)
- lottery winnings
- premium bond prizes
- income from qualifying life insurance policies that pay out on death – for example, mortgage protection policies, family income benefit policies (see p. 100)
- income from insurance policies to cover mortgage payments if you are sick or unemployed
- income from a permanent health insurance policy, creditor insurance and some long-term care policies
- what is paid out under some accident insurance policies (usually group ones)
- interest on a delayed settlement for damages for personal injury or death
- compensation for being wrongly sold a personal pension (paid following the review ordered by the Securities and Investments Board)
- interest on a tax rebate

# GROSSING-UP TABLES

Some forms of income are paid net – after some tax has been deducted from them. For example, 20 per cent tax is normally deducted from the interest on savings accounts in banks and building societies before it is paid out to you or added to your account (unless it is a tax-exempt special savings account or TESSA). In working out your tax bill, you may need to know how much the income was before the tax was deducted – the gross income.

You can find the gross income by grossing-up the net income using the ready reckoners below. With most forms of investment income, tax will have been deducted at 20 per cent, so that is the rate in the first ready reckoner. The other two are for grossing up income where tax has been deducted at the basic rate of 24 per cent for the tax year ending 5 April 1997, or for the basic rate of 23 per cent for the tax year beginning 6 April 1997.

If the tax rates change, you can use the following formula to work out the grossed-up income:

$$\text{Amount paid to you net} \times \left( \frac{100}{100 - \text{rate of tax}} \right)$$

So if, for argument's sake, the rate of tax was 15 per cent, and you received £85 after tax, the grossed-up amount of the income would be:

$$£85 \times \left( \frac{100}{100 - 15} \right)$$
$$= £85 \times \frac{100}{85}$$
$$= £100$$

## Grossing-up when tax is deducted at 20 per cent

| Net amount £ | Gross amount £ | Net amount £ | Gross amount £ | Net amount £ | Gross amount £ |
|---|---|---|---|---|---|
| 1 | 1.25 | 10 | 12.50 | 100 | 125.00 |
| 2 | 2.50 | 20 | 25.00 | 200 | 250.00 |
| 3 | 3.75 | 30 | 37.50 | 300 | 375.00 |
| 4 | 5.00 | 40 | 50.00 | 400 | 500.00 |
| 5 | 6.25 | 50 | 62.50 | 500 | 625.00 |
| 6 | 7.50 | 60 | 75.00 | 600 | 750.00 |
| 7 | 8.75 | 70 | 87.50 | 700 | 875.00 |
| 8 | 10.00 | 80 | 100.00 | 800 | 1,000.00 |
| 9 | 11.25 | 90 | 112.50 | 900 | 1,125.00 |
| | | | | 1,000 | 1,250.00 |

---

# EXAMPLE

Gary Loudon receives building society interest of £1,793 in the tax year ending 5 April 1997. He must gross up this net interest at 20 per cent as follows:

| Net income | Gross income |
|---|---|
| £1,000 | £1250.00 |
| £700 | £875.00 |
| £90 | £112.50 |
| £3 | £3.75 |
| TOTAL £1,793 | £2,241.25 |

---

## Grossing-up when tax is deducted at 24 per cent

| Net amount £ | Gross amount £ | Net amount £ | Gross amount £ | Net amount £ | Gross amount £ |
|---|---|---|---|---|---|
| 1 | 1.32 | 10 | 13.16 | 100 | 131.58 |
| 2 | 2.63 | 20 | 26.32 | 200 | 263.16 |
| 3 | 3.95 | 30 | 39.47 | 300 | 394.74 |
| 4 | 5.26 | 40 | 52.63 | 400 | 526.32 |
| 5 | 6.58 | 50 | 65.79 | 500 | 657.89 |
| 6 | 7.89 | 60 | 78.95 | 600 | 789.47 |
| 7 | 9.21 | 70 | 92.10 | 700 | 921.05 |
| 8 | 10.53 | 80 | 105.26 | 800 | 1,052.63 |
| 9 | 11.84 | 90 | 118.42 | 900 | 1,184.21 |
| | | | | 1,000 | 1,315.79 |

| Net income | Gross income |
|---|---|
| £2,000 | £2,631.58 |
| £100 | £131.58 |
| £90 | £118.42 |
| £6 | £7.89 |
| TOTAL £2,196 | £2,889.47 |

## Grossing-up when tax is deducted at 23 per cent

| Net amount £ | Gross amount £ | Net amount £ | Gross amount £ | Net amount £ | Gross amount £ |
|---|---|---|---|---|---|
| 1 | 1.30 | 10 | 12.99 | 100 | 129.87 |
| 2 | 2.60 | 20 | 25.97 | 200 | 259.74 |
| 3 | 3.90 | 30 | 38.96 | 300 | 389.61 |
| 4 | 5.19 | 40 | 51.95 | 400 | 519.48 |
| 5 | 6.49 | 50 | 64.94 | 500 | 649.35 |
| 6 | 7.79 | 60 | 77.92 | 600 | 779.22 |
| 7 | 9.09 | 70 | 90.91 | 700 | 909.09 |
| 8 | 10.39 | 80 | 103.90 | 800 | 1,038.96 |
| 9 | 11.69 | 90 | 116.88 | 900 | 1,168.83 |
| | | | | 1,000 | 1,298.70 |

## EXAMPLE

Peggy Cronin receives net income of £4,375 in the tax year beginning 6 April 1997, from which tax has been deducted at the basic rate of 23 per cent. She finds the gross income as follows:

| Net income | Gross income |
|---|---|
| £4,000 | £5,194.80 |
| £300 | £389.61 |
| £70 | £90.91 |
| £5 | £6.49 |
| TOTAL £4,375 | £5,681.81 |

# INHERITANCE TAX

There is no space on the 1997 tax return for inheritance tax. This is because it is largely a tax on what you leave when you die (including gifts made in the seven years before). And few people are affected by inheritance tax – just one in 45 estates currently falls in its net.

Do not ignore it, however. The tax rate is a hefty 40 per cent of anything much over £200,000. There is plenty that can be done to reduce the amount paid – as long as you plan carefully. As the chancellor said in his budget speech in November 1996: 'It is largely paid by people of modest means who either cannot or simply do not make careful plans to avoid it.'

This appendix tells you how inheritance tax works and how to reduce the amount that goes to the Inland Revenue. It also has some guidance on what can be done to reduce an inheritance tax bill after the event; there is some scope to ease the burden even then.

## How inheritance tax works
When you die, everything you own – your home, possessions, investments and savings – goes into your estate. So does money paid out by life insurance policies unless they are written in trust (see p. 350), and the value of things you have given away but reserved the right to use for yourself (gifts with reservation – see p. 352). Debts such as outstanding mortgages and funeral expenses are deducted from the total to find the value of your estate.

Some or all your estate may be free of inheritance tax: anything left to your husband or wife, or to a UK charity, for example (for a full list of what is tax-free, see p. 347). These tax-free bequests and legacies are deducted from the value of your estate before the tax bill is worked out.

Then any gifts to other people in the seven years before your death which are not tax-free are added. So are gifts made to a trust for a disabled person, or to an accumulation and maintenance trust for children and grandchildren under 25.

If the resulting total exceeds a certain limit – £215,000 for deaths on or after 6 April 1997 – inheritance tax is payable on the amount over the limit at 40 per cent.

So if the total is £250,000, tax is payable on £250,000 – £215,000 = £35,000. This gives a tax bill of 40 per cent of £35,000, that is £14,000.

Inheritance tax due on what you leave on death is paid out of your estate. But if inheritance tax is due on a gift made before your death, it must be paid by the person you made the gift to. They may be able to reduce the amount payable if the gift was made more than three years before death by claiming tapering relief:

| Years between gift and death | % of inheritance tax payable |
| --- | --- |
| Up to 3 | 100% |
| More than 3 and up to 4 | 80% |
| More than 4 and up to 5 | 60% |
| More than 5 and up to 6 | 40% |
| More than 6 and up to 7 | 20% |

Inheritance tax may also have to be paid on gifts to certain types of trust made more than seven years before death. The tax, which must be paid at the time of the gift, can also affect the tax payable on death. If you are

---

# EXAMPLE

Angela Framing died in April 1997, leaving an estate worth £287,000 (largely the value of her home counties house). In December 1992, she had made a taxable gift of £10,000 to help a grandchild with the cost of studying for an MBA at a leading business school. Subsequently, in August 1994, she gave another grandchild a taxable gift of £5,000 to start a business.

The calculation of the inheritance tax due starts with the earliest taxable gift – the £10,000 made just over four years before her death. There is no tax to pay on this gift, since it is well below the £215,000 threshold for inheritance tax applying in April 1997 when she died. Nor is there any inheritance tax to pay on the 1994 gift of £5,000. It brought her total of taxable gifts to £15,000 – still well below the £215,000 tax threshold.

In calculating the tax due on Angela's estate, the £15,000 of taxable lifetime gifts is added to the £287,000 left on death to produce a total of £302,000. The first £215,000 of that is free of tax, leaving £302,000 – £215,000 = £87,000 on which tax is due.

Tax at 40 per cent on £87,000 is £34,800 – tax that will be entirely paid out of Angela's estate.

involved with such trusts, you should seek professional advice from an accountant or solicitor – this appendix does not deal with their complexities.

## Gifts free of inheritance tax

Gifts that are always tax-free:

- gifts between husband and wife – even if the two are legally separated. But only the first £55,000 is tax-free if the gifts are to someone who is not domiciled in the UK (domicile reflects the individual's natural home, see p. 279)
- gifts to UK charities
- gifts to certain national institutions such as the National Trust, National Gallery, British Museum (and their Scottish, Welsh and Northern Irish equivalents)
- gifts of certain types of heritage property such as paintings, archives, land or historic buildings to non-profit-making concerns like local museums
- gifts of land in the UK to registered housing associations
- gifts of shares in a company into a trust for the benefit of most or all of the employees which will control the company.
- gifts to established political parties.

Gifts that are tax-free on death only:

- lump sums paid out on your death by a pension scheme provided the trustees of the scheme have discretion about who gets the money
- refunds of personal pension contributions (and interest) paid directly to someone else or a trust – in other words, not paid into your estate
- the estate of anyone killed on active military service in war or whose death was hastened by such service.

Gifts that are tax-free in lifetime only:

- anything given to an individual more than seven years before your death – unless there are strings attached (see p. 352)
- small gifts worth up to £250 to any number of people in any tax year. But you can't give anyone more than this limit and claim exemption on the first £250 – if you give someone £500, the whole £500 will be taxable unless it is tax-free for one of the other reasons below
- regular gifts made out of normal income. The gifts must come out of your usual after-tax income and not from your capital. After paying for the gifts, you should have enough income to maintain your normal standard of living
- gifts on marriage to a bride or groom: each parent of the bride or groom can give £5,000, grandparents or remoter relatives £2,500 and anyone else £1,000. The gifts must be made before the great day – and if the marriage is called off, the gift becomes taxable

- gifts for the maintenance of your family – an ex-husband or wife, certain dependent relatives and children under 18 or still in full-time education. The children can be yours, stepchildren, adopted children or any other children in your care
- up to £3,000 in total a year of other gifts. If you don't use the whole £3,000 annual exemption in one year, you can carry forward the unused part to the next tax year only. You can't use the annual exemption to top up the small gifts exemption. If you give someone more than £250 in a year, all of it must come off the annual exemption if it is to be free of inheritance tax.

## PLANNING FOR INHERITANCE TAX

If your estate is likely to be well below the threshold for paying inheritance tax, there is no need to worry about it. But if it looks as if you are above it, there is much you can do to reduce the tax bill. An important first step is to draw up a will which will make you think about what you own and how you want it to be disposed of after you die.

Most of the ways of minimising inheritance tax involve making gifts which are free of tax or making taxable gifts more than seven years before your death. But remember your heirs will still be better off even if tax is due on your estate. Don't give away so much that you or your spouse are left impoverished in old age, merely to cheat the Inland Revenue of every last penny of tax.

### Tax-free gifts

If you do have some resources to spare, make as full use as possible of the tax-free small gifts, gifts on marriage and such like. And make sure your spouse has enough to make similar gifts free of inheritance tax.

If you want to make larger gifts, the earlier you make them the better – because inheritance tax may have to be paid on a gift if you die within seven years of making it. (For this reason, lifetime gifts are often described as potentially exempt transfers (PETs). They are potentially free of inheritance tax but you must survive for seven years after they are made for the tax to be avoided.)

Even if you die within seven years of making a gift, the inheritance tax paid by the person you made the gift to will be reduced by tapering relief (see p. 346) if the gift is made more than three years before your death. Note that gifts in your lifetime, other than cash, may mean a capital gains tax bill.

## Share your wealth

A married couple can share their wealth – what they give to each other is free of inheritance tax. Each can then make tax-free gifts and leave a taxable estate of up to £215,000 without paying inheritance tax.

In practice, it may not be easy to split your worldly goods and give them away during your lifetime. It may make more sense to pass all or most of them on to the survivor so he or she has enough to live on. But this principle of estate-splitting is a basic strategy to be followed where possible.

## Your home

Your home is almost certainly your most valuable possession – and may be the main reason why your estate ends up over the threshold for paying inheritance tax. But it is one of the hardest assets to remove from the tax net – assuming you intend to go on living in it until you die.

For example, you can't make a lifetime gift of it to your children on condition you can continue to live in it. That would count as a gift with reservation (see p. 352), and the home would be treated as yours.

## EXAMPLE

Veronica McGrath wants to give away as much as possible free of inheritance tax before she dies.

First, she gives £1,000 a year to each of her three children – taking advantage of the £3,000 a year annual exemption. Then she makes £250 gifts every year to each of her ten grandchildren – a total of £2,500 a year free of inheritance tax as small gifts. She also gives the maximum £2,500 to any of her grandchildren who get married.

She can afford to pay the premiums on insurance policies on her own life out of her normal income. So she takes out policies written in trust (see p. 350) for each of her three children. The premiums come to £60 a month each and will be tax-free as regular gifts made out of normal income (when she dies, the money from the insurance policies will be paid straight to the children without being taxable).

Overall, Veronica manages to give away almost £7,000 a year free of inheritance tax. This is nearly £50,000 in a seven-year period, and even if she dies within seven years of starting this programme of gifts there will be no inheritance tax to pay on them.

You might be able to reduce the size of your estate somewhat by sharing the ownership of the house. If your home is jointly owned with someone under a joint tenancy, your share automatically goes to the survivor when one of you dies. But if you jointly own your home with someone else as a tenancy in common, you can bequeath your half-share to anyone you please.

For example, if you had a tenancy in common with your spouse, you could bequeath half of your half-share to your spouse and the other half to the next generation. This would reduce the size of your spouse's estate but leave him or her in control of the home.

There is no inheritance tax to pay if you leave part or all of a home to your spouse, since gifts between husband and wife are always tax-free. But a gift to anyone who is not your husband or wife is taxable.

### Life insurance
If you want to make sure there is enough money to pay an inheritance tax bill on a home or business, you can take out a term life insurance policy which pays out if you die within seven years of giving it away. And if you plan to leave a large asset on death, whole life insurance policies pay out whenever you die, again providing cash to pay the inheritance tax.

Make sure you have any such policies written in trust to the person you want to have the money. The proceeds will then be paid directly to that person on your death and be free of inheritance tax. If the policy is not written in trust, the money will be added to your estate and inheritance tax charged on it (there will also be a delay before your heirs can get their hands on it until probate is granted).

E X A M P L E

Alan and Meg Riordan realise they are going to face a hefty inheritance tax bill when they die, since most of their assets are in Alan's name. They decide to start an active programme of making tax-free gifts and estate-splitting.

They adopt a similar approach to Veronica McGrath in making gifts. Since each of them can make these tax-free gifts, they are soon passing on around £100,000 to their children and grandchildren every seven years.

They also divide their assets between them, and bequeath a further £200,000 each to their children in their wills, with the rest to each other. When the first dies, the £200,000 bequest to the children will be below the threshold for inheritance tax.

The second to die will thus leave £200,000 less to fall into the tax net. And the Riordans will have saved £100,000 from inheritance tax for each seven years of the lifetime gifts programme.

By starting 15 years before their deaths, the Riordans manage to pass on £400,000 more without tax than if they had left it all in Alan's name. This saves their heirs £160,000 in inheritance tax.

The premiums for a policy written in trust count as gifts, but will be free of inheritance tax if the policy is for your spouse. And if you pay the premiums out of your normal spending, they will be tax-free whoever benefits.

## Shares

The market value of any shares left on death (or given away in the previous seven years) must normally be included in your estate in working out the inheritance tax bill. But some sorts of shares qualify for business relief, which reduces the value for inheritance tax purposes – or even removes them from the calculation altogether:

- shares in a listed company which form a controlling interest – for gifts made on or after 10 March 1992 and inheritance tax bills which arise out of deaths on or after that date, the value of the shares is halved
- shares quoted on the Unlisted Securities Market (USM) or Alternative Investment Market (AIM) – no inheritance tax provided they have been held for at least two years
- unquoted shares and those traded on the Over the Counter (OTC) markets are also eligible for business relief on the same basis as AIM shares.

## Your own business or farm

If you own or have an interest in a small business or a farm, seek professional advice on inheritance tax, since there are substantial concessions which can reduce or eliminate the tax:

- business relief means there will be no inheritance tax to pay on business assets such as goodwill, land, buildings, plant, stock, patents and so on (reduced by debts incurred in the business)
- agricultural relief can mean no inheritance tax on the agricultural value of owner-occupied farmlands and farm tenancies (including cottages, farm buildings and farm houses). There are also reliefs for landowners who let farmland.

## Estate freezing

Estate freezing is a way of freezing some of the value of your wealth now so the increase in value in future years benefits someone else.

A simple way of doing this is by investing in an endowment or unit-linked life insurance policy written in trust for your children or grandchildren (see Life insurance, above). Any growth in its value accumulates in the policy free of inheritance tax. Some unit trust managers can do something similar with investments in unit trusts.

A more ambitious approach is to set up an accumulation and maintenance trust for your children or grandchildren. You put some capital in and any income from it is either reinvested or used for the maintenance, education or benefit of the beneficiaries at the discretion of the trustees. When the beneficiaries reach the age of 25, either the capital is shared out or they become entitled to the income from it. If you live for more than seven years after making gifts to such trusts, there is no inheritance tax to pay.

If you are thinking of setting up a family trust, consult a professional tax adviser such as a solicitor or accountant.

## INHERITANCE TAX PLANNING PITFALLS

You might think that there are some rather obvious wheezes that will help you avoid inheritance tax. It is unlikely that the Inland Revenue will not have thought of them and blocked their use.

### Gifts with strings attached

If you give something away but reserve the right to use it, it counts as a gift with reservation – and is treated as remaining your property. The gift would not be recognised for inheritance tax purposes and its value would be added to your estate when you died.

For example, if you give your home to a child on condition that you can go on living in it until your death, this would count as a gift with reservation. This could apply even if there was no formal agreement that you go on living in the home. If the gift was made after 17 March 1986, it counts as subject to a reservation if you go on using it.

### Associated operations

If you try to get round the inheritance tax rules by making a series of gifts, the Inland Revenue is allowed to treat them as associated operations which form a single direct gift.

For example, you might think you could give an extra £5,000 to an adult child by making ten tax-free gifts of £250 to friends which they pass on. The taxman will treat this as a single £5,000 gift, however – and one subject to inheritance tax.

### Related property

In working out the value of a bequest or gift, the Inland Revenue treats as yours property which it reckons is related to yours – in particular, anything owned by your husband or wife. This means you can't reduce its value by splitting it up with your spouse.

Suppose, for example, you own 30 per cent of the shares in a company and your spouse owns another 30 per cent. The Inland Revenue will value your 30 per cent as worth half the value of a 60 per cent controlling interest, which is generally higher than the value of a 30 per cent minority interest.

Property will also be treated as related if it has been owned at any time in the previous five years by a charity, political party or national institution to which you or your spouse gave it.

## EASING THE PAYMENT OF INHERITANCE TAX

Inheritance tax is due six months after the end of the month in which the death happened. In practice, it can often take longer for the executors or personal representatives to sort out the will and tidy up the dead person's affairs. As part of the process of seeking probate, they must submit an Inland Revenue account, listing the value of the dead person's property (including property owned jointly with anybody else) and the amounts of any debts. Probate will not be granted until the tax has been paid.

Interest is charged if the tax is paid after the six-month deadline, running from the time the tax was due. Likewise, if you pay too much inheritance tax, you will get interest on the over-payment from the Inland Revenue.

If you take out a loan to pay inheritance tax before probate is granted, you can get tax relief on the interest on it for up to 12 months.

### Payment by instalments
You can spread the pain of paying inheritance tax over ten equal yearly instalments with two sorts of assets:
• land and property
• a business, including certain holdings of unquoted shares.

This option is allowed only with bequests on death and lifetime gifts where the recipient still owns the property when the death occurs. Interest has to be paid on the delayed tax with land and property, unless it is business property or agricultural land.

If you want to pay in instalments, tell the Inland Revenue before the normal payment date for the tax. The first instalment is due on the date the whole tax would have been payable.

### Reducing the tax on bequests that have fallen in value
If you inherit investments or land and buildings which fall in value after the death of the person who bequeathed them, you might be able to reduce your inheritance tax bill.

For investments, this applies to quoted shares (including those quoted on the AIM) and authorised unit trusts which fall in value or become worthless in the year after death:

- if sold during this period for less than they were worth on death, the sale price can be used to value them for inheritance tax purposes instead of their value on death
- if cancelled without replacement, they are treated as having been sold immediately before the date of cancellation for the nominal sum of £1
- if suspended and remaining suspended a year after the death, their value at the first anniversary can be used for inheritance tax purposes instead of their value on death.

When this relief is claimed, however, all such investments sold in the year after death are revalued in this way. So if some shares or unit trusts have been sold for more than they were worth on death, this would offset any loss made on other shares or unit trusts.

For land or buildings, you can ask for the inheritance tax bill to be recalculated if you sell them within four years of the death for less than their probate value. The inheritance tax bill will be worked out on the actual sale proceeds instead. Again, if this relief is claimed, all land or property sold during the four-year period is revalued for inheritance tax purposes at what it was sold for, rather than what it was worth on death.

### Facing a second inheritance tax bill within five years?
If you inherit something that has only recently been subject to inheritance tax, the tax due on this second change of ownership is reduced by what is known as quick succession relief. Provided the death which led to the first payment was within five years of the death that has led to a second tax bill, the second bill can be reduced by a fraction of the first bill.

If the first death was within one year of the second death, the second bill is reduced by the following fraction of the first bill:

$$\frac{\text{Value of inheritance at the time of first transfer}}{\text{Value of inheritance at transfer + tax paid on first transfer}}$$

If the first death was more than one year before the second death, the fraction is reduced by 20 per cent for each complete year between the two. The example on p. 355 shows how quick succession relief works.

### Changing inheritances after a death
If you are facing an inheritance tax bill, one option to reduce it is to vary the inheritances covered. Whether or not there is a will, those who are entitled to a share of a dead person's estate can agree to vary the way the estate is divided up.

For example, the variation could direct some of the estate towards tax-free bequests – from the children to the dead person's husband or wife, for example. Or it might be used to jump a generation, so it goes straight to the grandchildren rather than adding further to the wealth of the children and the amount of tax that would have to be paid on their deaths.

The procedure is to draw up a deed of variation in writing, which must be signed within two years of the death by all those who will lose out. If it increases the amount of tax, the personal representatives of the dead person must also sign it. It should clearly state which inheritances are being changed and how.

A variation can be carried out only once, so it is important to get it right. A solicitor can advise on drawing up the document.

# EXAMPLE

Maurice Thornton inherits a half-share of his mother's estate, worth £150,000. Inheritance tax of £16,000 is due on this share.

However, Maurice's mother had inherited £80,000 from her father only two and a half years earlier – an inheritance on which tax of £20,000 had been paid. Because Maurice's legacy is within five years of his mother's own legacy, he is entitled to reduce the inheritance tax on his legacy by a fraction of what was paid on hers.

The fraction of the tax bill on his mother's legacy which can be taken into account is worked out as follows:

$$\frac{£80,000}{£80,000 + £20,000}$$
$$= \frac{£80,000}{£100,000}$$
$$= \frac{4}{5}$$

This, expressed as a decimal, is 0.8, which is reduced by 20 per cent for each complete year between Maurice's mother's legacy and her death. Since this period was two and a half years, the 0.8 is reduced by 2 x 20 per cent = 40 per cent. Forty per cent of 0.8 is 0.32.

Thus the tax on Maurice's estate is reduced by 0.8 – 0.32 = 0.48 of the tax due on the legacy when he got it (£20,000), that is, £9,600. This results in a tax bill of £16,000 – £9,600 = £6,400.

# USEFUL LEAFLETS

You can get all these leaflets free from your tax office.

## Introductions to self-assessment
SA/BK1      Self-assessment – a general guide
SA/BK2      Self-assessment – a guide for the self-employed
SA/BK3      Self-assessment – a guide to keeping records for the self-employed
SA/BK4      Self-assessment – a general guide to keeping records
SAT 3      Self-assessment – what it will mean for employers

## General guides to the Inland Revenue
IR37      Appeals against tax
IR73      Inland Revenue investigations: how settlements are negotiated
IR120      You and the Inland Revenue
IR141      Open government
SVD1      Shares Valuation Division – an introduction
AO1      How to complain about the Inland Revenue

## Income tax for particular groups
IR33      Income tax and school leavers
IR41      Income tax and the unemployed
IR60      Income tax and students
IR80      Income tax and married couples
IR90      Tax allowances and reliefs
IR91      A guide for widows and widowers
IR92      A guide for one-parent families
IR121      Income tax and pensioners

## Income tax and international issues

IR20     Residents and non-residents – liability to tax in the UK
IR58     Going to work abroad?
IR138    Living or retiring abroad – a guide to UK tax on your UK income and pension
IR139    Income from abroad? A guide to UK tax on overseas income
IR140    Non-resident landlords, their agents and tenants

## Income tax – general

IR1      Extra-statutory concessions (plus supplement with latest concessions)
IR45     What to do about tax when someone dies
IR46     Income tax and corporation tax – clubs, societies and associations
IR65     Giving to charity – how individuals can get tax relief
IR87     Letting and your home
IR93     Separation, divorce and maintenance payments
IR103    Tax relief for private medical insurance – for people aged 60 and over
IR113    Gift Aid – a guide for donors and charities
IR115    Tax and childcare
IR119    Tax relief for vocational training
IR122    Volunteer drivers
IR123    Mortgage interest relief: buying your home
IR144    Income tax and incapacity benefit

## Savings and investments

IR68     Accrued income scheme – taxing securities on transfer
IR78     Personal pensions: a guide for tax
IR89     Personal Equity Plans (PEPs) – a guide for potential investors
IR110    A guide for people with savings
IR114    TESSA – tax-free interest for taxpayers
IR127    Are you paying too much tax on your savings?
IR129    Occupational pension schemes – an introduction
IR137    The Enterprise Investment Scheme
IR152    Trusts – an introduction

## Employees

480       Expenses and benefits – a guide for tax
IR16     Share acquisitions by directors and employees – explanatory notes
IR17     Share acquisitions by directors and employees – an outline for employees
IR34     Pay As You Earn
IR42     Lay-offs and short-time work

IR43     Income tax and strikes
IR69     Expenses payments: Forms P11D – how to save yourself work
IR95     Approved profit-sharing schemes – an outline for employees
IR97     Approved save as you earn share option schemes – an outline for employees
IR101   Approved company share option plans – an outline for employees
IR133   Income tax and company cars from 6 April 1994 – a guide for employees
IR134   Income tax and relocation packages
IR136   Income tax and company vans – a guide for employees and employers

## Self-employed
CWL1   Starting your own business?
IR24     Class 4 National Insurance contributions
IR56     Employed or self-employed? A guide for tax and National Insurance
IR72     Investigations: the examination of business accounts
IR104   Simple tax accounts for businesses with a turnover of less than £15,000
IR105   How your profits are taxed

## Income tax – construction industry
IR14/15 Construction industry tax deduction scheme
IR40     Construction industry: conditions for getting a sub-contractor's tax certificate
IR116   Guide for sub-contractors with tax certificates
IR117   A sub-contractor's guide to the deduction scheme
IR148   Are your workers employed or self-employed – a guide to tax and National Insurance for contractors in the construction industry

## Employers
480      Expenses and benefits – a guide for tax
P7       Employer's guide to Pay As You Earn
IR53     Thinking of taking someone on? PAYE for employers
IR64     Giving to charity – how businesses can get tax relief
IR71     PAYE inspections: the inspection of employers' and contractors' records
IR109   PAYE: inspections and negotiations: employers' and contractors' records – how settlements are negotiated
IR132   The taxation of company cars from 6 April 1994: employers' guide
IR136   Income tax and company vans – a guide for employees and employers

## Capital gains tax

CGT4    Capital gains tax – owner-occupied houses
CGT6    Retirement relief on disposal of a business – capital gains tax
CGT11   Capital gains tax and small businesses
CGT14   Capital gains tax – an introduction
CGT16   Capital gains tax – indexation allowance, disposals after 5 April
        1988

## Inheritance tax

IHT2*   Inheritance tax on lifetime gifts
IHT3    An introduction to inheritance tax
IHT8*   Alterations to an inheritance following a death
IHT14*  Inheritance tax – the personal representatives' responsibilities
IHT15*  Inheritance tax – how to calculate the liability
IHT16*  Inheritance tax – settled property
IHT17*  Inheritance tax – businesses, farms and woodlands
IHT18*  Inheritance tax – foreign aspects

*Available from the three Capital Taxes Offices:
England and Wales: Ferrers House, PO Box 38, Castle Meadow Road, Nottingham, NG2 1BB
Scotland: Mulberry House, 16 Picardy Place, Edinburgh EH1 3NB
Northern Ireland: Dorchester House, 52-58 Great Victoria Street, Belfast BT2 7QL

## Business Economic Notes

These give information on how tax inspectors approach particular business-es such as travel agents, road hauliers, hairdressers and funeral directors. You can get them from:

The Reference Room
Inland Revenue Library
Room 8, New Wing
Somerset House
London WC2R 1LB

They cost £1.50 each.

# INDEX

accommodation expenses 170-1
accumulation unit trusts 272
additional personal allowance 10, 29, 42, 133-5
additional voluntary contributions 32, 69, 93, 94
  refunds 93, 103
  reliefs 116-17
administrative expenses 201
advertising
  furnished holiday lettings 223
  self-employment 202
age-related allowances 128
agency work 185
allowances 8
  *see also* expenses
  1996 budget 25-6
  additional personal 10, 29, 42, 133-5
  age-related 128
  amounts to be taken from 287
  blind person's 10, 128-9, 136
  capital gains 35
  childcare 92
  deadlines 23, 24
  income tax 3, 8, 9, 23
  late claims 28
  married couples *(see married couple's allowance)*
  meaning 3
  older people 38-40

  on PAYE coding notice 284-7
  personal *(see personal allowance)*
  restriction 287
  separation or divorce 42
  single parents 40-1

  in tax return 128-36
  transfer of surplus allowances 135-6
  transitional allowance 129-30, 136
  types 9
  widow's bereavement 10, 135
allowances (benefits) *(see social security benefits and individual allowances eg jobseeker's allowance)*
Alternative Investment Market 27, 73, 267
annuities 88
  retirement 71, 82, 108, 109, 113-14, 285
anti-avoidance provisions
  benefit test 188
  motive test 188
  self-employment 187-9
  too small to count test 188
appeals 20-1
attendance allowance 93
bad debts 202
bank interest 84
  paid after tax 63
  paid without deduction 65
benefit test, anti-avoidance provisions 188
benefits
  in kind 289
  welfare *(see social security benefits)*
bereavement allowance (widow) 10, 135
betting winnings 247
blind person's allowance 10, 128-9, 136
bravery decorations 247
bridging loans 52
budget changes (1996) 25-7
building society interest 84, 286
  paid after tax 63

paid without deduction 65
   in tax return 81
building society shares 272
business expansion scheme 73
   capital gains 247
Business Links 203
business loans relief 9
business mileage 30
   *see also* fuel
capital allowances
   amount claimable 205-6
   buying and selling capital items 206-8
   claiming 208-9
   furnished holiday lettings 224
   property 229
   scrapping short life asset 208
   writing down allowance 205
capital gains tax
   allowable expenses 257-8
   calculating gain or loss 248-9, 257-63,
   265-8
   caravan or houseboat 57, 247
   chattels 247, 262
   delaying bill 249-50
   dependant relatives 57-8
   documents needed 251
   ex spouse 57-8
   gardens 58
   gifts 266-7
   hold over relief 266
   home sale 245-6
   indexation allowance 259-60
   investment for gain 66
   letting relief 35
   lettings 60-1
   losses 263-5
      carrying over 264
      claiming 264-5
   main residence 245
   married couples 251, 263
   non-qualifying policies life assurance
   policy 102
   part disposals 258-9
   persons who have to pay 248
   private residence relief 34, 59-60
   rates 26
   record keeping 35
   reducing bill 249-50

reinvestment relief 35, 267-8
reliefs *(see individual reliefs eg hold
over relief)*
retirement relief 274-5
roll-over relief 275
saving tax payment 35
separation and divorce 48-9
shares 268-73
   accumulation unit trusts 272
   bought after 6 April (1965)
   269
   bought on or before 5 April
   (1982) 269
   building societies 272
   conversions or reorganisations
   272
   employee share schemes 271
   instalment payment 272
   insurance companies 272
   investment trusts 268
   mergers 272
   monthly savings schemes 273
   rights issues 272
   sale within 10 days of buying
   269, 271
   stock dividends 272
   takeovers 272
   unit trusts 268
   valuation 268
splitting disposals over years 35
tax free allowance 35
tax return 78, 251-7
tax-free gains 246-8
trusts 247, 250-1
valuing assets 257, 260-1
wasting assets 57, 247
when paid 246
which home 57-8
working from home 59
capital redemption policies 81
caravans 57, 247
cars 288
   company cars 146, 155-8
   business mileage 30
   changing, getting and losing
   157
   fuel for 158-9
   giving up for cash 158

private use of fuel 26
saving tax 30
two 158
expenses 201
fixed profit scheme 155
fuels
  benefit 288
  business mileage 30
  company cars 158-9
  mileage allowances 153-5
  private use 26
  sliding charges 159
private 247
self-employment expense 201
vans 159-60
casual earnings 103
charge cards 152
charitable giving
  capital gains tax and 35
  covenants 9, 28-9, 107, 123-4
  Gift Aid 9, 28-9, 107, 125
  income reliefs 107, 123-5
  PAYE coding notice 286
  payroll-giving schemes 28-9, 144
  reliefs 9
chattels 247, 262
child benefit 93
Child Support Agency 42-3
childcare 162, 172
  allowance 92
  provided by employer 30
children
  employment payments towards education 163
  investments for 81
  trust income for 240-2
Christmas bonus
  employees 144
  pensioners 92
cleaning services 225
clothing 204
cohabitees, mortgage interest relief 54
company cars 146, 155-8
  business mileage 30
  changing, getting and losing 157
  fuel for 158-9
  giving up for cash 158
  private use of fuel 26

saving tax 30
two 158
company credit cards 152
complaints (to IR) 20-1
corrections to tax return 17
council tax
  benefit 93
  paid by employer 149, 151-2
covenants 290
  charitable giving 9, 28-9, 107, 123-4
  commercial reasons 104
credit cards 152
  paid by employer 149, 151-2
credit unions income 87
damage award 248
  interest on 83
deadlines (see time limits)
death of half married couple 49
decorations for bravery 247
deductions, meaning 3
dental insurance 162
dependant relatives, property
  capital gains 57-8
  mortgage interest relief 55
dependent child benefits 92
determination, failure to send in tax return 15
disability
  disability living allowance 93
  disability working allowance 93
  employment income for 166
discovery assessment 18-19
discretionary share options, approved 175, 178-9
distributions
  foreign income 234
  investment income 5, 7
  non-qualifying 91
dividends 272
  foreign income 91, 234, 242
  investment income 5, 7, 81, 89-92
  non-qualifying distributions 91
  scrip 90-1, 242
  stock 272
  in tax return 81, 89-92
  unit trusts 89-90
divorce (see separation and divorce)

domicile 279
education
  *see also* training
  private, employment payments
    towards 163
employee share ownership trusts (ESOTs)
  175
employee share schemes
  *see also* share options; shares
  capital gains tax 271
employees
  *see also* PAYE scheme
  1996 budget changes 26
  childcare provision 30
  expenses 26
  fringe benefits 29-30
  saving tax payments 29-31
  vocation training 26
employers' pension schemes
  approved 68-9
  AVCs *(see additional voluntary contri-
    butions)*
  contributions 68-9, 144
  limits on benefits 68
employment
  assets transferred to you 149, 150-1
  benefits 142
  cash or perks 149, 151
  childcare 163
  Christmas bonus 144
  contributions to pensions 144
  dates taxable 142
  directors 143
  disability 166
  documents required 142-3
  earnings 141
  education of children help 163
  employer details 141
  expenses 163-4
    in doing job 169-73
    exclusively incurred for work
      172-3
    fixed deductions for 172
    professional fees and subscrip-
      tions 172
    subsistence 170-1
    travel 170-1
  foreign service 166

fringe benefits 146-64
  gifts 143-4
  golden hellos 144
  holiday pay 144
  incentive awards 144-5
  living accommodation 152-3
  loans, cheap or free 160-1
  lump sums
    compensation 164-6
    retirement 142
  maternity pay 145
  matters to be taxed 141-2
  mileage allowances 153-5
  mobile phones 161-2, 289
  money from employment 143-6
  PAYE tax deducted 146
  payments made for you 149, 151-2
  payroll giving schemes 28-9, 144
  private medical or dental
    insurance 162
  professional society fees 163
  profit related pay 144, 145
  relocation expenses 162
  services provision 163
  share schemes or share options 163
  sick pay 144, 145
  status of employee 140
  subscriptions 163
  suggestion schemes 145
  in tax return 76, 140-73
  taxable benefits for all
    employees 149-55
  tips 144, 146
  voluntary payments 143-4
  vouchers 152
  when job ends 165-6
enquiries (by IR) 17-18
  demand for documents 18
  discovery assessment 18-19
  written notice 18
enterprise investment scheme 27, 33, 72-3,
  74, 287, 294
  capital gains 247
  reliefs 9, 107, 122-3
Enterprise Zone trusts 87
entertainment expense 202
ex spouse, property
  capital gains 57-8

mortgage interest relief 55
executive share options scheme 178
expenses 285
    *see also* fringe benefits
    accommodation 170-1
    administrative 201
    advertising 202, 223
    bad debts 202
    capital gains 257-8
    employee costs 199-200
    entertainment 202
    finance charges 203, 222, 227
    furnished holiday lettings 221-3
    interest 203
    legal costs 202, 222
    motor expenses 201
    payments and balancing charges 163-4
    premises costs 200
    professional costs 202, 222
    promotion 202
    property 227
    relief for 9
    repairs 200, 221-2, 227
    subsistence 26, 170-1, 201
    in tax return 197-204
    travel 26, 170-1, 201
    wear and tear 34-5, 229
family credit 92
finance charges
    furnished holiday lettings 222
    property 227
    self-employment expense 203
fiscal accounting 191-2
foreign currency 247
foreign earnings
    deduction 168-9
    foreign tax 169
    not taxable in UK 166-8
    in tax return 166-9
foreign estates 243-4
foreign income
    *see also* non-residence
    distributions 234
    dividends 91, 234, 242
    documents needed 233
    double taxation agreements 234
    how taxed 231-2

    land and property 235
    life insurance policies 236
    offshore funds 235-6
    pensions 233-5
    savings 233-5
    supplementary pages 78
    tax credit relief 231-2, 236-8
    tax-free 232-3
    unable to remit 233
foreign service income 166
freelance earnings 5, 103
friendly societies
    income from 87
    relief on payments to 107, 126-7

fringe benefits 29-30
    *(see also expenses)*
    company car 146
    dispensations 147
    as income 5, 7
    medical insurance 146
    PAYE settlement agreements 147
    payments not entered 147
    in tax return 146-64
    tax-free 147-9
fuel
    benefit 288
    business mileage 30
    for company cars 158-9
    mileage allowances 153-5
    private use 26
    sliding charges 159
furnished holiday lettings 220-5
    advertising 223
    capital allowances 224
    expenses 221-3
    finance charges 222
    income 221
    legal costs 222
    losses 224-5
    private use 223-4
    professional costs 222
    repairs 221-2
    services provided costs 223
    tax adjustments 223-4
    tax benefits 220-1
futures 104
gardening 225

general commissioners 21
Gift Aid 9, 28-9, 107, 125
gifts 6
    between married couples 37
    capital gains tax 266-7
    from employer 143-4
    public benefit 247
gilt strips 87
gilts
    capital gains 247
    interest 63, 84
    in tax return 86-7
golden hellos 144
government stock
    capital gains 247
    interest 63, 84
    in tax return 86-7
guardians allowance 93
hairdressing 162
hold over relief 266
holiday pay 144
home improvement loans 34, 55
home income schemes 9, 52
homeowners
    absence from home 34, 55-6
    saving tax 33-5
    separation and divorce 48
houseboats 57, 247
housing benefit 93
incapacity benefit 93, 288
    taxable 96-7
incentive awards 144-5
income
    casual earnings 103
    employment *(see employment)*
    filling in return 80-105
    foreign *(see foreign income)*
    freelance earnings 5, 103
    fringe benefits 5, 7
    from personal representative 7
    furnished holiday lettings 221
    inherited 242-4
    investments *(see investment income)*
    losses unable to be set against 104
    maintenance agreements 6
    maintenance income 5, 7
    meaning 3
    partnership 7

    payments considered as income 5, 7
    payments not income 5-6
    pensions 5, 7
    pensions and benefits 92-8
    permanent health insurance 104
    reliefs *(see reliefs main heading)*
    rent 5, 7
    salary 5, 7
    self-employment 195-7
    social security benefits 5, 7, 22
    tax-free 6
    taxable 4
    trusts and settlements *(see trusts)*
income support 93, 95-6
income tax
    allowances *(see allowances main heading)*
    deadlines 22-4
    deductions, meaning 3
    filling in return 80-105
    income *(see income)*
    investments *(see investment income)*
    PAYE *(see PAYE system)*
    payments
        deadlines 22-3
        instalments 16, 23
        interest and surcharge 17
        interim 15-16, 24
        overpayment 19
        PAYE 21-2
        small 16
        statement of accounts 16-17
        underpayment 21, 23
        unpaid 17
    rates 4, 25
    reliefs *(see reliefs main heading)*
    simple guide 2-4
    taxable income 4
indexation allowance 259-60
industrial death benefit 93, 95
industrial disablement benefit 93
inheritance tax
    gifts from normal income 36
    gifts on marriage 36
    life insurance 36
    rates 26
    reduction after death 36
    saving tax payments 36

separation and divorce 48-9
inherited income 242-4
    foreign estates 243-4
    personal representative's
    statement 242-3
Inland Revenue
    *see also* tax return
    appeals to 20-1
    changes occurring in 11
    complaints to 20-1
    enquiries 17-18
        demand for documents 18
        discovery assessment 18-19
        written notice 18
    obligation to 12-13
insurance policies, gains on 247
interest 5, 7
    bank interest 63, 65, 84
    building society 63, 65, 81, 84, 286
    damage award 83
    government stocks (gilts) 63, 84
    higher rate required 65-6
    investment income 5, 7
    loans 9, 107, 118-19, 286, 290
        restriction 290
    mortgages *see* mortgage
    interest
    National Savings Certificates 6
    paid after tax 63, 84-5
    paid before tax 83-4, 84-5
    PAYE coding notice 286
    personal injury award 83
    self-employment expense 203
    in tax return 83-8
    tax-free 6
    trusts 85, 247
    unit trusts 85-6
    untaxed 289
invalid care allowance 93, 96
investment income 5, 7, 81-92
    distributions 5, 7
    dividends 5, 7, 81, 89-92
    government stock 86-7
    grossing up 63
    interest 5, 7
        bank interest 63, 65, 84
        building society 63, 65, 81, 84,
        286

    higher rate required 65-6
        paid after tax 63
    not in tax return 82
    offshore funds 235-6
    partnership share 81
    shares and unit trusts 64
    tax free 62
    in tax return 81-92
    too much tax deducted 64-5
    trusts 81, 268
investments
    Alternative Investment Market 27, 73
    business expansion scheme 73, 247
    for capital gains 66
    enterprise investment scheme 27, 33,
    72-3, 74, 287, 294
    in growing businesses 72-4
    life insurance policies 67
    pensions 67-71
    personal equity plans (PEPs) 32-3, 71-
    2
    profit-sharing scheme 26, 33, 175-6
    saving tax payments 32-3
    savings-related share option scheme
    33
    tax-free 32
    TESSAs 33, 72
    venture capital trusts 27, 73-4, 107,
    121-2, 247
jobfinder's grant 93
jobseeker's allowance 5, 93, 95-6
jointly owned assets 41
land *(see property)*
leasing equipment income 104
legal costs
    furnished holiday lettings 222
    self-employment expense 202
lettings 34-5, 287
    advertising 223
    capital allowances 224
    capital gains tax 60-1
    expenses 221-3
    finance charges 222
    furnished holiday lets 220-5
    income 221
    income record keeping 13
    legal costs 222
    losses 224-5

mortgage interest relief 56-7
own home 34
private use 223-4
professional costs 222
rent a room scheme 26-7, 34, 218-20
repairs 221-2
second home 34
services provided costs 223
tax adjustments 223-4
tax benefits 220-1
wear and tear 34-5, 229
life annuities 87
life insurance policies 33, 81
foreign 236
income in tax return 100-3
investment 67
losses 102-3
nomination to avoid inheritance tax 36
non-qualifying policies 101-3
qualifying policies 101
relief on premiums 67
savings-type 67
literary works, profits from 103
living accommodation 152-3
loan stocks 87, 88
loans
*see also* mortgage interest relief
bridging 52
business 9
home improvement 34
income from guaranteeing 104
interest 9, 107, 118-19, 286, 290
restriction 290
local authority 63, 84, 88
not income 6
paid by employer 288
local authority loans 84, 88
interest paid after tax 63
losses
capital gains tax 263-5
furnished holiday lettings 224-5
property 230
self-employment 209-11, 287
closing down 210-11
future profits 210
previous year 209-10
lottery winnings 6, 247

lump sums
retirement 70, 142
in tax return 164-6
maintenance arrangements
from parents for over 21s 99
income 5, 6, 7
new rules 43-4, 120
switching from old rules 46-8
old rules 44, 99, 120-1
PAYE coding notice 286, 289
payments received 44
PAYE coding notice 289
reliefs 9
payment received 119-21
payments made 44-5
saving tax 29
separation and divorce 42-4
tax return 98-100
married couples
allowance *see* married couple's allowance
capital gains tax 251, 263
death of one partner 49
divorce *see* separation and divorce
employment of spouse 31
gifts between 37
jointly owned assets 41
methods of saving tax 29
mortgage interest relief 34, 53
newlyweds 53
older people 38
separation *see* separation and divorce
married couple's allowance 10, 23, 37-8, 130-2, 285
deadlines 23
married men 131-2
married women 132
splitting and transferring 29, 38, 40, 130, 288
tax return 130-2
year of marriage 40-1
maternity allowance 92
maternity pay 94, 96, 145
medical insurance 146, 162
relief for 3
mileage allowances 30, 153-5
mistakes in tax return 17
mobile phones 161-2, 289

money
  capital gains 247
  foreign currency 247
monthly savings schemes 273
mortgage interest relief 9, 33-4
  absence from home 55-6
  bigger mortgages 51-2
  bridging loans 52
  cohabitees 54
  dependant relatives 55
  home improvement loans 55
  home income schemes 52
  how to get 50-1
  letting home 56-7
  married couples 34, 53
  MIRAS 50-1, 53, 56-7
  negative equity 53
  newlyweds 53
  qualifying loans 51
  rolling over mortgage to new home 53
  sharers 54
  to buy house for let 9
  to buy own home 9
  working from home 56
motive test, anti-avoidance
  provisions 188
motor expenses *(see cars)*
National Insurance contributions
  class 2 211-12, 213
  class 4 212-13
  deferred payment 213
National Savings, interest before deduction of tax 86
National Savings Capital Bonds 86, 247
National Savings Certificates 83, 241, 247
  interest tax-free 6
National Savings Children's Bonus Bonds
  83
National Savings Deposit Bonds 86
National Savings First Option Bonds 84,
  86
  interest paid after tax 63
National Savings Income Bonds 86
National Savings Investment Account 86
National Savings Ordinary Account 83,
  86
National Savings Stock Register 88
non-residence 276-9

domicile 279
status determination 276-7
  91 day test 277, 278-9
  183 day test 277, 278
  absent for whole tax year test
  277, 278
  motive test 277-8
  supplementary pages 78
NVQ training relief 9, 26, 107, 117-18
offshore funds 235-6
older people, personal allowance 38
one-parent benefit 93
overpayment of tax 19
part-time earnings 289
partnerships
  becoming a partner 215
  ceasing to be partner 215
  changing partners 216-17
  full version 214
  income 7
  investment income 81
  joint responsibility 214
  new partnerships 215-16
  old partnerships 215-16
  partnership statement 214
  penalties 20
  short version 214
  supplementary pages 77
  tax return 214-17
patent rights 103
PAYE
  deadlines 22-4
  refunds 137
  system 21-2
  tax deducted on tax return 146
PAYE coding notice 280-91
  amounts to be taken from allowances
  287
  balance of allowances 286
  basic rate restriction 290
  car, van and fuel benefit 288
  charitable giving 286
  checking 281-7
  employer's loan benefit 288
  expenses 285
  higher rate adjustment 290
  interest 286
  K codes 284

loan interest restriction 290
lower rate allowances 286
lower rate tax adjustment 290
maintenance 286, 289
married couples allowance 288
more than one source of income 284
part-time earnings 289
property income 289
restriction of allowance 287
retirement annuities 285
state pension and benefits 288
superannuation 285
tax allowances 284-7
tips 289
unpaid tax 290
payment of tax
  deadlines 22-3
  instalments 16, 23
  interest and surcharge 17
  interim 15-16, 24
  methods of saving *see* saving
  tax payment
  overpayment 19
  PAYE 21-2
  small 16
  statement of accounts 16-17
  underpayment 21, 23
  unpaid 17
payroll-giving schemes 28-9, 144
penalties 19-20
Pensioners' Guaranteed Income Bonds 86
pensions
  100 per cent deduction 98
  additional voluntary contributions 32, 69, 93, 94
    refunds 103
    reliefs 116-17
  cap on earnings 27
  contributions to employer's scheme 144
  documents needed 94
  employers' pension schemes 68-9
    approved 68-9
    contributions 68-9, 144
    limits on benefits 68
  foreign income 233-5
  income from 5, 7
  income tax relief 107-17

  non-approved, payments from 165
  old person's pension (over 80) 93
  personal pension plans 32, 69-71, 81, 94, 108
    backdating contributions 32
    contracting out of SERPS 70
    death before drawing 70
    income withdrawals from scheme 94
    limits to contributions 70
    limits to tax-free lump sum 70
    reliefs 9, 108, 111, 114-16
    tax return 94
  reliefs 9
    personal pension plans 108, 111, 114-16
    retirement annuity 108, 109, 113-14
  retirement annuities 71, 81, 82, 88, 108, 109, 285
    reliefs 108, 109, 113-14
  state retirement pension 93, 94-5, 288
  tax incentives 32, 67-71
  tax return 93-4
  tax-free 98
  through PAYE 9
  war widows 93
  widow's 93, 95
permanent health insurance 104
personal allowance 10, 128, 285
  additional 10, 29, 42, 133-5
  older people 38-40
  single parents 40-1
personal equity plans (PEPs) 32-3, 71-2, 83, 247
personal injury compensation 83, 248
personal pensions 69-71, 81, 108
  backdating contributions 32
  contracting out of SERPS 70
  death before drawing 70
  income withdrawals from scheme 94
  limits to contributions 70
  limits to tax-free lump sum 70
  reliefs 9, 108, 111, 114-16
  tax return 94
personal representatives
  income from 7
  statement supplied by 242-3

phasing out 26
pools winnings 247
post-cessation
  expenses income relief 107, 125-6
  receipts 103
  recovery of debts for which relief claimed 103
premises costs 200
premium bonds 6, 83
presents *(see gifts)*
private dental insurance 162
private education, employment payments towards 163
private medical insurance 9, 162, 289
private residence relief 34, 59-60
professional costs
  furnished holiday lettings 222
  self-employment expense 202
professional society fees 163, 172
profit-related pay scheme 26, 144, 145
profit-sharing schemes 33, 175-6
promotion, self-employment expense 202
property
  *see also* lettings
  1996 budget changes 26-7
  agent's commission 225
  bridging loans 52
  capital allowances 229
  capital gains 245-6
    caravan or houseboat 57
    dependent relatives 57-8
    ex spouse 57-8
    gardens 58
    lettings 60-1
    private residence relief 34, 59-60
  wasting assets 57
  which home 57-8
  working from home 59
  dealings in 61
  expenses 227
  finance charges 227
  home improvement loans 34
  homeowners
    absence from home 34, 55-6
    saving tax 33-5
    separation and divorce 48
  income

  chargeable premiums 226
  rents 225-6
  services provided 225-6
  income tax *(see mortgage interest relief)*
  lettings *(see lettings main heading)*
  losses 230
  more than one home 34
  mortgages *(see mortgage interest relief)*
  overseas 235
  PAYE coding notice 289
  private residence relief 34, 59-60
  repairs 227
  sale of home 245-6
  supplementary pages 77
  tax adjustments 227-30
  working from home 59
public benefit gifts 247
rates of tax
  allowances 25-6
  capital gains tax 26
  income tax 4, 25
  inheritance tax 26
record keeping 28
  business mileage 154
  new requirements 12-13
  period 13
  valuables purchase and sale 35
reinvestment relief 35
reliefs
  additional voluntary contributions 116-17
  charitable giving 107, 123-5
  claiming 111
  deadline for claiming unused 24
  deductions makeable 107
  documents required 106
  enterprise investment scheme 107, 122-3
  friendly society payments 107, 126-7
  hold over relief 266
  letting relief 35
  loan interest 107, 118-19
  maintenance payments 119-21
  mortgage interest 33-4
  pensions 107-17
  personal pension plans 108, 111, 114-

16
post-cessation expenses 107, 125-6
private residence relief 34, 59-60
reinvestment relief 35, 266-8, 267-8
retirement annuity 108, 109, 113-14
retirement relief 274-5
roll-over relief 275
tax return 107-27
trade unions payments 107, 126-7
unused, deadline for claiming 24
venture capital trusts 107, 121-2
vocational training 26, 107, 117-18
year claimed 111-13
relocation expenses 162
rent
income 5, 7
paid by employer 149, 152
rent a room scheme 34, 218-20
1996 budget 26-7
rent just above scheme level 219-20
repairs
furnished holiday lettings 221-2
property 227
self-employment 200
retirement annuity 71, 81, 82, 88, 285
reliefs 108, 109, 113-14
retirement relief 274-5
rights issues 272
roll-over relief 275
salary, as income 5, 7
Save-As-You-Earn 83, 177
terminal bonuses 247
saving tax payments
all taxpayers 28-9
capital gains 35
employees 29-31
inheritance tax 36
investments 32-3
married couples 29
self-employed 31-2
savings
1996 budget changes 26-7
foreign 233-5
monthly savings schemes 273
savings-related share options 33, 175,
177-8
school uniform grants 93
scrip dividends 90-1, 242

season tickets 152
self-assessment
deadlines 23
inland revenue to calculate 14
self calculation 14-15
penalties 19-20
responsibilities 1
start of regime 2
tax return not received 12-13
self-employment
accounting year 185-6
agency work 185
anti-avoidance provisions 187-9
business details 185-9
capital allowances 204-9
amount claimable 205-6
buying and selling capital items
206-8
claiming 208-9
scrapping short life asset 208
writing down allowance 205
closing down 192-4
clothing 204
expenses
administrative 201
advertising 202
bad debts 202
employee costs 199-200
entertainment 202
expenses 197-204
finance charges 203
interest 203
legal costs 202
motor expenses 201
premises costs 200
professional costs 202
promotion 202
repairs 200
subsistence 201
in tax return 197-204
travel 201
first year of trading 189-90
fiscal accounting 191-2
gross profits 196-7
income in tax return 195-7
losses 209-11, 287
closing down 210-11
future profits 210

previous year 209-10
National Insurance
contributions
    class 2 211-12, 213
    class 4 212-13
    deferred payment 213
overlap profits 188, 190-1
saving tax payments 31-2
second year of trading 190
status establishment 184
tax adjustments to net profit and loss
204
tax return 77, 184-230
    expenses 197-204
    income 195-7
third year of trading 190
transitional rules 186-7
value added tax 196
separation and divorce
additional personal allowances 42
capital gains tax 48-9
children 42
home and 48
informing inspector 41-2
inheritance tax 48-9
maintenance payments 42-4
tax allowances 42
settlements *(see trusts)*
severe disablement allowance 93
share, supplementary pages 77
share options 163, 175, 176-7
capital gains tax 271
discretionary share options 175, 178-9
executive share options scheme 178
exercise of 181
long options 179-80
savings-related schemes 33, 175, 177-8
taxable amounts 180
unapproved 175, 179-80
    free or cheap shares through
    175, 180-3
sharers, mortgage interest relief 54
shares 163
*(see also dividends)*
accumulation unit trusts 272
benefits 174, 183
bought after 6 April (1965) 269

bought on or before 5 April (1982)
269
building societies 272
capital gains tax 268-73
conversions or reorganisations 272
documents required 175
employee share ownership trusts
(ESOTs) 175
employee share schemes 271
foreign income 234
instalment payment 272
insurance companies 272
investment income 64
investment trusts 268
mergers 272
monthly savings schemes 273
options *(see share options)*
post-acquisition charges 183
profit-sharing schemes, approved 175-6
received from employment 182
rights issues 272
sale within 10 days of buying 269, 271
stock dividends 272
takeovers 272
in tax return 174-83
transfer of securities 104
in UK companies 89
unit trusts 89-90, 268
valuation 268
sick pay 94, 96, 144, 145
single parents, personal allowances 40-1
social fund maternity payments 92
social fund payments 93
social security benefits 288
*(see also individual benefits eg widowed mother's allowance)*
deadlines 22
incapacity 288
tax return 93-4
    not included in 92-3
unemployment 288
social security payments
income 5, 7
jobseeker's allowance 5
special commissioners 21
Specialist Taxpayer Service Office 11

spouse
*(see also married couples; married couple's allowance)*
employment of 31
state retirement pension 93, 94-5
statement of account 291-4
  checking 293
  payments on account 292-3
    reduction 293-4
statutory maternity pay 94, 96
statutory sick pay 94, 96
stock dividends 272
student grants 93
subscriptions 163, 172
subsistence expenses 26, 170-1, 201
suggestion schemes 145
superannuation 285
supplementary pages *(see tax return)*
tax bill, paid by employer 149, 152
Tax Calculation Guide 75
tax exempt special savings accounts (TESSAs) 33, 72
tax free allowance, capital gains 35
tax return
  capital gains 78, 251-7
  checking correct ones 76-9
  correct details in 138
  corrections 17
  date of birth 138
  deadlines 14-15, 24
  declaration 139
  determination 15
  dividends 81, 89-92
  documents included 75
  employment 76, 140-73
  enquiries 17-18
  foreign 78
  foreign earnings 166-9
  fringe benefits 146-64
  how to fill in 75-9
  income reliefs 107-27
  income tax 80-105
  interest
    with tax deducted 84-5
    unit trusts 85-6
    without tax deducted 83-4, 84-5
  investment income 81-92

land and property 77-8
life insurance policies income 100-3
maintenance income 98-100
mistakes 17
new 13-15
non-residence 79, 276-9
not received 12-13
partnerships 77, 214-17
pensions and benefits 92-8
request for 75
self-employment 77, 184-230
share schemes 77
shares 174-83
supplementary pages 14
trusts 78
working on own tax bill 137
Tax Return Guide 75
tax-free income 6
tax-free investments 32
Taxpayer Enquiry Centres 11
Taxpayer Service Office 11
telephones
  mobiles 161-2, 289
  payment of bill 149, 151-2, 289
TESSAs 33, 72, 83
time limits
  deadlines for tax return 14-15
  income tax 22-4
    allowances 23, 24
    claiming unused reliefs 24
    payments 22-3
  inland revenue to calculate 14
  self calculation 14-15
  self-assessment deadlines 14-15, 23, 24
tips 144, 146, 289
too small to count test 188
trade unions, relief on payments to 107, 126-7
training
  income reliefs 107, 117-18
  NVQ costs 9, 26, 107, 117-18, 287
transfer of securities 104
transitional allowance 129-30, 136
travel expenses 26, 170-1
  self-employment 201
trusts 33
  capital gains tax 247, 250-1

    children 240-2
    discretionary 240
    income from 33, 239-40
    interest 85, 247
    with interest in possession 240
    supplementary pages 78
    tax return 81
Ulster Savings Certificates 83
underwriting income 104
unemployment benefit 93, 95-6, 288
unit trusts
    accumulation 272
    capital gains tax 268
    interest 85-6
    investment income 64
    tax return 89-90
unpaid tax 290
value added tax 196
vans 159-60, 288
vehicles (see cars)
venture capital trusts 27, 73-4
    capital gains 247
    income relief 107, 121-2
vocational training costs 9, 26, 107, 117-
    18, 287
vouchers 152
war disablement benefits 93
war orphan's benefit 93
war widow's pension 93
wasting assets 57, 247
wear and tear 34-5, 229
widowed mother's allowance 93, 95
widow's bereavement allowance 9, 135
widow's payment 93
widow's pension 93, 95
winnings 6, 247
working from home
    capital gains 59
    mortgage interest relief 56
YT training scheme allowance 93